Two Wheels To War is a scholarly but entertaining look at the largely forgotten world of the motorcycle despatch rider in the early months of the First World War, then a new phenomenon in the field of conflict. At the heart of the book is an illustrated and annotated edition of the underrated – and initially uncensored – classic first published in 1915, *Adventures of a Despatch Rider*, written by Captain WHL Watson, one of the well-educated young men who volunteered for the Signal service. He and over 400 other motorcyclists were sent to France, some mounted on their own machines, direct from the recruiting office. Sometimes uncomfortably close to the fast evolving action, Watson and his colleagues played a little known but key part in the early campaigns at Mons, Le Cateau, on the Retreat and on the Aisne. They accompanied the BEF returning to the north in October 1914 when the Western Front extended to Flanders, enduring the harsh winter that followed.

His book, which initially escaped scrutiny by the censor, was a graphic and particularly well-written account of the reality of war from the Retreat from Mons to the First Battle of Ypres. To illustrate his classic prose, we have unearthed a treasure trove of contemporary photographs, mainly taken by three of his fellow despatch riders in the 5th Signal company, Pollers, Sadders and Cecil Burney, using the soldier's camera, the VPK, as the iconic Vest Pocket Kodak camera became known.

As well as Watson's book itself, we continue his story until April 1915, when he was wounded and repatriated to England. His book was based on his letters home which were serialised in *Blackwood's Magazine* (the famous '*Maga*'), an Edinburgh-based publisher responsible for other classics of the time such as *The Thirty Nine Steps* and *The First Hundred Thousand*. While convalescing from a shrapnel wound, Watson was persuaded to edit his letters into a book which was released in late 1915. Now commissioned, Watson resumed writing (but in a less personal style than before) about his experiences as an officer commanding a Cyclist's battalion, articles which appeared in *Maga* under the title *Tales of a Gaspipe Officer*. Plans to publish these in book form were thwarted by the censor who had by now spotted that his first book had slipped through the censor's net and had been withdrawn awaiting review. These *Maga* articles are republished here for the first time since 1916.

Our introduction offers a new perspective on their story – how the Signal service hurriedly recruited and sent to France more than 400 motorcyclists with their own machines. We have also researched the biographical details of the twelve despatch riders of 5th Signal company. These reveal their real identities, hidden until now behind the nicknames they used such as "Huggie" and "Spuggy" and the ironically named "Fat Boy". The appendices describe the motorcycles and equipment the despatch riders used, and finally there is a database of the 400 men who went to France in this role in 1914, which will prove an invaluable tool for their descendants researching their forebears.

Martin Shelley, VMCC Blackburne and OEC Marque specialist, and Nick Shelley, secretary of the Marston Sunbeam Club & Register, are both vintage motorcycle enthusiasts and amateur historians of the early motor industry.

The Shelley brothers discovered the Burney brothers' photograph albums and medals in an auction, and quickly realised they featured in the classic *Adventures of a Despatch Rider* by W.H.L. Watson. Critically, the captions and names written on the backs of some pictures in the album helped them to identify the 12 despatch riders whose exploits Watson had written about.

They have used these striking pictures to illustrate the book, which also seeks to place Watson's thoughtful memoirs into a wider context through further detailed research. Over the course of six years they have found the despatch riders' families, unearthed unpublished material written by other members of the unit, read the war diaries and Watson's correspondence with his publisher, and visited France and Belgium, where they followed the tracks of the despatch riders from Mons to the Aisne, and then to Flanders.

The pictures and information they have uncovered are used here to enrich the original text, and to paint a fuller picture of the experiences of the early despatch riders in 1914 and beyond.

TWO WHEELS TO WAR

A Tale of Twelve Bright Young Men Who
Volunteered Their Own Motorcycles for the
British Expeditionary Force 1914

Incorporating the full text of
Adventures of a Despatch Rider

Martin Shelley & Nick Shelley

Helion & Company

Helion & Company Limited
26 Willow Road
Solihull
West Midlands
B91 1UE
England
Tel. 0121 705 3393
Fax 0121 711 4075
Email: info@helion.co.uk
Website: www.helion.co.uk
Twitter: @helionbooks
Visit our blog at http://blog.helion.co.uk/

Published by Helion & Company 2017
Designed and typeset by Mach 3 Solutions Ltd (www.mach3solutions.co.uk)
Cover designed by Paul Hewitt, Battlefield Design (www.battlefield-design.co.uk)
Printed by Short Run Press, Exeter, Devon

ISBN 978-1-911096-58-0

British Library Cataloguing-in-Publication Data.
A catalogue record for this book is available from the British Library.

For details of other military history titles published by Helion & Company
Limited, contact the above address, or visit our website: http://www.helion.co.uk

We always welcome receiving book proposals from prospective authors.

Contents

Foreword

by Roger Polhill

Most of us regret not asking our parents more about their lives before it is too late. I am no exception and my father was quite reticent about the war. I only remember him referring once to the stench of dead horses. Fortunately he was engaged to my mother in the first days of the war and she meticulously kept all his letters. In fact his first letter from Ireland during the transit was his proposal with apologies for not having done so while they were together. He was also the first of the despatch riders in the 5th Signal Company to publish an account in the September issue of *The Trident*, the magazine of Trent College, his old school where his youngest brother was still a pupil. A copy of *Blackwood's Magazine* and two small boxes of photographic negatives were among the mementos my mother kept.

Of the twelve original despatch riders in the unit of which my father took charge, ten survived the war. All were commissioned during the conflict, and most went on to have contented lives. Three daughters and two sons are still living and have been able to contribute to this wonderful

Roger Polhill holding his
father's copy of the menu
for the motorcyclists' 1914
Christmas dinner

book. Valerie Upton is the daughter of Hugh Trepess, who continued his architectural career after the war. Sue Elphick is the daughter of Cecil Hayes-Sadler, who followed his uncle into the Colonial Service in Kenya. She was brought up in Nairobi where her father had to postpone his retirement from a senior post until the end of the Second World War in 1945. Roselle Bonney and David Danson have resided in England though their father Jack, the youngest of the despatch riders, was earlier involved with the family business in Burma. Cecil and Jack were friends and became brothers in law.

My father trained as a pilot in the Royal Flying Corps at Turnberry in Scotland and now married with a small child, he stayed on, it seems, to teach aerial photography. After the war he was made redundant from engineering firms three times and opted to take his skills to farming in Kenya. He only returned to England once, for my graduation.

We all have the greatest admiration for the wealth of enthusiasm and scholarly perseverance that Nick and Martin have put into this exceedingly well illustrated book that covers so many aspects of the crucial role these men played in the campaign from Mons to Ypres. We hope it will have a great appeal to all those interested in vintage motor cycles and the social and military history of the period.

Introduction:
A new perspective on the
August 1914 despatch riders

'Two Wheels to War' is the distillation of our efforts to create a definitive illustrated edition of 'Adventures of a Despatch Rider', and in so doing to analyse the distinctive rôle played by motorcycle despatch riders in the 1914 campaign. The book shows how these men – predominantly in their early 20s along with a few older colleagues – decided on the spur of the moment to offer themselves as despatch riders. Within a few days of that decision – and having received no serious training – they found themselves in action in France.

This photograph captured the moment when the 5th Signals despatch riders gathered for their 1914 Christmas party. When we came across it for the first time in the Burney brothers' album, it caught our imagination. The real names noted on the back of this photograph helped us to track down the true identities of the members of the group – and gave us the key to unlock the code with which Watson concealed the identities of all his colleagues.

Even though the Army had made few realistic preparations for their use, the despatch riders generally took a positive view of what they were called on to do. They were selected for their unique combination of skills – proficient motorcyclists, communicative messengers, and the ability to think on their feet. Those demanding selection criteria meant that, for the most part, they came from similar backgrounds. The army allowed friends, and even brothers, to serve together, and as a result, many of them readily bonded into effective teams. The despatch riders quickly made a distinctive contribution to the Signal companies to which they were assigned, and we are sure that Watson and his colleagues greatly enhanced the effectiveness of the Signal companies.

The dramatic story of the highly mobile early campaign reflects the chaotic conditions that developed in the autumn of 1914. The shock of total war, and particularly the impact of modern weapons, exposed the shortcomings of years of careful military planning. The presence of the motorcyclists gave the Army's leadership greater control and helped to preserve order in the Retreat and the fast-moving campaign which followed.

We have expanded Watson's work in various ways. The book features over 60 previously unpublished photographs taken by the despatch riders' own cameras. The CAST chapter is made up of their detailed life-stories, and of other soldiers who appear in the book. The TIMELINE includes accounts by Watson's fellow DRs, based on their own letters and diaries. It also includes instalments from Watson's *Tales of a Gaspipe Officer*, which followed on from 'Adventures of a Despatch Rider'. In mid-February 1915 Watson was commissioned as a Cyclist officer, and the new material takes his story up to that summer, when he was recovering from the wound he sustained at the Second Battle of Ypres.

All this additional material deepens our understanding of Watson's 'adventures'. Our aim is to show the campaign as the despatch riders saw it, and to describe what was at stake for them. We've added notes to the text where they were needed to make the book accessible to the general reader unfamiliar with the world of 1914.

In the first weeks of the First World War, the British Army recruited some four hundred motorcycle despatch riders. Although the Expeditionary Force was otherwise planned down to the last detail, the despatch riders were, essentially, an afterthought. Motorcyclists had proved their worth at the summer manoeuvres in 1913 and 1914, yet the Army had recruited only a handful to the Special Reserve.

The recruitment of despatch riders was a minor footnote in the vast campaign launched in August 1914. Kitchener's face on the posters led to the recruitment of volunteer Armies on a previously unimagined scale. Those citizen armies, each of one hundred thousand men, eventually won the war. Meanwhile, the task was not to lose the war in the first month. Most of the eager candidates for the rôle of despatch rider wanted to be involved in front line action without delay. There was, after all, a respectable case for thinking that the war would be over by Christmas.

The motorcyclists were recruited through general newspaper advertisements, through messages to Officer Training Corps in schools and universities, and by word of mouth through the community of motorcycle journalists and sporting organisers. Once recruited, the despatch riders were assigned, in groups of around a dozen, to Signal companies and squadrons. The creation of "Kitchener's Armies" swung ponderously into action, bringing hundreds of thousands of citizens into makeshift barracks or under canvas, training for their initiation in the 1915 battles or on the Somme. Meanwhile the despatch riders were already in France or en route.

As soon as they arrived, the motorcyclists found themselves, with scant preparation, in a hard fought and fast-moving campaign. The war of movement lasted from August till October. From then till late November 1914, when an early winter arrived, the allied armies, in rudimentary trenches, held off the enemy's attempts to break through and bring the war to an end.

Though their rôle has rarely been acknowledged, the despatch riders played a crucial part in keeping the Expeditionary Force together. We believe they should have some credit for the fact that the British Army remained a coherent force during the long and exhausting Retreat from Mons to the Marne. In two weeks the first six British divisions covered more than 200 miles. They hastened south from Mons, across the Belgian border and through Picardy, not stopping until they reached the Marne well to the south east of Paris. There the tide turned, and the pursued became the pursuers – the German army turned and retreated until it dug in at the Aisne. Then the British Army found that it was unable to break through the well-defended terrain between the river and the Chemin des Dames which ran along the heights behind the river Aisne.

In the second half of Watson's story, starting with 'The move to the North', the Expeditionary Force was transferred, division by division, to Flanders and northern France, where they held the left wing of the Allied front. The despatch riders played their part there, too, helping to manage the British efforts to fight off the sustained German attacks which so nearly broke the Allied line in front of Ypres, Festubert and Bethune.

The men in this book were the first twelve motorcyclists recruited to 5th Signal Company in August 1914. All but two survived the war. All those who survived were commissioned, and all of them served on the Western Front and other theatres of war – most of them for the entire war. The ten survivors recovered, more or less, from the war and most of them enjoyed successful, and sometimes lengthy and distinguished, civilian careers.

'Adventures of a Despatch Rider' was one of the earliest books about the war published by a serving soldier. It was serialised first in *Blackwood's Magazine*. Its publisher commissioned the book version immediately after the first instalment appeared. However, the book was on sale for only a few months before it was withdrawn on the orders of the Army Council, and Watson was severely reprimanded for publishing it without official approval. Later, the censors relented, and in 1917 they allowed Blackwood's to republish the book in an expurgated 'Shilling' edition. We have shown what was changed or removed as annotations in this edition. Comparison of the two versions reveals what matters offended official sensibilities. Then the book disappeared from sight after the war, and was not reprinted for eighty years.

We hope that 'Two Wheels to War' will contribute to the re-appraisal of Watson's classic. Notwithstanding the claims of other publishers to have produced an 'illustrated' edition, this is the first time that 'Adventures of a Despatch Rider' has included pictures of, and by, those despatch riders who are the subject of the book. Along with studio portraits and scenes from later life, almost all the pictures are previously unpublished. They include scenes of everyday life near the front as well as informal group shots of 5th Signal Company despatch riders.

Our project began when we discovered Cecil Burney's photograph album. At the time we were researching Cecil's rôle as one of the men who founded the firm of Burney & Blackburne in 1912, which manufactured an innovative range of motorcycles. Much later he became one of the pioneers of the vintage vehicle movement in the UK. We knew that he had been a despatch rider, and we were excited to realise that he was one of the despatch riders who had featured in Watson's book.

The next task in our research was to identify the other despatch riders. That was much easier than it might have been because many of the pictures in the album had detailed labels. The men in the album were identified by their nicknames as well as their real names, and that helped us to find their surviving relatives. Those relatives, in turn, gave us much help and encouragement, and, as a result, this book also contains unpublished photographs taken by Cecil Hayes-Sadler and Stanley Polhill.

Though we have identified when and where most of them were taken, sadly the pictures are of variable quality because of the limitations of the Vest Pocket Kodak (VPK) camera used and the circumstances under which they were taken. However, even the poorer images convey the atmosphere of the time when they were taken. The book also includes pictures of the men who appear in the book taken at other times in their lives. There are also photographs and stories of other despatch riders who were recruited at the same time as these men.

During our research we visited many of the places around which the book revolves. We have been to Chatham and Carlow, and, using Watson as our guide, we travelled to France and Belgium. We found that, using his text alone, it was possible to trace the route he followed a hundred years earlier. Many of the sites around Mons and Le Cateau are unchanged, but around Bailleul and Beuvry all that is visible are the reconstructed towns and villages. But a 'Maison Commune Estaminet' at St Jans Cappel is still in business, and Serches and the Aisne remain much as Watson described.

We've researched the life stories of the despatch riders, some of whom are still in the living memories of their sons and daughters and other relatives. We learned how they came to be recruited through those unusual channels. We've also learned about the families they came from, how they were educated, their prior military experience, and what they did after the war.

Another feature of our edition is the accounts taken from letters and diaries written by the men with whom Watson campaigned. The author was a reliable historian and thoughtful commentator, and his account of the campaign needs no amplification. There is nothing which suggests that he made factual mistakes or indulged in exaggeration. Nonetheless, he was only one of several who wrote letters and diaries to help them make sense of what they saw and did. The book includes unpublished contributions by many of those Watson campaigned with. There are letters written by Polhill, Hayes-Sadler, and Overton. Bagshaw's impressions of the first four months were recorded by an academic in December 1914. We have included the recollections of George Owen, written in 1926, and extracts from the autobiography of Frank Merchant, the company pay Sergeant when war was declared, who wrote his life story when he retired in the 1930s.

Many of the books about the First World War have been written or edited by scholars with extensive military training and with first-hand knowledge of war. We recognise that neither of us has that experience. However, we looked at 'Adventures' from another perspective – our experience as motorcyclists. Each of us became motorcyclists at about the age that the despatch riders were when they joined up, and we have a deep appreciation of the value of two wheeled machines, and a lifetime's experience of their limitations! We are now both retired, with time to reflect on those experiences, and to evaluate the despatch riders in the light of our experience. We're familiar with machines of the 1914 period, not only in terms of their history and development but also in terms of hands-on experience of running veteran motorbikes.

We believe this is a timely moment to draw attention to the rôle of the motorcycle in the study of technology in war. The modern motorcycle owes its existence to the combination, early in the twentieth century, of two inventions which occurred in the Victorian age – the safety bicycle and the high speed internal combustion engine. The diamond pattern frame quickly established itself as the standard bicycle design, once the inadequacies of the high bicycle or 'Penny Farthing' were acknowledged. Then it was soon realised that the diamond frame was suitable for the addition of the kind of light but powerful engine that was developed soon after the safety bicycle arrived. The 'motorcycle' concept went through many iterations before a standard design was adopted, based on the machine produced by the Werner brothers in Paris in 1901, but even before then, people had adapted these primitive machines to carry weapons or imagined them as useful in military applications.

It was only in the first decade of the twentieth century that the motorcycle advanced to the point where it was a capable, reliable machine, but still well short of the modern (motorcycle) design. Belt drive was the transmission of choice for most machines, and the gearbox was mainly located inside the rear hub rather than as a countershaft device. Ideas of using the motorcycle for military purposes began to be explored tentatively quite early in the century, but the Army was still largely committed to the horse as the primary means of individual transport.

In the final two or three years before the outbreak of war, the authorities began to perceive the possibility that the motorcycle could play an important rôle in maintaining communications. By 1914 the motorcycle industry was producing a large range of machines, many of which could meet the Army's minimum requirements (see Appendix II). Thus it was credible for the Army to advertise in the motorcycle press for able-bodied motorcyclists to join territorial units as despatch riders, in the knowledge that many able men would be available, and would own machines which met military specifications.

However, it was only after the declaration of war that the Army recognised the need to recruit despatch riders in large numbers. Men were asked to sign up as soon as possible, along with their own machines. The minimum requirement was for machines equipped with gears, and with four stroke engines of at least 350cc capacity. Some machines were rejected for arcane reasons. For example, Henry Blower's Singer was not accepted because it had a German-made NSU two speed gear.[1] The 'before and after' pictures of Alick Burney's own Blackburne machine registered AR3348 – at a Brooklands photo-call in 1913 and written off at Serches in September 1914 – are definitive proof that this method of procurement really happened, and is no urban myth.

Another theme identified was how the Army set the manpower standards for despatch riders. The War Office issued their call to motorcyclists through the Officer Training Corps, the national press and the motorcycle press. Although national newspapers reached a wide audience, the use of the OTC and motorcycling journalists focussed the recruitment drive on quite a small field of possible recruits – filtering out a large number of capable motorcyclists in favour of better-educated men from the layer of society which initially supplied most of the officers. Officer Training Corps units were based in universities, the public schools and kindred organisations. The editor of *The Motor Cycle* also played an important role in the selection process, and he approached the task with similar values. Thus, the first recruits were overwhelmingly either leading motorcycle professionals or educated men from middle-class backgrounds.

To the extent that many of the latter group already owned motorcycles or had motorcycling experience, they were not entirely typical as in 1914, the middle-class male was more likely to be a motorist or horseman than a motorcyclist.

Among the former group, the Burney brothers had been building machines under the Burney & Blackburne badge for two years before war broke out. They were among the very first to volunteer at Chatham. They rode machines they had manufactured themselves, which proved to be amongst the finest machines used in the war. They were older than most of their fellow despatch riders, and were widely respected because of their knowledge and experience. Before the Signal company embarked for France, the Burneys persuaded Sergeant Merchant, a practiced horseman who ended the war as officer commanding 5th Signal Company, to experiment with a motorcycle. While we would not expect a Royal Engineers NCO to be a technophobe, it is remarkable how quickly Merchant mastered the basic skills, and became an enthusiastic motorcyclist within a few weeks of landing in France.

We noticed an unconventional streak in many of the recruits. Overton, Polhill, and Watson were all sons of clergymen, who might have been expected either to follow their father to the cloth, or to rebel against their upbringing. Many motorcyclists had succeeded in training as engineers against parental wishes. Equally, motorcycling had developed to the point where it could be an appealing hobby for the young. For example, Cecil Hayes-Sadler and Jack Danson formed a life-long friendship while they were at Oxford University through their shared interest in motorcycling. George Owen, who had only owned a motorcycle briefly, recorded how pleased he was that

---

1   Imperial War Museum, Oral History. Ref 4074.

he had taken up a hobby, purely by chance, which qualified him to become a despatch rider while his brothers lacked that experience.

Early in our research we widened the net to include men other than the 5th Signal company DRs, and we have identified more than 400 motorcyclists who reached France as despatch riders in 1914. We also draw tentative conclusions about the men in our database by comparing the fortunes of those who arrived as motorcyclists and those who arrived with the fighting units.

Motorcycle despatch riders in 1914 were exposed to all the ordinary dangers of motorcycling – they rode high mileages at speed over dangerous road conditions, where a collision, or even a puncture, could be fatal. They were, in addition, exposed to the hazards of shellfire, snipers, machine guns, and out of control military hardware and horses. It seems that motorcyclists had a better rate of survival than men who served with the fighting arms, such as the infantry or artillery. Their competitive urge, fuelled by the desire to get to the Front straightaway, had unplanned beneficial consequences in their lives later in the war.

We also looked at what the book itself, and our research, taught us about motorcycling. A motorcyclist never forgets that riding motorcycles has many dangers – riding a motorcycle is an absorbing experience. A motorcyclist must live in the moment, for lapses of concentration may be fatal. The motorcycle quickly teaches the rider the necessary skills. Those who can't, or won't, acquire the skills needed to survive on two wheels either don't survive, or give up motorcycling as a bad job. Even today, the ordinary risks faced by every rider require the motorcyclist to prepare properly, to anticipate, to read the road, to take nothing for granted.

Throughout 'Adventures', and in nearly all the literature written by motorcyclists referred to in these pages, one frequent theme is how riders felt safer with cautious behaviour and steady progress rather than haste and hurry. The men who volunteered as despatch rides were almost all accomplished riders in their own right, whether with extensive competition experience in events like the Tourist Trophy races in the Isle of Man or simply intelligent, articulate men who used their self-preservation instincts to the best effect.

In summary, it seems to us that the rôle of despatch riders in the First World War, specifically their achievements in the 1914 campaign, have been under-appreciated. We hope that this book sets the record straight. Even well-trained, capable and experienced motorcyclists today would be challenged by the conditions which the 1914 despatch riders and their motorcycles faced. Ultimately they should be remembered for their crucial efforts, round the clock and sometimes against impossible odds, to locate destinations and deliver messages reliably. Their success in doing so made a major contribution to keeping the Expeditionary Force together throughout the entire 1914 campaign from Mons to Ypres.

ADVENTURES OF A DESPATCH RIDER

By

Captain W. H. L. Watson

With Maps

William Blackwood and Sons
Edinburgh and London
1915

WHL Watson in 1915, at the time he wrote the book.

To

The perfect mother,

My Own

A Letter by Way of Introduction[1]

To 2nd Lieut. R. B. WHYTE,[2]
      1st Black Watch,
          B.E.F.

MY DEAR ROBERT, –

Do you remember how in the old days we used to talk about my first book? Of course it was to be an Oxford novel full of clever little character-sketches – witty but not unkind: of subtle and pleasurable hints at our own adventures, for no one had enjoyed Balliol and the city of Oxford so hugely: of catch-words that repeated would bring back the thrills and the laughter – *Psych. Anal.* and *Steady, Steady!* of names crammed with delectable memories – the Paviers', Cloda's Lane, and the notorious Square and famous Wynd: of acid phrases, beautifully put, that would show up once and for all those dear abuses and shams that go to make Oxford. It was to surpass all Oxford Novels and bring us all eternal fame.

    You remember, too, the room? It was stuffy and dingy and the pictures were of doubtful taste, but there were things to drink and smoke. The imperturbable Ikla would be sitting in his chair pulling at one of his impossibly luxurious pipes. You would be snorting in another – and I would be holding forth … but I am starting an Oxford novelette already and there is no need. For two slightly senior contemporaries of ours have already achieved fame. The hydrangeas have blossomed. "The Home" has been destroyed by a Balliol tongue. The flower-girl has died her death. The Balliol novels have been written – and my first book is this.

    We have not even had time to talk it over properly. I saw you on my week's leave in December, but then I had not thought of making a book. Finally, after three months in the trenches you came home in August. I was in Ireland and you in Scotland, so we met at Warrington just after midnight and proceeded to staggering adventures. Shall we ever forget that six hours' talk, the mad ride and madder breakfast with old Peter M'Ginn, the solitary hotel at Manchester and the rare dash to London? But I didn't tell you much about my book.

    It is made up principally of letters to my mother and to you. My mother showed these letters to Mr Townsend Warner, my old tutor at Harrow,[3] and he, who was always my godfather in letters, passed them on until they have appeared in the pages of 'Maga.' I have filled in the gaps these letters leave with narrative, worked the whole into some sort of connected account, and added maps and an index.

    This book is not a history, a military treatise, an essay, or a scrap of autobiography. It has no more accuracy or literary merit than letters usually possess. So I hope you will not judge it too harshly. My only object is to try and show as truthfully as I can the part played in this monstrous

---

1   The Letter by Way of Introduction appeared in the first edition in 1915, but was not included in the Shilling
    edition in 1917.

2   See Cast, page 130.

3   George Townsend Warner (1865-1916). For more details, see Appendix I, page 246.

war by a despatch rider during the months from August 1914 to February 1915. If that object is gained I am content.

Because it is composed of letters, this book has many faults.

Firstly, I have written a great deal about myself. That is inevitable in letters. My mother wanted to hear about me and not about those whom she had never met. So do not think my adventures are unique. I assure you that if any of the other despatch riders were to publish their letters you would find mine by comparison mild indeed. If George now could be persuaded[1] … !

Secondly, I have dwelt at length upon little personal matters. It may not interest you to know when I had a pork-chop – though, as you now realise, on active service a pork-chop is extremely important – but it interested my mother. She liked to know whether I was having good and sufficient food, and warm things on my chest and feet, because, after all, there was a time when I wanted nothing else.

Thirdly, all letters are censored. This book contains nothing but the truth, but not the whole truth. When I described things that were actually happening round me, I had to be exceedingly careful – and when, as in the first two or three chapters, my letters were written several weeks after the events, something was sure to crop up in the meantime that unconsciously but definitely altered the memory of experiences. …

We have known together two of the people I have mentioned in this book – Alec and Gibson.[2] They have both advanced so far that we have lost touch with them. I had thought that it would be a great joy to publish a first book, but this book is ugly with sorrow. I shall never be able to write "Alec and I" again – and he was the sweetest and kindest of my friends, a friend of all the world. Never did he meet a man or woman that did not love him. The Germans have killed Alec. Perhaps among the multitudinous Germans killed there are one or two German Alecs. Yet I am still meeting people who think that war is a fine bracing thing for the nation, a sort of national week-end at Brighton.

Then there was Gibson, who proved for all time that nobody made a better soldier than the young don – and those whose names do not come into this book. …

Robert, you and I know what to think of this Brighton theory. We are only just down from Oxford, and perhaps things strike us a little more passionately than they should.

You have seen the agony of war. You have seen those miserable people that wander about behind the line like pariah dogs in the streets. You know what is behind "Tommy's invincible gaiety." Let us pray together for a time when the publishing of a book like this will be regarded with fierce shame.

So long and good luck!

Ever yours,

WILLIAM.

PIRBRIGHT HUTS
1/10/15.

The day after I had written this letter the news came to me that Robert Whyte had been killed. The letter must stand – I have not the heart to write another.

W. H. L. W.
PIRBRIGHT HUTS

---

1 George was indeed persuaded – see Timeline Part 1.
2 See Cast, page 131.

1

Enlisting

At 6.45 p.m. on Saturday, July 25, 1914, Alec and I determined to take part in the Austro-Servian War. I remember the exact minute, because we were standing on the "down" platform of Earl's Court Station, waiting for the 6.55 through train to South Harrow, and Alec had just remarked that we had ten minutes to wait. We had travelled up to London, intending to work in the British Museum for our "vivas" at Oxford,[1] but in the morning it had been so hot that we had strolled round Bloomsbury, smoking our pipes. By lunch-time we had gained such an appetite that we did not feel like work in the afternoon. We went to see Elsie Janis.[2]

The evening papers were full of grave prognostications. War between Servia and Austria seemed inevitable. Earl's Court Station inspired us with the spirit of adventure. We determined to take part, and debated whether we should go out as war correspondents or as orderlies in a Servian hospital. At home we could talk of nothing else during dinner. Ikla, that wisest of all Egyptians, mildly encouraged us, while the family smiled.

On Sunday we learned that war had been declared. Ways and means were discussed, but our great tennis tournament on Monday, and a dance in the evening, left us with a mere background of warlike endeavour. It was vaguely determined that when my "viva" was over we should go and see people of authority in London. …

On the last day of July a few of us met together in Gibson's rooms, those neat, white rooms in Balliol that overlook St Giles. Naymier,[3] the Pole, was certain that Armageddon was coming. He proved it conclusively in the Quad with the aid of large maps and a dissertation on potatoes. He also showed us the probable course of the war.

We lived in strained excitement. Things were too big to grasp. It was just the other day that 'The Blue Book,' most respectable of Oxford magazines, had published an article showing that a war between Great Britain and Germany was almost unthinkable. It had been written by an undergraduate who had actually been at a German university. Had the multitudinous Anglo-German societies at Oxford worked in vain? The world came crashing round our ears. Naymier was urgent for an Oxford or a Balliol Legion – I do not remember which – but we could not take him seriously. Two of us decided that we were physical cowards, and would not under any circumstances enlist. The flower of Oxford was too valuable to be used as cannon-fodder.

The days passed like weeks. Our minds were hot and confused. It seemed that England must come in. On the afternoon of the fourth of August I travelled up to London. At a certain club in St James's there was little hope. I walked down Pall Mall. In Trafalgar Square a vast, serious crowd was anxiously waiting for news. In Whitehall Belgians were doing their best to rouse the mob.

---

1 An oral examination for a degree.
2 Elsie Janis (1889–1956), American singer, songwriter and actress, later known as "the sweetheart of the AEF".
3 Sir Lewis Bernstein Namier (1888–1960), born Ludwik Niemerovski, emigrated from the Polish territories in 1907 and studied at Balliol College from 1908. He served as a private in the Royal Fusiliers 1914–15, but was discharged due to poor eyesight. Later he achieved distinction as an historian of 18th-century English politics.

Beflagged cars full of wildly gesticulating Belgians were driving rapidly up and down. Belgians were haranguing little groups of men. Everybody remained quiet but perturbed.

War was a certainty. I did not wish to be a spectator of the scenes that would accompany its declaration, so I went home. All the night in my dreams I saw the quiet, perturbed crowds.

War was declared. All those of us who were at Balliol together telephoned to one another so that we might enlist together. Physical coward or no physical coward – it obviously had to be done. Teddy and Alec were going into the London Scottish. Early in the morning I started for London to join them, but on the way up I read the paragraph in which the War Office appealed for motor-cyclists.[1]

So I went straight to Scotland Yard. There I was taken up to a large room full of benches crammed with all sorts and conditions of men. The old fellow on my right was a sign-writer. On my left was a racing motor-cyclist.[2] We waited for hours. Frightened-looking men were sworn in and one phenomenally grave small boy. Later I should have said that a really fine stamp of man was enlisting. Then they seemed to me a shabby crew.

At last we were sent downstairs, and told to strip and array ourselves in moderately dirty blue dressing-gowns. Away from the formality of the other room we sang little songs, and made the worst jokes in the world – being continually interrupted by an irritable sergeant, whom we called "dearie."

One or two men were feverishly arguing whether certain physical deficiencies would be passed. Nobody said a word of his reason for enlisting except the sign-writer, whose wages had been low.

The racing motor-cyclist and I were passed one after another, and, receiving warrants, we travelled down to Fulham. Our names, addresses, and qualifications were written down. To my overwhelming joy I was marked as "very suitable."

I went to Great Portland Street, arranged to buy a motor-cycle, and returned home.[3] That evening I received a telegram from Oxford advising me to go down to Chatham.

I started off soon after breakfast, and suffered three punctures. The mending of them put despatch-riding in an unhealthy light. At Rochester I picked up Wallace and Marshall of my college, and together we went to the appointed place.[4]

There we found twenty or thirty enlisted or unenlisted. I had come only to make inquiries, but I was carried away. After a series of waits I was medically examined and passed. At 5.45 p.m. I kissed the Book, and in two minutes I became a corporal in the Royal Engineers. During the ceremony my chief sensation was one of thoroughgoing panic.

In the morning four of us, who were linguists, were packed off to the War Office. We spent the journey in picturing all the ways we might be killed, until, by the time we reached Victoria, there was not a single one of us who would not have given anything to un-enlist. The War Office rejected us on the plea that they had as many Intelligence Officers as they wanted. So we returned glumly.

---

1   *Call for All Motorcyclists – The War Office announce that civilian medical practitioners desiring to serve at home or abroad as surgeons with the army should communicate with the Secretary, War Office. Motorcyclists for service with the army are also required. Their pay will be 35s weekly, all found. A bounty of £10 will be paid to each man approved and a further £5 on discharge. Men are required to enlist for one year, or as long as the war continues. A certain number of foreman artificers, electricians, blacksmiths etc, are also required for service with the army.* (Watson)

2   Probably Frank Begley (1890–1963) who rode a Martin JAP in the 1913 Senior TT.

3   In 1914 Great Portland Street was centre of the motorcycle trade in London's West End.

4   Alan Wallace (1891–1915), a New Zealand Rhodes Scholar at Balliol, enlisted in the New Zealand Engineers and was killed at Gallipoli. Alfred George Marshall (1888–1973), also a New Zealand Rhodes Scholar at Balliol, served with 5th Cavalry Brigade in France, ending the war as Captain in the Royal Engineers.

The next few days we were drilled, lectured, and given our kit. We began to know each other, and make friends. Finally, several of us, who wanted to go out together, managed by slight misstatements to be put into one batch. We were chosen to join the 5th Division. The Major in command told us – to our great relief – that the Fifth would not form part of the first Expeditionary Force.[1]

I remember Chatham as a place of heat, intolerable dirt, and a bad sore throat. There we made our first acquaintance with the army, which we undergraduates had derided as a crowd of slavish wastrels and empty-headed slackers.[2] We met with tact and courtesy from the mercenary. A sergeant of the Sappers we discovered to be as fine a type of man as any in the wide earth. And we marvelled, too, at the smoothness of organisation, the lack of confusing hurry. …

We were to start early on Monday morning. My mother and sister rushed down to Chatham, and my sister has urgently requested me to mention in "the book" that she carried, with much labour, a large and heavy pair of ski-ing boots. Most of the others had enlisted like myself in a hurry. They did not see "their people" until December.

All of us were made to write our names in the visitors' book, for, as the waiter said – "They ain't nobodies now, but in these 'ere times yer never knows what they may be."

Then, when we had gone in an ear-breaking splutter of exhausts, he turned to comfort my mother –

"Pore young fellers! Pore young fellers! I wonder if any of 'em will return."

That damp chilly morning I was very sleepy and rather frightened at the new things I was going to do. I imagined war as a desperate continuous series of battles, in which I should ride along the trenches picturesquely haloed with bursting shell, varied by innumerable encounters with Uhlans,[3] or solitary forest rides and immense tiring treks over deserted country to distant armies. I wasn't quite sure I liked the idea of it all. But the sharp morning air, the interest in training a new motor-cycle in the way it should go, the unexpected popping-up and grotesque salutes of wee gnome-like Boy Scouts, soon made me forget the war. A series of the kind of little breakdowns you always have in a collection of new bikes delayed us considerably, and only a race over greasy setts through the southern suburbs, over Waterloo Bridge and across the Strand, brought us to Euston just as the boat-train was timed to start. In the importance of our new uniforms we stopped it, of course, and rode joyfully from one end of the platform to the other, much to the agitation of the guard, while I posed delightfully against a bookstall to be photographed by a patriotic governess.

Very grimy we sat down to a marvellous breakfast, and passed the time reading magazines and discussing the length of the war. We put it at from three to six weeks. At Holyhead we carefully took our bikes aboard, and settled down to a cold voyage. We were all a trifle apprehensive at our lack of escort, for then, you will remember, it had not yet been proved how innocuous the German fleet is in our own seas.[4]

Ireland was a disappointment. Everybody was dirty and unfriendly, staring at us with hostile eyes. Add Dublin grease, which beats the Belgian, and a crusty garage proprietor who only after persuasion supplied us with petrol, and you may be sure we were glad to see the last of it. The road

---

1 The Expeditionary Force was to consist of six Infantry Divisions and a Cavalry Division, but it was the 4th and 6th Divisions which were held back in England against a possible invasion.
2 For an explanation of how the book came to be re-issued in an expurgated version in 1917, see Appendix I, page 247. The first two sentences of this paragraph were deleted by the censors, and the word "mercenary" was replaced by "professionals".
3 Mobile and lightly armed German cavalry used for scouting.
4 *This was written before the days of the "Submarine Blockade."* (Watson)

to Carlow was bad and bumpy. But the sunset was fine, and we liked the little low Irish cottages in the twilight. When it was quite dark we stopped at a town with a hill in it. One of our men had a brick thrown at him as he rode in, and when we came to the inn we didn't get a gracious word, and decided it was more pleasant not to be a soldier in Ireland.

The daughter of the house was pretty and passably clean, but it was very grimly that she had led me through an immense gaudy drawing-room disconsolate in dust wrappings, to a little room where we could wash. She gave us an exiguous meal at an extortionate charge, and refused to put more than two of us up; so, on the advice of two gallivanting lancers who had escaped from the Curragh for some supper, we called in the aid of the police, and were billeted magnificently on the village. A moderate breakfast at an unearthly hour, a trouble with the starting up of our bikes, and we were off again. It was about nine when we turned into Carlow Barracks.

The company sighed with relief on seeing us. We completed the establishment on mobilisation. Our two "artificers," Cecil and Grimers, had already arrived.[1] We were overjoyed to see them. We realised that what they did not know about motor-cycles was not worth knowing, and we had suspected at Chatham what we found afterwards to be true, that no one could have chosen for us pleasanter comrades or more reliable workers.

A fine breakfast was soon prepared for us and we begun looking round. The position should have been a little difficult – a dozen or so 'Varsity men, very fresh from their respective universities, thrown as corporals at the head of a company of professional soldiers. We were determined that, whatever vices we might have, we should not be accused of "swank." The sergeants, after a trifle of preliminary stiffness, treated us with fatherly kindness, and did all they could to make us comfortable and teach us what we wanted to learn.

Carlow was a fascinating little town. The National Volunteers still drilled just behind the barracks. It was not wise to refer to the Borderers or to Ulster, but the war had made all the difference in the world. We were to represent Carlow in the Great War. Right through the winter Carlow never forgot us. They sent us comforts and cigarettes and Christmas Puddings. When the 5th Signal Company returns, Carlow will go mad.

My first "official" ride was to Dublin. It rained most of the way there and all the way back, but a glow of patriotism kept me warm. In Dublin I went into a little public-house for some beer and bread and cheese. The landlord told me that though he wasn't exactly a lover of soldiers, things had changed now. On my return I was given lunch in the Officers' Mess, for nobody could consider their men more than the officers of our company.

The next day we were inoculated. At the time we would much rather have risked typhoid. We did not object to the discomfort, though two of us nearly fainted on parade the following morning – it was streamingly hot – but our farewell dinner was absolutely spoilt. Bottles of the best Moselle Carlow could produce were left untouched. Songs broke down in curses. It was tragic.

---

1   Cecil and Alick Burney (see Cast, page 132). Alick no doubt earned his nickname from the state of his hands, which was the inevitable result of maintaining the motorcycles, and occasionally he and his brother were known collectively as 'the Grimers'.

2

The Journey to the Front

We made a triumphant departure from Carlow, preceded down to the station by the band of the N.V.[1] We were told off to prevent anybody entering the station, but all the men entered magnificently, saying they were volunteers, and the women and children rushed us with the victorious cry, "We've downed the p'lice." We steamed out of the station while the band played "Come back to Erin" and "God save Ireland," and made an interminable journey to Dublin. At some of the villages they cheered, at others they looked at us glumly. But the back streets of Dublin were patriotic enough, and at the docks, which we reached just after dark, a small, tremendously enthusiastic crowd was gathered to see us off.

They sang songs and cheered, and cheered and sang songs. "I can generally bear the separation, but I don't like the leave-taking."[2]

The boat would not go off. The crowd on the boat and the crowd on the wharf made patriotic noises until they were hoarse. At midnight our supporters had nearly all gone away. We who had seen our motor-cycles carefully hoisted on board ate the buns and apples provided by "Friends in Dublin" and chatted. A young gunner told me of all his amours, and they were very numerous. Still –

> For my uncle *Toby's* amours running all the way in my head, they had the same effect upon me as if they had been my own – I was in the most perfect state of bounty and goodwill.[3]

So I set about finding a place for sleep.

The whole of the Divisional Headquarters Staff, with all their horses, were on the *Archimedes*, and we were so packed that when I tried to find a place to sleep I discovered there was not an inch of space left on the deck, so I passed an uncomfortable night on top of some excruciatingly hard ropes.

We cast off about one in the morning. The night was horribly cold, and a slow dawn was never more welcomed. But day brought a new horror. The sun poured down on us, and the smell from the horses packed closely below was almost unbearable; while, worst of all, we had to go below to wash and to draw our rations.

Then I was first introduced to bully. The first tin tastes delicious and fills you rapidly. You never actually grow to dislike it, and many times when extra hungry I have longed for an extra tin. But when you have lived on bully for three months (we have not been served out with fresh meat more than a dozen times altogether),[4] how you long for any little luxuries to vary the monotony of your food!

---

1 The National Volunteers were a political movement loyal to John Redmond, a politician who opposed Unionism but supported the British involvement in the European war.

2 Watson is quoting from The Notebooks of Samuel Butler, a posthumous collection of aphorisms by the iconoclastic Victorian author which was a publishing sensation in 1912.

3 Uncle Toby, a soldier and ladies' man, was a character in Laurence Sterne's bawdy novel "Tristram Shandy" (1767).

4 *This was written in the middle of October.* (Watson)

Due to overcrowding and the stench of horses in the hold of SS Archimedes, the motorcyclists preferred to stay on deck in the benign weather conditions

On the morning of the third day we passed a French destroyer with a small prize in tow, and rejoiced greatly, and towards evening we dropped anchor off Havre. On either side of the narrow entrance to the docks there were cheering crowds, and we cheered back, thrilled, occasionally breaking into the soldier's anthem, "It's a long, long way to Tipperary."[1]

---

1   *We became bored with the song, and dropped it soon after for less printable songs.* (Watson)

French civilians mingle with the Expeditionary Force. The motor lorries indicate that much of the Army Service Corps transport was already motorized, although many specialist vehicles, such as cable-carts and cooks' wagons, were horse-drawn.

We disembarked at a secluded wharf, and after waiting about for a couple of hours or so – we had not then learned to wait – we were marched off to a huge dim warehouse, where we were given gallons of the most delicious hot coffee, and bought scrumptious little cakes.

It was now quite dark, and, for what seemed whole nights, we sat wearily waiting while the horses were taken off the transport. We made one vain dash for our quarters, but found only another enormous warehouse, strangely lit, full of clattering waggons and restive horses. We watched with wonder a battery clank out into the night, and then returned sleepily to the wharf-side. Very late we found where we were to sleep, a gigantic series of wool warehouses. The warehouses were full of wool and the wool was full of fleas. We were very miserable, and a little bread and wine we managed to get hold of hardly cheered us at all. I feared the fleas, and spread a waterproof sheet on the bare stones outside. I thought I should not get a wink of sleep on such a Jacobean resting-place, but, as a matter of fact, I slept like a top, and woke in the morning without even an ache. But those who had risked the wool – !

We breakfasted off the strong, sweet tea that I have grown to like so much, and some bread, butter, and chocolate we bought off a smiling old woman at the warehouse gates. Later in the morning we were allowed into the town. First, a couple of us went into a café to have a drink, and when we came out we found our motor-cycles garlanded with flowers by two admiring flappers.[1]

Everywhere we went we were the gods of a very proper worship, though the shopkeepers in their admiration did not forget to charge. We spent a long, lazy day in lounging through the town, eating a lot of little meals and in visiting the public baths – the last bath I was to have, if I had only known it, for a month. A cheery, little, bustling town Havre seemed to us, basking in a bright

---

1   Attractive young single women were known as "flappers" well before the 1920s.

sunshine, and the hopes of our early overwhelming victory. We all stalked about, prospective conquerors, and talked fluently of the many defects of the German army.

Orders came in the afternoon that we were to move that night. I sat up until twelve, and gained as my reward some excellent hot tea and a bit of rather tough steak. At twelve everybody was woken up and the company got ready to move. We motor-cyclists were sent off to the station. Foolishly I went by myself. Just outside what I thought was the station I ran out of petrol. I walked to the station and waited for the others. They did not come. I searched the station, but found nothing except a cavalry brigade entraining. I rushed about feverishly. There was no one I knew, no one who had heard anything of my company. Then I grew horribly frightened that I should be left behind. I pelted back to the old warehouses, but found everybody had left two hours ago. I thought the company must surely have gone by now, and started in my desperation asking everybody I knew if they had seen anything of the company. Luckily I came across an entraining officer, who told me that the company were entraining at "Point Six-Hangar de Laine," – three miles away. I simply ran there, asking my way of surly, sleepy sentries, tripping over ropes, nearly falling into docks.

I found the Signal Company. There was not a sign of our train. So Johnson[1] took me on his carrier back to the station I had searched in such fear. We found the motor-cycle, Johnson gave me some petrol, and we returned to Point Six. It was dawn when the old train at last rumbled and squeaked into the siding.

I do not know how long we took to entrain, I was so sleepy. But the sun was just rising when the little trumpet shrilled, the long train creaked over the points, and we woke for a moment to murmur – By Jove, we're off now, – and I whispered thankfully to myself – Thank heaven I found them at last.

We were lucky enough to be only six in our compartment, but, as you know, in a French IIIme there is very little room, while the seats are fiercely hard. And we had not yet been served out with blankets. Still, we had to stick it for twenty-four hours. Luckily the train stopped at every station of any importance, so, taking the law into our own hands, we got out and stretched our legs at every opportunity.

We travelled *viâ* Rouen and Amiens to Landrecies. The Signal Company had a train to itself. Gradually we woke up to find ourselves travelling through extraordinarily pretty country and cheering crowds. At each level-crossing the curé was there to bless us. If we did not stop the people threw in fruit, which we vainly endeavoured to catch. A halt, and they were round us, beseeching us for souvenirs, loading us with fruit, and making us feel that it was a fine thing to fight in a friendly country.

At Rouen we drew up at a siding, and sent porters scurrying for bread and butter and beer, while we loaded up from women who came down to the train with all sorts of delicious little cakes and sweets. We stopped, and then rumbled slowly towards Amiens. At St Roche we first saw wounded, and heard, I do not know with what truth, that four aviators had been killed, and that our General, Grierson, had died of heart failure.[2] At Ham they measured me against a lamp-post, and ceremoniously marked the place.[3] The next time I passed through Ham I had no time to look for the mark! It began to grow dark, and the trees standing out against the sunset reminded me of our two lines of trees at home. We went slowly over bridges, and looked fearfully from our windows for bursting shells. Soon we fell asleep, and were wakened about midnight by shouted orders. We had arrived at Landrecies, near enough the Frontier to excite us.

---

1   Henry Goode Fielding-Johnson. See Cast, page 138.

2   Lieutenant-General Sir James Grierson (1859–1914) died of a heart attack shortly after his arrival in France as commanding officer of 2 Corps.

3   See Cast, page 128.

The approach to the station in Landrecies is little changed – one can visualize this scene today. Beyond the closed wagons the flat-bed trucks carry cable-carts – the last surviving example is displayed at the Royal Signals Museum, Blandford Forum.

I wonder if you realise at home what the Frontier meant to us at first? We conceived it as a thing guarded everywhere by intermittent patrols of men staring carefully towards Germany and Belgium in the darkness, a thing to be defended at all costs, at all times, to be crossed with triumph and recrossed with shame. We did not understand what an enormous, incredible thing modern war was – how it cared nothing for frontiers, or nations, or people.

Very wearily we unloaded our motor bicycles and walked to the barracks, where we put down our kit and literally feel asleep, to be wakened for fatigue work.

We rose at dawn, and had some coffee at a little *estaminet* [1] where a middle-aged dame, horribly arch, cleaned my canteen for me, "pour l'amour de toi." We managed an excellent breakfast of bacon and eggs before establishing the Signal Office at the barracks. A few of us rode off to keep touch with the various brigades that were billeted round. The rest of us spent the morning across the road at an inn drinking much wine-and-water and planning out the war on a forty-year-old map.

In the afternoon I went out with two others to prospect some roads, very importantly. We were rather annoyed to lose our way out of the town, and were very short with some inquisitive small boys who stood looking over our shoulders as we squatted on the grass by the wayside studying our maps.

We had some tea at a mad village called Hecq. All the inhabitants were old, ugly, smelly, and dirty; and they crowded round us as we devoured a magnificent omelette, endeavouring to incite us to do all sorts of things to the German women if ever we reached Germany. We returned home in the late afternoon to hear rumours of an advance next day.

---

1   *The word used in Flanders for a tavern that does not aspire to the dignity of "restaurant" or "hotel."* (Watson)

Three of us wandered into the Square to have a drink. There I first tried a new pipe that had been given me. The one pipe I brought with me I had dropped out of the train between Amiens and Landrecies. It had been quite a little tragedy, as it was a pipe for which I had a great affection. It had been my companion in Switzerland and Paris.

Coming back from the Square I came across an excited crowd. It appears that an inoffensive, rather buxom-looking woman had been walking round the Square when one of her breasts cooed and flew away. We shot three spies at Landrecies.

I hung round the Signal Office, nervous and excited, for "a run." The night was alive with the tramp of troops and the rumble of guns. The old 108th passed by – huge good-natured guns, each drawn by eight gigantic plough-horses.[1] I wonder if you can understand – the thrilling excitement of waiting and listening by night in a town full of troops.

At midnight I took my first despatch. It was a dark, starless night; very misty on the road. From the brigade I was sent on to an ambulance – an unpleasant ride, because, apart from the mist and the darkness, I was stopped every few yards by sentries of the West Kents, a regiment which has now about the best reputation of any battalion out here.[2] I returned in time to snatch a couple of hours of sleep before we started at dawn for Belgium.

When the Division moves we ride either with the column or go in advance to the halting-place. That morning we rode with the column, which meant riding three-quarters of a mile or so and then waiting for the main guard to come up, – an extraordinarily tiring method of getting along.

The day (August 21) was very hot indeed, and the troops who had not yet got their marching feet suffered terribly, even though the people by the wayside brought out fruit and eggs and drinks. There was murmuring when some officers refused to allow their men to accept these gifts. But a start had to be made some time, for promiscuous drinks do not increase marching efficiency.

We, of course, could do pretty well what we liked. A little coffee early in the morning, and then anything we cared to ask for. Most of us in the evening discovered, unpleasantly enough, forgotten pears in unthought-of pockets.

About 1.30 we neared Bavai, and I was sent on to find out about billeting arrangements, but by the time they were completed the rest had arrived.

For a long time we were hutted in the Square. Spuggy[3] found a "friend," and together we obtained a good wash. The people were vociferously enthusiastic. Even the chemist gave us some "salts" free of charge.

My first ride from Bavai began with a failure, as, owing to belt-slip, I endeavoured vainly to start for half an hour (or so it seemed) in the midst of an interested but sympathetic populace.[4] A smart change saw me tearing along the road to meet with a narrow escape from untimely death in the form of a car, which I tried to pass on the wrong side. In the evening we received our first batch of pay, and dining magnificently at a hotel, took tearful leave of Huggie[5] and Spuggy. They had been chosen, they said, to make a wild dash through to Liege. We speculated darkly on their probable fate. In the morning we learned that we had been hoaxed, and used suitable language.

We slept uncomfortably on straw in a back yard, and rose again just before dawn. We break-fasted hastily at a café, and were off just as the sun had risen.

---

1   108 Heavy Battery, Royal Garrison Artillery, was equipped with 60-pdr guns (illustration, page 187).
2   1st Battalion Queen's Own (Royal West Kent Regiment) was one of four infantry battalions which made up 13th Infantry Brigade.
3   Eric Bagshaw (see Cast, page 139).
4   Watson's motorcycle was probably a Rudge – belt-driven rather than chain-driven (see Appendix II, page 262).
5   Hugh Trepess (see Cast, page 143).

One happy task for a Pay Sergeant was the weekly ritual of handing out pay packets. Watson can be seen signing for his pay, while the man on the left is counting the contents of his envelope.

Our day's march was to Dour, in Belgium, and for us a bad day's march it was. My job was to keep touch with the 14th Brigade, which was advancing along a parallel road to the west.[1] That meant riding four or five miles across rough country roads, endeavouring to time myself so as to reach the 14th column just when the S.O.[2] was passing, then back again to the Division, riding up and down the column until I found our captain. In the course of my riding that day I knocked down "a civvy" in Dour, and bent a foot-rest endeavouring to avoid a major, but that was all in the day's work.

The Signal Office was first established patriarchally with a table by the roadside, and thence I made my last journey that day to the 14th. I found them in a village under the most embarrassing attentions. As for myself, while I was waiting, a curé photographed me, a woman rushed out and washed my face, and children crowded up to me, presenting me with chocolate and cigars, fruit and eggs, until my haversack was practically bursting.

When I returned I found the S.O. had shifted to the station of Dour. We were given the waiting-room, which we made comfortable with straw. Opposite the station was a hotel where the Staff lived. It was managed by a curiously upright old man in a threadbare frock-coat, bright check trousers, and carpet slippers. Nadine, his pretty daughter, was tremulously eager to make us comfortable, and the two days we were at Dour we hung round the hotel, sandwiching omelettes and drink between our despatches.

---

1   *The Bavai-Andregnies-Elouges road.* (Watson)
2   Signal Office.

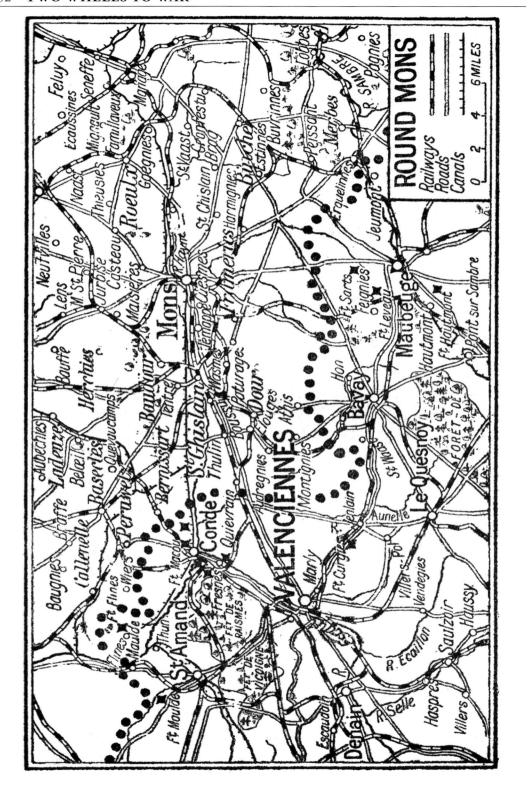

3

The Battle of Mons

We knew nothing of what was going on. There was a rumour that Namur had fallen, and I heard certain officers say we had advanced dangerously far. The cavalry was on our left and the Third Division on our right. Beyond the Third Division we had heard of the First Corps, but nothing of the French. We were left, to the best of our knowledge, a tenuous bulwark against the German hosts.

The 14th Brigade had advanced by the Andregnies road to Elouges and the Canal. The 13th was our right brigade, and the 15th, at first in reserve, extended our line on the second day to Frameries. The Cyclists were reconnoitring north of the Canal.

The roads round Dour were of the very worst *pavé*, and, if this were not enough, the few maps we had between us were useless. The villages of Waasmes, Paturages, and Frameries were in the midst of such a network of roads that the map could not possibly be clear. If the country had been flat, we might at least have found our way by landmarks. It was not. The roads wandered round great slag-heaps, lost themselves in little valleys, ran into pits and groups of buildings. Each one tried to be exactly like all its fellows. Without a map to get from Elouges to Frameries was like asking an American to make his way from Richmond Park to Denmark Hill.

About ten o'clock on the morning of August 23rd I was sent out to find General Gleichen, who was reported somewhere near Waasmes.[1] I went over nightmare roads, uneven cobbles with great pits in them. I found him, and was told by him to tell the General that the position was unfortunate owing to a weak salient. We had already heard guns, but on my way back I heard a distant crash, and looked round to find that a shell had burst half a mile away on a slag-heap, between Dour and myself. With my heart thumping against my ribs I opened the throttle, until I was jumping at 40 m.p.h. from cobble to cobble. Then, realising that I was in far greater danger of breaking my neck than of being shot, I pulled myself together and slowed down to proceed sedately home.

The second time I went out to General Gleichen I found him a little farther back from his former position. This time he was on the railway. While I was waiting for a reply we had an excellent view of German guns endeavouring to bring down one of our aeroplanes. So little did we know of aeroplanes then, that the General was persuaded by his brigade-major to step back into shelter from the falling bits, and we all stared anxiously skywards, expecting every moment that our devoted aviator would be hit.

That evening Huggie and I rode back to Bavai and beyond in search of an errant ammunition column. Eventually we found it and brought news of it back to H.Q. I shall never forget the captain reading my despatch by the light of my lamp, the waggons guarded by Dorsets,[2] with fixed bayonets appearing to disappear shadowy in the darkness. We showed the captain a short-cut that avoided Bavai, then left him. His horses were tired, but he was forced to push them on another ten

---

1   Brigadier-General Count Gleichen (1863–1937) commanded the 15th Infantry Brigade.
2   1st Battalion The Dorsetshire Regiment belonged to the 15th Brigade.

miles to Dour. We got back at 10, and found Nadine weeping. We questioned her, but she would not tell us why.

There was a great battle very early the next morning, a running-about and set, anxious faces. We were all sent off in rapid succession. I was up early and managed to get a wash at the station-master's house, his wife providing me with coffee, which, much to my discomfiture, she liberally dosed with rum. At 6.30 Johnson started on a message to the 15th Brigade. We never saw him again.

At 9.15 three despatch riders who had gone to the 15th, George,[1] Johnson, and Grimers, had not returned. I was sent. Two miles out I met George with Grimers' despatches. Neither of them had been able to find the 15th. I took the despatches and sent George back to report. I went down a road, which I calculated ought to bring me somewhere on the left of the 15th, who were supposed to be somewhere between Paturages and Frameries.

There were two villages on hills, one on each side. I struck into the north end of the village on my left; there was no road to the one on my right.[2] I came across a lot of disheartened stragglers retreating up the hill.[3] I went a little farther and saw our own firing line a quarter of a mile ahead. There was a bit of shrapnel flying about, but not much. I struck back up the hill and came upon a crowd of fugitive infantry men, all belonging to the 13th Brigade. At last I found General Cuthbert, the Brigadier of the 13th, sitting calmly on his horse watching the men pass.[4] I asked him where the 15th was. He did not know, but told me significantly that our rallying-point was Athis.

I rode a little farther, and came upon his signal officer. He stopped me and gave me a verbal message to the General, telling me that the 15th appeared to be cut off. As I had a verbal message to take back there was no need for me to go farther with my despatches, which, as it appeared later, was just as well. I sprinted back to Dour, picking my way through a straggling column of men sullenly retreating. At the station I found everybody packing up. The General received my message without a word, except one of thanks.

> The right flank of the 13th has been badly turned.
> Most of our officers have been killed.
> Some companies of the K.O.S.B.[5] are endeavouring to cover our retreat.[6]

We viciously smashed all the telegraph instruments in the office and cut all the wires. It took me some time to pack up my kit and tie it on my carrier. When I had finished, everybody had gone. I could hear their horses clattering up the street. Across the way Nadine stood weeping. A few women with glazed, resigned eyes, stood listlessly round her. Behind me, I heard the first shell crash dully into the far end of the town. It seemed to me I could not just go off. So I went across to Nadine and muttered "Nous reviendrons, Mademoiselle." But she would not look at me, so I jumped on my bicycle, and with a last glance round at the wrecked, deserted station, I rode off, shouting to encourage more myself than the others, "Ça va bien."

---

1   George Owen (see Cast, page 144).
2   *I had no map with me. All the maps were in use. Looking afterwards at the map which I obtained later in the day, I am unable to trace my route with any accuracy. It is certain that the Germans temporarily thrust in a wedge between the 13th and 15th Brigades.* (Watson)
3   The censor required "disheartened" to be replaced with the words "lost and weary."
4   Brigadier-General Gerald Cuthbert (1861–1931) commanded 13th Brigade.
5   2nd Battalion King's Own Scottish Borderers was also part of 13th Brigade.
6   These three sentences were deleted by the censor.

I caught up the General, and passed him to ride on ahead of the Signal Company. Never before had I so wished my engine to turn more slowly. It seemed a shame that we motor-cyclists should head the retreat of our little column. I could not understand how the men could laugh and joke. It was blasphemous. They ought to be cursing with angry faces, – at the least, to be grave and sorrowful.

I was told that Divisional Headquarters would be established at Villers-Pol, a little country village about ten miles west of Bavai and eight miles south-east of Valenciennes. I rode to St Waast, a few miles out of Bavai, and, finding there a cavalry colonel (of the 2nd Life Guards, I think), gave him all the news. I hurried on to Jenlain, thinking I might be of some use to the troops on our right flank, but Jenlain was peaceful and empty. So I cut across low rolling downs to Villers-Pol. There was nobody there when I arrived. The sun was shining very brightly. Old women were sleeping at the doors; children were playing lazily on the road. Soon one or two motor-cyclists dribbled in, and about an hour later a section of the Signal Company arrived after a risky dash along country lanes. They outspanned,[1] and we, as always, made for the inn.

There was a mother in the big room. She was a handsome little woman of about twenty-four. Her husband was at the war. She asked me why we had come to Villers-Pol. I said we were retreating a little – pour attaquer le mieux – un mouvement strategique. She wept bitterly and loudly, "Ah, my baby, what will they do to us? They will kill you, and they will ill-treat me so that never again shall I be able to look my husband in the eyes – his brave eyes; but now perhaps they are closed in death!" There was an older, harsh-featured woman who rated the mother for her silliness, and, while we ate our omelette, the room was filled with the clamour of them until a dog outside began to howl. Then the mother went and sat down in a chair by the fire and stopped crying, but every now and then moaned and clasped her baby strongly to her breast, murmuring, "My poor baby, my poor baby, what shall we do?"

We lounged about the place until a cavalry brigade came through. The General commandeered me to find his transport. This I did, and on the way back waited for the brigade to pass. Then for the first time I saw that many riderless horses were being led, that some of the horses and many of the men were wounded, and that one regiment of lancers was pathetically small. It was the 2nd Cavalry Brigade, that had charged the enemy's guns, to find them protected by barbed wire.[2]

Sick at heart I rode back into Villers-Pol, and found the Signal Company hastily harnessing up. Headquarters had been compelled to go farther back still – to St Waast, and there was nobody, so far as we knew, between us and the Germans. The order caught George with his gear down.[3] We made a marvellously rapid repair, then went off at the trot. A mile out, and I was sent back to pick up our quartermaster and three others who were supposed to have been left behind. It was now quite dark. In the village I could not find our men, but discovered a field ambulance that did not know what to do. Their horses were dead tired, but I advised them strongly to get on. They took my advice, and I heard at Serches that they left Villers-Pol as the Germans[4] entered it. They were pursued, but somehow got away in the darkness.

---

1   Unharnessed the horses from the wagons.
2   A handful of cavalry charges occurred in 1914 – on this occasion 800 men of 4th Dragoon Guards and 9th Lancers charged infantry at Elouges. They lost 234 officers and men, killed and wounded, before they got within half a mile of the German position.
3   George was riding a Rudge Multi on which changing gear is effected by a pair of expanding and contracting pulleys, which cannot be moved when the bike is stationary, hence starting out in a high gear is very difficult.
4   *A small patrol of cavalry, I should imagine, if the tale I heard at Serches be true.* (Watson)

I went on, and at some cross-roads in a black forest came across a regiment of hussars. I told them where their B.H.Q.[1] was, and their Colonel muttered resignedly, "It's a long way, but we shall never get our wounded horses there to-morrow." I put two more companies right, then came across a little body of men who were vainly trying to get a horse attached to a S.A.A. limber[2] out of the ditch. It was a pitch-black night, and they were bravely endeavouring to do it without catching a glimpse of the horse. I gave them the benefit of my lamp until they had got the brute out. Two more bodies of stragglers I directed, and then pushed on rapidly to St Waast, where I found all the other motor-cyclists safe except Johnson. Two had come on carts, having been compelled to abandon their motor-cycles.

George had been attached to the 14th. He had gone with them to the canal, and had been left there with the Cornwalls[3] when the 14th had retired to its second position. At last nobody remained with him except a section. They were together in a hut, and outside he could hear the bullets singing.

He noticed some queer-looking explosives in a corner, and asked what they were for. He was told they were to blow up the bridge over the canal, so decided it was time for him to quit, and did so with some rapidity under a considerable rifle fire. Then he was sent up to the Manchesters,[4] who were holding a ready-made trench across the main road. As he rode up he tells me men shouted at him, "Don't go that way, it's dangerous," until he grew quite frightened; but he managed to get to the trench all right, slipped in, and was shown how to crawl along until he reached the colonel.

N'Soon and Sadders[5] were with the 13th. On the Sunday night they had to march to a new position more towards their right. The Signal Section went astray and remained silently on a byroad while their officer reconnoitred. On the main road between them and their lines were some lights rapidly moving – Germans in armoured motor-cars. They successfully rejoined, but in the morning there was something of a collision, and Sadders' bicycle was finished. He got hold of a push-bike alongside the waggons for some distance, finishing up on a limber.

Spuggy was sent up to the trenches in the morning. He was under heavy shell fire when his engine seized up. His brigade was retreating, and he was in the rear of it, so, leaving his bicycle, he took to his heels, and with the Germans in sight ran till he caught up a waggon. He clambered on, and so came into St Waast.

I had not been in many minutes when I was sent off to our Army H.Q. at Bavai. It was a miserable ride. I was very tired, the road was full of transport, and my lamp would not give more than a feeble glimmer.

I got to bed at 1 a.m. About 3.30 (on August 24) I was called and detailed to remain with the rear-guard. First I was sent off to find the exact position of various bodies posted on roads to stem the German advance. At one spot I just missed a shell-trap. A few minutes after I had left, some of the Manchesters, together with a body of the D. Cyclists[6] who were stationed three miles or so out of St Waast, were attacked by a body of Jaegers,[7] who appeared on a hill opposite. Foolishly they disclosed their position by opening rifle fire. In a few minutes the Jaegers went, and to our utter discomfiture a couple of field-guns appeared and fired point-blank at 750 yards. Luckily the range

---

1   Brigade Headquarters.
2   Small Arms Ammunition limber.
3   1st Battalion Duke of Cornwall's Light Infantry was part of 14th Brigade.
4   2nd Battalion Manchester Regiment was also part of 14th Brigade.
5   Jack Danson and Cecil Hayes-Sadler (see Cast, pages 146 and 148) became friends at Oxford.
6   The Divisional Cyclist Company.
7   Jaeger regiments were light infantry trained for reconnaissance and skirmishing.

was not very exact, and only a few were wounded – those who retired directly backwards instead of transversely out of the shells' direction.

The H.Q. of the rear-guard left St Waast about 5.30. It was cold and chilly. What happened I do not quite know. All I remember was that at a given order a battery would gallop off the road into action against an enemy we could not see. So to Bavai, where I was sent off with an important despatch for D.H.Q.[1] I had to ride past the column, and scarcely had I gone half a mile when my back tyre burst. There was no time to repair it, so on I bumped, slipping all over the road. At D.H.Q., which of course was on the road, I borrowed some one else's bicycle and rode back by another road. On the way I came across Huggie filling up from an abandoned motor-lorry. I did likewise, and then tore into Bavai. A shell or two was bursting over the town, and I was nearly slaughtered by some infantrymen, who thought they were firing at an aeroplane. Dodging their bullets, I left the town, and eventually caught up the H.Q. of the rear-guard.

It was now about 10.30. Until five the troops tramped on, in a scorching sun, on roads covered with clouds of dust. And most pitiful of all, between the rear-guard and the main body shuffled the wounded; for we had been forced to evacuate our hospital at Bavai. Our men were mad at retreating. The Germans had advanced on them in the closest order. Each fellow firmly believed he had killed fifty, and was perfectly certain we could have held our line to the crack of doom. They trudged and trudged. The women, who had cheerily given us everything a few days before, now with anxious faces timorously offered us water and fruit.

Great ox-waggons full of refugees, all in their best clothes, came in from side-roads. None of them were allowed on the roads we were retreating along, so I suppose they were pushed across the German front until they fell into the Germans' hands.[2]

For us it was column-riding the whole day – half a mile or so, and then a halt, – heart-breaking work.

I was riding along more or less by myself in a gap that had been left in the column. A curé stopped me. He was a very tall and very thin young man with a hasty, frightened manner. Behind him was a flock of panic-stricken, chattering old women. He asked me if there was any danger. Not that he was afraid, he said, but just to satisfy his people. I answered that none of them need trouble to move. I was too ashamed to say we were retreating, and I had an eye on the congestion of the roads. I have sometimes wondered what that tall, thin curé, with the sallow face and the frightened eyes, said about me when, not twelve hours later, the German advance-guard triumphantly defiled before him.

Late in the afternoon we passed through Le Cateau, a bright little town, and came to the village of Reumont, where we were billeted in a large barn.

We were all very confident that evening. We heard that we were holding a finely entrenched position, and the General made a speech – I did not hear it – in which he told us that there had been a great Russian success, and that in the battle of the morrow a victory for us would smash the Germans once and for all.[3] But our captain was more pessimistic. He thought we should suffer a great disaster. Doubting, we snuggled down in the straw, and went soundly to sleep.

---

1   Divisional Headquarters.

2   The final sentence of this paragraph was deleted by the censor.

3   General Sir Horace Smith-Dorrien (1863–1931), commanding officer of 2 Corps, conferred with General Allenby (Cavalry Division) and General Snow (4th Infantry Division). Allenby and Snow agreed to make a stand under his orders. The intention was to deliver a "stopping blow" before resuming the Retreat.

4

The Battle of Le Cateau

The principal thing about Le Cateau is that the soldiers pronounce it to rhyme with Waterloo – Leacatoo – and all firmly believe that if the French cavalry had come up to help us, as the Prussians came up at Waterloo, there would have been no Germans to fight against us now.[1]

It was a cold misty morning when we awoke, but later the day was fine enough. We got up, had a cheery and exiguous breakfast to distant, intermittent firing, then did a little work on our bicycles. I spent an hour or so watching through glasses the dim movement of dull bodies of troops and shrapnel bursting vaguely on the horizon. Then we were all summoned to H.Q., which were stationed about a mile out from Reumont on the Le Cateau road. In front of us the road dipped sharply and rose again over the brow of a hill about two miles away. On this brow, stretching right and left of the road, there was a line of poplars. On the slope of the hill nearer to us there were two or three field batteries in action. To the right of us a brigade of artillery was limbered up ready to go anywhere. In the left, at the bottom of the dip the 108th was in action, partially covered by some sparse bushes. A few ambulance waggons and some miscellaneous first-line transport were drawn up along the side of the road at the bottom of the dip. To the N.W. we could see for about four miles over low, rolling fields. We could see nothing to the right, as our view was blocked by a cottage and some trees and hedges. On the roof of the cottage a wooden platform had been made. On it stood the General and his Chief of Staff and our Captain[2]. Four telephone operators worked for their lives in pits breast-high, two on each side of the road. The Signal Clerk sat at a table behind the cottage, while round him, or near him, were the motor-cyclists and cyclists.

About the battle itself you know as much as I. We had wires out to all the brigades, and along them the news would come and orders would go. The ———— are holding their position satisfactorily. Our flank is being turned. Should be very grateful for another battalion. We are under very heavy shell fire. Right through the battle I did not take a single message. Huggie took a despatch to the 13th, and returned under very heavy shrapnel fire, and for this was very properly mentioned in despatches.

How the battle fluctuated I cannot now remember. But I can still see those poplars almost hidden in the smoke of shrapnel. I can still hear the festive crash of the Heavies as they fired slowly, scientifically, and well. From 9 to 12.30 we remained there kicking our heels, feverishly calm, cracking the absurdest jokes. Then the word went round that on our left things were going very badly. Two battalions were hurried across, and then, of course, the attack developed even more fiercely on our right.

Wounded began to come through – none groaning, but just men with their eyes clenched and great crimson bandages.

An order was sent to the transport to clear back off the road. There was a momentary panic. The waggons came through at the gallop and with them some frightened footsloggers, hanging on and

---

1   The first paragraph of this Chapter was deleted by the Censor.
2   Captain Doherty Holwell (see Cast, page 158).

running for dear life.[1] Wounded men from the firing line told us that the shrapnel was unbearable in the trenches.

A man came galloping up wildly from the Heavies. They had run out of fuses. Already we had sent urgent messages to the ammunition lorries, but the road was blocked and they could not get up to us. So Grimers was sent off with a haversack – mine – to fetch fuses and hurry up the lorries. How he got there and back in the time that he did, with the traffic that there was, I cannot even now understand.

It was now about two o'clock, and every moment the news that we heard grew worse and worse, while the wounded poured past us in a continuous stream. I gave my water-bottle to one man who was moaning for water. A horse came galloping along. Across the saddle-bow was a man with a bloody scrap of trouser instead of a leg, while the rider, who had been badly wounded in the arm, was swaying from side to side.

A quarter of an hour before the brigade on our right front had gone into action on the crest of the hill. Now they streamed back at the trot, all telling the tale – how, before they could even unlimber, shells had come crashing into them. The column was a lingering tragedy. There were teams with only a limber and without a gun. And you must see it to know what a twistedly pathetic thing a gun team and limber without a gun is. There were bits of teams and teams with only a couple of drivers. The faces of the men were awful. I smiled at one or two, but they shook their heads and turned away. One sergeant as he passed was muttering to himself, as if he were repeating something over and over again so as to learn it by rote – "My gun, my gun, my gun!"

At this moment an order came from some one for the motor-cyclists to retire to the farm where we had slept the night. The others went on with the crowd, but I could not start my engine. After trying for five minutes it seemed to me absurd to retreat, so I went back and found that apparently nobody had given the order. The other motor-cyclists returned one by one as soon as they could get clear, but most of them were carried on right past the farm.

A few minutes later there was a great screaming crash overhead – shrapnel. I ran to my bicycle and stood by waiting for orders.

The General suggested mildly that we might change our headquarters. There was a second crash. We all retired about 200 yards back up the road. There I went to the captain in the middle of the traffic and asked him what I should do. He told us to get out of it as we could not do anything more – "You have all done magnificently" – then he gave me some messages for our subaltern. I shouted, "So long, sir," and left him, not knowing whether I should ever see him again. I heard afterwards that he went back when all the operators had fled and tried to get into communication with our Army H.Q.

Just as I had started up my engine another shell burst about 100 yards to the left, and a moment later a big waggon drawn by two maddened horses came dashing down into the main street. They could not turn, so went straight into the wall of a house opposite. There was a dull crash and a squirming heap piled up at the edge of the road.

I pushed through the traffic a little and came upon a captain and a subaltern making their way desperately back. I do not know who they were, but I heard a scrap of what they said –

"We must get back for it," said the captain.
"We shall never return," replied the subaltern gravely.
"It doesn't matter," said the captain.
"It doesn't matter," echoed the subaltern.

---

1   The words "frightened footsloggers, hanging on for dear life" were deleted by the censor.

But I do not think the gun could have been saved.

About six of us collected in a little bunch at the side of the road. On our left we saw a line of infantry running. The road itself was impassable. So we determined to strike off to the right. I led the way, and though we had not the remotest conception whether we should meet British or German, we eventually found our way to 2nd Corps H.Q.[1]

I have only a dim remembrance of what happened there. I went into the signal-office and reported that, so far as I knew, the 5th Division was in flight along the Reumont – Saint-Quentin road.

The sergeant in charge of the 2nd Corps Motor-cyclists offered us some hard-boiled eggs and put me in charge of our lot. Then off we went, and hitting the main road just ahead of our muddled column, halted at the desolate little village of Estrées.

It now began to rain.

Soon the column came pouring past, so miserably and so slowly, – lorries, transport, guns, limbers, small batches of infantrymen, crowds of stragglers. All were cursing the French, for right through the battle we had expected the French to come up on our right wing. There had been a whole corps of cavalry a few miles away, but in reply to our urgent request for help their general had reported that his horses were too tired. How we cursed them and cursed them.[2]

After a weary hour's wait our subaltern came up, and, at my request, sent me to look for the captain. I found him about two miles this side of Reumont, endeavouring vainly to make some sort of ordered procession out of the almost comically patchwork medley. Later I heard that the last four hundred yards of the column had been shelled to destruction as it was leaving Reumont, and a tale is told – probably without truth – of an officer shooting the driver of the leading motor-lorry in a hopeless endeavour to get some ammunition into the firing line.[3]

I scooted back and told the others that our captain was still alive, and a little later we pushed off into the flood. It was now getting dark, and the rain, which had held off for a little, was pouring down.

Finally, we halted at a tiny cottage, and the Signal Company outspanned.

We tried to make ourselves comfortable in the wet by hiding under damp straw and putting on all available bits of clothing. But soon we were all soaked to the skin, and it was so dark that horses wandered perilously near. One hungry mare started eating the straw that was covering my chest. That was enough. Desperately we got up to look round for some shelter, and George, our champion "scrounger," discovered a chicken house. It is true there were nineteen fowls in it. They died a silent and, I hope, a painless death.

The order came round that the motor-cyclists were to spend the night at the cottage – the roads were utterly and hopelessly impassable – while the rest of the company was to go on. So we presented the company with a few fowls and investigated the cottage.

It was a startling place. In one bedroom was a lunatic hag with some food by her side. We left her severely alone. Poor soul, we could not move her! In the kitchen we discovered coffee, sugar, salt, and onions. With the aid of our old Post Sergeant we plucked some of the chickens and put on a great stew. I made a huge basin full of coffee.

The others, dead tired, went to sleep in a wee loft. I could not sleep. I was always seeing those wounded men passing, passing, and in my ear – like the maddening refrain of a musical comedy ditty – there was always murmuring – "We shall never return. It doesn't matter." Outside was the

---

1   2 Corps, commanded by Smith-Dorrien, consisted of 3rd and 5th Infantry Divisions.
2   The last three sentences of this paragraph were deleted by the censor.
3   The last sentence of this paragraph was deleted by the censor.

clink and clatter of the column, the pitiful curses of tired men, the groaning roar of the motor-lorries as they toiled up the slope.

Then the Staff began to wander in one by one – on foot, exhausted and bedraggled. They loved the coffee, but only played with the chicken – I admit it was tough. They thought all was lost and the General killed. One murmured to another: "Magersfontein, Dour, and this – you've had some successful battles." And one went to sleep, but kept starting up, and giving a sort of strangled shout – "All gone! All gone!" When each had rested awhile he would ask gently for a little more coffee, rub his eyes, and disappear into the column to tramp through the night to Saint Quentin. It was the purest melodrama.[1]

And I, too tired to sleep, too excited to think, sat sipping thick coffee the whole night through, while the things that were happening soaked into me like petrol into a rag. About two hours before dawn I pulled myself together and climbed into the loft for forty minutes' broken slumber.

An hour before dawn we wearily dressed. The others devoured cold stew, and immediately there was the faintest glimmering of light we went outside. The column was still passing, – such haggard, broken men! The others started off, but for some little time I could not get my engine to fire. Then I got going. Quarter of a mile back I came upon a little detachment of the Worcesters[2] marching in perfect order, with a cheery subaltern at their head. He shouted a greeting in passing. It was Urwick, a friend of mine at Oxford.[3]

I cut across country, running into some of our cavalry on the way. It was just light enough for me to see properly when my engine jibbed. I cleaned a choked petrol pipe, lit a briar – never have I tasted anything so good – and pressed on.

Very bitter I felt, and when nearing Saint Quentin, some French soldiers got in my way, I cursed them in French, then in German, and finally in good round English oaths for cowards, and I know not what. They looked very startled and recoiled into the ditch. I must have looked alarming – a gaunt, dirty, unshaven figure towering above my motor-cycle, without hat, bespattered with mud, and eyes bright and weary for want of sleep. How I hated the French! I hated them because, as I then thought, they had deserted us at Mons and again at Le Cateau; I hated them because they had the privilege of seeing the British Army in confused retreat; I hated them because their roads were very nearly as bad as the roads of the Belgians. So, wet, miserable, and angry, I came into Saint Quentin just as the sun was beginning to shine a little.[4]

---

1   This entire paragraph was deleted by the censor.
2   3rd Battalion Worcestershire Regiment was part of 7th Brigade in 3rd Infantry Division.
3   2nd Lt Lyndall Fownes Urwick (1891–1983) became a management consultant. He was an influential management thinker between the wars, and published his last work in 1980 aged 89.
4   This entire paragraph, save for the last sentence, was deleted by the censor.

5

The Great Retreat

On the morning of the 27th we draggled into Saint Quentin. I found the others gorged with coffee and cakes provided by a kindly Staff-Officer. I imitated them and looked around. Troops of all arms were passing through very wearily. The people stood about, listless and sullen. Everywhere proclamations were posted beseeching the inhabitants to bring in all weapons they might possess. We found the Signal Company, and rode ahead of it out of the town to some fields above a village called Castres. There we unharnessed and took refuge from the gathering storm under a half-demolished haystack. The Germans didn't agree to our remaining for more than fifty minutes. Orders came for us to harness up and move on. I was left behind with the H.Q.S., which had collected itself, and was sent a few minutes later to 2nd Corps H.Q. at Ham, a ride of about fifteen miles.

On the way I stopped at an inn and discovered there three or four of our motor-cyclists, who had cut across country, and an officer. The officer[1] told us how he had been sent on to construct trenches at Le Cateau. It seems that although he enlisted civilian help, he had neither the time nor the men to construct more than very makeshift affairs, which were afterwards but slightly improved by the men who occupied them.[2]

Five minutes and I was on the road again. It was an easy run, something of a joy-ride until, nearing Ham, I ran into a train of motor-lorries, which of all the parasites that infest the road are the most difficult to pass. Luckily for me they were travelling in the opposite direction to mine, so I waited until they passed and then rode into Ham and delivered my message.

The streets of Ham were almost blocked by a confused column retreating through it. Officers stationed at every corner and bend were doing their best to reduce it to some sort of order, but with little success.

Returning I was forced into a byroad by the column, lost my way, took the wrong road out of the town, but managed in about a couple of hours to pick up the Signal Co., which by this time had reached the Chateau at Oleezy.

There was little rest for us that night. Twice I had to run into Ham. The road was bad and full of miscellaneous transport. The night was dark, and a thick mist clung to the road. Returning the second time, I was so weary that I jogged on about a couple of miles beyond my turning before I woke up sufficiently to realise where I was.

The next morning (the 28th) we were off before dawn. So tired were we that I remember we simply swore at each other for nothing at all. We waited, shivering in the morning cold, until the column was well on its way.

At Oleezy the Division began to find itself. Look at the map and think for a moment what the men had done. On the 21st they had advanced from Landrecies to Bavai, a fair day's march on a blazing day. On the 22nd they had marched from Bavai to the Canal. From the morning of the

---

1   *I do not know who the officer was, and I give the story as I wrote it in a letter home – for what it is worth.* (Watson)
2   This entire paragraph was deleted by the censor.

23rd to midday or later on the 24th they had fought hard. On the afternoon and evening of the 24th they had retired to the Bavai-Saint-Waast line. Before dawn on the morning of the 25th they had started off again and marched in column of route on another blazing day back to a position a few miles south of Le Cateau. The battle had begun as the sun rose on the 26th, and continued until three o'clock or later in the afternoon. They plodded through the darkness and the rain. No proper halt was made until midday of the 27th.

The General, who had escaped, and the Staff worked with ferocious energy, as we very painfully knew. Battalions bivouacked in the open fields round Oleezy collected the stragglers that came in and reorganised themselves. The cavalry were between us and Saint Quentin. We were in communication with them by despatch rider. Trains full of French troops passed westwards over Oleezy bridge. There were, I believe, General d'Amade's two reserve divisions. We had walked away from the Germans.

We rode after the column. On the way we passed a battalion of men who had been on outpost duty with nothing but a biscuit and a half apiece. They broke their ranks to snatch at some meat that had been dumped by the roadside, and gnawed it furiously as they marched along until the blood ran down from their chins on to their jackets.

I shall never forget how our General saw a batch of Gordons and K.O.S.B. stragglers trudging listlessly along the road. He halted them. Some more came up until there was about a company in all, and with one piper. He made them form fours, put the piper at the head of them. "Now, lads, follow the piper, and remember Scotland"; and they all started off as pleased as Punch with the tired piper playing like a hero.[1]

Oving or the Fat Boy[2] volunteered to take a message to a body of cavalry that was covering our rear. He found them, and then, being mapless (maps were very scarce in those days), he lost his way. There was no sun, so he rode in what he thought was the right direction, until suddenly he discovered that he was two kilometres from Saint Quentin. As the Germans were officially reported to be five miles south of the town he turned back and fled into the darkness. He slept that night at a cottage, and picked up the Division in the morning.

I was sent on to fill up with petrol wherever I could find it. I was forced to ride on for about four miles to some cross-roads. There I found a staff-car that had some petrol to spare. It was now very hot, so I had a bit of a sleep on the dusty grass by the side of the road, then sat up to watch lazily the 2nd Corps pass.

The troops were quite cheerful and on the whole marching well. There were a large number of stragglers, but the majority of them were not men who had fallen out, but men who had become separated from their battalions at Le Cateau. A good many were badly footsore. These were being crowded into lorries and cars.

There was one solitary desolate figure. He was evidently a reservist, a feeble little man of about forty, with three days' growth on his chin. He was very, very tired, but was struggling along with an unconquerable spirit. I gave him a little bit of chocolate I had; but he wouldn't stop to eat it. "I can't stop. If I does, I shall never get there." So he chewed it, half-choking, as he stumbled along. I went a few paces after him. Then Captain Dillon came up, stopped us, and put the poor fellow in a staff-car and sent him along a few miles in solitary grandeur, more nervous than comfortable.

---

1 'Our General', Major-General Sir Charles Fergusson (1865–1951), was a Scot. The 1st Battalion, Gordon Highlanders, from the 3rd Division, had become mixed up with 2nd Battalion, Kings Own Scottish Borders, from the 5th Division.

2 Arnold Overton (see Cast, page 150).

Eventually the company came along and I joined. Two miles farther we came to a biggish town with white houses that simply glared with heat.[1] My water-bottle was empty, so I humbly approached a good lady who was doling out cider and water at her cottage door. It did taste good! A little farther on I gave up my bicycle to Spuggy, who was riding in the cable-cart.

We jolted along at about two miles an hour. For some time two spies under escort walked beside the limber. Unlike most spies they looked their part. One was tall and thin and handsome. The other was short and fat and ugly. The fear of death was on their faces, and the jeers of our men died in their mouths.[2] They were marched along for two days until a Court could be convened. Then they were shot.

Just before Noyon we turned off to the left and halted for half an hour at Landrimont, a little village full of big trees. We had omelettes and coffee at the inn, then basked in the sun and smoked. Noyon was unattractive. The people did not seem to care what happened to anybody. Perhaps we thought that, because we were very tired. Outside Noyon I dozed, then went off to sleep.

When I awoke it was quite dark, and the column had halted. The order came for all except the drivers to dismount and proceed on foot. The bridge ahead was considered unsafe, so waggons went across singly.

I walked on into the village, Pontoise. There were no lights, and the main street was illuminated only by the lanterns of officers seeking their billets. An A.S.C. officer gave me a lift. Our H.Q. were right the other end of the town in the Chateau of the wee hamlet called La Pommeraye. I found them, stumbled into a loft, and dropped down for a sleep.

We were called fairly late.[3] George and I rode into Pontoise and "scrounged" for eggs and bread. These we took to a small and smelly cottage. The old woman of the cottage boiled our eggs and gave us coffee. It was a luxurious breakfast. I was looking forward to a slack lazy day in the sun, for we were told that we had for the moment outdistanced the gentle Germans. But my turn came round horribly soon, and I was sent off to Compiegne with a message for G.H.Q., and orders to find our particularly elusive Div. Train. It was a gorgeous ride along a magnificent road, through the great forest, and I did the twenty odd miles in forty odd minutes.

G.H.Q. was installed in the Palace. Everybody seemed very clean and lordly, and for a moment I was ashamed of my dirty, ragged, unshorn self. Then I realised that I was "from the Front" – a magic phrase to conjure with for those behind the line – and swaggered through long corridors.

After delivering my message I went searching for the Div. Train. First, I looked round the town for it, then I had wind of it at the station, but at the station it had departed an hour or so before. I returned to G.H.Q., but there they knew nothing. I tried every road leading out of the town. Finally, having no map, and consequently being unable to make a really thorough search, I had a drink, and started off back.

When I returned I found everybody was getting ready to move, so I packed up. This time the motor-cyclists rode in advance of the column. About two miles out I found that the others had dropped behind out of sight. I went on into Carlepont, and made myself useful to the Billeting Officer. The others arrived later. It seems there had been a rumour of Uhlans[4] on the road, and they had come along fearfully.

The troops marched in, singing and cheering. It was unbelievable what half a day's rest had done for them. Of course you must remember that we all firmly believed, except in our moments

---

1   *It must have been Guiscard.* (Watson)
2   The second half of this sentence was deleted by the censor.
3   *August 29th.* (Watson)
4   See footnote 3, page 23.

of deepest despondency, first, that we could have held the Germans at Mons and Le Cateau if the French had not "deserted" us, and second,[1] that our retreat was merely a "mouvement stratégique."

There was nothing doing at the Signal Office, so we went and had some food – cold sausage and coffee. Our hostess was buxom and hilarious. There was also a young girl about the place, Hélène. She was of a middle size, serious and dark, with a mass of black lustreless hair. She could not have been more than nineteen. Her baby was put to bed immediately we arrived. We loved them both, because they were the first women we had met since Mons who had not wanted to know why we were retreating and had not received the same answer – "mouvement strategique pour attaquer le mieux." I had a long talk that night with Hélène as she stood at her door. Behind us the dark square was filled with dark sleeping soldiers, the noise of snoring and the occasional clatter of moving horses. Finally, I left her and went to sleep on the dusty boards of an attic in the Chateau.

We were called when it was still dark and very cold (August 30). I was vainly trying to warm myself at a feeble camp fire when the order came to move off – without breakfast. The dawn was just breaking when we set out – to halt a hundred yards or so along. There we shivered for half an hour with nothing but a pipe and a scrap of chocolate that had got stuck at the bottom of my greatcoat pocket. Finally, the motor-cyclists, to their great relief, were told that they might go on ahead. The Grimers and I cut across a country to get away from the column. We climbed an immense hill in the mist, and proceeding by a devious route eventually bustled into Attichy, where we found a large and dirty inn containing nothing but some bread and jam. The column was scheduled to go ten miles farther, but "the situation being favourable" it was decided to go no farther. Headquarters were established by the road-side, and I was sent off to a jolly village right up on the hill to halt some sappers, and then back along the column to give the various units the names of their billets.

We supped off the sizzling bacon and slept on the grass by the side of the road. That night George burned his Rudge. It was an accident, but we were none too sorry, for it had given much trouble. There were messages right through the night. At one in the morning I was sent off to a Chateau in the Forest of Compiegne. I had no map, and it was a pure accident that I found my way there and back.

The next day (Aug. 31) was a joyous ride. We went up and down hills to a calm, lazy little village, Haute Fontaine. There we took a wrong turning and found ourselves in a blackberry lane. It was the hottest, pleasantest of days, and forgetting all about the more serious things – we could not even hear the guns – we filled up with the softest, ripest of fruit. Three of us rode together, N'Soon, Grimers, and myself. I don't know how we found our way. We just wandered on through sleepy, cobbled villages, along the top of ridges with great misty views and by quiet streams. Just beyond a village stuck on to the side of a hill, we came to a river, and through the willows we saw a little church. It was just like the Happy Valley that's over the fields from Burford.

We all sang anything we could remember as we rattled along. The bits of columns that we passed did not damp us, for they consisted only of transport, and transport can never be tragic – even in a retreat. The most it can do is to depress you with a sense of unceasing monotonous effort.

About three o'clock we came to a few houses – Béthancourt. There was an omelette, coffee, and pears for us at the inn. The people were frightened.

Why are the English retreating? Are they defeated?
No, it is only a strategical movement.
Will the dirty Germans pass by here?
We had better pack up our traps and fly.

---

1   From "first, that we could have held the Germans at Mons" to "second" deleted by the censor.

We were silent for a moment, then I am afraid I lied blandly.

Oh no, this is as far as we go.

But I had reckoned without my host, a lean, wiry old fellow, a bit stiff about the knees. First of all he proudly showed me his soldier's book – three campaigns in Algeria. A crowd of smelly women pressed round us – luckily we had finished our meal – while with the help of a few knives and plates he explained exactly what a strategical movement was, and demonstrated to the satisfaction of everybody except ourselves that the valley we were in was obviously the place "pour reculer le mieux."

We had been told that our H.Q. were going to be at a place called Béthisy St Martin, so on we went. A couple of miles from Béthisy we came upon a billeting party of officers sitting in the shade of a big tree by the side of the road. Had we heard that the Germans were at Compiegne, ten miles or so over the hill? No, we hadn't. Was it safe to go on into Béthisy? None of us had an idea. We stopped and questioned a "civvy" push-cyclist. He had just come from Béthisy and had seen no Germans. The officers started arguing whether or no they should wait for an escort. We got impatient and slipped on. Of course there was nothing in Béthisy except a wide-eyed population, a selection of smells, and a vast congregation of chickens. The other two basked on some hay in the sun, while I went back and pleased myself immensely by reporting to the officers who were timorously trotting along that there wasn't a sign of a Uhlan.[1]

We rested a bit. One of us suggested having a look round for some Uhlans from the top of the nearest hill. It was a terrific climb up a narrow track, but our bicycles brought us up magnificently. From the top we could see right away to the forest of Compiegne, but a judicious bit of scouting produced nothing.

Coming down we heard from a passing car that H.Q. were to be at Crépy-en-Valois, a biggish old place about four miles away to the south the other side of Béthancourt. We arrived there just as the sun was going to set. It was a confusing place, crammed full of transport, but I found my way to our potential H.Q. with the aid of a joyous little flapper on my carrier.

Then I remembered I had left my revolver behind on the hill above Béthisy. Just before I started I heard that there were bags of Uhlans coming along over the hills and through the woods. But there was nothing for it but to go back, and back I went. It was a bestial climb in the dusk. On my way back I saw some strange-looking figures in the grounds of a chateau. So I opened my throttle and thundered past.

Later I found that the figures belonged to the rest of the motor-cyclists. The chateau ought to have been our H.Q., and arriving there they had been entertained to a sit-down tea and a bath.

We had a rotten night – nothing between me and a cold, hard tiled floor except a waterproof sheet, but no messages.

We woke very early (September 1st) to the noise of guns. The Germans were attacking vigorously, having brought up several brigades of Jaegers by motor-bus. The 15th was on our left, the 13th was holding the hill above Béthancourt, and the 14th was scrapping away on the right. The guns were ours, as the Germans didn't appear to have any with them. I did a couple of messages out to the 15th. The second time I came back with the news that their left flank was being turned.

A little later one of our despatch riders rode in hurriedly. He reported that, while he was riding along the road to the 15th, he had been shot at by Uhlans whom he had seen distinctly. At the

---

1   See footnote 3, page 23.

moment it was of the utmost importance to get a despatch through to the 15th. The Skipper[1] offered to take it, but the General refused his offer.

A second despatch rider was carefully studying his map. It seemed to him absolutely inconceivable that Uhlans should be at the place where the first despatch rider had seen them. They must either have ridden right round our left flank and left rear, or else broken through the line. So he offered boldly to take the despatch.

He rode by a slightly roundabout road, and reached the 15th in safety. On his way back he saw a troop of North Irish Horse. In the meantime the Divisional Headquarters had left Crépy in great state, the men with rifles in front, and taken refuge on a hill south-east of the town. On his return the despatch rider was praised mightily for his work, but to this day he believes the Uhlans were North Irish Horse and the bullets "overs "[2] – to this day the first despatch rider contradicts him.

The Division got away from Crépy with the greatest success. The 13th slaughtered those foolish Huns that tried to charge up the hill in the face of rifle, machine-gun, and a considerable shell fire. The Duke of Wellington's laid a pretty little ambush and hooked a car containing the general and staff of the 1st Cavalry Division. The prisoners were remorsefully shot, as it would have been impossible to bring them away under the heavy fire.[3]

We jogged on to Nanteuil, all of us very pleased with ourselves, particularly the Duke of Wellington's, who were loaded with spoils, and a billeting officer who, running slap into some Uhlans, had been fired at all the way from 50 yards' range to 600 and hadn't been hit.

I obtained leave to give a straggler a lift of a couple of miles. He was embarrassingly grateful. The last few miles was weary work for the men. Remember they had marched or fought, or more often both, every day since our quiet night at Landrecies. The road, too, was the very roughest *pavé*, though I remember well a little forest of bracken and pines we went through. Being "a would-be literary bloke," I murmured "Scottish"; being tired I forgot it from the moment after I saw it until now.

There was no rest at Nanteuil. I took the Artillery Staff Captain round the brigades on my carrier, and did not get back until 10. A bit of hot stew and a post-card from home cheered me. I managed a couple of hours' sleep.

We turned out about 3, the morning of September 2nd. It was quite dark and bitterly cold. Very sleepily indeed we rode along an exiguous path by the side of the cobbles. The sun had risen, but it was still cold when we rattled into that diabolical city of lost souls, Dammartin.

Nobody spoke as we entered. Indeed there were only a few haggard, ugly old women, each with a bit of a beard and a large goitre. One came up to me and chattered at me. Then suddenly she stopped and rushed away, still gibbering. We asked for a restaurant. A stark, silent old man, with a goitre, pointed out an *estaminet*. There we found four motionless men, who looked up at us with expressionless eyes. Chilled, we withdrew into the street. Silent, melancholy soldiers – the H.Q. of some army or division – were marching miserably out. We battered at the door of a hotel for twenty minutes. We stamped and cursed and swore, but no one would open. Only a hideous and filthy crowd stood round, and not one of them moved a muscle. Finally, we burst into a bare little inn, and had such a desolate breakfast of sour wine, bread, and bully. We finished as soon as we could to leave the nightmare place. Even the houses were gaunt and ill-favoured.

On our way out we came across a deserted motor-cycle. Some one suggested sending it on by train, until some one else remarked that there were no trains, and this was fifteen miles from Paris.

---

1   Captain Doherty Holwell, see Cast, page 158.

2   *Stray bullets that, fired too high, miss their mark, and occasionally hit men well behind the actual firing line.* (Watson)

3   This sentence deleted by the censor.

We cut across country, rejoined the column, and rode with it to Vinantes, passing on the way a lost motor-lorry. The driver was tearing his hair in an absolute panic. We told him the Germans were just a few miles along the road; but we wished we hadn't when, in hurriedly reversing to escape, he sent a couple of us into the ditch.

At Vinantes we "requisitioned" a car, some chickens, and a pair of boots. There was a fusty little tavern down the street, full of laughing soldiers. In the corner a fat, middle-aged woman sat weeping quietly on a sack. The host, sullen and phlegmatic, answered every question with a shake of the head and a muttered "N'importe." The money he threw contemptuously on the counter. The soldiers thought they were spies. "As speaking the langwidge," I asked him what the matter was.

"They say, sir, that this village will be shelled by the cursed Germans, and the order has gone out to evacuate."

Then, suddenly his face became animated, and he told me volubly how he had been born in the village, how he had been married there, how he had kept the *estaminet* for twenty years, how all the leading men of the village came of an evening and talked over the things that were happening in Paris.

He started shouting, as men will –

"What does it matter what I sell, what I receive? What does it matter, for have I not to leave all this?"

Then his wife came up and put her hand on his arm –

"Now, now; give the gentlemen their beer."

I bought some cherry brandy and came away.

I was sent on a couple of messages that afternoon: one to trace a telephone wire to a deserted station with nothing in it but a sack of excellent potatoes, another to an officer whom I could not find. I waited under a tree eating somebody else's pears until I was told he had gone mad, and was wandering aimlessly about.

It was a famous night for me. I was sent off to Dammartin, and knew something would go wrong. It did. A sentry all but shot me. I nearly rode into an unguarded trench across the road, and when I started back with my receipt my bicycle would not fire. I found that the mechanic at Dammartin had filled my tank with water. It took me two hours, two lurid hours, to take that water out. It was three in the morning when I got going. I was badly frightened the Division had gone on, because I hadn't the remotest conception where it was going to. When I got back H.Q. were still at Vinantes. I retired thankfully to my bed under the stars, listening dreamily to Grimers, who related how a sentry had fired at him, and how one bullet had singed the back of his neck.

We left Vinantes not too early after breakfast, – a comfort, as we had all of us been up pretty well the whole night. Grimers was still upset at having been shot at by sentries. I had been going hard, and had had only a couple of hours' sleep. We rode on in advance of the company. It was very hot and dusty, and when we arrived at Crécy with several hours to spare, we first had a most excellent omelette and then a shave, a hair-cut, and a wash. Crécy was populous and excited. It made us joyous to think we had reached a part of the country where the shops were open, people pursuing their own business, where there was no dumbly reproaching glance for us in our retreat.

We had been told that our H.Q. that night were going to be at the chateau of a little village called La Haute Maison. Three of us arrived there and found the caretaker just leaving. We obtained the key, and when he had gone did a little bit of looting on our own. First we had a great meal off lunch

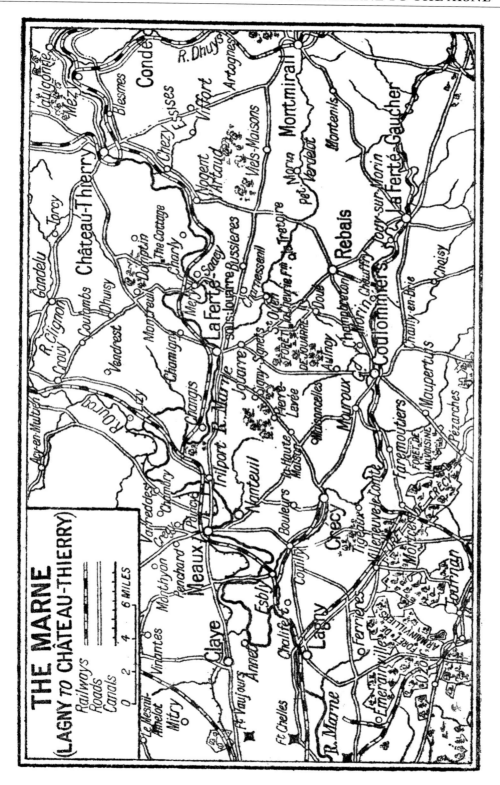

THE MARNE
(LAGNY TO CHÂTEAU-THIERRY)

Railways
Roads
Canals

0   2   4   6 MILES

his ditch to see what was wanted. The rifle fire seemed to increase. The air was buzzing, and just in front of his bicycle multitudinous little spurts of dust flecked the road.

It was distinctly unpleasant, and, as Major Buckle persisted in standing in the middle of the road instead of taking the despatch rider with him into his ditch, the despatch rider had to stand there too, horribly frightened. The Major said it was impossible to go farther. There was only a troop of cavalry, taking careful cover, at the farm in front, and –

"My God, man, you're under machine-gun fire."

So that's what it is, murmured the despatch rider to himself, not greatly cheered. He saw he could not get to any vantage point by that road, and it seemed best to get back at once. He absolutely streaked along back to D.H.Q., stopping on the way very much against his will to deliver a message from Major Buckle to the Duke of Wellington's who were in support.

He gave in his report, such as it was, to Colonel Romer, and was praised. Moral: Be called away by some pressing engagement *before* the captain calls for volunteers. May *Gott strafe* thoroughly all interfering sergeants![1]

The Headquarters Staff advanced in an hour or so to some houses. The 3rd Corps, consisting of the 4th Division and the unlucky 19th Brigade, had pushed on with tremendous dash towards Jouarre, and we learnt from an aeroplane which dropped a message on the hill at Doué that the general situation was favourable. The Germans were crowding across the bridge at La Ferté under heavy shell fire, but unluckily we could not hit the blighted bridge.

It was now midday and very hot. There was little water. We had been advancing over open fields without a vestige of shade.

Under cover of their guns the Germans fled across the Petit Morin in such confusion that they did not even hold the very defensible heights to the north of the river. We followed on their heels through St Ouen and up the hill behind the village. Three of us went on ahead and sat for two hours in a trench with borrowed rifles waiting for the Germans to come out of a wood. But it began to rain very hard, and the Germans came on the other side and were taken by the Cyclists.

It was just getting dark when we rendezvoused at the cross-roads of Charnesseuil. The village was battered by our guns, but the villagers did not mind a scrap and welcomed us with screams of joy. The local inn was reopened with cheers, and in spite of the fact that there were two dead horses, very evil-smelling, just outside, we had drinks all round.

We were interrupted by laughter and cheers. We rushed out to see the quaintest procession coming from the west into Charnesseuil. Seventy odd immense Prussian Guards were humbly pushing in the bicycles of forty of our Divisional Cyclists, who were dancing round them in delight. They had captured a hundred and fifty of them, but our guns had shelled them, luckily without doing much damage to the Cyclists, so loading up the prisoners with all their kit and equipment, and making them lead their captors' bicycles, the Cyclists brought them in triumph for the inspection of the Staff. It was a great moment.

I was very tired, and, careless of who passed, stretched myself at the side of the road for a sleep. I was wakened an hour later, and we all went along together to the chateau. There we slept in the hall before the contented faces of some fine French pictures – or the majority of them, – the rest were bestially slashed.

At the break of dawn (Sept. 9th) I was sent off to the 14th Brigade, which composed the advance-guard. Scouts had reported that Saacy had been evacuated by the enemy. So we pushed on cautiously and took possession of the bridge.

---

1   The second and third sentences of this paragraph were deleted by the censor.

I came up with the Brigade Staff on a common at the top of the succeeding hill, having been delayed by a puncture. Nixon, the S.O., told me that a battery of ours in position on the common to the south of the farm would open fire in a few minutes.

The German guns would reply, but would be quickly silenced. In the meantime I was to take shelter in the farm.

I had barely put my bicycle under cover in the courtyard when the Germans opened fire, not at our guns but at a couple of companies of the Manchesters who were endeavouring to take cover just north of the farm.

In the farm I found King and his platoon of Cyclists. Shrapnel bullets simply rattled against the old house, and an occasional common shell dropped near by way of variety. The Cyclists were restive, and I was too, so to relieve the situation I proposed breakfast. King and I had half a loaf of Saacy bread and half a pot of jam I always carried about with me. The rest went to the men. Our breakfast was nearly spoilt by the Manchesters, who, after they had lost a few men, rushed through the farm into the wood, where, naturally enough, they lost a few more. They besought the Cyclists to cover their retreat, but as it was from shrapnel we mildly suggested it was impossible.[1]

The courtyard was by this time covered with tiles and pitted with bullets. We, close up against the wall, had been quite moderately safe. The shelling slackened off, so we thought we had better do a bunk. With pride of race the motor-cyclist left last.

The 14th Brigade had disappeared. I went back down the track and found the General and his staff, fuming, half-way up the hill. The German guns could not be found, and the German guns were holding up the whole Division.

See overleaf. Overton also described "two of our 18 pounders firing on a German transport convoy. Considerable execution was done and we finally saw the Germans bolt across country."

---

1   The last two sentences of this paragraph were deleted by the censor.

I slept by the roadside for an hour. I was woken up to take a message to 2nd Corps at Saacy. On my return I was lucky enough to see a very spectacular performance.

From the point which I call A to the point B is, or ought to be, 5000 yards. At A there is a gap in the wood, and you get a gorgeous view over the valley. The road from La Ferté to the point B runs on high ground, and at B there is a corresponding gap, the road being open completely for roughly 200 yards. A convoy of German lorries was passing with an escort of infantry, and the General thought we might as well have a shot at them. Two 18-pdrs. were man-handled to the side of the hill and opened fire, while six of us with glasses and our lunch sat behind and watched.

It was a dainty sight – the lorries scooting across, while the escort took cover. The guns picked off a few, completely demolishing two lorries, then with a few shells into some cavalry that appeared on the horizon, they ceased fire.

The affair seemed dangerous to the uninitiated despatch rider. Behind the two guns was a brigade of artillery in column of route on an exceedingly steep and narrow road. Guns firing in the open can be seen. If the Germans were to spot us, we shuddered to think what would become of the column behind us on the road.

That afternoon I had nothing more to do, so, returning to the common, I dozed there for a couple of hours, knowing that I should have little sleep that night. At dusk we bivouacked in the garden of the chateau at Méry. We arrived at the chateau before the Staff and picked up some wine.

In the evening I heard that a certain captain in the gunners went reconnoitring and found the battery – it was only one – that had held up our advance. He returned to the General, put up his eyeglass and drawled, "I say, General, I've found that battery. I shall now deal with it." He did. In five minutes it was silenced, and the 14th attacked up the Valley of Death, as the men called it. They were repulsed with very heavy losses; their reinforcements, which had arrived the day before, were practically annihilated.[1]

It was a bad day.

That night it was showery, and I combined vain attempts to get to sleep between the showers with a despatch to 2nd Corps at Saacy and another to the Division Ammunition Column the other side of Charnesseuil.

Towards morning the rain became heavier, so I took up my bed – *i.e.*, my greatcoat and ground-sheet – and, finding four free square feet in the S.O., had an hour's troubled sleep before I was woken up half an hour before dawn to get ready to take an urgent message as soon as it was light.

On September 9th, just before dawn – it was raining and very cold – I was sent with a message to Colonel Cameron at the top of the hill, telling him he might advance. The Germans, it appeared, had retired during the night. Returning to the chateau at Méry, I found the company had gone on, so I followed them along the Valley of Death to Montreuil.

It was the dismallest morning, dark as if the sun would never rise, chequered with little bursts of heavy rain. The road was black with mud. The hedges dripped audibly into watery ditches. There was no grass, only a plentiful coarse vegetation. The valley itself seemed enclosed by unpleasant hills from joy or light. Soldiers lined the road – some were dead, contorted, or just stretched out peacefully; some were wounded, and they moaned as I passed along. There was one officer who slowly moved his head from side to side. That was all he could do. But I could not stop; the ambulances were coming up. So I splashed rapidly through the mud to the cross-roads north of Montreuil.

To the right was a barn in which the Germans had slept. It was littered with their equipment. And in front of it was a derelict motor-car dripping in the rain.

---

1   The words from "reinforcements" were deleted by the censor.

At Montreuil we had a scrap of bully with a bit of biscuit for breakfast, then we ploughed slowly and dangerously alongside the column to Dhuizy, where a house that our artillery had fired was still burning. The chalked billeting marks of the Germans were still on the doors of the cottages. I had a despatch to take back along the column to the Heavies. Grease a couple of inches thick carpeted the road. We all agreed that we should be useless in winter.

At Dhuizy the sun came out.

A couple of miles farther on I had a talk with two German prisoners – R.A.M.C. They were sick of the war. Summed it up thus:

Wir weissen nichts: wir essen nichts: immer laufen, laufen, laufen.[1]

In bright sunshine we pushed on towards Gandeln. On the way we had a bit of lunch, and I left a pipe behind. As there was nothing doing I pushed on past the column, waiting for a moment to watch some infantry draw a large wood, and arrived with the cavalry at Gandeln, a rakish old town at the bottom of an absurdly steep hill. Huggie passed me with a message. Returning he told me that the road ahead was pitiably disgusting.

You must remember that we were hotly pursuing a disorganised foe. In front the cavalry and horse artillery were harassing them for all they were worth, and whenever there was an opening our bigger guns would gallop up for a trifle of blue murder.

From Gandeln the road rises sharply through woods and then runs on high ground without a vestige of cover for two and a half miles into Chézy. On this high, open ground our guns caught a German convoy, and we saw the result.

First there were a few dead and wounded Germans, all muddied. The men would look curiously at each, and sometimes would laugh. Then at the top of the hill we came upon some smashed and abandoned waggons. These were hastily looted. Men piled themselves with helmets, greatcoats, food, saddlery, until we looked a crowd of dishevelled bandits. The German wounded watched – they lay scattered in a cornfield, like poppies. Sometimes Tommy is not a pleasant animal, and I hated him that afternoon. One dead German had his pockets full of chocolate. They scrambled over him, pulling him about, until it was all divided.[2]

Just off the road was a small sandpit. Three or four waggons – the horses, frightened by our shells, had run over the steep place into the sand. Their heads and necks had been forced back into their carcasses, and on top of this mash were the splintered waggons. I sat for a long time by the well in Chézy and watched the troops go by, caparisoned with spoils. I hated war.

Just as the sun was setting we toiled out of Chézy on to an upland of cornfields, speckled with grey patches of dead men and reddish-brown patches of dead horses. One great horse stood out on a little cliff, black against the yellow of the descending sun. It furiously stank. Each time I passed it I held my nose, and I was then pretty well used to smells. The last I saw of it – it lay grotesquely on its back with four stiff legs sticking straight up like the legs of an overturned table – it was being buried by a squad of little black men billeted near. They were cursing richly. The horse's revenge in death, perhaps, for its ill-treatment in life.

It was decided to stay the night at Chézy. The village was crowded, dark, and confusing. Three of us found the signal office, and made ourselves very comfortable for the night with some fresh straw that we piled all over us. The roads were for the first time too greasy for night-riding. The rest slept in a barn near, and did not discover the signal office until dawn.

---

1   "We know nothing; we eat nothing; we're always running, running, running."
2   The entire paragraph, save for the first sentence, was deleted by the censor.

We awoke, stiff but rested, to a fine warm morning. It was a quiet day. We rode with the column along drying roads until noon through peaceful rolling country – then, as there was nothing doing, Grimers and I rode to the head of the column, and inquiring with care whether our cavalry was comfortably ahead, came to the village of Noroy-sur-Ourcq. We "scrounged" for food and found an inn. At first our host, a fat well-to-do old fellow, said the Germans had taken everything, but, when he saw we really were hungry, he produced sardines, bread, butter, sweets, and good red wine. So we made an excellent meal – and were not allowed to pay a penny.

He told that the Germans, who appeared to be in great distress, had taken everything in the village, though they had not maltreated any one. Their horses were dropping with fatigue – that we knew – and their officers kept telling their men to hurry up and get quickly on the march. At this point they were just nine hours in front of us.

Greatly cheered we picked up the Division again at Chouy, and sat deliciously on a grass bank to wait for the others. Just off the road on the opposite side was a dead German. Quite a number of men broke their ranks to look curiously at him – anything to break the tedious, deadening monotony of marching twenty-five miles day after day: as a major of the Dorsets said to us as we sat there, "It is all right for us, but it's hell for them!"

The Company came up, and we found that in Chouy the Germans had overlooked a telephone – great news for the cable detachment. After a glance at the church, a gorgeous bit of Gothic that we had shelled, we pushed on in the rain to Billy-sur-Ourcq. I was just looking after a convenient loft when I was sent back to Chouy to find the Captain's watch. A storm was raging down the valley. The road at any time was covered with tired foot sloggers. I had to curse them, for they wouldn't get out of the way. Soon I warmed and cursed them crudely and glibly in four languages. On my return I found some looted boiled eggs and captured German Goulasch hot for me. I fed and turned in.

This day my kit was left behind with other unnecessary "tackle," to lighten the horses' load. I wish I had known it.

The remaining eggs for breakfast – delicious.

Huggie and I were sent off just before dawn on a message that took us to St Rémy, a fine church, and Hartennes, where we were given hot tea by that great man, Sergeant Croucher of the Divisional Cyclists. I rode back to Rozet St Albin, a pleasant name, along a road punctuated with dead and very evil-smelling horses. Except for the smell it was a good run of about ten miles. I picked up the Division again on the sandy road above Chacrise.

Sick of column riding I turned off the main road up a steep hill into Ambrief, a desolate black-and-white village totally deserted. It came on to pour, but there was a shrine handy. There I stopped until I was pulled out by an ancient captain of cuirassiers, who had never seen an Englishman before and wanted to hear all about us.

On into Acy, where I decided to head off the Division at Ciry, instead of crossing the Aisne and riding straight to Vailly, our proposed H.Q. for that night. The decision saved my life, or at least my liberty. I rode to Sermoise, a bright little village where the people were actually making bread. At the station there was a solitary cavalry man. In Ciry itself there was no one. Half-way up the Ciry hill, a sort of dry watercourse, I ran into some cavalry and learnt that the Germans were holding the Aisne in unexpected strength. I had all but ridden round and in front of our own cavalry outposts.

Two miles farther back I found Huggie and one of our brigades. We had a bit of bully and biscuit under cover of a haystack, then we borrowed some glasses and watched bodies of Germans on the hills the other side of the Aisne. It was raining very fast. There was no decent cover, so we sat on the leeward side of a mound of sand.

When we awoke the sun was setting gorgeously. Away to the west in the direction of Soissons there was a tremendous cannonade. On the hills opposite little points of flame showed that the

Germans were replying. On our right some infantry were slowly advancing in extended order through a dripping turnip-field.

The Battle of the Aisne had begun.

We were wondering what to do when we were commandeered to take a message down that precipitous hill of Ciry to some cavalry. It was now quite dark and still raining. We had no carbide,[1] and my carburetter had jibbed, so we decided to stop at Ciry for the night. At the inn we found many drinks – particularly some wonderful cherry brandy – and a friendly motor-cyclist who told us of a billet that an officer was probably going to leave. We went there. Our host was an old soldier, so, after his wife had hung up what clothes we dared take off to dry by a red-hot stove, he gave us some supper of stewed game and red wine, then made us cunning beds with straw, pillows, and blankets. Too tired to thank him we dropped asleep.

That, though we did not know it then, was the last night of our little Odyssey. We had been advancing or retiring without a break since my tragic farewell to Nadine. We had been riding all day and often all night. But those were heroic days, and now as I write this in our comfortable slack winter quarters, I must confess – I would give anything to have them all over again. Now we motor-cyclists are middle-aged warriors. Adventures are work. Experiences are a routine.

Then, let's be sentimental, we were young.[2]

---

1 The despatch riders' motorcycles used acetylene lights which had a canister of calcium carbide into which water was dripped slowly, generating acetylene gas which burned with a very bright white light. Replacement water was often improvised, but finding carbide was more difficult!

2 This sentence deleted in the 1917 edition.

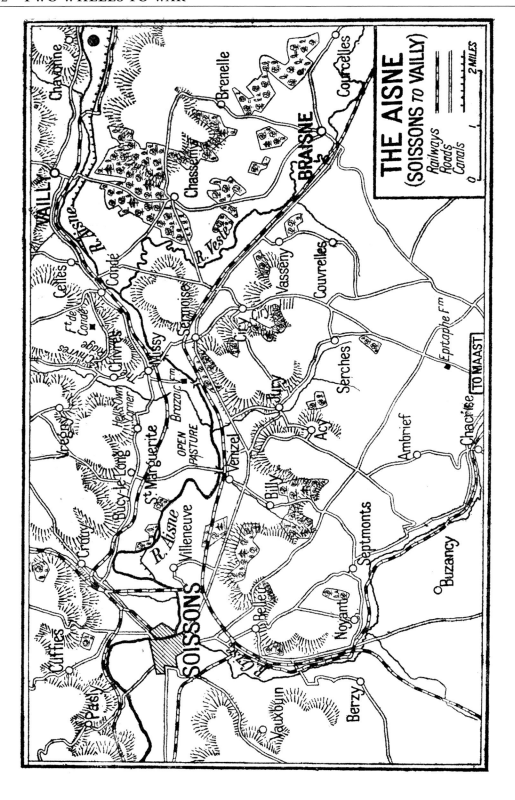

7

The Battle of the Aisne

I'm going to start by giving you an account of what we thought of the military situation during the great marches and the battle of the Aisne – for my own use. What happened we shall be able to look up afterwards in some lumbersome old history, should we forget, but, unless I get down quickly what we thought, it will disappear in after-knowledge.

You will remember how the night we arrived on the Aisne Huggie and I stretched ourselves on a sand-heap at the side of the road – just above Ciry – and watched dim columns of Germans crawling like grey worms up the slopes the other side of the valley. We were certain that the old Division was still in hot cry on the heels of a rapidly retreating foe. News came – I don't know how: you never do – that our transport and ammunition were being delayed by the fearsome and lamentable state of the roads. But the cavalry was pushing on ahead, and tired infantry were stumbling in extended order through the soaked fields on either side of us. There was hard gunnery well into the red dusk. Right down the valley came the thunder of it, and we began to realise that divisions, perhaps even corps, had come up on either flank.

The ancient captain of cuirassiers, who had hauled me out of my shrine into the rain that afternoon, made me understand there was a great and unknown number of French on our left. From the Order before the Marne I had learnt that a French Army had turned the German right, but the first news I had had of French on our own right was when one staff-officer said in front of me that the French away to the east had been held up. That was at Doué.

Our retreat had been solitary. The French, everybody thought, had left us in the lurch at Mons and again at Le Cateau, when the cavalry we knew to be there refused to help us. For all we knew the French Army had been swept off the face of the earth. We were just retiring, and retiring before three or four times our own numbers. We were not even supported by the 1st Corps on our right. It was smashed, and had all it could do to get itself away. We might have been the Ten Thousand.[1]

But the isolation of our desperate retreat dismayed nobody, for we all had an unconquerable belief in the future. There must be some French somewhere, and in spite – as we thought then – of our better judgments, we stuck to the story that was ever being circulated: "We are luring the Germans into a trap." It was impressed upon us, too, by "the Div." that both at Mons and Le Cateau we were strategically victorious. We had given the Germans so hard a knock that they could not pursue us at once; we had covered the retirement of the 1st Corps; we had got away successfully ourselves. We were sullen and tired victors, never defeated. If we retreated, it was for a purpose. If we advanced, the Germans were being crushed.

The Germans thought we were beaten, because they didn't realise we knew we were victorious the whole time.

I do not say that we were always monotonously cheerful. The night after Le Cateau we all thought the game was up, – until the morning, when cheerfulness came with the sun. Then we sighed with relief and remembered a little bitterly that we were "luring the Germans on."

---

1   The second and third sentences of this paragraph were deleted by the censor.

Many a time I have come across isolated units in hot corners who did not see a way out. Yet if a battery or a battalion were hard hit, the realisation of local defeat was always accompanied by a fervent faith that "the old Fifth" was doing well. Le Cateau is a victory in the soldier's calendar.

> Le Cateau and La Bassée,
> It jolly well serves them right.

We had been ten days or more on the Aisne before we grasped that the force opposite us was not merely a dogged, well-entrenched rearguard, but a section of the German line.

Soon after we arrived a French cavalry officer had ridden into D. H.Q., and after his departure it was freely rumoured that he had ridden right round the German position. News began to trickle in from either flank. Our own attacks ceased, and we took up a defensive position. It was the beginning of trench-warfare, though owing to the nature of the country there were few trenches. Then we heard vaguely that the famous series of enveloping movements had begun, but by this time the Division was tired to death, and the men were craving for a rest.

Strategy in the ranks – it was elementary stuff pieced vaguely together. But perhaps it will interest you at home to know what we thought out here on this great little stage. What we did you have heard. Still, here is the play as we acted in it.

Along the Aisne the line of our Division stretched from Venizel to the bridge of Condé. You must not think of the river as running through a gorge or as meandering along the foot of slopes rising directly from the river bank. On the southern side lie the Heights of Champagne, practically a tableland. From the river this tableland looks like a series of ridges approaching the valley at an angle. Between the foothills and the river runs the Soissons-Rheims road, good *pavé*, and for the most part covered by trees. To the north there is a distance of two miles or so from the river to the hills.

Perhaps I shall make this clearer if I take the three main points about the position.

First. If you are going to put troops on the farther side of the river you must have the means of crossing it, and you must keep those means intact. The bridges running from left to right of our line were at Venizel, Missy, Sermoise, and Condé. The first three were blown up. Venizel bridge was repaired sufficiently to allow of light traffic to cross, and fifty yards farther down a pontoon-bridge was built fit for heavy traffic. Missy was too hot: we managed an occasional ferry. I do not think we ever had a bridge at Sermoise. Once when in search of the C.R.E. I watched a company of the K.O.S.B. being ferried across under heavy rifle fire. The raft was made of ground-sheets stuffed, I think, with straw. Condé bridge the Germans always held, or rather neither of us held it, but the Germans were very close to it and allowed nobody to cross. Just on our side of the bridge was a car containing two dead officers. No one could reach them. There they sat until we left, ghastly sentinels, and for all I know they sit there still.

Now all communication with troops on the north bank of the river had to pass over these bridges, of which Venizel alone was comparatively safe. If ever these bridges should be destroyed, the troops on the north bank would be irrevocably cut off from supplies of every sort and from orders. I often used to wonder what would have happened if the Germans had registered accurately upon the bridges, or if the river had risen and swept the bridges away.

Second. There was an open belt between the river and the villages which we occupied – Bucy-le-Long, St Marguerite, Missy. The road that wound through this belt was without the veriest trace of cover – so much so, that for a considerable time all communication across it was carried on by despatch riders, for a cable could never be laid. So if our across-the-river brigades had ever been forced to retire in daylight they would have been compelled, first to retire two miles over absolutely open country, and then to cross bridges of which the positions were known with tolerable accuracy to the Germans.

Third. On the northern bank four or five spurs came down into the plain, parallel with each other and literally at right angles to the river. The key to these was a spur known as the Chivres hill or plateau. This we found impregnable to the attack of two brigades. It was steep and thickly wooded. Its assailants, too, could be heavily enfiladed from either flank.

Now you have the position roughly. The tactics of our Division were simple. In the early days, when we thought that we had merely a determined rearguard in front of us, we attacked. Bridges – you will remember the tale – were most heroically built. Two brigades (14th and 15th) crossed the river and halted at the very foot of the hills, where they were almost under cover from alien fire. The third brigade was on their right in a position I will describe later.

Well, the two brigades attacked, and attacked with artillery support, but they could not advance. That was the first phase. Then orders came that we were to act on the defensive, and finally of our three brigades, one was on the right, one across the river, and one in a second line of trenches on the southern bank of the river acted as divisional reserve. That for us was the battle of the Aisne. It was hard fighting all through.[1]

Under these conditions there was plentiful work for despatch riders. I am going to try and describe it for you.

When D.H.Q. are stationary, the work of despatch riders is of two kinds. First of all you have to find the positions of the units to which you are sent. Often the Signal Office gives you the most exiguous information. "The 105th Brigade is somewhere near Ciry," or "The Div. Train is at a farm just off the Paris-Bordeaux" road.

Starting out with these explicit instructions, it is very necessary to remember that they may be wrong and are probably misleading. That is not the fault of the Signal Office. A Unit changes ground, say from a farm on the road to a farm off the road. These two farms are so near each other that there is no need to inform the Div. just at present of this change of residence. The experienced despatch rider knows that, if he is told the 105th Brigade is at 1904 Farm, the Brigade is probably at 1894 Farm, half a mile away.

Again, a despatch rider is often sent out after a unit has moved and before the message announcing the move has "come through" to the Division.

When the Division is advancing or retiring this exploration-work is the only work. To find a given brigade, take the place at which it was last reported at the Signal Office and assume it was never there. Prefer the information you get from your fellow despatch riders. Then find out the road along which the brigade is said to be moving. If the brigade may be in action, take a road that will bring you to the rear of the brigade. If there are troops in front of the brigade, strike for the head of it. It is always quicker to ride from van to rear of a brigade than from rear to van.

The second kind of work consists in riding along a road already known. A clever despatch rider may reduce this to a fine art. He knows exactly at which corner he is likely to be sniped, and hurries accordingly. He remembers to a yard where the sentries are. If the road is under shell fire, he recalls where the shells usually fall, the interval between the shells and the times of shelling. For there is order in everything, and particularly in German gunnery. Lastly, he does not race along with nose on handlebar. That is a trick practised only by despatch riders who are rarely under fire, who have come to a strange and alarming country from Corps or Army Headquarters. The experienced motor-cyclist sits up and takes notice the whole time. He is able at the end of his ride to give an account of all that he has seen on the way.

D.H.Q. were at Serches, a wee village in a hollow at the head of a valley. So steeply did the hill rise out of the hollow to the north that the village was certainly in dead ground. A fine road went

---

1   *I do not pretend for a moment that all these details are meticulously accurate. They are what I knew or thought I knew at the time this was written.* (Watson)

to the west along the valley for three miles or so to the Soissons-Rheims road. For Venizel you crossed the main road and ran down a little hill through a thick wood, terribly dark of nights, to the village; you crossed the bridge and opened the throttle.

The first time I rode north from Venizel, Moulders[1] was with me. On the left a few hundred yards away an ammunition section that had crossed by the pontoon was at full gallop. I was riding fast – the road was loathsomely open – but not too fast, because it was greasy. A shell pitched a couple of hundred yards off the road, and then others, far enough away to comfort me.

A mile on the road bends sharp left and right over the railway and past a small factory of some sort. The Germans loved this spot, and would pitch shells on it with a lamentable frequency. Soon it became too much of a routine to be effective. On shelling-days three shells would be dropped one after another, an interval of three minutes, and then another three. This we found out and rode accordingly.

A hundred yards past the railway you ride into Bucy-le-Long and safety. The road swings sharp to the right, and there are houses all the way to St Marguerite.

Once I was riding with despatches from D.H.Q. It was a heavy, misty day. As I sprinted across the open I saw shrapnel over St Marguerite, but I could not make out whether it was German shrapnel bursting over the village or our shrapnel bursting over the hills beyond. I slowed down.

Now, as I have told you, on a motor-cycle, if you are going rapidly, you cannot hear bullets or shells coming or even shells bursting unless they are very near. Running slowly on top, with the engine barely turning over, you can hear everything. So I went slow and listened. Through the air came the sharp "woop-wing" of shrapnel bursting towards you, the most devilish sound of all. Some prefer the shriek of shrapnel to the dolorous wail and deep thunderous crash of high explosive. But nothing frightens me so much as the shrapnel-shriek.[2]

Well, as I passed the little red factory I noticed that the shrapnel was bursting right over the village, which meant that as 80 per cent of shrapnel bullets shoot forward the village was comparatively safe. As a matter of fact the street was full of ricocheting trifles.

Transport was drawn up well under cover of the wall and troops were marching in single file as near to the transport as possible. Two horses were being led down the middle of the street. Just before they reached me the nose of one of the horses suddenly was gashed and a stream of blood poured out. Just a ricochet, and it decided me. Despatch riders have to take care of themselves when H.Q. are eight miles away by road and there is no wire. I put my motor-cycle under cover and walked the remaining 200 yards.

Coming back I heard some shouting, a momentary silence, then a flare of the finest blasphemy. I turned the bend to see an officer holding his severed wrist and cursing. He was one of those dashing fellows. He had ridden alongside the transport swearing at the men to get a move on. He had held up his arm to give the signal when a ricochet took his hand off cleanly. His men said not a word, – sat with an air of calm disapproval like Flemish oxen.

It was one in the morning and dark on the road when I took my next despatch to St Marguerite. Just out of Bucy I passed Moulders, who shouted, "Ware wire and horses." Since last I had seen it the village had been unmercifully shelled. Where the transport had been drawn up there were shattered waggons. Strewn over the road were dead horses, of all carcasses the most ludicrously pitiful, and wound in and out of them, a witches' web, crawled the wire from the splintered telegraph posts. There was not a sound in the village except the gentle thump of my engine. I was forced to pull up, that I might more clearly see my way between two horses. My engine silent, I could only hear a little whisper from the house opposite and a dripping that I did not care to

---

1   Roy Meldrum (see Cast, page 157).
2   *Curiously enough, months after this was written the author was wounded by shrapnel.* (Watson)

understand. Farther on a house had fallen half across the road. I scarcely dared to start my engine again in the silence of this desolate destruction. Then I could not, because the dripping was my petrol and not the gore of some slaughtered animal. A flooded carburettor is a nuisance in an unsavoury village.

At the eastern end of St Marguerite the road turns sharply south. This is "Hell's Own Corner." From it there is a full and open view of the Chivres valley, and conversely those in the Chivres valley can see the corner very clearly. When we were acting on the offensive, a section of 4.5 in. howitzers were put into position just at the side of the road by the corner. This the Germans may have discovered, or perhaps it was only that the corner presented a tempting target, for they shelled to destruction everything within a hundred yards. The howitzers were rapidly put out of action though not destroyed, and a small orchard just behind them was ploughed, riven, and scarred with high explosive and shrapnel.

The day St Marguerite was shelled one of the two brigadiers determined to shift his headquarters to a certain farm. N'Soon and Grimers were attached to the brigade at the time. "Headquarters" came to the corner. N'Soon and Grimers were riding slowly in front. They heard a shell coming. Grimers flung himself off his bicycle and dropped like a stone. N'Soon opened his throttle and darted forward, foolishly. The shell exploded. Grimers' bicycle was covered with branches and he with earth and dust. N'Soon for some reason was not touched.

The General and his staff were shelled nearly the whole way to the farm, but nobody was hit. The brigade veterinary officer had a theory that the safest place was next the General, because generals were rarely hit, but that day his faith was shaken, and the next day – I will tell you the story – it tottered to destruction.

I had come through St Marguerite the night after the brigade had moved. Of course I was riding without a light. I rounded Hell's Own Corner carefully, very frightened of the noise my engine was making. A little farther on I dismounted and stumbled to the postern-gate of a farm. I opened it and went in. A sentry challenged me in a whisper and handed me over to an orderly, who led me over the black bodies of men sleeping to a lean-to where the General sat with a sheltered light, talking to his staff. He was tired and anxious. I delivered my despatch, took the receipted envelope and stumbled back to the postern-gate. Silently I hauled my motor-cycle inside, then started on my tramp to the General who had moved.

After Hell's Own Corner the road swings round again to the east, and runs along the foot of the Chivres hill to Missy. A field or so away to the left is a thick wood inhabited for the most part by German snipers. In the preceding days N'Soon and Sadders had done fine work along this road in broad daylight, carrying despatches to Missy.

I was walking, because no motor-cyclist goes by night to a battalion, and the noise of a motor-cycle would have advertised the presence of brigade headquarters somewhere on the road. It was a joyous tramp of two miles into the village of dark, ominous houses. I found a weary subaltern who put me on my way, a pitch-black lane between high walls. At the bottom of it I stepped upon an officer, who lay across the path asleep with his men. So tired was he that he did not wake. On over a field to the farm. I delivered my despatch to the Brigade-Major, whose eyes were glazed with want of sleep. He spoke to me in the pitiful monotone of the unutterably weary. I fed off bully, hot potatoes, bread and honey, then turned in.

In the morning I had just finished my breakfast when a shell exploded fifty yards behind the farm, and others followed. "Headquarters" turned out, and we crawled along a shallow ditch at the side of a rough country road until we were two hundred yards from the farm. We endeavoured to get into communication with the other brigade by flag, but after the first message a shell dropped among the farther signallers and we saw no more of them.

Shells began to drop near us. One fellow came uncomfortably close. It covered us with dirt as we "froze" to the bottom of the ditch. A little scrap of red-hot metal flew into the ground between me and the signal sergeant in front of me. I grabbed it, but dropped it because it was so hot; it was sent to the signal sergeant's wife and not to you.

We crawled a hundred yards farther along to a place where the ditch was a little deeper, and we were screened by some bushes, but I think the General's red hat must have been marked down, because for the next hour we lay flat listening to the zip-zip of bullets that passed barely overhead.

Just before we moved the Germans started to shell Missy with heavy howitzers. Risking the bullets, we saw the village crowned with great lumps of smoke. Our men poured out of it in more or less extended order across the fields. I saw them running, poor little khaki figures, and dropping like rabbits to the rifles of the snipers in the wood.

Two hundred yards south of the St Marguerite-Missy road – that is, between the road and the ditch in which we were lying – there is a single line of railway on a slight embankment. Ten men in a bunch made for the cover it afforded. One little man with an enormous pack ran a few yards in front. Seven reached the top of the embankment, then three almost simultaneously put their hands before their eyes and dropped across the rails. The little man ran on until he reached us, wide-eyed, sweaty, and breathing in short gasps. The Brigade-Major shouted to him not to come along the road but to make across the field. Immediately the little man heard the voice of command he halted, stood almost to attention, and choked out, "But they're shelling us" – then, without another word he turned off across the fields and safely reached cover.

In the ditch we were comfortable if confined, and I was frightened when the order came down, "Pass the word for the motor-cyclist." I crawled up to the General, received my despatch, and started walking across the field. Then I discovered there is a great difference between motor-cycling under rifle fire, when you can hear only the very close ones, and walking across a heavy turnip-field when you can hear all. Two-thirds of the way a sharp zip at the back of my neck and a remembrance of the three men stretched across the rails decided me. I ran.

At the farm where the other brigade headquarters were stationed I met Sadders with a despatch for the general I had just left. When I explained to him where and how to go he blenched a little, and the bursting of a shell a hundred yards or so away made him jump, but he started off at a good round pace. You must remember we were not used to carrying despatches on foot.

I rode lazily through St Marguerite and Bucy-le-Long, and turned the corner on to the open stretch. There I waited to allow a battery that was making the passage to attract as many shells as it liked. The battery reached Venizel with the loss of two horses. Then, just as I was starting off, a shell plunged into the ground by the little red factory. As I knew it to be the first of three I waited again.

At that moment Colonel Seely's car came up, and Colonel Seely himself got out[1] and went forward with me to see if the road had been damaged. For three minutes the road should have been safe, but the German machine became human, and in a couple of minutes Colonel Seely and I returned covered with rich red plough and with a singing in our ears. I gave the Colonel a couple of hundred yards start, and we sprinted across into the safe hands of Venizel.

Beyond Missy, which we intermittently occupied, our line extended along the foot of the hills and crossed the Aisne about three-quarters of a mile short of Condé bridge – and that brings me to a tale.

One night we were healthily asleep after a full day. I had been "next for duty" since ten o'clock, but at two I began to doze, because between two and five there is not often work for the despatch rider. At three I awoke to much shouting and anxious hullabaloo. The intelligence officer was

---

1   John E B Seely, M.P. (1868–1947) was Secretary of State for War but resigned in 1914 to become a Staff Officer at GHQ. He remained an M.P. while on active service throughout the war. Watson would have seen him as a celebrity, but he has recently become well-known once more for his long relationship with his charger 'Warrior', the subject of *War Horse: the real story*.

rousing us hurriedly – "All motor-cyclists turn out. Pack up kit. Seven wanted at once in the Signal Office."

This meant, firstly, that Divisional Headquarters were to move at once, in a hurry, and by night; secondly, that the same despatch was to be sent simultaneously to every unit in the Division. I asked somebody to get my kit together, and rushed upstairs to the Signal Office. There on the table I saw the fateful wire.

"Germans entrenched south side of Condé bridge and are believed to be crossing in large numbers." I was given a copy of this message to take to the 15th Brigade, then at St Marguerite. Away on the road at full speed I thought out what this meant. The enemy had broken through our line – opposite Condé there were no reserves – advance parties of the Germans might even now be approaching headquarters – large numbers would cut us off from the Division on our right and would isolate the brigade to which I was going; it would mean another Le Cateau.

I tore along to Venizel, and slowing down at the bridge shouted the news to the officer in charge – full speed across the plain to Bucy, and caring nothing for the sentries' shouts, on to St Marguerite. I dashed into the general's bedroom and aroused him. Almost before I had arrived the general and his brigade-major – both in pyjamas – were issuing commands and writing messages. Sleepy and amazed orderlies were sent out at the double. Battalion commanders and the C.R.E. were summoned.

I started back for D.H.Q. with an acknowledgment, and rattling through the village came out upon the plain.

Over Condé bridge an ochreous, heavy dawn broke sullenly. There was no noise of firing to tell me that the men of our right brigade were making a desperate resistance to a fierce advance. A mile from Serches I passed a field-ambulance loaded up for instant flight; the men were standing about in little groups talking together, as if without orders. At Headquarters I found that a despatch rider had been sent hot-foot to summon two despatch riders, who that night were with the corps, and others to every unit. Everybody carried the same command – load up and be ready to move at a moment's notice.

Orders to move were never sent. Our two ghastly sentinels still held the bridge. It was a scare.

The tale that we heard at the time was the tale of a little German firing – a lost patrol of ours, returning by an unauthorised road, mistaken in the mist for Germans – a verbal message that had gone wrong. As for the lieutenant who – it was said – first started the hare, his name was burnt with blasphemy for days and days. The only men who came out of it well were some of our cyclists, who, having made their nightly patrol up to the bridge, returned just before dawn to D.H.Q. and found the Division trying to make out that it had not been badly frightened.

I did not hear what really happened at the bridge that night until I published my paper, "The Battle of the Aisne," in the May 'Blackwood.' Here is the story as I had it from the officer principally concerned: –

Condé bridge was under our control by shell-fire alone, so that we were obliged to patrol its unpleasant neighbourhood by night. For this purpose an "officer's patrol" was organised (in addition to the "standing patrol" provided by the Cyclists) and supplied every night by different battalions. So many conflicting reports were received nightly about the bridge that the officer who told me the story was appointed Brigade Patrolling Officer.

He established himself in a certain wood, and on the night in question worked right up beyond Condé bridge – until he found a burning house about 200 yards beyond the bridge on the south side of it. In the flare of the house he was surprised to discover Germans entrenched in an old drain on the British side of the river. He had unknowingly passed this body of the enemy.

He heard, too, a continuous stream of Germans in the transport marching through the woods towards the bridge. Working his way back, he reported the matter personally to the Brigadier of the 13th, who sent the famous message to the Division.

It appears that the Germans had come down to fill their water-carts that night, and to guard against a surprise attack had pushed forward two platoons across the bridge into the drain. Unfortunately one of our patrols disobeyed its orders that night and patrolled a forbidden stretch of road. The officer shot two of these men in the dark.[1]

Three days later the outpost company on Vesle bridge of the Aisne was surrounded, and, later still, Condé bridge passed out of our artillery control, and was finally crossed by the Germans.

I have written of this famous scare of Condé bridge in detail, not because it was characteristic, but because it was exceptional. It is the only scare we ever had in our Division, and amongst those who were on the Aisne, and are still with the Division, it has become a phrase for encouragement – "Only another Condé."

During the first days on this monotonous river, the days when we attacked, the staff of our right brigade advanced for a time into open country and took cover behind the right haystack of three. To this brigade Huggie took a message early one morning, and continued to take messages throughout the day because – this was his excuse – he knew the road. It was not until several months later that I gathered by chance what had happened on that day, for Huggie, quite the best despatch rider in our Division, would always thwart my journalistic curiosity by refusing resolutely to talk about himself. The rest of us swopped yarns of an evening.

These haystacks were unhealthy: so was the approach to them. First one haystack was destroyed. The brigade went to the next. This second was blown to bits. The staff took refuge behind the third. In my letters I have told you of the good things the other despatch riders in our Division have done, but to keep up continuous communication all day with this be-shelled and refugee brigade was as fine a piece of despatch riding as any. It received its proper reward, as you know.

Afterwards the brigade emigrated to a hillside above Ciry, and remained there. Now the German gunner in whose sector Ciry was included should not be dismissed with a word. He was a man of uncertain temper and accurate shooting, for in the first place he would shell Ciry for a few minutes at any odd time, and in the second he knocked a gun out in three shells and registered accurately, when he pleased, upon the road that led up a precipitous hill to the edge of the Serches hollow. On this hill he smashed some regimental transport to firewood and killed a dozen horses, and during one of his sudden shellings of the village blew a house to pieces just as a despatch rider, who had been told the village that morning was healthy, rode by.

You must not think that we were for ever scudding along, like the typical "motor-cyclist scout" in the advertisements, surrounded with shells. There was many a dull ride even to Bucy-le-Long. An expedition to the Div. Train (no longer an errant and untraceable vagabond) was safe and produced jam. A ride to Corps Headquarters was only dangerous because of the innumerable and bloodthirsty sentries surrounding that stronghold.

One afternoon a report came through to the Division that a motor-car lay derelict at Missy. So "the skipper" called for two volunteers who should be expert mechanics. Divisional Signal companies were not then provided with cars, and if the C.O. wished to go out to a brigade, which might be up to or over eight miles away, he was compelled to ride a horse, experiment with a motor-cycle that was probably badly missed by the despatch riders, or borrow one of the staff cars. Huggie and the elder Cecil volunteered.

As soon as it was dusk they rode down to Sermoise, and crossing by the ferry – it was perilous in the dark – made their way with difficulty across country to Missy, which was then almost in front of our lines. They found the car, and examining it discovered that to outward appearance it was sound, – a great moment when after a turn or two of the handle the engine roared into the darkness, but the noise was alarming enough because the Germans were none too far away.

---

1   The last sentence of this paragraph was deleted by the censor.

OCTOBER 1914   LA BASSÉE

CAR (BARRE') CAPTURED AT MISSY BY CECIL & HUGGIE

Cecil Burney and Hugh Trepess 'scrounged' the car but it was Alick Burney who drove it regularly – it was a valued trophy and remained with the Signal company for some months.

They started on their journey home – by St Marguerite and Venizel. Just after they had left the village the beam of an alien searchlight came sweeping along the road. Before the glare had discovered their nakedness they had pulled the car to the side of the road under the shelter of the hedge nearest the Germans, and jumping down had taken cover. By all the rules of the game it was impossible to drive a car that was not exactly silent along the road from Missy to Hell's Own Corner. The searchlight should have found them, and the fire of the German snipers should have done the rest. But their luck was in, and they made no mistakes. Immediately the beam had passed they leaped on to the car and tore scathless into St Marguerite and so back to the Division.

After its capture the car was exhibited with enormous pride to all that passed by. We should not have been better pleased if we had captured the whole Prussian Guard. For prisoners disappear and cannot always be shown to prove the tale. The car was an *ἀεὶ κτῆμα*.[1]

In the morning we rode down into Sermoise for the motor-cycles. Sermoise had been shelled to pieces, but I shall never forget a brave and obstinate inhabitant who, when a shell had gone through his roof and demolished the interior of his house, began to patch his roof with bully-tins and biscuit-tins that he might at least have shelter from the rain.

Elated with our capture of the car we scented greater victories. We heard of a motor-boat on the river near Missy, and were filled with visions of an armoured motor-boat, stuffed with

1   An object that is "yours to keep" (literally, "a possession for ever").

machine-guns, plying up and down the Aisne. Huggie and another made the excursion. The boat was in an exposed and altogether unhealthy position, but they examined it, and found that there was no starting-handle. In the village forge, which was very completely fitted up, they made one that did not fit, and then another, but however much they coaxed, the engine would not start. So regretfully they left it.

To these adventures there was a quiet background of uncomfortable but pleasant existence. Life on the Aisne was like a "reading party" – only instead of working at our books we worked at soldiering.

The night that Huggie and I slept down at Ciry, the rest of the despatch riders, certain that we were taken, encamped at Ferme d'Epitaphe, for the flooded roads were impassable. There we found them in the morning, and discovered they had prepared the most gorgeous stew of all my recollection.

Now, to make a good stew is a fine art, for a stew is not merely a conglomeration of bully and vegetables and water boiled together until it looks nice. First the potatoes must be cut out to a proper size and put in; of potatoes there cannot be too many. As for the vegetables, a superfluity of carrots is a burden, and turnips should be used with a sparing hand. A full flavour of leek is a great joy. When the vegetables are nearly boiled, the dixie should be carefully examined by all to see if it is necessary to add water. If in doubt spare the water, for a rich thick gravy is much to be desired. Add bully, and get your canteens ready.

This particular stew made by Orr was epic. At all other good stews it was recalled and discussed, but never did a stew come up to the stew that we so scrupulously divided among us on the bright morning of Sept. 12, 1914, at Ferme d'Epitaphe, above Serches.

Later in the day we took over our billet, a large bicycle shed behind the school in which D.H.Q. were installed. The front of it was open, the floor was asphalt, the roof dripped, and we shared it with the Divisional Cyclists. So close were we packed that you could not turn in your sleep without raising a storm of curses, and if you were called out of nights you were compelled to walk boldly over prostrate bodies, trusting to luck that you did not step on the face of a man who woke suddenly and was bigger than yourself.

On the right of our dwelling was a little shed that was once used as a guard-room. A man and woman were brought in under suspicion of espionage. The woman was put in the shed. There she shrieked the night through, shouted for her husband (he had an ugly-sounding name that we could not understand), and literally tore her hair. The language of the Cyclists was an education even to the despatch riders, who once had been told by their Quartermaster-Sergeant that they left the cavalry standing. Finally, we petitioned for her removal, and once again slept peacefully. The Court of Inquiry found the couple were not spies, but unmarried. So it married them and let them go.

The Cyclists were marvellous and indefatigable makers of tea. At any unearthly hour you might be gently shaken by the shoulder and a voice would whisper –

"'Ave a drop o' tea – real 'ot and plenty o' sugar."

Never have I come back from a night ride without finding a couple of cyclists squatting out in the gloom round a little bright fire of their own making, with some fine hot tea. Wherever they go may they never want a drink!

And never shall I forget that fine bit of roast pork my friend Sergeant Croucher insisted on sharing with me one evening! I had not tasted fresh meat for weeks.

George was our unofficial Quartermaster. He was and is a great man, always cheerful, able to coax bread, vegetables, wine, and other luxuries out of the most hardened old Frenchwoman; and the French, though ever pathetically eager to do anything for us, always charged a good round price.[1] Candles were a great necessity, and could not be bought, but George always had candles for us. I forget at the moment whether they were for "Le General French, qui arrive," or "Les pauvres, pauvres, blessés." On two occasions George's genius brought him into trouble, for military law consists mainly of the commandment –

Thou shalt not allow thyself to be found out.

We were short of firewood. So George discovered that his engine wanted a little tuning, and started out on a voyage of discovery. Soon he came upon a heap of neatly cut, neatly piled wood. He loaded up until he heard shouts, then fled. That night we had a great fire, but in the morning came tribulation. The shouts were the shouts of the C.R.E. and the wood was an embryonic bridge. Severely reprimanded.

Then there was the Honey Question. There were bees in the village and we had no honey. The reputation of George was at stake. So one night we warily and silently approached some hives with candles; unfortunately we were interfered with by the military police. Still an expedition into the hedgerows and woods always had an excuse in time of war, and we made it.

The village of Acy, high on the hill above the road to Venizel, was the richest hunting-ground. First, there was a bread-shop open at certain hours. George was often late, and, disdaining to take his place in the long line of those who were not despatch riders, would march straight in and demand bread for one of his two worthy charities. When these were looked upon with suspicion he engineered a very friendly understanding with the baker's wife.

Then there was a dark little shop where you could buy good red wine, and beyond it a farmer with vegetables to sell. But his greatest find was the chateau, which clung to the edge of the hill and overlooked the valley of the Aisne to Condé Fort and the Hill of Chivres.

Searching one morning amongst a pile of captured and derelict stuff we discovered a canvas bath. Now, not one of us had had a bath since Havre, so we made arrangements. Three of us took the bath up to the chateau, then inhabited by a caretaker and his wife. They brought us great pails of hot water, and for the first time in a month we were clean. Then we had tea and talked about the Germans who had passed through. The German officer, the old woman told us, had done them no harm, though he had seized everything without paying a sou. Just before he left bad news was brought to him. He grew very angry, and shouted to her as he rode off –

"You shall suffer for this when we return;" but she laughed and shouted back at him, mocking – "When you return!"

And then the English came.

After tea we smoked our pipes in the terraced garden, watched the Germans shelling one of our aeroplanes, examined the German lines, and meditated in safety on the war just like newspaper correspondents.

It was in Serches itself that George received the surprise of his life. He was after potatoes, and seeing a likely-looking old man pass, D.H.Q. ran after him. In his best French – "Avez-vous pommes-de-terre a vendre?" The old man turned round, smiled, and replied in broadest Yorkshire, "Wanting any 'taters?" George collapsed.

It seems that the old fellow had settled in Serches years and years before. He had a very pretty daughter, who spoke a delectable mixture of Yorkshire and the local dialect. Of course she was

---

1 The second half of this sentence was deleted by the censor.

suspected of being a spy – in fact, probably was – so the military police were set to watch her, – a job, I gathered later from one of them, much to their liking.

Our life on the Aisne, except for little exciting episodes, was restful enough. We averaged, I should think, a couple of day messages and one each night, though there were intermittent periods of high pressure. We began to long for the strenuous first days, and the Skipper, finding that we were becoming unsettled, put us to drill in our spare time and gave some of us riding lessons. Then came rumours of a move to a rest-camp, probably back at Compiegne.

The 6th Division arrived to take over from us, or so we were told, and Rich and Cuffe[1] came over with despatches. We had not seen them since Chatham. They regarded us as veterans, and we told them the tale.

One afternoon some artillery of this division came through the valley. They were fine and fresh, but not a single one of us believed they equalled ours. There was a line of men to watch them pass, and everybody discovered a friend until practically at every stirrup there was a man inquiring after a pal, answering questions, and asking what they thought in England, and how recruiting was going. The air rang with crude, great-hearted jokes. We motor-cyclists stood aside just criticising the guns and men and horses. We felt again that shyness we had felt at Chatham in front of the professional soldier. Then we remembered that we had been through the Retreat and the Advance, and went back to tea content.

---

1   Corporals George Cuffe and Neville Rich were both sworn in at Chatham the same day as Watson. Cuffe, who was described in *The Motor Cycle* as "a well-known competition rider", was knighted in 1946 for his work on the Indian railways.

8

The Move to the North

We left Serches at dusk with little regret and pushed on over the hill past Ferme d'Epitaphe of gluttonous memory, past the Headquarter clerks, who were jogging peacefully along on bicycles, down the other side of the hill, and on to the village of Maast.

Headquarters were in a curious farm. One side of its court was formed by a hill in which there were caves – good shelter for the men. There was just one run that night to Corps H.Q. in a chateau three miles farther on.

The morning was clear and sunny. A good, lazy breakfast preluded a great wash. Then we chatted discreetly with a Paris *midinette* at the gate of the farm. Though not in Flanders, she was of the Flemish type, – bright colouring, high cheek-bones, dark eyes. On these little social occasions – they came all too rarely; that is why I always mention them – there was much advantage in being only a corporal. Officers, even Staff Officers, as they passed threw at us a look of admiration and envy. A salute was cheap at the price. In the afternoon there was a run, and when I returned I found that the rest-camp rumour had been replaced by two others – either we were going into action immediately a little farther along the line beyond Soissons, or we were about to make a dash to Ostend for the purpose of outflanking the Germans.

We moved again at dusk, and getting clear of the two brigades with H.Q. rode rapidly twenty miles across country, passing over the road by which we had advanced, to Longpont, a big dark chateau set in a wood and with a French sentry at the gate. Our third brigade was trekking away into the darkness as we came in. We slept in a large room on straw mattresses – very comforting to the bones.

The morning was again gorgeous, and again we breakfasted late and well. The chateau we discovered to be monumental, and beside it, set in a beautiful garden, was a ruined chapel, where a service was held – the first we had been able to attend since the beginning of the war.

Our host, an old man, thin and lithe, and dressed in shiny black, came round during the day to see that we had all we needed. We heard a tale – I do not know how true it was – that the Crown Prince had stayed at the chateau. He had drunk much ancient and good wine, and what he had not drunk he had taken away with him, together with some objects of art. The chateau was full of good things.

During the day I had a magnificent run of forty miles over straight dry roads to Hartennes, where, if you will remember, that great man, Sergeant Croucher of the cyclists, had given us tea, and on to Chacrise and Maast. It was the first long and open run I had had since the days of the retreat, when starting from La Pommeraye I had ridden through the forest to Compiegne in search of the Divisional Train.

Just after I had returned we started off again – at dusk. I was sent round to a place, the name of which I cannot remember, to a certain division; then I struck north along a straight road through the forest to Villers-Cotterets. The town was crammed with French motor-lorries and crowded with French troops, who greeted me hilariously as I rode through to Veze.

There we slept comfortably in the lodge of the chateau, all, that is, except Grimers, who had been seized with a puncture just outside the main hotel in Villers-Cotterets.

The despatch riders prepare breakfast in the farmyard at Maast on 3rd October – the surviving Blackburne and the other motorcycles lined up behind them to the right.
Seated are Bagshaw (left) and Cecil Burney (right).

The despatch riders posed for a group photograph in the abbey ruins at Longpont on Sunday 4th October. Between the two poilus, most of the motorcyclists are identifiable, including Danson, Meldrum, and Watson leaning forward. Behind them, Alick Burney has rolled up sleeves. Trepess holds out his mug to Orr, partly concealing both Bagshaw and Cecil Burney. Owen is on the far right.

In the morning I had a fine run to a brigade at Béthancourt, the little village, you will remember, where we lunched off an excellent omelette, and convinced the populace, with the help of our host, that the Germans would come no farther.

While I was away the rest discovered some excellent white wine in the cellar of the lodge, and before starting again at dusk we made a fine meal. Cecil and I remained after the others had gone, and when the wife of the lodge-keeper came in and expressed her utter detestation of all troops, we told her that we were shedding our blood for France, and offered her forgetfully a glass of her own good wine.

That night we slept at Béthisy St Martin. On the retreat, you will remember, the lord of the chateau had given some of the despatch riders dinner, before they learnt that D.H.Q. had been diverted to Crécy-en-Valois. He recognised us with joy, allowed us to take things from the kitchen, and in the morning hunted out for us a tennis set. Four of us who were not on duty played a great game on a very passable gravel court.

We now heard that "the Division" was convinced that we were going to make a dash for Ostend, and rumour seemed to crystallise into truth when orders came that we were to entrain that night at Pont St Maxence.

The despatch riders rode ahead of the column, and received a joyous welcome in the town. We stalked bravely into a café, and drank loud and hearty toasts with some friendly but rather drunk French soldiers. Gascons they were, and d'Artagnans all, from their proper boasting – the heart of a lion and the cunning of a fox, they said. One of us was called into a more sober chamber to drink ceremonious toasts in champagne with their officers. In the street another of us – I would not give even his initial – selecting the leading representative of young, demure, and ornamental maiden-hood, embraced her in the middle of the most admiring crowd I have ever seen, while the rest of us explained to a half-angry mother that her daughter should be proud and happy – as indeed she was – to represent the respectable and historic town of Pont St Maxence.

Then, amidst shrieks and cheers and cries of "Brave Tommy" and "We love you," the despatch riders of the finest and most famous of all Divisions rode singing to the station, where we slept peacefully on straw beside a large fire until the train came in and the Signal Company arrived.

Our entraining at Pont St Maxence began with a carouse and ended with a cumulative disappointment. In the middle was the usual wait, a tiresome but necessary part of all military evolutions. To entrain a Signal Company sounds so simple. Here is the company – there is the train. But first comes the man-handling of cable-carts on to trucks that were built for the languid conveyance of perambulators. Then follows a little horseplay, and only those who, like myself, regard horses as unmechanical and self-willed instruments of war, know how terrifying a sight and how difficult a task the emboxing of a company's horses can be. Motor-cycles are heavy and have to be lifted, but they do not make noises and jib and rear, and look every moment as if they were going to fall backward on to the interested spectator.

We despatch riders fetched a great deal of straw and made ourselves comfortable in one of those waggons that are marked outside, with such splendid optimism –

Chevaux 8
Hommes 40–5

With our friend the Post-Sergeant and his underling there were roughly a dozen of us and no super-fluity of space, but, seeing men wandering fiercely up and down the train under the command of our Sergeant-Major, we took in a H.Q. clerk. This ruffled us, but it had to be done. The Sergeant-Major came to our waggon. We stood at the door and pointed out to him that we had in our waggon not only all the despatch riders, but also the whole of the Postal and Headquarters Staffs. He said nothing to us – only told ten more men to get in. Finally we were twenty-five in all, with full equipment. Thinking of the 40-5 we settled down and managed to effect a compromise of room which, to our amazement, left us infinitely more comfortable than we had been in the IIIme coming up from Havre to Landrecies.

The train shuffled out of the station just before dawn. We slept a bit, and then, just as it was getting light, started our pipes and began to talk of the future.

The general opinion favoured Ostend, though a sergeant hazarded that we were going to be shipped swiftly across to England to defend the East Coast. This suggestion was voted impossible and tactless – at least, we didn't put it quite like that. Ostend it was going to be – train to Abbeville, and then boat to Ostend, and a rapid march against the German flank.

The discussion was interrupted by somebody saying he had heard from somebody who had been told by his Major, that 60,000 Germans had been killed in the last two days, Von Kluck had been killed by a lucky shell, and the Crown Prince had committed suicide. We were bringing the cynicism of youth to bear on the trustfulness of a mature mercenary when the train arrived at Amiens.

Some washed. Some meditated on a train of French wounded and another train of Belgian refugees, humble and pitiful objects, very smelly. Two, not waiting for orders, rushed to the buffet and bought beer and sardines and chocolate and bread. One of these was cut off from his waggon by a long goods train that passed through, but he knew the ways of military trains, waited till the goods had passed, then ran after us and caught us up after a mile's jog-trot. The good people of Amiens, who had not so very long before been delivered from the Germans, were exceedingly affectionate, and threw us fruit, flowers, and kisses. Those under military age shrieked at the top of their shrill little trebles –

Engleesh – Tipperary – Biskeet – Biskeet – Souvenir.

We have never understood the cry of "Biskeet." The fat little fellows were obviously well nourished. Perhaps, dog-like, they buried their biscuits with a thought for the time when the English should be forgotten and hunger should take their place as something very present.

The motorcyclists played "a little football" in the parade ground of the Great Barracks at Abbeville, known as La Caserne Courbet.

So joyously we were rushed north at about five miles an hour, or eight kilometres per hour, which sounds better. Early in the afternoon we came to Abbeville, a hot and quiet station, and, with the aid of some London Scottish, disembarked. From these Scots we learnt that the French were having a rough time just north of Arras, that train-load upon train-load of wounded had come through, that our Corps (the 2nd) was going up to help.

So even now we do not know whether we really were going to Ostend and were diverted to the La Bassée district to help the French who had got themselves into a hole, or whether Ostend was somebody's little tale.

We rode through the town to the Great Barracks, where we were given a large and clean ward. The washing arrangements were sumptuous and we had truckle-beds to sleep upon, but the sanitation, as everywhere in France, was vile. We kicked a football about on the drill-ground. Then some of us went down into the town, while the rest of us waited impatiently for them to come back, taking a despatch or two in the meanwhile.

From the despatch rider's point of view Abbeville is a large and admiring town, with good restaurants and better baths. These baths were finer than the baths of Havre – full of sweet-scented odours and the deliciously intoxicating fumes of good soap and plenteous boiling-water.

In a little restaurant we met some friends of the 3rd Division and a couple of London Scots, who were getting heartily sick of the L. of C., though taking prisoners round the outskirts of Paris had, I gather, its charm even for the most ardent warriors.[1]

In the morning there was parade, a little football, and then a stroll into the town. I had just finished showing an Intelligence Officer how to get a belt back on to the pulley of his motor-cycle when Cecil met me and told me we were to move north that evening.

We had a delectable little tea, bought a map or two, and then strolled back to the barracks. In half an hour we were ready to move off, kit piled high upon our carriers, looking for all the world (said our C.O.) like those funny little animals that carry their houses upon their backs and live at the bottom of ponds. Indeed it was our boast that – such was our ingenuity – we were able to carry more kit than any regimental officer.

It was dusk when N'Soon and I pushed off, – we had remained behind to deal with messages that might come in foolishly after the Division had left. We took the great highroad to Calais, and, carefully passing the General, who was clattering along with his staff and an escort of Hussars, we pulled up to light our lamps at a little estaminet with glowing red blinds just like the blinds of certain hospitable taverns in the city of Oxford. The coincidence was so remarkable that we were compelled to enter.

We found a roaring, leaping log-fire, a courteous old Frenchman who drank our healths, an immense omelette, some particularly good coffee, and the other despatch riders.

That night it was freezing hard. With our chairs drawn in close to the fire, a glass of something to keep the cold out ready to hand, and pipes going strong, we felt sorry for the general and his escort who, probably with chilled lips and numbed fingers, jogged resoundingly through the village street.

Twenty minutes later we took the road, and soon, pretending that we had lost our way, again passed the general – and lost our way, or at least rode well past our turning. Finally, colder than we had ever been before, we reached the Chateau at Gueschart. There we found a charming and hospitable son of the house and a pleasantly adoring lad. With their aid we piled the floor of the harness-room with straw, and those of us who were not on duty slept finely.

---

1   1st Battalion London Scottish landed in September 1914 – the first Territorial regiment to reach France. To their disappointment they were first deployed as 'Line of Communication' troops. Alec Hepburne-Scott (see Cast, page 130) may have been one of the London Scottish with whom Watson dined.

From the dawn of the next morning we were working at top pressure right through the day, keeping in touch with the brigades which were billeted in villages several miles distant.

Late in the afternoon we discovered we were very short of petrol, so I was sent off to Crécy in our famous captured car, with a requisition. We arrived amidst cheers. I strode into the nearest garage and demanded 100 litres of petrol. It was humbly brought and placed in the car: then I sent boys flying round the town for jam and bread and butter, and in the meantime we entertained the crowd by showing them a German helmet. I explained volubly that my bandaged fingers – there was an affair of outposts with an ambulance near Serches – were the work of shrapnel, and they nearly embraced me. A boy came back and said there was no jam, so the daughter of the house went to her private cupboard and brought me out two jars of jam she had made herself, and an enormous glass of wine. We drove off amidst more cheers, to take the wrong road out of the town in our great excitement.

The brigades moved that night; headquarters remained at Gueschart until dawn, when the general started off in his car with two of us attendant.

Now before the war a motor-cyclist would consider himself ill-used if he were forced to take a car's dust for a mile or so. Your despatch rider was compelled to follow in the wake of a large and fast Daimler for twenty-five miles, and at the end of it he did not know which was him and which dust.

We came upon the 15th, shivering in the morning cold, and waiting for some French motor-buses. Then we rushed on to St Pol, which was crammed full of French transport, and on to Chateau Brias. Until the other despatch riders came up there was no rest for the two of us that had accompanied the car. The roads, too, were blocked with refugees flying south from Lille and men of military age who had been called up. Once again we heard the distant sound of guns – for the first time since we had been at the Chateau of Longpont.

At last we were relieved for an hour, and taking possession of a kitchen we fried some pork-chops with onions and potatoes. It was grand. We washed them down with coffee, and went back to duty. For the remainder of that day and for the whole of the night there was no rest for us.

At dawn the Division marched in column of route north-east towards the sound of the guns.

Half of us at a time slipped away and fed in stinking taverns – but the food was good.

I cannot remember a hotter day, and we were marching through a thickly-populated mining district – the villages were uncomfortably like those round Dour. The people were enthusiastic and generous with their fruit and with their chocolate. It was very tiring work, because we were compelled to ride with the Staff, for first one of us was needed and then another to take messages up and down the column or across country to brigades and divisions that were advancing along roads parallel to ours. The old Division was making barely one mile an hour. The road was blocked by French transport coming in the opposite direction, by 'buses drawn up at the side of the road, and by cavalry that, trekking from the Aisne, crossed our front continuously to take up their position away on the left.

At last, about three o'clock in the afternoon, we reached the outskirts of Béthune. The sound of the guns was very near, and to the east of the town we could see an aeroplane haloed in bursting shrapnel.

The Staff took refuge first in an unsavoury field and afterwards in a little house. Despatch after despatch until evening – and then, ordered to remain behind to direct others, and cheered by the sight of our most revered and most short-sighted staff-officer walking straight over a little bridge into a deep, muddy, and stinking ditch, I took refuge in the kitchen and experienced the discreeter pleasures of "the Force." The handmaidens brought coffee, and brushed me and washed me and talked to me. I was sorry when the time came for me to resume my beat, or rather to ride with Cecil after the Division.

We passed some Turcos, happy-looking children but ill companions in a hostile country, and some Spahis with flowing burnous, who looked ridiculously out of place, and then, after a long search – it was dark on the road and very cold – we found the Division.

I dined off a maconochie,[1] and was wondering whether I dare lie down to sleep, when I was called out to take a message to and remain at the 13th Brigade. It was a bad night. Never was a man so cold in his life, and the brigade had taken up its quarters in a farm situated in the centre of a very labyrinth of country roads. But I had four hours' sleep when I got there, while the others were up all the night.

There was no hurry in the morning. The orders were to join the Division at a bridge just outside Béthune, a point which they could not possibly reach before ten. So I got up late and had a glorious meal of soup, omelette, and fruit in the town, waited on by a most excellent flapper who wanted to know everything about everything. I reported at the Signal Office, then occupying the lodge of the town cemetery, and was sent off to catch the Devons. At the village where I waited for them I found some Cuirassiers, genial fellows; but living helios in the burning sun. When I returned the Division had moved along the north bank of the Canal to Beuvry Station. The post picked us up, and in the joyous possession of two parcels and some letters I unpacked my kit. We all settled down on some moderately clean straw in the waiting-room of the station, and there we remained for three full weeks.

Men talk of the battle of Ypres[2] as the finest achievement of the British Army. There was one brigade there that had a past. It had fought at Mons and Le Cateau, and then plugged away cheerfully through the Retreat and the Advance. What was left of it had fought stiffly on the Aisne. Some hard marching, a train journey, more hard marching, and it was thrown into action at La Bassée. There it fought itself to a standstill. It was attacked and attacked until, shattered, it was driven back one wild night. It was rallied, and turning on the enemy held them. More hard marching – a couple of days' rest, and it staggered into action at Ypres, and somehow – no one knows how – it held its bit of line. A brigade called by the same name, consisting of the same regiments, commanded by the same general, but containing scarce a man of those who had come out in August, marched very proudly away from Ypres and went – not to rest – but to hold another bit of the line.

And this brigade was not the Guards Brigade. There were no picked men in the brigade. It contained just four ordinary regiments of the line – the Norfolks, the Bedfords, the Cheshires, and the Dorsets. What the 15th Brigade did, other brigades have done.

Now little has been heard of this fighting round La Bassée in October, so I wish I could tell you about it in more detail than I can. To my thinking it was the finest fighting I have seen.

You will understand, then, how difficult it is for me to describe the country round La Bassée. I might describe it as it appeared to me when first we arrived – sunny and joyous, with many little farms and thick hedges and rare factories – or as I saw it last, on a horrible yellowish evening, shattered and black and flooded and full of ghosts.

Now when first we arrived news filtered through to us that La Bassée was held only by a division of Jägers, plentifully supplied with artillery and machine guns. I believe this was the fact. The Jägers held on stubbornly until reinforcements came up. Instead of attacking we were hard pressed, and had more than we could do to prevent the Germans in their turn from breaking through. Indeed we had not a kick left in us when the Division was relieved.

At the beginning it looked so simple. The British Army was wheeling round on to the German right flank. We had the shortest distance to go, because we formed the extreme British right. On our left was the 3rd Division, and beyond the 3rd was the First Corps. On the left of the First the Third Corps was sweeping on to Armentières.

---

1 A tinned meat and vegetable stew produced in Aberdeen for the Army by the Maconochie Company.
2 *The first – in October and November.* (Watson)

Then Antwerp fell suddenly. The First Corps was rushed up to help the Seventh Division which was trying to guard the right flank of the Belgians in retirement along the coast. Thus some sort of very weak line was formed from the sea to La Bassée. The Germans, reinforced by the men, and more particularly by the guns that the fall of Antwerp had let loose, attacked violently at Ypres and La Bassée. I do not say this is what really happened. I am trying to tell you what we thought was happening.

Think of us, then, in the heat of early October going into action on the left of the French, confident that we had just a little opposition to brush away in front of us before we concentrated in the square at La Bassée.

At first the 13th Brigade was put into position south of the canal, the 15th Brigade attacked from the canal to the La Bassée-Estaires road, and the 14th from the main road roughly to the Richebourgs. In the second stage the French extended their line to the Canal, and the 13th became a reserve brigade. In the third stage we had every man in the line – the 13th Brigade being split up between the 14th and 15th, and the French sent two battalions to the north bank of the canal.

The work of the despatch riders was of two kinds. Three-quarters of us rode between the divisional and the brigade headquarters. The rest were attached to the brigades, and either used for miscellaneous work or held in reserve so that communication might not be broken if the wires were cut or smashed by shells.

One motor-cyclist went out every day to Lieutenant Chapman, who was acting as liaison officer with the French. This job never fell to my lot, but I am told it was exciting enough. The French general was an intrepid old fellow, who believed that a general should be near his fighting men. So his headquarters were always being shelled. Then he would not retire, but preferred to descend into the cellar until the evil times were overpast.

The despatch rider with Chapman had his bellyful of shells. It was pleasant to sit calmly in a cellar and receive food at the hands of an accomplished *chef*, and in more peaceful times there was opportunity to study the idiosyncrasies of German gunners and the peculiar merits of the Soixante-Quinze.[1] But when the shelling was hottest there was usually work for the despatch rider – and getting away from the unhealthy area before scooting down the Annequin road was a heart-thumping job.

French generals were always considerate and hospitable to us despatch riders. On our arrival at Béthune Huggie was sent off with a message to a certain French Corps Commander. The General received him with a proper French embrace, congratulated him on our English bravery, and set him down to some food and a glass of good wine.

It was at La Bassée that we had our first experience of utterly unrideable roads. North of the canal the roads were fair macadam in dry weather and to the south the main road Béthune-Beuvry-Annequin was of the finest pavé. Then it rained hard. First the roads became greasy beyond belief. Starting was perilous, and the slightest injudicious swerve meant a bad skid. Between Gorre and Festubert the road was vile. It went on raining, and the roads were thickly covered with glutinous mud. The front mud-guard of George's Douglas choked up with a lamentable frequency. The Blackburne alone, the finest and most even-running of all motor-cycles,[2] ran with unswerving regularity.

---

1   The renowned French 75mm artillery.

2   *This is not an unthinking advertisement. After despatch riding from August 16 to February 18 my judgment should be worth something. I am firmly convinced that if the Government could have provided all despatch riders with Blackburnes, the percentage – at all times small – of messages undelivered owing to mechanical breakdowns or the badness of the roads would have been reduced to zero. I have no interest in the Blackburne Company beyond a sincere admiration of the machine it produces.* (Watson)

"Ginger" the cook, and his assistant, probably taken at Beuvry.

Finally, to our heartburning sorrow, there were nights on which motor-cycling became impossible, and we stayed restlessly at home while men on the despised horse carried our despatches. This we could not allow for long. Soon we became so skilled that, if I remember correctly, it was only on half a dozen nights in all right through the winter that the horsemen were required.

It was at La Bassée too that we had our second casualty. A despatch rider whom we called "Moulders" came in one evening full of triumph. A bullet had just grazed his leg and the Government was compelled to provide him with a new puttee. We were jealous, and he was proud.

We slept in that room which was no room, the entrance-hall of Beuvry Station. It was small and crowded. The floor was covered with straw which we could not renew. After the first fortnight the population of this chamber increased rapidly; one or two of us spoke of himself hereafter in the plural. They gave far less trouble than we had expected, and, though always with some of us until the spring, suffered heavy casualties from the use of copious petrol and the baking of washed shirts in the village oven.

We had been given a cook of our own. He was a youth of dreamy habits and acquisitive tastes, but sometimes made a good stew. Each one of us thought he himself was talented beyond the ordinary, so the cook never wanted assistance – except perhaps in the preparing of breakfast. Food was good and plentiful, while the monotony of army rations was broken by supplies from home and from Béthune. George, thank heaven, was still with us. Across the bridge was a shop where you could buy anything from a pair of boots to a kilo of vermicelli. Those of us who were not on duty would wander in about eleven in the morning, drink multitudinous bowls of coffee at two sous the bowl, and pass the time of day with some of the cyclists who were billeted in the big brewery. Just down the road was a tavern where infernal cognac could be got and occasionally good red wine.

Even when there was little to do, the station was not dull. French hussars, dainty men with thin and graceful horses, rode over the bridge and along the canal every morning. Cuirassiers would clatter and swagger by – and guns, both French and English. Behind the station much ammunition was stored, a source of keen pleasure if ever the Germans had attempted to shell the station. It was well within range. During the last week His Majesty's armoured train, "Jellicoe," painted in wondrous colours, would rumble in and on towards La Bassée. The crew were full of Antwerp tales and late newspapers. The first time the train went into action it demolished a German battery, but afterwards it had little luck.

The corps was at Hinges. If work were slack and the Signal Sergeant were kind, he would give one of us a bunch of messages for the corps, with the hint that the return might be made at leisure. Between Hinges and Beuvry lay Béthune. Hinges deserves a word.

When first the corps came to Hinges, the inhabitants were exalted. The small boys came out in puttees and the women put ribbons in their hair. Now, if you pronounce Hinges in the French fashion, you give forth an exclamation of distressful pain. The name cannot be shouted from a motor-cycle. It has its difficulties even for the student of French. So we all called it, plainly and bluntly, Hinges, as though it were connected to a door. The inhabitants noticed this. Thinking that they and their forefathers had been wrong – for surely these fine men with red hats knew better than they – the English pronunciation spread. The village became 'Ingees, and now only some unfashionable dotards in Béthune preserve the tradition of the old pronunciation. It is not only Hinges that has been thus decently attired in British garb. Le Cateau is Lee Catòo. Boescheppe is Bo-peep. Ouderdon is Eiderdown.

Béthune was full of simple pleasures. First there were the public baths, cheap and good, and sundry coiffeurs who were much in demand, for they made you smell sweetly. Then there was a little blue and white café. The daughter of the house was well-favoured and played the piano with some skill. One of us spent all his spare time at this café in silent adoration – of the piano, for his French was exiguous in the extreme. There was a patisserie crammed full of the most delicious cream-cakes. The despatch rider who went to Hinges about 3.30 p.m. and did not return with cakes for tea, found life unpleasant. Near the station three damsels ruled a tavern. They were friendly and eager to teach us French. We might have left them with a sigh of regret if we had not once arrived as they were eating their mid-day meal.

At one time the Germans dropped a few shells into Béthune, but did little damage. Bombs fell too. One nearly ended the existence of "Sadders" – also known as "Boo." It dropped on the other side of the street; doing our despatch rider no damage, it slightly wounded Sergeant Croucher of the Cyclists in a portion of his body that made him swear when he was classed as a "sitting-up case."

Of all the towns behind the lines – Béthune, Estaires, Armentieres, Bailleul, Poperinghe – Béthune is the pleasantest. The people are charming. There is nothing you cannot buy there. It is clean and well-ordered, and cheerful in the rain. I pray that Béthune may survive the war – that after peace has been declared and Berlin has been entered, I may spend a week there and much money to the profit of the people and the satisfaction of myself.

Now I will give some account of our adventures out with the brigades round La Bassée.

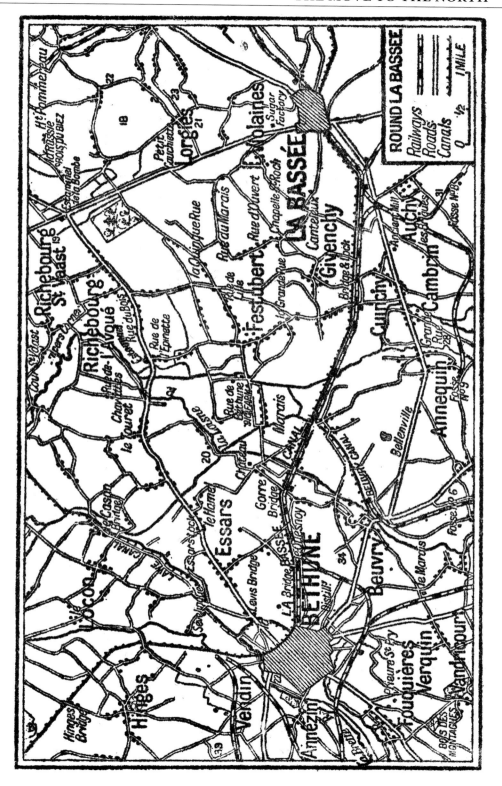

9

Round La Bassée

It had been a melancholy day, full of rain and doubting news. Those of us who were not "out" were strolling up and down the platform arranging the order of cakes from home and trying to gather from the sound of the gunning and intermittent visits to the Signal Office what was happening.

Someone had been told that the old 15th was being hard pressed. Each of us regretted loudly that we had not been attached to it, though our hearts spoke differently. Despatch riders have muddled thoughts. There is a longing for the excitement of danger and a very earnest desire to keep away from it.

The C.O. walked on to the platform hurriedly, and in a minute or two I was off. It was lucky that the road was covered with unholy grease, that the light was bad and there was transport on the road – for it is not good for a despatch rider to think too much of what is before him. My instructions were to report to the general and make myself useful. I was also cheerfully informed that the H.Q. of the 15th were under a robust shell-fire. Little parties of sad-looking wounded that I passed, the noise of the guns, and the evil dusk heartened me.

I rode into Festubert, which was full of noise, and, very hastily dismounting, put my motor-cycle under the cover of an arch and reported to the general. He was sitting at a table in the stuffy room of a particularly dirty tavern. At the far end a fat and frightened woman was crooning to her child. Beside her sat a wrinkled, leathery old man with bandaged head. He had wandered into the street, and he had been cut about by shrapnel. The few wits he had ever possessed were gone, and he gave every few seconds little croaks of hate. Three telephone operators were working with strained faces at their highest speed. The windows had been smashed by shrapnel, and bits of glass and things crunched under foot. The room was full of noises – the crackle of the telephones, the crooning of the woman, the croak of the wounded old man, the clear and incisive tones of the general and his brigade-major, the rattle of not too distant rifles, the booming of guns and occasionally the terrific, overwhelming crash of a shell bursting in the village.

I was given a glass of wine. Cadell, the Brigade Signal Officer, and the Veterinary Officer, came up to me and talked cheerfully in whispered tones about our friends.

There was the sharp cry of shrapnel in the street and a sudden rattle against the whole house. The woman and child fled somewhere through a door, followed feebly by the old man. The brigade-major persuaded the general to work in some less unhealthy place. The telephone operators moved. A moment's delay as the general endeavoured to persuade the brigade-major to go first, and we found ourselves under a stalwart arch that led into the courtyard of the tavern. We lit pipes and cigarettes. The crashes of bursting shells grew more frequent, and the general remarked in a dry and injured tone – "Their usual little evening shoot before putting up the shutters, I suppose."

But first the Germans "searched" the village. Now to search a village means to start at one end of the village and place shells at discreet intervals until the other end of the village is reached. It is an unpleasant process for those in the middle of the village, even though they be standing, as we were, in comparatively good shelter.

We heard the Germans start at the other end of the village street. The crashes came nearer and nearer, until a shell burst with a scream and a thunderous roar just on our right. We puffed away at our cigarettes for a second, and a certain despatch rider wished he were anywhere but in the cursed village of Festubert by Béthune. There was another scream and overwhelming relief. The next shell burst three houses away on our left. I knocked my pipe out and filled another.

The Germans finished their little evening shoot. We marched back very slowly in the darkness to 1910 Farm.

This farm was neither savoury nor safe. It was built round a courtyard which consisted of a gigantic hole crammed with manure in all the stages of unpleasant putrefaction. One side is a barn; two sides consist of stables, and the third is the house inhabited not only by us but by an incredibly filthy and stinking old woman who was continually troubling the general because some months ago a French cuirassier took one of her chickens. The day after we arrived at this farm I had few despatches to take, so I wrote to Robert.[1]

Here is some of the letter and bits of other letters I wrote during the following days. They will give you an idea of our state of mind:[2] –

If you want something of the dramatic – I am writing in a farm under shrapnel fire, smoking a pipe that was broken by a shell. For true effect I suppose I should not tell you that the shrapnel is bursting about fifty yards the other side of the house, that I am in a room lying on the floor, and consequently that, so long as they go on firing shrapnel, I am perfectly safe.

It's the dismallest of places. Two miles farther back the heavies are banging away over our heads. There are a couple of batteries near the farm. Two miles along the road the four battalions of our brigade are holding on for dear life in their trenches.

The country is open plough, with little clumps of trees, sparse hedges, and isolated cottages giving a precarious cover. It's all very damp and miserable, for it was raining hard last night and the day before.

I am in a little bare room with the floor covered with straw. Two telegraph operators are making that infernal jerky clicking sound I have begun so to hate. Half a dozen men of the signal staff are lying about the floor looking at week-old papers. In the next room I can hear the general, seated at a table and intent on his map, talking to an officer that has just come from the firing line. Outside the window a gun is making a fiendish row, shaking the whole house. Occasionally there is a bit of a rattle – that's shrapnel bullets falling on the tiles of an outhouse.

If you came out you might probably find this exhilarating. I have just had a talk with our mutual friend Cadell, the Signal Officer of this brigade, and we have decided that we are fed up with it. For one thing – after two months' experience of shell fire the sound of a shell bursting within measurable distance makes you start and shiver for a moment – reflex action of the nerves. That is annoying. We both decided we would willingly change places with you and take a turn at defending your doubtless excellently executed trenches at Liberton.[3]

The line to the ——[4] has just gone. It's almost certain death to relay it in the daytime. Cadell and his men are discussing the chances while somebody else has started a musical-box. A man has gone out; I wonder if he will come back. The rest of the men have gone to sleep again. That gun outside the window is getting on my nerves. Well, well!

---

1 Robert Whyte, see Cast, page 130.
2 *The letters were written on the 14th October et seq. The censor was kind.* (Watson)
3 Watson may be gently mocking Whyte's rôle as a Territorial soldier safe at home in practice trenches at Liberton, an Edinburgh suburb – however, by that date Whyte had already applied for a commission, and he transferred to the Black Watch in November 1914.
4 *Dorsets, I think.* (Watson).

The shrapnel fire appears to have stopped for the present. No, there's a couple together. If they fire over this farm I hope they don't send me back to D.H.Q.

Do you know what I long for more than anything else? A clean, unhurried breakfast with spotless napery and shining silver and porridge and kippers. I don't think these long, lazy after-breakfast hours at Oxford were wasted. They are a memory and a hope out here. The shrapnel is getting nearer and more frequent. We are all hoping it will kill some chickens in the courtyard. The laws against looting are so strict.

What an excellent musical-box, playing quite a good imitation of *Cavalleria Rusticana*. I guess we shall have to move soon. Too many shells. Too dark to write any more

After all, quite the most important things out here are a fine meal and a good bath. If you consider the vast area of the war the facts that we have lost two guns or advanced five miles are of very little importance. War, making one realise the hopeless insignificance of the individual, creates in one such an immense regard for self, that so long as one does well it matters little if four officers have been killed reconnoitring or some wounded have had to be left under an abandoned gun all night. I started with an immense interest in tactics. This has nearly all left me and I remain a more or less efficient despatch-carrying animal – a part of a machine realising the hopeless, enormous size of the machine.

The infantry officer after two months of modern war is a curious phenomenon.[1] He is probably one of three survivors of an original twenty-eight. He is not frightened of being killed; he has forgotten to think about it. But there is a sort of reflex fright. He becomes either cautious and liable to sudden panics, or very rash indeed, or absolutely mechanical in his actions. The first state means the approach of a nervous breakdown, the second a near death. There are very few, indeed, who retain a nervous balance and a calm judgment. And all have a harsh frightened voice. If you came suddenly out here, you would think they were all mortally afraid. But it is only giving orders for hours together under a heavy fire.

Battle noises are terrific. At the present moment a howitzer is going strong behind this, and the concussion is tremendous. The noise is like dropping a traction-engine on a huge tin tray. A shell passing away from you over your head is like the loud crackling of a newspaper close to your ear. It makes a sort of deep reverberating crackle in the air, gradually lessening, until there is a dull boom, and a mile or so away you see a thick little cloud of white smoke in the air or a pear-shaped cloud of grey-black smoke on the ground. Coming towards you a shell makes a cutting, swishing note, gradually getting higher and higher, louder and louder. There is a longer note one instant and then it ceases. Shrapnel bursting close to you has the worst sound.

It is almost funny in a village that is being shelled. Things simply disappear. You are standing in an archway a little back from the road – a shriek of shrapnel. The windows are broken and the tiles rush clattering into the street, while little bullets and bits of shell jump like red-hot devils from side to side of the street, ricochetting until their force is spent. Or a deeper bang, a crash, and a whole house tumbles down.[2]

¾-hour later. – Curious life this. Just after I had finished the last sentence, I was called out to take a message to a battery telling them to shell a certain village. Here am I wandering out, taking orders for the complete destruction of a village and probably for the death of a couple of hundred men[3] without a thought, except that the roads are very greasy and that lunch time is near.

---

1   *I do not say this paragraph is true. It is what I thought on 15th October 1914. The weather was depressing.* (Watson)
2   This paragraph and the preceding paragraph commencing "Battle noises" were deleted by the censor.
3   *Optimist!* (Watson)

LA BASSEE   OCTOBER 1914.

Nʳ FESTUBERT.

This image was so striking that it featured at the front of the Burneys' album and was also used by Sadders.

Again, yesterday, I put our Heavies in action, and in a quarter of an hour a fine old church, with what appeared from the distance a magnificent tower, was nothing but a grotesque heap of ruins. The Germans were loopholing it for defence.

Oh the waste, the utter damnable waste of everything out here – men, horses, buildings, cars, everything. Those who talk about war being a salutary discipline are those who remain at home. In a modern war there is little room for picturesque gallantry or picture-book heroism. We are all either animals or machines, with little gained except our emotions dulled and brutalised and nightmare flashes of scenes that cannot be written about because they are unbelievable. I wonder what difference you will find in us when we come home

Do you know what a night scare is? In our last H.Q. we were all dining when suddenly there was a terrific outburst of rifle-fire from our lines. We went out into the road that passes the farm and stood there in the pitch darkness, wondering. The fire increased in intensity until every soldier within five miles seemed to be revelling in a lunatic succession of "mad minutes." Was it a heavy attack on our lines? Soon pom-poms joined in sharp, heavy taps – and machine guns. The lines to the battalions were at the moment working feebly, and what the operators could get through was scarcely intelligible. Ammunition limbers were hurried up, and I stood ready to dart anywhere. For twenty minutes the rifle-fire seemed to grow wilder and wilder. At last stretcher-bearers came in with a few wounded and reported that we seemed to be holding our own. Satisfactory so far. Then there were great flashes of shrapnel over our lines; that comforted us, for if your troops are advancing you don't fire shrapnel over the enemy's lines. You never know how soon they may be yours. The firing soon died down until we heard nothing but little desultory bursts. Finally an orderly came – the Germans had half-heartedly charged our trenches but had been driven off with loss. We returned to the farm and found that in the few minutes we had been outside everything had been packed and half-frightened men were standing about for orders.

The explanation of it all came later and was simple enough. The French, without letting us know, had attacked the Germans on our right, and the Germans to keep us engaged had made a feint attack upon us. So we went back to dinner.

In modern war the infantryman hasn't much of a chance. Strategy nowadays consists in arranging for the mutual slaughter of infantry by the opposing guns, each general trusting that his guns will do the greater slaughter. And half gunnery is luck. The day before yesterday we had a little afternoon shoot at where we thought the German trenches might be. The Germans unaccountably retreated, and yesterday when we advanced we found the trenches crammed full of dead. By a combination of intelligent anticipation and good luck we had hit them exactly.

From these letters you will be able to gather what mood we were in and something of what the brigade despatch rider was doing. After the first day the Germans ceased shrapnelling the fields round the farm and left us nearly in peace. There I met Major Ballard, commanding the 15th Artillery Brigade, one of the finest officers of my acquaintance, and Captain Frost, the sole remaining officer of the Cheshires. He was charming to me; I was particularly grateful for the loan of a razor, for my own had disappeared and there were no despatch riders handy from whom I could borrow.

Talking of the Cheshires reminds me of a story illustrating the troubles of a brigadier. The general was dining calmly one night after having arranged an attack. All orders had been sent out. Everything was complete and ready. Suddenly there was a knock at the door and in walked Captain M—, who reported his arrival with 200 reinforcements for the Cheshires, a pleasant but irritating addition. The situation was further complicated by the general's discovery that M— was senior to the officer then in command of the Cheshires. Poor M— was not left long in command. A fortnight later the Germans broke through and over the Cheshires, and M— died where a commanding officer should.[1]

From 1910 Farm I had one good ride to the battalions, through Festubert and along to the Cuinchy bridge. For me it was interesting because it was one of the few times I had ridden just behind our trenches, which at the moment were just north of the road and were occupied by the Bedfords.

In a day or two we returned to Festubert, and Cadell gave me a shake-down on a mattress in his billet – gloriously comfortable. The room was a little draughty because the fuse of a shrapnel had gone right through the door and the fireplace opposite. Except for a peppering on the walls and some broken glass the house was not damaged; we almost laughed at the father and mother and daughter who, returning while we were there, wept because their home had been touched.

Orders came to attack. A beautiful plan was drawn up by which the battalions of the brigade were to finish their victorious career in the square of La Bassée.

In connection with this attack I was sent with a message for the Devons. It was the blackest of black nights and I was riding without a light. Twice I ran into the ditch, and finally I piled up myself and my bicycle on a heap of stones lying by the side of the road. I did not damage my bicycle. That was enough. I left it and walked.

When I got to Cuinchy bridge I found that the Devon headquarters had shifted. Beyond that the sentry knew nothing. Luckily I met a Devon officer who was bringing up ammunition. We searched the surrounding cottages for men with knowledge, and at last discovered that the Devons had moved farther along the canal in the direction of La Bassée. So we set out along the tow-path, past a house that was burning fiercely enough to make us conspicuous.

---

1   Captain Frederick Henry Mahony (1874–1914) served with 3rd Battalion Cheshire Regiment in South Africa – he was killed on 22 October 1914.

We felt our way about a quarter of a mile and stopped, because we were getting near the Germans. Indeed we could hear the rumble of their transport crossing the La Bassée bridge. We turned back, and a few yards nearer home some one coughed high up the bank on our right. We found the cough to be a sentry, and behind the sentry were the Devons.

The attack, as you know, was held up on the line Cuinchy-Givenchy-Violaines; we advanced our headquarters to a house just opposite the inn by which the road to Givenchy turns off. It was not very safe, but the only shell that burst anywhere near the house itself did nothing but wound a little girl in the leg.

On the previous day I had ridden to Violaines at dawn to draw a plan of the Cheshires' trenches for the general. I strolled out by the sugar factory, and had a good look at the red houses of La Bassée. Half an hour later a patrol went out to explore the sugar factory. They did not return. It seems that the factory was full of machine-guns. I had not been fired upon, because the Germans did not wish to give their position away sooner than was necessary.

A day or two later I had the happiness of avenging my potential death. First I took orders to a battery of 6-inch howitzers at the Rue de Marais to knock the factory to pieces, then I carried an observing officer to some haystacks by Violaines, from which he could get a good view of the factory. Finally I watched with supreme satisfaction the demolition of the factory, and with regretful joy the slaughter of the few Germans who, escaping, scuttled for shelter in some trenches just behind and on either side of the factory.

I left the 15th Brigade with regret, and the regret I felt would have been deeper if I had known what was going to happen to the brigade. I was given interesting work and made comfortable. No despatch rider could wish for more.

At Beuvry the despatch riders were constantly on hand to keep themselves updated from the flow of signals. In the front row, left to right: Trepess, Hayes-Sadler, M. Mayer (French official), Polhill, and Bagshaw. Back row, left to right: Giblett (who joined 5th Signal company at Beuvry), Owen, Alick Burney, and Cecil Burney.

Not long after I had returned from the 15th Brigade, the Germans attacked and broke through. They had been heavily reinforced and our tentative offensive had been replaced by a stern and anxious defensive.

Now the Signal Office was established in the booking-office of Beuvry Station. The little narrow room was packed full of operators and vibrant with buzz and click. The Signal Clerk sat at a table in a tiny room just off the booking-office. Orderlies would rush in with messages, and the Clerk would instantly decide whether to send them over the wire, by push-cyclist, or by despatch rider. Again, he dealt with all messages that came in over the wire. Copies of these messages were filed. This was our tape; from them we learned the news. We were not supposed to read them, but, as we often found that they contained information which was invaluable to despatch riders, we always looked through them and each passed on what he had found to the others. The Signal Clerk might not know where a certain unit was at a given moment. We knew, because we had put together information that we had gathered in the course of our rides and information which – though the Clerk might think it unimportant – supplemented or completed or verified what we had already obtained.

So the history of this partially successful attack was known to us. Every few minutes one of us went into the Signal Office and read the messages. When the order came for us to pack up, we had already made our preparations, for Divisional Headquarters, the brain controlling the actions of seventeen thousand men, must never be left in a position of danger. And wounded were pouring into the Field Ambulances.

The enemy had made a violent attack, preluded by heavy shelling, on the left of the 15th, and what I think was a holding attack on the right. Violaines had been stormed, and the Cheshires had been driven, still grimly fighting, to beyond the Rue de Marais. The Norfolks on their right and the K.O.S.B.'s on their left had been compelled to draw back their line with heavy loss, for their flanks had been uncovered by the retreat of the Cheshires.

The Germans stopped a moment to consolidate their gains. This gave us time to throw a couple of battalions against them. After desperate fighting Rue de Marais was retaken and some sort of line established. What was left of the Cheshires gradually rallied in Festubert.

This German success, together with a later success against the 3rd Division, that resulted in our evacuation of Neuve Chapelle, compelled us to withdraw and readjust our line. This second line was not so defensible as the first. Until we were relieved the Germans battered at it with gunnery all day and attacks all night. How we managed to hold it is utterly beyond my understanding. The men were dog-tired. Few of the old officers were left, and they were "done to the world." Never did the Fighting Fifth more deserve the name. It fought dully and instinctively, like a boxer who, after receiving heavy punishment, just manages to keep himself from being knocked out until the call of time.

Yet, when they had dragged themselves wearily and blindly out of the trenches, the fighting men of the Fighting Fifth were given but a day's rest or two before the 15th and two battalions of the 13th were sent to Hooge, and the remainder to hold sectors of the line farther south. Can you wonder that we despatch riders, in comparative safety behind the line, did all we could to help the most glorious and amazing infantry that the world has ever seen?[1] And when you praise the deeds of Ypres of the First Corps, who had experienced no La Bassée, spare a word for the men of the Fighting Fifth who thought they could fight no more and yet fought.

A few days after I had returned from the 15th Brigade I was sent out to the 14th. I found them at the Estaminet de l'Epinette on the Béthune–Richebourg road. Headquarters had been

---

1   *After nine months at the Front – six and a half months as a despatch rider and two and a half months as a cyclist officer – I have decided that the English language has no superlative sufficient to describe our infantry.* (Watson)

Auberge de la Bombe at Richebourg was briefly occupied as Headquarters of the 14th Brigade, but destroyed by shell-fire an hour or so after this picture was taken – Cecil's Blackburne is visible parked outside.

compelled to shift, hastily enough, from the Estaminet de La Bombe on the La Bassée–Estaires road. The estaminet had been shelled to destruction half an hour after the Brigade had moved. The Estaminet de l'Epinette was filthy and small. I slept in a stinking barn, half-full of dirty straw, and rose with the sun for the discomfort of it.

Opposite the estaminet a road goes to Festubert. At the corner there is a cluster of dishevelled houses. I sat at the door and wrote letters, and looked for what might come to pass. In the early dawn the poplars alongside the highway were grey and dull. There was mist on the road; the leaves that lay thick were black. Then as the sun rose higher the poplars began to glisten and the mist rolled away, and the leaves were red and brown.

An old woman came up the road and prayed the sentry to let her pass. He could not understand her and called to me. She told me that her family were in the house at the corner fifty yards distant. I replied that she could not go to them – that they, if they were content not to return, might come to her. But the family would not leave their chickens, and cows, and corn. So the old woman, who was tired, sank down by the wayside and wept. This sorrow was no sorrow to the sorrow of the war. I left the old woman, the sentry, and the family, and went into a fine breakfast.

At this time there was much talk about spies. Our wires were often cut mysteriously. A sergeant had been set upon in a lane. The enemy were finding our guns with uncanny accuracy. All our movements seemed to be anticipated by the enemy. Taking for granted the extraordinary efficiency of the German Intelligence Corps, we were particularly nervous about spies when the Division was worn out, when things were not going well.

At the Estaminet de l'Epinette I heard a certain story, and hearing it set about to make a fool of myself. This is the story – I have never heard it substantiated, and give it as an illustration and not as fact.

There was once an artillery brigade billeted in a house two miles or so behind the lines. All the inhabitants of the house had fled, for the village had been heavily bombarded. Only a girl had had the courage to remain and do hostess to the English. She was so fresh and so charming, so clever in her cookery, and so modest in her demeanour that all the men of the brigade headquarters fell madly in love with her. They even quarrelled. Now this brigade was suffering much from espionage. The guns could not be moved without the Germans knowing their new position. No transport or ammunition limbers were safe from the enemy's guns. The brigade grew mightily indignant. The girl was told by her numerous sweethearts what was the matter. She was angry and sympathetic, and swore that through her the spy should be discovered. She swore the truth.

One night a certain lewd fellow of the baser sort pursued the girl with importunate pleadings. She confessed that she liked him, but not in that way. He left her and stood sullenly by the door. The girl took a pail and went down into the cellar to fetch up a little coal, telling the man with gentle mockery not to be so foolish. This angered him, and in a minute he had rushed after her into the cellar, snorting with disappointed passion. Of course he slipped on the stairs and fell with a crash. The girl screamed. The fellow, his knee bruised, tried to feel his way to the bottom of the stairs and touched a wire. Quickly running his hand along the wire he came to a telephone. The girl rushed to him, and, clasping his knees, offered him anything he might wish, if only he would say nothing. I think he must have hesitated for a moment, but he did not hesitate long. The girl was shot.

Full of this suspiciously melodramatic story I caught sight of a mysterious document fastened by nails to the house opposite the inn. It was covered with coloured signs which, whatever they were, certainly did not form letters or make sense in any way. I examined the document closely. One sign looked like an aeroplane, another like a house, a third like the rough drawing of a wood. I took it to a certain officer, who agreed with me that it appeared suspicious.

We carried it to the staff-captain, who pointed out very forcibly that it had been raining lately, that colour ran, that the signs left formed portions of letters. I demanded the owner of the house upon which the document had been posted. She was frightened and almost unintelligible, but supplied the missing fragments. The document was a crude election appeal. Being interpreted it read something like this: –

SUPPORT LEFEVRE. HE IS NOT A LIAR LIKE DUBOIS.

Talking of spies, here is another story. It is true.

Certain wires were always being cut. At length a patrol was organised. While the operator was talking there was a little click and no further acknowledgment from the other end. The patrol started out and caught the man in the act of cutting a second wire. He said nothing.

He was brought before the Mayor. Evidence was briefly given of his guilt. He made no protest. It was stated that he had been born in the village. The Mayor turned to the man and said – "You are a traitor. It is clear. Have you anything to say?"

The man stood white and straight. Then he bowed his head and made answer – "Priez pour moi."

That was no defence. So they led him away.

The morning after I arrived at the 14th the Germans concentrated their fire on a large turnip-field and exhumed multitudinous turnips. No further damage was done, but the field was unhealthily near the Estaminet de l'Epinette. In the afternoon we moved our headquarters back a mile or so to a commodious and moderately clean farm with a forgettable name.

That evening two prisoners were brought in. They owned to eighteen, but did not look more than sixteen. The guard treated them with kindly contempt. We all sat round a makeshift table in the loft where we slept and told each other stories of fighting and love and fear, while the boys, squatting a little distance away, listened and looked at us in wonder. I came in from a ride about one in the morning and found those of the guard who were off duty and the two German boys sleeping side by side. Literally it was criminal negligence – some one ought to have been awake

– but, when I saw one of the boys was clasping tightly a packet of woodbines, I called it something else and went to sleep.

A day or two later I was relieved. On the following afternoon I was sent to Estaires to bring back some details about the Lahore Division which had just arrived on the line. I had, of course, seen Spahis and Turcos and Senegalese, but when riding through Lestrem I saw these Indian troops of ours the obvious thoughts tumbled over one another.

We despatch riders when first we met the Indians wondered how they would fight, how they would stand shell-fire and the climate – but chiefly we were filled with a sort of mental helplessness, riding among people when we could not even vaguely guess at what they were thinking. We could get no deeper than their appearance, dignified and clean and well-behaved.

In a few days I was back again at the 14th with Huggie. At dusk the General went out in his car to a certain village about three miles distant. Huggie went with him. An hour or so, and I was sent after him with a despatch. The road was almost unrideable with the worst sort of grease, the night was pitch-black and I was allowed no light. I slithered along at about six miles an hour, sticking out my legs for a permanent scaffolding. Many troops were lying down at the side of the road. An officer in a strained voice just warned me in time for me to avoid a deep shell-hole by inches. I delivered my despatch to the General. Outside the house I found two or three officers I knew. Two of them were young captains in command of battalions. Then I learned how hard put to it the Division was, and what the result is of nervous strain.

They had been fighting and fighting and fighting until their nerves were nothing but a jangling torture. And a counter-attack on Neuve Chapelle was being organised. Huggie told me afterwards that when the car had come along the road, all the men had jumped like startled animals and a few had turned to take cover. Why, if a child had met one of these men she would have taken him by the hand instinctively and told him not to be frightened, and defended him against anything that came. Yet it is said there are still those at home who will not stir to help. I do not see how this can possibly be true. It could not be true.

First we talked about the counter-attack, and which battalion would lead; then with a little manipulation we began to discuss musical comedy and the beauty of certain ladies. Again the talk would wander back to which battalion would lead.

I returned perilously with a despatch and left Huggie, to spend a disturbed night and experience those curious sensations which are caused by a shell bursting just across the road from the house.

The proposed attack was given up. If it had been carried out, those men would have fought as finely as they could. I do not know whether my admiration for the infantry or my hatred of war is the greater. I can express neither.[1]

On the following day the Brigadier moved to a farm farther north. It was the job of Huggie and myself to keep up communication between this farm and the brigade headquarters at the farm with the forgettable name. To ride four miles or so along country lanes from one farm to another does not sound particularly strenuous. It was. In the first place, the neighbourhood of the advanced farm was not healthy. The front gate was marked down by a sniper who fired not infrequently but a little high. Between the back gate and the main road was impassable mud. Again, the farm was only three-quarters of a mile behind our trenches, and "overs" went zipping through the farm buildings at all sorts of unexpected angles. There were German aeroplanes about, so we covered our stationary motor-cycles with straw.

Starting from brigade headquarters the despatch rider in half a mile was forced to pass the transport of a Field Ambulance. The men seemed to take a perverted delight in wandering aimlessly and deafly across the road, and in leaving anything on the road which could conceivably obstruct

---

1   The last two sentences of this paragraph were deleted by the censor.

or annoy a motor-cyclist. Then came two and a half miles of winding country lanes. They were covered with grease. Every corner was blind. A particularly sharp turn to the right and the despatch rider rode a couple of hundred yards in front of a battery in action that the Germans were trying to find. A "hairpin" corner round a house followed. This he would take with remarkable skill and alacrity, because at this corner he was always sniped. The German's rifle was trained a trifle high. Coming into the final straight the despatch rider or one despatch rider rode for all he was worth. It was unpleasant to find new shell-holes just off the road each time you passed, or, as you came into the straight, to hear the shriek of shrapnel between you and the farm.

Huggie once arrived at the house of the "hairpin" bend simultaneously with a shell. The shell hit the house, the house did not hit Huggie, and the sniper forgot to snipe. So every one was pleased.

On my last journey I passed a bunch of wounded Sikhs. They were clinging to all their kit. One man was wounded in both his feet. He was being carried by two of his fellows. In his hands he clutched his boots.

The men did not know where to go or what to do. I could not make them understand, but I tried by gestures to show them where the ambulance was.

I saw two others – they were slightly wounded – talking fiercely together. At last they grasped their rifles firmly, and swinging round, limped back towards the line.

Huggie did most of the work that day, because during the greater part of the afternoon I was kept back at brigade head-quarters.

In the evening I went out in the car to fetch the general. The car, which was old but stout, had been left behind by the Germans. The driver of it was a reservist who had been taken from his battalion. Day and night he tended and coaxed that car. He tied it together when it fell to pieces. At all times and in all places he drove that car, for he had no wish at all to return to the trenches.

On the following day Huggie and I were relieved. When we returned to our good old musty quarters at Beuvry men talked of a move. There were rumours of hard fighting in Ypres. Soon the Lahore Division came down towards our line and began to take over from us. The 14th Brigade was left to strengthen them. The 15th and 13th began to move north.

Early on the morning of October 29 we started, riding first along the canal by Béthune. As for Festubert, Givenchy, Violaines, Rue de Marais, Quinque Rue, and La Bassée, we never want to see them again.

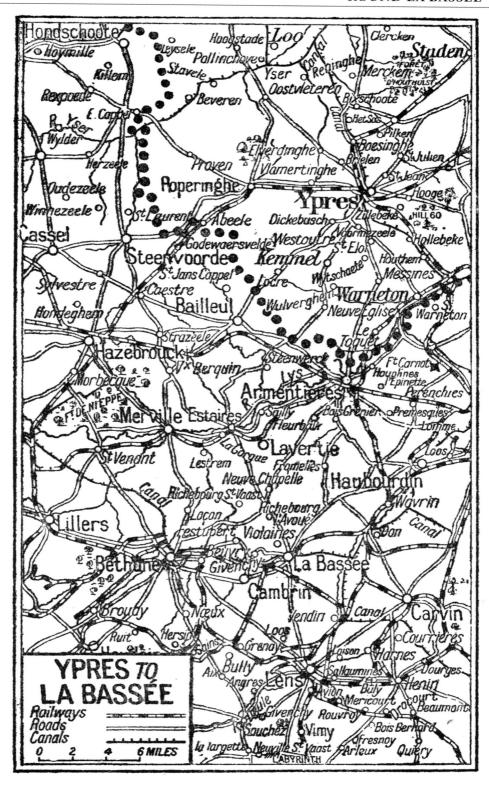

YPRES TO
LA BASSÉE

Railways
Roads
Canals

0   2   4   6 MILES

10

The Beginning of Winter

Before we came, Givenchy had been a little forgettable village upon a hill, Violaines a pleasant afternoon's walk for the working men in La Bassée, Festubert a gathering-place for the people who lived in the filthy farms around. We left Givenchy a jumble of shuttered houses and barricaded cellars. A few Germans were encamped upon the site of Violaines. The great clock of Festubert rusted quickly against a tavern wall. We hated La Bassée, because against La Bassée the Division had been broken. There are some square miles of earth that, like criminals, should not live.

Our orders were to reach Caestre not later than the Signal Company. Caestre is on the Cassel-Bailleul road, three miles north-east of Hazebrouck. These unattached rides across country are the most joyous things in the world for a despatch rider. There is never any need to hurry. You can take any road you will. You may choose your tavern for lunch with expert care. And when new ground is covered and new troops are seen, we capture sometimes those sharp delightful moments of thirsting interest that made the Retreat into an epic and the Advance a triumphant ballad.

N'Soon and myself left together. We skidded along the tow-path, passed the ever-cheerful cyclists, and, turning due north, ran into St Venant. The grease made us despatch riders look as if we were beginning to learn. I rode gently but surely down the side of the road into the gutter time after time. Pulling ourselves together, we managed to slide past some Indian transport without being kicked by the mules, who, whenever they smelt petrol, developed a strong offensive. Then we came upon a big gun, discreetly covered by tarpaulins. It was drawn by a monster traction-engine, and sad-faced men walked beside it. The steering of the traction-engine was a trifle loose, so N'Soon and I drew off into a field to let this solemn procession pass. One of the commands in the unpublished "Book of the Despatch Rider" is this:

> When you halt by the roadside to let guns pass or when you leave your motor-cycle unat-tended, first place it in a position of certain safety where it cannot possibly be knocked over, and then move it another fifty yards from the road. It is impossible for a gunner to see some-thing by the roadside and not drive over it. Moreover, lorries when they skid, skid furiously.

Four miles short of Hazebrouck we caught up the rest. Proceeding in single file along the road, we endeavoured not to laugh, for – as one despatch rider said – it makes all the difference on grease which side of your mouth you put your pipe in. We reached Hazebrouck at midday. Spreading out – the manoeuvre had become a fine art – we searched the town. The "Chapeau Rouge" was well reported on, and there we lunched.

All those tourists who will deluge Flanders after the war should go to the "Chapeau Rouge" in Hazebrouck. There we had lentil soup and stewed kidneys, and roast veal with potatoes and leeks, fruit, cheese, and good red wine. So little was the charge that one of us offered to pay it all. There are other more fashionable hotels in Hazebrouck, but, trust the word of a despatch rider, the "Chapeau Rouge" beats them all.

Very content we rode on to Caestre, arriving there ten minutes before the advance-party of the Signal Company. Divisional Headquarters were established at the House of the Spy. The owner of the house had been well treated by the Germans when they had passed through a month before. Upon his door had been written this damning legend:

HIER SIND GUETIGE LEUTE[1]

and, when on the departure of the Germans the house had been searched by an indignant populace, German newspapers had been discovered in his bedroom.

It is the custom of the Germans to spare certain houses in every village by chalking up some laudatory notice. We despatch riders had a theory that the inhabitants of these marked houses, far from being spies, were those against whom the Germans had some particular grievance. Imagine the wretched family doing everything in its power to avoid the effusive affection of the Teuton, breaking all its own crockery, and stealing all its own silver, defiling its beds and tearing its clothing. For the man whose goods have been spared by the German becomes an outcast. He lives in a state worse than death. He is hounded from his property, and driven across France with a character attached to him, like a kettle to a cat's tail. Genuine spies, on the other hand – so we thought – were worse treated than any and secretly recompensed. Such a man became a hero. All his neighbours brought their little offerings.

The House of the Spy had a fine garden, hot and buzzing in the languorous heat. We bathed ourselves in it. And the sanitary arrangements were good.

Grimers arrived lunchless an hour later. He had been promoted to drive the captured car. We took him to the tavern where beauty was allied with fine cooking. There he ate many omelettes.

In the evening he and I suffered a great disappointment. We wandered into another tavern and were about to ask for our usual "Grenadine" when we saw behind the bar two bottles of Worthington. For a moment we were too stupefied to speak. Then, pulling ourselves together, we stammered out an order for beer, but the girl only smiled. They were empty bottles, souvenirs left by some rascally A.S.C. for the eternal temptation of all who might pass through. The girl in her sympathy comforted us with songs, one of which, "Les Serments," I translated for the benefit of Grimers, who knew no French. We sang cheerfully in French and English until it was time to return to our billet.

In the morning a German aeroplane passed over at a great height. All the youngsters in the village tumbled over each other for shelter, shouting – Caput! caput![2]

Alick Burney took charge of the Barré car which was captured at Missy.

1   *Here are kindly people.* (Watson)
2   *French, Flemish, and German slang expression. Done for!* (Watson)

Watson (left) and Alick Burney are pictured in the Barré with their backs to the camera. On the right Bagshaw is now equipped with an Ariel 3 ½ HP motorcycle. Behind them is a row of London buses used to transport troops during the First Battle of Ypres.

Later in the day we advanced to Bailleul, where we learnt that the 1st Corps was fighting furiously to the north. The square was full of motor-buses and staff-officers. They were the first of our own motor-buses we had seen out in Flanders. They cheered us greatly, and after some drinks we sat in one and tried to learn from the map something of the new country in which we were to ride. We rejoiced that we had come once again upon a Belgian sheet, because the old French map we had used, however admirable it might have been for brigadiers and suchlike people, was extremely unsuited to a despatch rider's work.

Infantry were pouring through, the stern remnants of fine battalions. Ever since the night after Le Cateau infantry in column of route have fascinated us, for a regiment on the march bares its character to the world.

First there were our brigades marching up to Mons, stalwart and cheering. After Le Cateau there were practically no battalions, just a crowd of men and transport pouring along the road to Paris. I watched the column pass for an hour, and in it there was no organised unit larger than a platoon, and only one platoon. How it happened I do not know, but, when we turned on the Germans, battalions, brigades, divisions, corps had been remade. The battalions were pitifully small. Many a time we who were watching said to one another: Surely that's not the end of the K.O.Y.L.I., or the Bedfords, or whatever regiment it might be!

A battalion going into action has some men singing, some smiling vaguely to themselves, some looking raptly straight ahead, and some talking quickly as if they must never stop.

A battalion that has come many miles is nearly silent. The strong men stride tirelessly without a word. Little weak men, marching on their nerves, hobble restlessly along. The men with bad feet limp and curse, wilting under the burden of their kit, and behind all come those who have fallen out by the way – men dragging themselves along behind a waggon, white-faced men with uneasy smiles on top of the waggons. A little farther back those who are trying to catch up: these are tragic figures, breaking into breathless little runs, but with a fine wavering attempt at striding out, as though they might be connecting files, when they march through a town or past an officer of high rank.

A battalion that has just come out of action I cannot describe to you in these letters, but let me tell you now about Princess Pat's.[1] I ran into them just as they were coming into Bailleul for the first time and were hearing the sound of the guns. They were the finest lot of men I have ever seen on the march. Gusts of great laughter were running through them. In the eyes of one or two were tears. And I told those civilians I passed that the Canadians, the fiercest of all soldiers, were come. Bailleul looked on them with more fright than admiration. The women whispered fearfully to each other – Les Canadiens, les Canadiens! …

We despatch riders were given a large room in the house where the Divisional Staff was billeted. It had tables, chairs, a fireplace and gas that actually lit; so we were more comfortable than ever we had been before – that is, all except N'Soon, who had by this time discovered that continual riding on bad roads is apt to produce a fundamental soreness. N'Soon hung on nobly, but was at last sent away with blood-poisoning. Never getting home, he spent many weary months in peculiar convalescent camps, and did not join up again until the end of January. Moral – before going sick or getting wounded become an officer and a gentleman.

The day after we arrived I was once more back in Belgium with a message to the C.R.A.[2] at Neuve Eglise. I had last been in Belgium on August 23, the day we left Dour.

The general might have been posing for a war artist. He was seated at a table in the middle of a field, his staff-captain with him. The ground sloped away to a wooded valley in which two or three batteries, carefully concealed, were blazing away. To the north shrapnel was bursting over Kemmel. In front the Messines ridge was almost hidden with the smoke of our shells. I felt that each point of interest ought to have been labelled in Mr Frederic Villiers' handwriting[3] – *"German shrapnel bursting over Kemmel – our guns – this is a dead horse."*

I first saw Ypres on the 6th November. I was sent off with a bundle of routine matter to the 1st Corps, then at Brielen, a couple of miles N.W. of Ypres. It was a nightmare ride. The road was *pavé* in the centre – villainous *pavé*. At the side of it were glutinous morasses about six feet in width, and sixteen inches deep. I started off with two 2nd Corps motor-cyclists. There was an almost continuous line of transport on the road – motor-lorries that did not dare deviate an inch from the centre of the road for fear of slipping into the mire, motor ambulances, every kind of transport, and some infantry battalions. After following a column of motor-lorries a couple of miles – we stuck twice in trying to get past the rearmost lorry – we tried the road by Dranoutre and Locre. But these country lanes were worse of surface that the main road – greasy *pavé* is better than greasy rocks – and they were filled with odd detachments of French artillery. The two 2nd Corps motor-cyclists turned back. I crawled on at the risk of smashing my motor-cycle and myself, now skidding perilously between waggons, now clogging up, now taking to the fields, now driving frightened pedestrians off what the Belgians alone would call a footpath. I skidded into a subaltern, and each of us turned to curse, when – it was Gibson, a junior "Greats" don at Balliol, and the finest of fellows.[4]

---

1   1st Battalion Princess Patricia's Canadian Light Infantry, raised in August 1914, was the first Canadian regular regiment. It landed in France in December 1914, and went into the front line for the first time in January 1915.

2   *An abbreviation for the general in command of the Divisional Artillery.* (Watson)

3   Frederick Villiers (1852–1922) was an early war artist and war correspondent.

4   Robert Gibson (see Cast, see page 131).

Beyond Dickebusch French artillery were in action on the road. The houses just outside Ypres had been pelted with shrapnel but not destroyed. Just by the station, which had not then been badly knocked about, I learnt where to go. Ypres was the first half-evacuated town I had entered. It was like motor-cycling into a village from Oxford very early on a Sunday morning.

Half an hour later I saw the towers of the city rising above a bank of mist which had begun to settle on the ground: then out rose great clouds of black smoke.

I came back by Poperinghe to avoid the grease and crowding of the direct road, and there being no hurry I stopped at an inn for a beefsteak. The landlord's daughter talked of the many difficulties before us, and doubted of our success. I said, grandiloquently enough, that no victory was worth winning unless there were difficulties. At which she smiled and remarked, laughing – "There are no roses without thorns."

She asked me how long the war would last. I replied that the good God alone knew. She shook her head – "How can the good God look down without a tear on the miseries of his people? Are not the flower of the young cut off in the spring of their youth?"

Then she pointed to the church across the way, and said humbly – "On a beaucoup prié."

She was of the true Flemish type, broad and big-breasted, but with a slight stoop, thick hips, dark and fresh-coloured, with large black eyes set too closely. Like all the Flemings, she spoke French slowly and distinctly, with an accent like the German. She was easy to understand.

I stopped too long at Poperinghe, for it was dark and very misty on the road. Beyond Boescheppe – I was out of my way – the mist became a fog. Once I had to take to the ditch when some cuirassiers galloped out of the fog straight at me. It was all four French soldiers could do to get my motorcycle out. Another time I stuck endeavouring to avoid some lorries. It is a diabolical joke of the Comic Imps to put fog upon a greasy road for the confusion of a despatch rider.

On the next day I was sent out to the 14th Brigade at the Rue de Paradis near Laventie. You will remember that the 14th Brigade had been left to strengthen the Indian Corps when the 2nd Corps had moved north. I arrived at Rue de Paradis just as the Brigade Headquarters were coming into the village. So, while everybody else was fixing wires and generally making themselves useful, I rushed upstairs and seized a mattress and put it into a dark little dressing-room with hot and cold water, a mirror and a wardrobe. Then I locked the door. There I slept, washed, and dressed in delicious luxury.

The brigade gave another despatch rider and myself, who were attached, very little to do beyond an occasional forty-mile run to D.H.Q. and back over dull roads. The signal office was established in a large room on the side of the house nearest to the Germans. It was constructed almost entirely of glass. Upon this the men commented with a grave fluency. The windows rattled with shrapnel bursting 600 yards away. The house was jarred through and through by the concussion of a heavy battery firing over our heads. The room was like a toy-shop with a lot of small children sounding all the musical toys. The vibrators and the buzzers were like hoarse toy trumpets.

Our only excitement was the nightly rumour that the General was going to move nearer the trenches, that one of us would accompany him – I knew what that meant on greasy misty roads.

After I had left, the Germans by chance or design made better practice. A shell burst in the garden and shattered all the windows of the room. The Staff took refuge in dug-outs that had been made in case of need. Tommy, then attached, took refuge in the cellar. According to his own account, when he woke up in the morning he was floating. The house had some corners taken off it and all the glass was shattered, but no one was hurt.

When I returned to Bailleul, Divisional Headquarters were about to move.

A puncture kept me at Bailleul after the others had gone on to Locre. Grimers stood by to help. We lunched well, and buying some supplies started off along the Ypres road. By this time our kit had accumulated. It is difficult enough to pass lorries on a greasy road at any time. With an immense weight on the carrier it is almost impossible. So we determined to go by Dranoutre.

NOVEMBER 24th 1914.

DESPATCH RIDERS 5th DIV. AT LOCRE.

Captain Doherty Holwell suggested the DRs get acquainted with "unmechanical horses"
when snow stopped them motorcycling.

An unfortunate bump dispersed my blankets and my ground-sheet in the mud. Grimers said my language might have dried them. Finally, that other despatch rider arrived swathed about with some filthy, grey, forlorn indescribables.

We were quartered in a large schoolroom belonging to the Convent. We had plenty of space and a table to feed at. Fresh milk and butter we could buy from the nuns, while a market-gardener just across the road supplied us with a sack of miscellaneous vegetables – potatoes, carrots, turnips, onions, leeks – for practically nothing. We lived gloriously. There was just enough work to make us feel we really were doing something, and not enough to make us wish we were on the Staff. Bridge we played every hour of the day, and "Pollers," our sergeant, would occasionally try a little flutter in Dominoes and Patience.

At Bailleul the Skipper had suggested our learning to manage the unmechanical horse. The suggestion became an order. We were bumped round unmercifully at first, until many of us were so sore that the touch of a motor-cycle saddle on *pavé* was like hot-iron to a tender skin. Then we were handed over to a friendly sergeant, who believed in more gentlemanly methods, and at Locre we had great rides – though Pollers, who was gently unhorsed, is still firmly convinced that wind-mills form the finest deterrent to cavalry.

In an unlucky moment two of us had suggested that we should like to learn signaller's work, so we fell upon evil days. First we went out for cable-drill. Sounds simple? But it is more arduous and dangerous than any despatch riding. If you "pay out" too quickly, you get tangled up in the wire and go with it nicely over the drum. If you pay out too slowly, you strangle the man on the horse behind you. The worst torture in the world is paying out at the fast trot over cobbles. First you can't hold on, and if you can you can't pay out regularly. Cable-drill is simply nothing compared to the real laying of cable. We did it twice – once in rain and once in snow. The rainy day I paid out, I was never more miserable in my life than I was after two miles. Only hot coffee and singing good songs past cheery Piou-pious[1] brought me home. The snowy day I ran with ladders, and, perched on the topmost rung, endeavoured to pass the wire round a buxom tree-trunk. Then, when it was round, it would always go slack before I could get it tied up tightly.

It sounds so easy, laying a wire. But I swear it is the most wearying business in the world – punching holes in the ground with a 16-lb. hammer, running up poles that won't go straight, unhooking wire that has caught in a branch or in the eaves of a house, taking the strain of a cable to prevent man and ladder and wire coming on top of you, when the man who pays out has forgotten to pay. Have a thought for the wretched fellows who are getting out a wire on a dark and snowy night, troubled perhaps by persistent snipers and frequent shells! Shed a tear for the miserable linesman sent out to find where the line is broken or defective. …

When there was no chance of "a run" we would go walks towards Kemmel. At the time the Germans were shelling the hill, but occasionally they would break off, and then we would unofficially go up and see what had happened.

Now Mont Kemmel is nearly covered with trees. I have never been in a wood under shell fire, and I do not wish to be. Where the Germans had heavily shelled Kemmel there were great holes, trees thrown about and riven and scarred and crushed – a terrific immensity of blasphemous effort. It was as if some great beast, wounded mortally, had plunged into a forest, lashing and biting and tearing in his agony until he died.

On one side of the hill was a little crazy cottage which had marvellously escaped. Three shells had fallen within ten yards of it. Two had not burst, and the other, shrapnel, had exploded in the earth. The owner came out, a trifling, wizened old man in the usual Belgian cap and blue overalls. We had a talk, using the *lingua franca* of French, English with a Scottish accent, German, and the few words of Dutch I could remember.

We dug up for him a large bit of the casing of the shrapnel. He examined it fearfully. It was an 11-inch shell, I think, nearly as big as his wee grotesque self. Then he made a noise, which we took to be a laugh, and told us that he had been very frightened in his little house (häusling), and his cat, an immense white Tom, had been more frightened still. But he knew the Germans could not hit him. Thousands and thousands of Germans had gone by, and a little after the last German came the English. "Les Anglais sont bons."

This he said with an air of finality. It is a full-blooded judgment which, though it sounds a trifle exiguous to describe our manifold heroic efforts, is a sort of perpetual epithet. The children use it confidingly when they run to our men in the cafes. The peasants use it as a parenthetical verdict whenever they mention our name. The French fellows use it, and I have heard a German prisoner say the same. A few days later those who lived on Kemmel were "evacuated." They were rounded up into the Convent yard, men and women and children, with their hens and pigs. At first they were angry and sorrowful; but nobody, not even the most indignant refugee, could resist our military policemen, and in three-quarters of an hour they all trudged off, cheerfully enough, along the road to Bailleul.

The wee grotesque man and his immense white cat were not with them. Perhaps they still live on Kemmel. Some time I shall go and see. …

If we did not play Bridge after our walks, we would look in at the theatre or stroll across to dinner and Bridge with Gibson and his brother officers of the K.O.S.B., then billeted at Locre.

Not all convents have theatres: this was a special convent. The Signal Company slept in the theatre, and of an evening all the kit would be moved aside. One of the military policemen could

---

1   Young French soldiers (slang).

play anything; so we danced and sang until the lights went out. The star performer was "Spot," the servant of an A.D.C.

"Spot" was a little man with a cheerful squint. He knew everything that had ever been recited, and his knowledge of the more ungodly songs was immense. He would start off with an imitation of Mr H. B. Irving, and a very good imitation it would be – with soft music. He would leave the Signallers thrilled and silent. The lights flashed up, and "Spot" darted off on some catchy doggerel of an almost talented obscenity. In private life Spot was the best company imaginable. He could not talk for a minute without throwing in a bit of a recitation and striking an attitude. I have only known him serious on two subjects – his master and Posh. He would pour out with the keenest delight little stories of how his master endeavoured to correct his servant's accent. There was a famous story of "a n'orse" – but that is untellable.

Posh may be defined, very roughly, as a useless striving after gentlemanly culture. Sometimes a chauffeur or an H.Q. clerk would endeavour to speak very correct English in front of Spot.

"'E was poshy, my dear boy, positively poshy. 'E made me shiver until I cried. 'Smith, old man,' I said to 'im, 'you can't do it. You're not born to it nor bred to it. Those that try is just demeaning themselves. Posh, my dear boy, pure posh.'"

And Spot would give a cruel imitation of the wretched Smith's mincing English. The punishment was the more bitter, because all the world knew that Spot could speak the King's English as well as anybody if only he chose. To the poshy alone was Spot unkind. He was a generous, warm-hearted little man, with real wisdom and a fine appreciation of men and things. … There were other performers of the usual type, young men who sang about the love-light in her eyes, older men with crude songs, and a Scotsman with an expressionless face, who mumbled about we could never discover what.

The audience was usually strengthened by some half-witted girls that the Convent educated, and two angelic nuns. Luckily for them, they only understood a slow and grammatical English, and listened to crude songs and sentimental songs with the same expression of maternal content.

Our work at Locre was not confined to riding and cable-laying. The 15th Brigade and two battalions of the 13th were fighting crazily at Ypres, the 14th had come up to Dranoutre, and the remaining two battalions of the 13th were at Neuve Eglise.

I had two more runs to the Ypres district before we left Locre. On the first the road was tolerable to Ypres, though near the city I was nearly blown off my bicycle by the fire of a concealed battery of 75's. The houses at the point where the Rue de Lille enters the Square had been blown to bits. The Cloth Hall had barely been touched. In its glorious dignity it was beautiful.

Beyond Ypres, on the Hooge Road, I first experienced the extreme neighbourhood of a "J.J."[1] It fell about 90 yards in front of me and 20 yards off the road. It makes a curiously low droning sound as it falls, like the groan of a vastly sorrowful soul in hell, – so I wrote at the time: then there's a gigantic rushing plunk and overwhelming crash as if all the houses in the world were falling.

On the way back the road, which had been fairly greasy, became practically impassable. I struggled on until my lamp failed (sheer carelessness – I ought to have seen to it before starting), and a gale arose which blew me all over the road. So I left my motor-bicycle safely behind a cottage, and started tramping back to H.Q. by the light of my pocket flash-lamp. It was a pitch-black night. I was furiously hungry, and stopped at the first inn and gorged coffee with rum, and a large sandwich of bread and butter and fat bacon. I had barely started again – it had begun to pour – when a car came along with a French staff-officer inside. I stopped it, saying in hurried and

---

1   A 'Jack Johnson' was a heavy German artillery shell – named after the world heavyweight boxing champion from 1908 to 1915.

weighty tones that I was carrying an important despatch (I had nothing on me, I am afraid, but a trifling bunch of receipts), and the rest of the way I travelled lapped luxuriously in soft furs.

The second time I rode along a frozen road between white fields. All the shells sounded alarmingly near. The noise in Ypres was terrific. At my destination I came across some prisoners of the Prussian Guard, fierce and enormous men, nearly all with reddish hair, very sullen and rude.

From accounts that have been published of the first battle of Ypres, it might be inferred that the British Army knew it was on the point of being annihilated. A despatch rider, though of course he does not know very much of the real meaning of the military situation, has unequalled opportunities for finding out the opinions and spirit of the men. Now one of us went to Ypres every day and stopped for a few minutes to discuss the state of affairs with other despatch riders and with signal-sergeants. Right through the battle we were confident; in fact the idea that the line might be broken never entered our heads. We were suffering very heavily. That we knew. Nothing like the shell fire had ever been heard before. Nobody realised how serious the situation must have been until the accounts were published.

Huggie has a perfect mania for getting frightened; so one day, instead of leaving the routine matter that he carried at a place whence it might be forwarded at leisure, he rode along the Menin road to the Chateau at Hooge, the headquarters of the 15th Brigade. He came back quietly happy, telling us that he had had a good time, though the noise had been a little overwhelming. We learned afterwards that the enemy had been registering very accurately upon the Hooge road.

So the time passed without any excitement until November 23, when first we caught hold of a definite rumour that we should be granted leave. We existed in restless excitement until the 27th. On that great day we were told that we should be allowed a week's leave. We solemnly drew lots, and I drew the second batch.

We left the Convent at Locre in a dream, and took up quarters at St Jans Cappel, two miles west of Bailleul. We hardly noticed that our billet was confined and uncomfortable. Certainly we never realised that we should stop there until the spring. The first batch went off hilariously, and with slow pace our day drew nearer and nearer.

You may think it a little needless of me to write about my leave, if you do not remember that we despatch riders of the Fifth Division enlisted on or about August 6. Few then realised that England had gone to war. Nobody realised what sort of a war the war was going to be. When we returned in the beginning of December we were Martians. For three months we had been vividly soldiers. We had been fighting not in a savage country, but in a civilised country burnt by war; and it was because of this that the sights of war had struck us so fiercely that when we came back our voyage in the good ship *Archimedes* seemed so many years distant. Besides, if I were not to tell you of my leave it would make such a gap in my memories that I should scarcely know how to continue my tale. …

The week dragged more slowly than I can describe. Short-handed, we had plenty of work to do, but it was all routine work, which gave us too much time to think. There was also a crazy doubt of the others' return. They were due back a few hours before we started. If they fell ill or missed the boat …! And the fools were motor-cycling to and from Boulogne!

On the great night we prepared some food for them, and having packed our kits, tried to sleep. As the hour drew near we listened excitedly for the noise of their engines. Several false alarms disturbed us: first, a despatch rider from the Third Division, and then another from the Corps. At last we heard the purr of three engines together, and then a moment later the faint rustle of others in the distance. We recognised the engines and jumped up. All the birds came home save one. George had never quite recovered from his riding exercises. Slight blood poisoning had set in. His leave had been extended at home. So poor "Tommy,"[1] who had joined us at Beuvry, was compelled to remain behind.

Violent question and answer for an hour, then we piled ourselves on our light lorry. Singing like angels we rattled into Bailleul. Just opposite Corps Headquarters, our old billet, we found a little crowd waiting. None of us could talk much for the excitement. We just wandered about greeting friends. I met again that stoutest of warriors, Mr Potter of the 15th Artillery Brigade, a friend of Festubert days. Then a battalion of French infantry passed through, gallant and cheerful men. At last the old dark-green buses rolled up, and about three in the morning we pounded off at a good fifteen miles an hour along the Cassel road.

Two of us sat on top, for it was a gorgeous night. We rattled over the *pavé* alongside multitudinous transport sleeping at the side of the road – through Metern, through Caestre of pleasant memories, and south to Hazebrouck. Our driver was a man of mark, a racing motorist in times of peace. He left the other buses and swung along rapidly by himself. He slowed down for nothing. Just before Hazebrouck we caught up a French convoy. I do not quite know what happened. The Frenchmen took cover in one ditch. We swayed past, half in the other, at a good round pace. Waggons seemed to disappear under our wheels, and frightened horses plunged violently across the road. But we passed them without a scratch – to be stopped by the level-crossing at Hazebrouck. There we filled up with coffee and cognac, while the driver told us of his adventures in Antwerp.

We rumbled out of Hazebrouck towards St Omer. It was a clear dawn in splashes of pure colour. All the villages were peaceful, untouched by war. When we came to St Omer it was quite light. All the soldiers in the town looked amateurish. We could not make out what was the matter with them, until somebody noticed that their buttons shone. We drew up in the square, the happiest crew imaginable, but with a dignity such as befitted chosen N.C.O.'s and officers.

That was the first time I saw St Omer. When last I came to it I saw little, because I arrived in a motor-ambulance and left in a hospital-train.

The top of the bus was crowded, and we talked "shop" together. *Sixth Division's having a pretty cushy time, what? – So you were at Mons!* (in a tone of respect) *– I don't mind their shells, and I don't mind their machine-guns, but their Minenwerfer [2] are the frozen limit! – I suppose there's no chance of our missing the boat. Yes, it was a pretty fair scrap – Smith? He's gone. Silly fool, wanted to have a look round – Full of buck? Rather! Yes, heard there's a pretty good show on at the Frivolity – Beastly cold on top of this old wheezer.*

It was, but none of us cared a scrap. We looked at the sign-posts that showed the distance to Boulogne, and then pretended that we had not seen them. Lurching and skidding and toiling we came to the top of the hill above Boulogne. With screaming brakes we rattled down to the harbour. That old sinner, Sergeant Maguire, who was in charge of us corporals, made all arrangements efficiently. We embarked, and after a year of Sundays cast off.

There was a certain swell on, and Mr Potter, the bravest of men, grew greener and greener. My faith in mankind went.

We saw a dark line on the horizon.

"By Jove, there's England!" We all produced our field-glasses and looked through them very carefully for quite a long time.

"So it is. Funny old country" – a pause – "Makes one feel quite sentimental, just like the books. That's what we're fighting for, I suppose. Wouldn't fight for dirty old Dover! Wonder if they still

---

1   Charles Turner Tomlinson (1887-1965) from Rochdale joined 5th Signal company in October 1914.
2   Short range mortars.

charge you a penny for each sardine. I suppose we'll have to draw the blinds all the way up to London. Not a safe country by any means, far rather stop in the jolly old trenches."

"You'll get the white feather, old man."

"No pretty young thing would give it you. Why, you wouldn't look medically fit in mufti!"[1]

"Fancy seeing a woman who isn't dirty and can talk one's own lingo!"

So we came to Folkestone, and all the people on the pier smiled at us. We scuttled ashore and shook ourselves for delight. There was a policeman, a postman. Who are these fussy fellows with badges on their arms? Special constables, of course!

Spurning cigarettes and bovril we rushed to the bar. We all noticed the cleanness of the barmaid, her beauty, the neatness of her dress, her cultivated talk. We almost squabbled about what drinks we should have first. Finally, we divided into parties – the Beers and the Whisky-and-Sodas. Then there were English papers to buy, and, of course, we must have a luncheon-basket. …

The smell of the musty S.–E. & C.R.[2] compartment was the scent of eastern roses. We sniffed with joy in the tunnels. We read all the notices with care. Nearing London we became silent. Quite disregarding the order to lower the blinds, we gazed from the bridge at a darkened London and the searchlight beams. Feverishly we packed our kit and stood up in the carriage. We jerked into the flare of Victoria. Dazzled and confused, we looked at the dense crowd of beaming, anxious people. There was a tug at my elbow, and a triumphant voice shouted –

"I've found him! Here he is! There's your Mother." …

This strange familiar country seemed to us clean, careless, and full of men. The streets were clean; the men and women were clean. Out in Flanders a little grime came as a matter of course. One's uniform was dirty. Well, it had seen service. There was no need to be particular about the set of the tunic and the exact way accoutrements should be put on. But here the few men in khaki sprinkled about the streets had their buttons cleaned and not a thing was out of place. We wondered which of them belonged to the New Armies. The women, too, were clean and beautiful. This sounds perhaps to you a foolish thing to say, but it is true. The Flemish woman is not so clean as she is painted, and as for women dressed with any attempt at fashionable display – we had seen none since August. Nadine at Dour had been neat; Hélène at Carlepont had been companionable; the pretty midinette at Maast had been friendly and not over-dirty. For a day or two after I returned to my own country I could not imagine how anybody ever could leave it.

And all the people were free from care. However cheerful those brave but irritating folk who live behind the line may be, they have always shadows in their eyes. We had never been to a village through which the Germans had not passed. Portly and hilarious the Teuton may have shown himself – kindly and well-behaved he undoubtedly was in many places – there came with him a terror which stayed after he had gone, just as a mist sways above the ground after the night has flown.

At first we thought that no one at home cared about the war – then we realised it was impossible for anybody to care about the war who had not seen war. People might be intensely interested in the course of operations. They might burn for their country's success, and flame out against those who threatened her. They might suffer torments of anxiety for a brother in danger, or the tortures of grief for a brother who had died. The FACT of war, the terror and the shame, the bestiality and the awful horror, the pity and the disgust – they could never *know* war. So we thought them careless. …

---

1   Civilian clothes.
2   South-Eastern & Chatham Railway.

Again, though we had been told very many had enlisted, the streets seemed ludicrously full of men. In the streets of Flanders there are women and children and old men and others. These others would give all that they had to put on uniform and march gravely or gaily to the trenches. In Flanders a man who is fit and wears no uniform is instantly suspected of espionage. I am grinding no axe. I am advocating nothing or attacking nothing. I am merely stating as a fact that, suspicious and contemptuous as we had been in Flanders of every able-bodied man who was not helping to defend his country, it seemed grotesque to us to find so many civilian men in the streets of the country to which we had returned.

Of the heavenly quietness and decency of life, of late breakfasts and later dinners, there is no need to tell, but even before the week was up unrest troubled us. The Division might go violently into action. The Germans might break through. The "old Div." would be wanting us, and we who felt towards the Division as others feel towards their Regiments were eager to get back. ...

On the boat I met Gibson. At Boulogne we clambered into the same bus and passed the time in sipping old rum, eating chocolate biscuits, reading the second volume of 'Sinister Street,' and sleeping. At St Omer our craving for an omelette nearly lost us the bus. Then we slept. All that I can remember of the rest of the journey is that we stopped near Bailleul. An anxious corporal popped his head in.

"Mr Brown here?"

"Ye – e – s," sleepily, "what the devil do you want?"

"Our battery's in action, sir, a few miles from here. I've got your horses ready waiting, sir."

Mr Brown was thoroughly awake in a moment. He disturbed everybody collecting his kit. Then he vanished.

We were late at Bailleul, and there was no one to meet us. The Cyclists as usual came to our help. Their gig was waiting, and climbing into it we drove furiously to St Jans Cappel. Making some sort of beds for ourselves, we fell asleep. When we woke up in the morning our leave was a dream.

11

St Jans Cappel

Soon after our return there were rumours of a grand attack. Headquarters positively sizzled with the most expensive preparations. At a given word the Staff were to dash out in motor-cars to a disreputable tavern, so that they could see the shells bursting. A couple of despatch riders were to keep with them in order to fetch their cars when the day's work was over. A mobile reserve of motor-cyclists was to be established in a farm under cover.

The whole scheme was perfect. There was good rabbit-shooting near the tavern. The atmosphere inside was so thick that it actually induced slumber. The landlady possessed an excellent stove, upon which the Staff's lunch, prepared with quiet genius at St Jans, might be heated up. The place was dirty enough to give all those in authority, who might come round to see that the British Army was really doing something, a vivid conception of the horrors of war. And, as I have said, there was a slope behind the road from which lots and lots of shells could be seen bursting.

The word came. We arrived at the tavern before dawn. The Staff sauntered about outside in delicious anticipation. We all looked at our watches. Punctually at six the show began. Guns of all shapes and sizes had been concentrated. They made an overwhelming noise. Over the German trenches on the near slope of the Messines ridge flashed multitudinous points of flame. The Germans were being furiously shelled. The dawn came up while the Staff were drinking their matutinal tea. The Staff set itself sternly to work. Messages describing events at La Bassée poured in. They were conscientiously read and rushed over the wires to our brigades. The guns were making more noise than they had ever made before. The Germans were cowering in their trenches. It was all our officers could do to hold back their men, who were straining like hounds in a leash to get at the hated foe. A shell fell among some of the gunners' transport and wounded a man and two horses. That stiffened us. The news was flashed over the wire to G.H.Q. The transport was moved rapidly, but in good order, to a safer place. The guns fired more furiously than ever.

As soon as there was sufficient light, the General's A.D.C., crammed full of the lust for blood, went out and shot some rabbits and some indescribable birds, who by this time were petrified with fear. They had never heard such a noise before. That other despatch rider sat comfortably in a car, finished at his leisure the second volume of 'Sinister Street,' and wrote a lurid description of a modern battle.

Before the visitors came, the scene was improved by the construction of a large dug-out near the tavern. It is true that if the Staff had taken to the dug-out they would most certainly have been drowned. That did not matter. Every well-behaved Divisional Staff must have a dug-out near its Advanced Headquarters. It is always "done."

Never was a Division so lucky in its visitors. A certain young prince of high lineage arrived.[1] Everybody saluted at the same time. He was, I think, duly impressed by the atmosphere of the tavern, the sight of the Staff's maps, the inundated dug-outs, the noise of the guns and the funny balls of smoke that the shells made when they exploded over the German lines.

---

1   The Prince of Wales (later King Edward VIII and Duke of Windsor).

What gave this battle a humorous twist for all time was the delectable visit of a Cabinet Minister. He came in a car and brought with him his own knife and fork and a loaf of bread as his contribution to the Divisional Lunch. When he entered the tavern he smelt among other smells the delicious odour of rabbit-pie. With hurried but charming condescension he left his loaf on the stove, where it dried for a day or two until the landlady had the temerity to appropriate it. He was fed, so far as I remember on –

Soup.

Fish.

Rabbit-pie. Potatoes. Cabbage.

Apple-tart.

Fruit. Coffee. Liqueurs.

and after lunch, I am told, showed a marked disinclination to ascend the hill and watch the shells bursting. He was only a "civvy."[1] The battle lasted about ten days. Each morning the Staff, like lazy men who are "something in the city," arrived a little later at the tavern. Each afternoon they departed a little earlier. The rabbits decreased in number, and finally, when two days running the A.D.C. had been able to shoot nothing at all, the Division returned for good to the Chateau at St Jans Cappel.

For this mercy the despatch riders were truly grateful. Sitting the whole day in the tavern, we had all contracted bad headaches. Even chess, the 'Red Magazine,' and the writing of letters, could do nothing to dissipate our unutterable boredom. Never did we pass that tavern afterwards without a shudder of disgust. With joyous content we heard a month or two later that it had been closed for providing drinks after hours.

Officially the grand attack had taken this course. The French to the north had been held up by the unexpected strength of the German defence. The 3rd Division on our immediate left had advanced a trifle, for the Gordons had made a perilous charge into the Petit Bois, a wood at the bottom of the Wytschaete Heights. And the Royal Scots had put in some magnificent work, for which they were afterwards very properly congratulated. The Germans in front of our Division were so cowed by our magniloquent display of gunnery that they have remained moderately quiet ever since.

After these December manoeuvres nothing of importance happened on our front until the spring, when the Germans, whom we had tickled with intermittent gunnery right through the winter, began to retaliate with a certain energy.

The Division that has no history is not necessarily happy. There were portions of the line, it is true, which provided a great deal of comfort and very little danger. Fine dug-outs were constructed – you have probably seen them in the illustrated papers. The men were more at home in such trenches than in the ramshackle farms behind the lines. These show trenches were emphatically the exception. The average trench on the line during last winter was neither comfortable nor safe. Yellow clay, six inches to four feet or more of stinking water, many corpses behind the trenches buried just underneath the surface-crust, and in front of the trenches not buried at all, inveterate sniping from a slightly superior position – these are not pleasant bedfellows. The old Division (or rather the new Division – the infantrymen of the old Division were now pitifully few) worked right hard through the winter. When the early spring came and the trenches were dry, the Division was sent north to bear a hand in the two bloodiest actions of the war. So far as I know, in the whole

---

1   *The soldier's contemptuous expression for the inhabitants of the civilian world.* (Watson)

history of British participation in this war there has never been a more murderous fight than one of these two actions – and the Division, with slight outside help, managed the whole affair.

Twice in the winter there was an attempted *rapprochement* between the Germans and ourselves. The more famous gave the Division a mention by "Eyewitness," so we all became swollen with pride.

On the Kaiser's birthday one-and-twenty large shells were dropped accurately into a farm suspected of being a battalion or brigade headquarters. The farm promptly acknowledged the compliment by blowing up, and all round it little explosions followed. Nothing pleases a gunner more than to strike a magazine. He always swears he knew it was there the whole time, and, as gunners are dangerous people to quarrel with, we always pretended to believe the tale.

There are many people in England still who cannot stomach the story of the Christmas truce. "Out there," we cannot understand why. Good fighting men respect good fighting men. On our front, and on the fronts of other divisions, the Germans had behaved throughout the winter with a passable gentlemanliness. Besides, neither the British nor the German soldier – with the possible exception of the Prussians – has been able to stoke up that virulent hate which devastates so many German and British homes. A certain lance-corporal puts the matter thus:[1] –

"We're fightin' for somethink what we've got. Those poor beggars is fightin' cos they've got to. An' old Bill Kayser's fightin' for somethin' what 'e'll never get. But 'e will get somethink, and that's a good 'iding!"[2]

We even had a sneaking regard for that "cunning old bird, Kayser Bill." Our treatment of prisoners explains the Christmas Truce. The British soldier, except when he is smarting under some dirty trick, suffering under terrible loss, or maddened by fighting or fatigue, treats his prisoners with a tolerant, rather contemptuous kindness. May God in His mercy help any poor German who falls into the hands of a British soldier when the said German has "done the dirty" or has "turned nasty"! There is no judge so remorseless, no executioner so ingenious in making the punishment fit the crime.[3]

This is what I wrote home a day or two after Christmas: From six on Christmas Eve to six in the evening on Christmas Day there was a truce between two regiments of our Division and the Germans opposite them. Heads popped up and were not sniped. Greetings were called across. One venturesome, enthusiastic German got out of his trench and stood waving a branch of Christmas Tree. Soon there was a fine pow-wow going on. Cigars were exchanged for tobacco. Friendship was pledged in socks. The Germans brought out some beer and the English some rum. Finally, on Christmas Day, there was a great concert and dance. The Germans were spruce, elderly men, keen and well fed, with buttons cleaned for the occasion. They appeared to have plenty of supplies, and were fully equipped with everything necessary for a winter campaign. A third battalion, wisely but churlishly, refused these seasonable advances, and shot four men who appeared with a large cask of what was later discovered to be beer. …

"The Div." were billeted in a chateau on the slope of a hill three-quarters of a mile above St Jans Cappel. This desirable residence stands in two acres of garden, just off the road. At the gate was a lodge. Throughout the winter we despatch riders lived in two small rooms of this lodge. We averaged fourteen in number. Two were out with the brigades, leaving twelve to live, eat, and sleep in two rooms, each about 15 ft. by 8 ft. We were distinctly cramped, and cursed the day that had brought us to St Jans. It was a cruel stroke that gave us for our winter quarters the worst billets we had ever suffered.

---

1   *I retired with some haste from Flanders the night after the Germans first began to use gas. Militant chemistry may have altered the British soldier's convictions.* (Watson)

2   *I have left out the usual monotonous epithet. Any soldier can supply it.* (Watson)

3   The last two sentences of this paragraph were deleted by the censor.

As we became inclined to breakfast late, nine o'clock parade was instituted. Breakfast took place before or after, as the spirit listed. Bacon, tea, and bread came from the cook. We added porridge and occasionally eggs. The porridge we half-cooked the night before.

After breakfast we began to clean our bicycles, no light task, and the artificers started on repairs. The cleaning process was usually broken into by the arrival of the post and the papers of the day before. Cleaning the bicycles, sweeping out the rooms, reading and writing letters, brought us to dinner at 1.

This consisted of bully or fresh meat stew with vegetables (or occasionally roast or fried meat), bread and jam. As we became more luxurious we would provide for ourselves Yorkshire pudding, which we discovered trying to make pancakes, and pancakes, which we discovered trying to make Yorkshire pudding. Worcester Sauce and the invaluable curry powder were never wanting. After dinner we smoked a lethargic pipe.

In the afternoon it was customary to take some exercise. To reduce the strain on our back tyres we used to trudge manfully down into the village, or, if we were feeling energetic, to the ammunition column a couple of miles away. Any distance over two miles we covered on motor-cycles. Their use demoralised us. Our legs shrunk away.

Sometimes two or three of us would ride to a sand-pit on Mont Noir and blaze away with our revolvers. Incidentally, not one of us had fired a shot in anger since the war began. We treated our revolvers as unnecessary luggage. In time we became skilled in their use, and thereafter learnt to keep them moderately clean. We had been served out with revolvers at Chatham, but had never practised with them – except at Carlow for a morning, and then we were suffering from the effects of inoculation. They may be useful when we get to Germany.

Shopping in Bailleul was less strenuous. We were always buying something for supper – a kilo of liver, some onions, a few sausages – anything that could be cooked by the unskilled on a paraffin-stove. Then after shopping there were cafes we could drop into, sure of a welcome. It was impossible to live from November to March "within easy reach of town" and not make friends.

Milk for tea came from the farm in which No. I Section of the Signal Company was billeted. When first we were quartered at St Jans this section wallowed in some mud a little above the chateau.

Because I had managed to make myself understood to some German prisoners, I was looked upon as a great linguist, and vulgarly credited with a knowledge of all the European languages. So I was sent, together with the Quartermaster-Sergeant and the Sergeant-Major, on billeting expeditions. Arranging for quarters at the farm, I made great friends with the farmer. He was a tall, thin, lithe old man, with a crumpled wife and prodigiously large family. He was a man of affairs, too, for once a month in peace time he would drive into Hazebrouck. While his wife got me the milk, we used to sit by the fire and smoke our pipes and discuss the terrible war and the newspapers. One of the most embarrassing moments I have ever experienced was when he bade me tell the sergeants that he regarded them as brothers, and loved them all. I said it first in French, that he might hear, and then in English. The sergeants blushed, while the old man beamed.

We loved the Flemish, and, for the most part, they loved us. When British soldiers arrived in a village the men became clean, the women smart, and the boys inevitably procured putties and wore them with pride. The British soldier is certainly not insular. He tries hard to understand the words and ways of his neighbours. He has a rough tact, a crude courtesy, and a great-hearted generosity. In theory no task could be more difficult than the administration of the British Area. Even a friendly military occupation is an uncomfortable burden. Yet never have I known any case of real ill-feeling. Personally, during my nine months at the Front, I have always received from the French and the Belgians amazing kindness and consideration. As an officer I came into contact with village and town officials over questions of billets and requisitions. In any difficulty I received courteous assistance. No trouble was too great; no time was too valuable. …

After tea of cakes and rolls the bridge-players settled down to a quiet game, with pipes to hand and whisky and siphons on the sideboard. We took it in turns to cook some delicacy for supper at 8 – sausages, curried sardines, liver and bacon, or – rarely but joyously – fish. At one time or another we feasted on all the luxuries, but fish was rarer than rubies. When we had it we did not care if we stank out the whole lodge with odours of its frying. We would lie down to sleep content in a thick fishy, paraffin-y, dripping-y atmosphere. When I came home I could not think what the delicious smell was in a certain street. Then my imagination struck out a picture – Grimers laboriously frying a dab over a smoky paraffin-stove.

On occasions after supper we would brew a large jorum of good rum-punch, sing songs with roaring choruses, and finish up the evening with a good old scrap over somebody else's bed. The word went round to "mobilise," and we would all stand ready, each on his bed, to repel boarders. If the sanctity of your bed were violated, the intruder would be cast vigorously into outer darkness. Another song, another drink, a final pipe, and to bed.

Our Christmas would have been a grand day if it had not been away from home.

At eight o'clock there was breakfast of porridge, bacon and eggs, and bloaters – everybody in the best of spirits. About nine the Skipper presented us with cards from the King and Queen. Then the mail came in, but it was poor. By the time we had tidied up our places and done a special Christmas shave and wash, we were called upon to go down to the cookhouse and sign for Princess Mary's Christmas gift – a good pipe, and in a pleasant little brass box lay a Christmas card, a photograph, a packet of cigarettes, and another of excellent tobacco.

It was now lunch-time – steak and potatoes.

The afternoon was spent on preparations for our great and unexampled dinner. Grimers printed the menu, and while I made some cold curried sardines, the rest went down into the village to stimulate the landlady of the inn where we were going to dine.

In the village a brigade was billeted, and that brigade was, of course, "on the wire." It was arranged that the despatch riders next on the list should take their motor-cycles down and be summoned over the wire if they were needed. An order had come round that unimportant messages were to be kept until the morning.

We dined in the large kitchen of the *Maison Commune Estaminet*, at a long table decorated with mistletoe and holly. The dinner – the result of two days' "scrounging" under the direction of George – was too good to be true. We toasted each other and sang all the songs we knew. Two of the Staff clerks wandered in and told us we were the best of all possible despatch riders. We drank to them uproariously. Then a Scotsman turned up with a noisy recitation. Finally, we all strolled home up the hill singing loudly and pleasantly, very exhilarated, in sure and certain belief we had spent the best of all possible evenings.

In the dwelling of the Staff there was noise of revelry. Respectable captains with false noses peered out of windows. Our Fat Boy declaimed in the signal office on the iniquities of the artillery telegraphists. Sadders sent gentle messages of greeting over the wires. He was still a little piqued at his failure to secure the piper of the K.O.S.B., who had been commandeered by the Staff. Sadders waited for him until early morning and then steered him to our lodge, but the piper was by then too tired to play.

At least two of the original Christmas menus survive, in Sadders' and Pollers' archives. They were hand-written by Grimers, and each was signed by all those present.

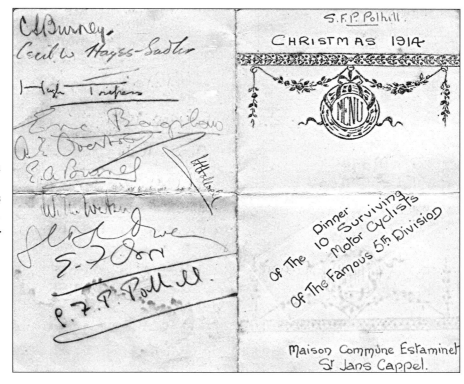

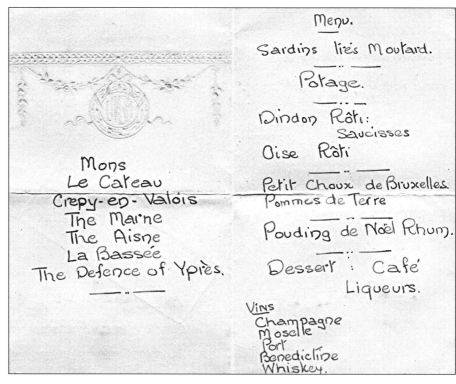

Here is our bill of fare:

CHRISTMAS, 1914.

———

DINNER OF THE
TEN SURVIVING MOTOR-CYCLISTS OF THE FAMOUS FIFTH DIVISION.

Sardins très Moutard.
Potage.
Dindon Rôti-Saucisses. Oise Rôti.
Petits Choux de Bruxelles.
Pommes de Terre.
Pouding de Noël Rhum.
Dessert. Café. Liqueurs.
Vins. – Champagne. Moselle. Port
Benedictine. Whisky.

On the reverse page we put our battle-honours – Mons, Le Cateau, Crêpy-en-Valois, the Marne, the Aisne, La Bassée, the Defence of Ypres.[1]

We beat the Staff on the sprouts, but the Staff countered by appropriating the piper.

Work dwindled until it became a farce. One run for each despatch rider every third day was the average. St Jans was not the place we should have chosen for a winter resort. Life became monotonous, and we all with one accord began applying for commissions. Various means were used to break the monotony. Grimers, under the Skipper's instructions, began to plant vegetables for the spring, but I do not think he ever got much beyond mustard and cress. On particularly unpleasant days we were told off to make fascines. N'Soon assisted the Quartermaster-Sergeant. Cecil did vague things with the motor-lorry. I was called upon to write the Company's War Diary. Even the Staff became restless and took to night-walks behind the trenches. If it had not been for the generous supply of "days off" that the Skipper allowed us, we should by February have begun to gibber.

Despatches were of two kinds – ordinary and priority. "Priority" despatches could only be sent by the more important members of the Staff. They were supposed to be important, were marked "priority" in the corner, and taken at once in a hurry. Ordinary despatches went by the morning and evening posts. During the winter a regular system of motor-cyclist posts was organised right through the British Area. A message could be sent from Neuve Eglise to Chartres in about two days. Our posts formed the first or last stage of the journey. The morning post left at 7.30 a.m., and the evening at 3.30 p.m. All the units of the division were visited.

If the roads were moderately good and no great movements of troops were proceeding, the post took about 1¾ hours; so the miserable postman was late either for breakfast or for tea. It was routine work pure and simple. After six weeks we knew every stone in the roads. The postman never came under fire. He passed through one village which was occasionally shelled, but, while I was with the Signal Company, the postman and the shells never arrived at the village at the same time. There was far more danger from lorries and motor ambulances than from shells.

As for the long line of "postmen" that stretched back into the dim interior of France – it was rarely that they even heard the guns. When they did hear them, they would, I am afraid, pluck a racing helmet from their pockets, draw the ear-flaps well down over their ears, bend down over

---

1   *To these may now be added – St Eloi, Hill 60, the Second Battle of Ypres.* (Watson)

their racing handle-bars, and sprint for dear life. Returning safely to Abbeville, they would write hair-raising accounts of the dangers they had passed through to the motor-cycling papers. It is only right that I should here once and for all confess – there is no finer teller of tall stories than the motor-cyclist despatch rider. …

From December to February the only time I was under shell fire was late in December, when the Grand Attack was in full train. A certain brigade headquarters had taken refuge inconsiderately in advanced dug-outs. As I passed along the road to them some shrapnel was bursting a quarter of a mile away. So long was it since I had been under fire that the noise of our own guns disturbed me. In the spring, after I had left the Signal Company, the roads were not so healthy. George experienced the delights of a broken chain on a road upon which the Germans were registering accurately with shrapnel. Church, a fine fellow, and quite the most promising of our recruits, was killed in his billet by a shell when attached to a brigade.[1]

Taking the post rarely meant just a pleasant spin, because it rained in Flanders from September to January.

One day I started out from D.H.Q. at 3.30 p.m. with the afternoon post, and reached the First Brigade well up to time. Then it began to rain, at first slightly, and then very heavily indeed, with a bagful of wind. On a particularly open stretch of road – the rain was stinging sharply – the engine stopped. With a heroic effort I tugged the bicycle through some mud to the side of a shed, in the hope that when the wind changed – it did not – I might be under cover. I could not see. I could not grip – and of course I could not find out what the matter was.

After I had been working for about half an hour the two artillery motor-cyclists came along. I stopped them to give me a hand and to do as much work as I could possibly avoid doing myself while preserving an appearance of omniscience.

We worked for an hour or more. It was now so dark that I could not distinguish one motor-cyclist from another. The rain rained faster than it had ever rained before, and the gale was so violent that we could scarcely keep our feet. Finally, we diagnosed a complaint that could not be cured by the roadside. So we stopped working, to curse and admire the German rockets.

There was an estaminet close by. It had appeared shut, but when we began to curse a light shone in one of the windows. So I went in and settled to take one of the artillery motor-cycles and deliver the rest of my quite unimportant despatches. It would not start. We worked for twenty minutes in the rain vainly, then a motor-cyclist turned up from the nearest brigade to see what had become of me, – the progress of the post is checked over the wire. We arranged matters – but then neither his motor-cycle nor the motor-cycle of the second artillery motor-cyclist would start. It was laughable. Eventually we got the brigade despatch rider started with my report.

A fifth motor-cyclist, who discreetly did not stop his engine, took my despatches back to "the Div." The second artillery motor-cycle we started after quarter of an hour's prodigious labour. The first and mine were still obstinate, so he and I retired to the inn, drank brandy and hot water, and conversed amiably with madame.

Madame, who together with innumerable old men and children inhabited the inn, was young and pretty and intelligent – black hair, sallow and symmetrical face, expressive mouth, slim and graceful limbs. Talking the language, we endeavoured to make our forced company pleasant. That other despatch rider, still steaming from the stove, sat beside a charming Flemish woman, and endeavoured, amid shrieks of laughter, to translate the jokes in an old number of 'London Opinion.'

---

1   William Henry Church (1896-1915) from Toxteth was the son of a policeman. He landed in France on 1st January 1915 and was assigned to 5th Signal company. He died on 5th March 1915.

A Welsh lad came in – a perfect Celt of nineteen, dark and lithe, with a momentary smile and a wild desire to see India. Then some Cheshires arrived. They were soaked and very weary. One old reservist staggered to a chair. We gave him some brandy and hot water. He chattered unintelligibly for a moment about his wife and children. He began to doze, so his companion took him out, and they tottered along after their company.

A dog of no possible breed belonged to the estaminet. Madame called him "Automobile Anglais," because he was always rushing about for no conceivable reason.

We were sorry when at 9.50 the lorry came for the bicycles. Our second driver was an ex-London cabby, with a crude wit expressed in impossible French that our hostess delightfully parried. On the way back he told me how he had given up the three taxis he had owned to do "his bit," how the other men had laughed at him because he was so old, how he had met a prisoner who used to whistle for the taxis in Russell Square. We talked also of the men in the trenches, of fright, and of the end of the war. We reached D.H.Q. about 10.30, and after a large bowl of porridge I turned in.

12

Behind the Lines

I had intended to write down a full description of the country immediately behind our present line. The Skipper, for fear we should become stale, allowed us plenty of leave. We would make little expeditions to Béthune for the baths, spend an afternoon riding round Armentières, or run over to Poperinghe for a chop. We even arranged for a visit to the Belgian lines, but that excursion was forbidden by a new order. Right through the winter we had "unrivalled opportunities" – as the journalists would say – of becoming intimate with that strip of Flanders which extends from Ypres to Béthune. Whether I can or may describe it is a matter for care. A too affectionate description of the neighbourhood of Wulverghem, for instance, would be unwise. But I see no reason why I should not state as a fact that a most excellent dry Martini could be obtained in Ypres up to the evening of April 22.

Wretched Ypres has been badly overwritten. Before the war it was a pleasant city, little visited by travellers because it lay on a badly served branch line. The inhabitants tell me it was never much troubled with tourists. One burgher explained the situation to me with a comical mixture of sentiment and reason.

"You see, sir, that our Cathedral is shattered and the Cloth Hall a ruin. May those devils, the dirty Germans, roast in Hell! But after the war we shall be the richest city in Belgium. All England will flock to Ypres. Is it not a monstrous cemetery? Are there not woods and villages and farms at which the brave English have fought like lions to earn for themselves eternal fame, and for the city an added glory? The good God gives His compensations after great wars. There will be many to buy our lace and fill our restaurants."

Mr John Buchan and Mr Valentine Williams and others have "written up" Ypres. The exact state of the Cloth Hall at any given moment is the object of solicitude. The shattered Belgian homes have been described over and over again. The important things about Ypres have been left unsaid.

Near the station there was a man who really could mix cocktails. He was no blundering amateur, but an expert with the subtlest touch. And in the Rue de Lille a fashionable dressmaker turned her *atelier* into a tea-room. She used to provide coffee or chocolate, or even tea, and the most delicious little cakes. Of an afternoon you would sit on comfortable chairs at a neat table covered with a fair cloth and talk to your hostess. A few hats daintily remained on stands, but, as she said, they were last year's hats, unworthy of our notice.

A pleasant afternoon could be spent on the old ramparts. We were there, as a matter of fact, to do a little building-up and clearing-away when the German itch for destruction proved too strong for their more gentlemanly feelings. We lay on the grass in the sun and smoked our pipes, looking across the placid moat to Zillebeke Vyver, Verbranden Molen, and the slight curve of Hill 60. The landscape was full of interest. Here was shrapnel bursting over entirely empty fields. There was a sapper repairing a line. The Germans were shelling the town, and it was a matter of skill to decide when the lumbersome old shell was heard exactly where it would fall. Then we would walk back into the town for tea and look in at that particularly enterprising grocer's in the Square to see his latest novelties in tinned goods.

From Ypres the best road in Flanders runs by Vlamertinghe to Poperinghe. It is a good macadam road, made, doubtless by perfidious Albion's money, just before the war.

Poperinghe has been an age-long rival of Ypres. Even to-day its inhabitants delight to tell you the old municipal scandals of the larger town, and the burghers of Ypres, if they see a citizen of Poperinghe in their streets, believe he has come to gloat over their misfortunes. Ypres is an Edinburgh and Poperinghe a Glasgow. Ypres was self-consciously "old world" and loved its buildings. Poperinghe is modern, and perpetrated a few years ago the most terrible of town halls. There are no cocktails in Poperinghe, but there is good whisky and most excellent beer.

I shall never forget my feelings when one morning in a certain wine-merchant's cellar I saw several eighteen-gallon casks of Bass's Pale Ale. I left Poperinghe in a motor-ambulance, and the Germans shelled it next day, but my latest advices state that the ale is still intact.

Across the road from the wine-merchant's is a delectable tea-shop. There is a teashop at Bailleul, the "Allies Tea-Rooms." It was started early in March. It is full of bad blue china and inordinately expensive. Of the tea-shop at Poperinghe I cannot speak too highly. There is a vast variety of the most delicious cakes. The proprietress is pleasant and her maids are obliging. It is also cheap. I have only one fault to find with it – the room is small. Infantry officers walk miles into Poperinghe for their tea and then find the room crowded with those young subalterns who supply us with our bully. They bring in bulldogs and stay a long time.

Dickebusch used to be a favourite Sunday afternoon's ride for the Poperinghe wheelers. They would have tea at the restaurant on the north of Dickebusch Vyver, and afterwards go for a row in the little flat-bottomed boats, accompanied, no doubt, by some nice dark Flemish girls. The village, never very pleasant, is now the worse for wear. I remember it with no kindly feelings, because, having spent a night there with the French, I left them in the morning too early to obtain a satisfactory meal, and arrived at Headquarters too late for any breakfast.

Not far from Dickebusch is the Desolate Chateau. Before the war it was a handsome place, built by a rich coal-merchant from Lille. I visited it on a sunny morning. At the southern gate there was a little black and shapeless heap fluttering a rag in the wind. I saluted and passed on, sick at heart. The grounds were pitted with shellholes: the cucumber-frames were shattered. Just behind the chateau was a wee village of dug-outs. Now they are slowly falling in. And the chateau itself?

It had been so proud of its finery, its pseudo-Greek columns, and its rich furnishings. Battered and confused – there is not a room of it which is not open to the wind from the sea. The pictures lie prostrate on the floor before their ravisher. The curtains are torn and faded. The papers of its master are scattered over the carpet and on the rifled desk. In the bedroom of its mistress her linen has been thrown about wildly; yet her two silver brushes still lie on the dressing-table. Even the children's room had been pillaged, and the books, torn and defaced, lay in a rough heap.

All was still. At the foot of the garden there was a little village half hidden by trees. Not a sound came from it. Away on the ridge miserable Wytschaete stood hard against the sky, a mass of trembling ruins. Then two soldiers came, and finding a boat rowed noisily round the tiny lake, and the shells murmured harshly as they flew across to Ypres. Some ruins are dead stones, but the broken houses of Flanders are pitifully alive – like the wounded men who lie between the trenches and cannot be saved. ...

Half a mile south from Dickebusch are cross-roads, and the sign-post tells you that the road to the left is the road to Wytschaete – but Wytschaete faces Kemmel and Messines faces Wulverghem.

I was once walking over the hills above Witzenhausen,[1] – the cherries by the roadside were wonderful that year, – and coming into a valley we asked a man how we might best strike a path into the next valley over the shoulder of the hill. He said he did not know, because he had never

---

1   Between school and university, Watson studied in Germany at the nearby University of Göttingen.

been over the hill. The people of the next valley were strangers to him. When first I came to a sign-post that told me how to get to a village I could not reach with my life, I thought of those hills above Witzenhausen. From Wulverghem to Messines is exactly two kilometres. It is ludicrous.

Again, one afternoon I was riding over the pass between Mont Noir and Mont Vidaigne. I looked to the east and saw in the distance the smoke of a train, just as from Harrow you might see the Scottish Express on the North-Western main line. For a moment I did not realise that the train was German, that the purpose of its journey was to kill me and my fellow-men. But it is too easy to sentimentalise, to labour the stark fact that war is a grotesque, irrational absurdity. …

Following the main road south from Dickebusch you cross the frontier and come to Bailleul, a town of which we were heartily sick before the winter was far gone. In peace it would be once seen and never remembered. It has no character, though I suppose the "Faucon" is as well known to Englishmen now as any hotel in Europe. There are better shops in Béthune and better cafes in Poperinghe. Of the "Allies TeaRooms" I have already written.

Bailleul is famous for one thing alone – its baths. Just outside the town is a large and modern asylum that contains a good plunge-bath for the men and gorgeous hot baths for officers. There are none better behind the line. Tuesdays and Fridays were days of undiluted joy.

Armentières is sprawling and ugly and full of dirt – a correct and middle-class town that reminded me of Bristol. In front of it are those trenches, of which many tales wandered up and down the line. Here the Christmas truce is said to have been prolonged for three weeks or more. Here the men are supposed to prefer their comfortable trenches to their billets, though when they "come out" they are cheered by the Follies and the Fancies. On this section of the line is the noto-rious Plugstreet Wood, that showplace to which all distinguished but valuable visitors are taken. Other corps have sighed for the gentle delights of this section of the line …

South-west from Armentières the country is as level as it can be. It is indeed possible to ride from Ypres to Béthune without meeting any hill except the slight ascent from La Clytte. Steenwerck, Erquinghem, Croix du Bac, and, farther west, Merris and Vieux Berquin, have no virtue what-soever. There is little country flatter and uglier than the country between Bailleul and Béthune.

One morning Huggie, Cecil, and I obtained leave to visit Béthune and the La Bassée district. It was in the middle of January, three months after we had left Beuvry. We tore into Bailleul and bumped along the first mile of the Armentières road. That mile is without any doubt the most excruciatingly painful *pavé* in the world. We crossed the railway and raced south. The roads were good and there was little traffic, but the sudden apparition of a motor-lorry round a sharp corner sent that other despatch rider into the ditch. Estaires, as always, produced much grease. It began to rain, but we held on by La Gorgue and Lestrem, halting only once for the necessary café-cognac.

We were stopped for our passes at the bridge into Béthune by a private of the London Scottish. I rejoiced exceedingly, and finding Alec, took him off to a bath and then to the restaurant where I had breakfasted when first we came to Béthune. The meal was as good as it had been three months before, and the flapper as charming.[1] After lunch we had our hair cut. Then Cecil took us to the little blue-and-white café for tea. She did play the piano, but two subalterns of the less combatant type came in and put us to flight. A corporal is sometimes at such a disadvantage.

We rode along the canal bank to Beuvry Station, and found that our filthy old quarters had been cleaned up and turned into an Indian dressing-station. We went on past the cross-roads at Gorre, where an Indian battalion was waiting miserably under the dripping trees. The sun was just setting behind some grey clouds. The fields were flooded with ochreous water. Since last I had been

---

1   *I cannot remember the name of the restaurant. Go to the north-east corner of the Square and turn down a lane to your right. It is the fourth or fifth house on your right. In Béthune there is also, of course, the big hotel where generals lunch. If you find the company of generals a little trying go to the flapper's restaurant.* (Watson)

along the road the country had been "searched" too thoroughly. One wall of 1910 farm remained. Chickens pecked feebly among the rest of it.

Coming into Festubert I felt that something was wrong. The village had been damnably shelled – that I had expected – and there was not a soul to be seen. I thought of the father and mother and daughter who, returning to their home while we were there in October, had wept because a fuse had gone through the door and the fireplace and all their glass had been broken. Their house was now a heap of nothing in particular. The mirror I had used lay broken on the top of about quarter of a wall. Still something was wrong, and Huggie, who had been smiling at my puzzled face, said gently in an off-hand way – "Seen the church?"

That was it! The church had simply disappeared. In the old days riding up from Gorre the fine tower of the church rose above the houses at the end of the street. The tower had been shelled and had fallen crashing through the roof.

We met a sapper coming out of a cottage. He was rather amused at our sentimental journey, and warned us that the trenches were considerably nearer the village than they had been in our time. We determined to push on as it was now dusk, but my engine jibbed, and we worked on it in the gloom among the dark and broken houses. The men in the trenches roused themselves to a sleepless night, and intermittent rifle-shots rang out in the damp air.

We rode north to the Estaminet de l'Epinette, passing a road which forking to the right led to a German barricade. The estaminet still lived, but farther down the road the old house which had sheltered a field ambulance was a pile of rubbish. On we rode by La Couture to Estaires, where we dined, and so to St Jans Cappel. …

Do you know what the Line means? When first we came to Landrecies the thought of the Frontier as something strong and stark had thrilled us again and again, but the Frontier was feeble and is nothing. A man of Poperinghe told me his brother was professor, his son was serving, his wife and children were "over there." He pointed to the German lines. Of his wife and children he has heard nothing for four months. Some of us are fighting to free "German" Flanders, the country where life is dark and bitter. Those behind our line, however confident they may be, live in fear, for if the line were to retire a little some of them would be cast into the bitter country. A day will come "when the whole line will advance," and the welcome we shall receive then from those who have come out of servitude! … There are men and women in France who live only for that day, just as there are those in this country who would welcome the day of death, so that they might see again those they love. …

You may have gathered from my former letters that no friction took place between the professional and amateur soldiers of the Signal Company. I have tried all through my letters to give you a very truthful idea of our life, and my account would not be complete without some description of the Signal Company and its domestic affairs.

Think for a moment of what happened at the beginning of August. More than a dozen 'Varsity men were thrown like Daniels into a den of mercenaries. We were awkwardly privileged persons – full corporals with a few days' service. Motor-cycling gave superlative opportunities of freedom. Our duties were "flashy," and brought us into familiar contact with officers of rank. We were highly paid, and thought to have much money of our own. In short, we who were soldiers of no standing possessed the privileges that a professional soldier could win only after many years' hard work.

Again, it did not help matters that our Corps was a Corps of intelligent experts who looked down on the ordinary "Tommy," that our Company had deservedly the reputation of being one of the best Signal Companies in the Army – a reputation which has been enhanced and duly rewarded in the present war. These motor-cyclists were not only experimental interlopers. They might even "let down" the Company.

We expected jealousy and unpleasantness, which we hoped to overcome by hard work. We found a tactful kindness that was always smoothing the rough way, helping us amusedly, and giving us more than our due, and a thorough respect where respect was deserved. It was astonishing, but then we did not know the professional soldier. During the winter there was a trifle of friction over cooking, the work of the Signal Office, and the use and abuse of motor-cycles. It would have been a poor-spirited company if there had been none. But the friction was transitory, and left no acid feeling.

I should like to pay my compliments to a certain commanding officer, but six months' work under him has convinced me that he does not like compliments. Still, there remains that dinner at the end of the war, and then … !

The Sergeant-Major frightened us badly at first. He looked so much like a Sergeant-Major, and a Sergeant-Major is more to be feared than the C.O., or the General, or the A.P.M., or anybody else in this disciplinary world. He can make life Hell or Heaven or a judicious compromise. Our Sergeant-Major believed in the judicious compromise with a tendency towards Heaven. When any question arose between professional and amateur, he dealt with it impartially. At other times he was inclined to let us work out our own salvation. I have always had a mighty respect for the Sergeant-Major, but have never dared tell him so. Perhaps he will read this.

The "Quarter-Bloke"[1] was a jewel. He was suddenly called upon to keep us supplied with things of which he had never even heard the names. He rose to the occasion like a hero or Mr Selfridge's buyer. Never did he pass by an unconsidered trifle. One day a rumour went round that we might get side-cars. That was enough for the Quarter-Bloke. He picked up every large-sized tyre he thought might come in useful. The side-cars came. There was a rush for tyres. The Quarter-Bloke did not rush. He only smiled.

His great triumph was the affair of the leather jackets. A maternal Government thought to send us out leather jackets. After tea the Q.-B. bustled in with them. We rode out with them the next morning. The 2nd Corps had not yet received theirs. We were the first motor-cyclists in our part of the world to appear in flaring chrome. The Q.-B. smiled again.

I always think the Quarter-Bloke is wasted. He ought to be put in charge of the Looting Department of a large invading army. Do not misunderstand me. The Q.-B. never "looted." He never stepped a hair's-breadth outside those regulations that hedge round the Quartermaster. He was just a man with a prophetic instinct, who, while others passed blindly by, picked up things because they might come in useful some day – and they always did. Finally, the Q.-B. was companionable. He could tell a good story, and make merry decorously, as befitted a Company Quartermaster-Sergeant.

Of the other sergeants I will make no individual mention. We took some for better, and some for worse, but they were all good men, who knew their job.

Then there was "Ginger," the cook. I dare not describe his personal appearance lest I should meet him again – and I want to – but it was remarkable. So was his language. One of us had a fair gift that way, and duels were frequent, but "Ginger" always had the last word. He would keep in reserve a monstrously crude sulphurous phrase with a sting of humour in its tail, and, when our fellow had concluded triumphantly with an exotic reference to Ginger's hereditary characteristics, Ginger would hesitate a moment, as if thinking, and then out with it. Obviously there was no more to be said.

I have ever so much more to tell about the Signal Company in detail and dialogue.

Perhaps some day I shall have the courage to say it, but I shall be careful to hide about whom I am writing. …

---

1   *Company Quartermaster-Sergeant, now a Sergeant-Major.* (Watson)

The "commission fever," which we had caught on the Aisne and, more strongly, at Beuvry, swept over us late in January. Moulders, who had lost his own company and joined on to us during the Retreat, had retired into the quietude of the A.S.C. Cecil was selected to go home and train the despatch riders of the New Armies.

There were points in being "an officer and a gentleman." Dirt and discomfort were all very well when there was plenty of work to do, and we all decided that every officer should have been in the ranks, but despatch-riding had lost its savour. We had become postmen. Thoughts of the days when we had dashed round picking-up brigades, had put battalions on the right road, and generally made ourselves conspicuous, if not useful, discontented us. So we talked it over.

Directing the operations of a very large gun seemed a good job. There would not be much moving to do, because monster guns were notoriously immobile. Hours are regular; the food is good, and can generally be eaten in comparative safety. If the gun had a very long range it would be quite difficult to hit. Unfortunately gunnery is a very technical job, and requires some acquaintance with Algebra. So we gave up the idea.

We did not dote on the cavalry, for many reasons. First, when cavalry is not in action it does nothing but clean its stables and exercise its horses. Second, if ever we broke through the German lines the cavalry would probably go ahead of anybody else. Third, we could not ride very well, and the thought of falling off in front of our men when they were charging daunted us.

The sappers required brains, and we had too great an admiration for the infantry to attempt commanding them. Besides, they walked and lived in trenches.

Two of us struck upon a corps which combined the advantages of every branch of the service. We drew up a list of each other's qualifications to throw a sop to modesty, sent in our applications, and waited. At the same time we adopted a slight tone of hauteur towards those who were not potential officers.

One night after tea "Ginger" brought in the orders. I had become a gentleman, and, saying good-bye, I walked down into the village and reported myself to the officer commanding the Divisional Cyclists. I was no longer a despatch rider but a very junior subaltern.

I had worked with the others for nearly seven months – with Huggie, who liked to be frightened; with George the arch scrounger; with Spuggy, who could sing the rarest songs; with Sadders, who is as brave as any man alive; with N'Soon, the dashing, of the tender skin; with Fat Boy, who loves "sustaining" food and dislikes frost; with Grimers and Cecil, best of artificers; with Pollers and Orr and Moulders and the Flapper.

I cannot pay them a more sufficient tribute than the tribute of the Commander-in-Chief:

> Carrying despatches and messages at all hours of the day and night, in every kind of weather, and often traversing bad roads blocked with transport, they have been conspicuously successful in maintaining an extraordinary degree of efficiency in the service of communications. … No amount of difficulty or danger has ever checked the energy and ardour which has distinguished their corps throughout the operations.

FINIS.

MORNING ABLUTIONS ON BEVRY STATION

The spirit of Adventures of a Despatch Rider is well captured in these two images from the Burney album: a mixture of camaraderie and dedicated hard work kept the show on the road

"GRIMERS" AT WORK.

The Cast:
Introducing the Men
at the Heart of the Story

THE AUTHOR – William Henry Lowe Watson (1891–1932)

The author, known to his colleagues as "Willie" described 'Adventures of a Despatch Rider' as a novice's insights into the war, assembled from the letters he sent home from France. In reality it was a significant literary achievement – the work of a new author who had long been preparing for this opportunity. The book was shaped as much by Watson's background and education as by the experiences which it recounts.

When he volunteered in 1914, Watson was the only surviving male member of a family which had suffered the premature deaths of his father and brother – both, coincidentally, named Patrick.

Watson's father, the Reverend Patrick Watson, was born in 1850, the son of a Dundee jute merchant. Instead of going into business Patrick devoted his life to a career in the Church.

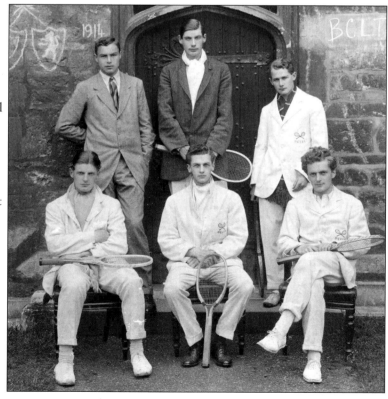

Watson (back row centre) was a member of the Balliol College tennis team in 1914. W A Stuart (top left) joined the US Army in 1917 and J E Norton (top right) served as an artillery officer. In the front row, Alasdair Macdonell (left) was killed at Loos in 1915 with the Cameron Highlanders, William Ker (centre) was killed on the Somme late in 1916 with the Royal Naval Division, and Archibald Gilmour (right) was also killed on the Somme in August 1916 with the King's Own Scottish Borderers.

He trained in Edinburgh for the Presbyterian ministry, but then moved to London where he trained for the Anglican ministry. Although he would have been seen as an outsider in the established Church of England, he had a reputation for scholarship and quickly developed a career in the church. His first ministries were in city parishes in London and Bristol, but shortly before he was 40, he was appointed Vicar of Earlsfield, a prosperous London suburb. He and his family – there were two sons and two daughters – would have been comfortably established there when the Reverend Watson died suddenly. He was 48 years of age, and it is known that he died in Egypt, but it's not clear whether he suffered an accident or illness on holiday, or whether he was abroad to convalesce. As a result, the family had to leave their home at the Vicarage to make room for his successor. However, it is a comment on the family's attachment to the parish that, when Watson entered Harrow in 1905, he was recorded as the "son of the Vicar of Earlsfield", as if his father were still alive and in post.

From Earlsfield the family moved first to Eastbourne, where William's elder brother Patrick was educated. Later they moved to Harrow-on-the-Hill, adjacent to the famous public school. Though Harrow was predominantly a boarding school, William was one of a small group of boys living nearby who were treated as 'home-boarders'. William followed his brother to Oxford but, a year before this picture was taken, the family suffered another tragic loss.

At Easter 1913 Patrick Watson had recently been ordained. He and his sisters went to Oxford to celebrate his graduation as an MA, but a happy outing on a punt went dreadfully wrong. The boat overturned and Patrick disappeared. His body was recovered from the river the next day. There is nothing in Watson's published work which deals with that incident or his father's sudden death, but it seems likely that those sad events would have reinforced his stoicism in the face of adversity which was part of the public school culture.

By any standards, Watson enjoyed an outstanding education. At Harrow his tutor was George Townsend Warner, a published historian with a national reputation who had also published a guide to the writing of history. Watson was awarded school prizes for his history essays, and won a scholarship to Balliol College to read modern history. Between Harrow and Oxford, he went to Germany where he studied economics and German at Göttingen – a

Sadders' picture taken at Carlow shows Watson's exceptional height. When he was commissioned in 1915 (see Timeline, pages 213–216) he was given special leave to have a uniform made to measure in Paris.

university which enjoyed a similar reputation for scholarship and liberal thought to Oxford. He evidently flourished once he reached Oxford – he was President of the College Debating Society, founded *The Blue Book* (a review), and was a member of the Inaugural Committee of University Liberal Club.

Balliol College, as it still does, enjoyed a reputation both for scholarship and the rôle it played in educating statesmen and academics. It was a college which had deep rooted connections to Scotland, and was named after its founder John Balliol, a mediaeval king of Scotland. Watson gravitated towards men with a Scottish background – his circle of friends included the young college tutor, Robert Gibson, from Glasgow, and Scottish undergraduates such as Alec Hepburne-Scott and Robert Whyte. All these men volunteered for the army when war came, and those three all served in Scottish regiments.

Nothing is known about Watson's experience of motorcycling before he enlisted. It's unlikely that he owned a machine when war broke out, for he followed the recruiting officer's suggestion of buying a new motorcycle for immediate delivery. In the first chapter he wrote that he offered himself for the Intelligence Corps – this was a new formation which recruited men with good modern languages and the analytic skills which Watson possessed in abundance. He was rejected only because they had enough recruits already. The Intelligence Corps officers who went to France with the Expeditionary Force were also mounted on motorcycles, so his riding skills would have been useful, but maybe he was fortunate to have been rejected because the Intelligence Corps sustained a high casualty rate in the first weeks of the war.

Watson's other defining characteristic was his exceptional height – at his medical examination he measured 6' 6½", and when the Signal company halted in the town of Ham on the way to Landrecies, he was "ceremoniously measured against a lamp-post".[1] Watson stood out from his colleagues, even though most of the original despatch riders in 5th Signal Company measured around 6 foot – only Stanley Polhill was significantly shorter than his colleagues.

The author's portrait was taken at a fashionable London studio, probably during his leave in December 1914.

---

1   See Chapter 2, page 28.

'Adventures of a Despatch Rider' is a faithful account of Watson's six months in the ranks, and there's no need to repeat here the story of Watson's rôle as a despatch rider. However, he does not mention that he was awarded the Distinguished Conduct Medal for his work on the Aisne and at Givenchy. He was commissioned in the field in February 1915 as Second Lieutenant in the 5th Division Cyclist Company. His unit went into the front line at the beginning of the Second Battle of Ypres, and he was wounded at Boesinghe on 23 April. A shell fragment was removed from his leg at the Duchess of Westminster's Hospital at Le Touquet, and from there he was repatriated to England on 4 May 1915.

By August 1915 he had made a full recovery and was promoted Captain, seemingly direct from Second Lieutenant. He was put in command of the Cyclist Company of the 16th (Irish) Division and joined them at Fermoy. After a period of intense training, he returned to France with his new unit early in December 1915.

On his return to France, he was temporarily assigned to the staff of the 16th Division. However, he preferred command to staff work, and in July 1916 he was promoted Major and given the command of X1 Corps Cyclist Battalion. He stayed in that position till December 1916. Meanwhile, he took the opportunity during home leave in August 1916 to marry Barbara Wake Walker, and he and his wife set up home at his mother's house in Harrow.

Moving next to the Tank Corps, he commanded D Battalion of the Tank Corps for twelve months from January 1917. He and his unit served at Bullecourt (April and May 1917), Third Ypres (July to September 1917), and various actions at Cambrai (November 1917).

He returned to England on 26 January 1918. The War Office recorded, candidly, that he was sent back to England as a "tired officer". He was then assigned to train a Carrier Tank Company. This was a new concept, described in detail in 'Company of Tanks',[1] in which obsolete tanks were deployed as armoured personnel carriers rather than fighting vehicles in their own right. He returned with this unit to France in June 1918, and served out the remainder of the war with them. By a strange coincidence, the company reached Le Cateau just before the Armistice. He had last seen the town when he and 5th Signal Company retreated from the battlefield in August 1914.

On demobilisation in January 1919, he went into the home Civil Service. He spent the rest of his career in the Ministry of Labour, concerned initially with the employment of juveniles. He served as Private Secretary to Ministers of Labour in the late 1920s and by the time of his death had reached the rank of Assistant Secretary.

He continued to write and publish after the success of 'Adventures'. Blackwood's published 'Tales of a Gaspipe Officer' in *Maga* in 1915 and 1916, but the serialisation was interrupted by the censors (see Appendix I) and the final instalment did not appear until 1917. 'Tales of a Gaspipe Officer' has less impact than 'Adventures of a Despatch Rider', and sometimes seems almost contrived. That may be partly due to the way that Watson distanced himself from the action by writing about "Gaspipe" and his exploits in the third person. When the expurgated 'Adventures' was ready for publication in 1917, a final instalment of 'Tales' appeared in *Maga*, but he published nothing more until 1920 when 'Company of Tanks' appeared. It covers the whole period from late 1916 to early 1919. During the 1920s he published two anthologies of historical stories written for schoolchildren.

He died just before Christmas 1932, leaving a widow and two teenage sons and a daughter. Apparently he died of pneumonia – it was a short illness following a chill caught while playing tennis. His widow believed that his heart had been weakened as a result of a bad attack of trench fever from which he nearly died during the war.

---

1   Watson, Company of Tanks (1920). Chapter 14.

THREE SCOTTISH SCHOLARS

Robert Barbour Whyte (1892–1915)

The outbreak of war found Robert Whyte, a close friend and colleague of Watson at Balliol, at home in Edinburgh. His father was the Principal of New College, the Free Church School of Divinity which was later incorporated into Edinburgh University. Robert had been educated at Clayesmore, an independent boarding school near Reading, before going up to Balliol a year ahead of Watson. When he graduated in 1913, he returned to the family home in Edinburgh's fashionable Charlotte Square and began his training as a chartered accountant.

Second Lieutenant Robert Whyte – pictured in the uniform of the The Black Watch in 1915.

Robert was even quicker off the mark than Watson in getting into uniform, for he signed up on 5 August 1914 as a private in the "Dandy Ninth", the 9th Battalion Royal Scots. As he had been born at Bonskeid, a village between Pitlochry and Blair Athol, this choice of regiment reflected his Highland background. The Dandy Ninth was the Edinburgh Territorial battalion of a Highland regiment, modelled on the "London Scottish" concept. It was initially deployed on coastal defence duties in Scotland but, if Robert had stayed with it, he would have arrived in France in February 1915.

However, he chose to apply for a commission in a Regular unit, and in October he was gazetted into the Black Watch. He joined the 1st Battalion in France early in 1915, just about the time that Watson was wounded. He and Watson corresponded frequently, and they met for the last time in early September when they were both on leave. He was killed at Hill 60 later that month.

Alexander Noel Hepburne Scott (1891–1915)

"Alec" was another Scot who had been educated at an English public school, before entering Balliol College, with its strong Scottish connections. The grandson of Lord Polwarth, he was one of seven children, having two brothers and four sisters. His housemasters at Repton School thought he was gentler and less assertive than his peers, but he was clearly well-liked, as he was at Balliol.

According to Chapter One of 'Adventures', Watson and Alec were in London, preparing for their final examinations at Oxford, when the crisis erupted. After war was declared and Watson signed on as a despatch rider, Alec joined the London Scottish as a private soldier. The regiment, part of the Territorial Army, was earmarked for home defence, but it was generally expected that the best-trained Territorial units such as the London Scottish would be sent to France before any New Army regiments were ready. And so it proved.

Alec was the only one of the three brothers to see active service. In September 1914 the London Scottish were the very first Territorial unit to land in France, where a disappointment awaited them. Instead of being sent into the front line, the battalion was used as 'line of communication' troops – they became railwaymen and dockers, escorted prisoners, and even provided a guard of honour for VIPs in Paris. Alec was probably among the London Scottish soldiers whom Watson met at Abbeville in October. Watson mentions meeting a couple of friends in a restaurant at Abbeville who complained about "L of C" duties. We can be sure Watson met Alec, probably for the last time, in Béthune in mid-January on the tour he described in Chapter Twelve.

Alexander Hepburne-Scott was known affectionately as "Alec" by Watson and his circle at Balliol.

It was not till late October that the London Scottish saw action for the first time at Wytschaete where it suffered heavy casualties. Alec survived that engagement, but he was invalided home with a bout of jaundice in January. On his recovery, rather than returning to France as a private soldier, he applied for a commission in the Regular army, and was gazetted Second Lieutenant in the Scots Guards on 9 March 1915. He was posted to France in April 1915, and was reported missing in the trenches near Festubert on 16 May. He was never seen again and in due course it was presumed that he had been killed that day.

Robert Gibson (1886–1915)

A Balliol Scot like Robert Whyte and Alec Hepburne-Scott, Gibson displayed the same characteristic combination of academic excellence with a commitment to the Officer Training Corps. As Watson put it, "he proved for all time that nobody made a better soldier than the young don". He came from an academic background – his father was headmaster of a Glasgow secondary school and his uncle was Professor of Mathematics at Glasgow University, where Robert completed his first degree. He entered Balliol in 1907 and graduated with 1st class honours in 1910. After a short period studying in Berlin, he became a Fellow of Balliol and Classics Tutor.

In August 1914 he applied for a commission rather than trying to enlist in the ranks. What is remarkable, however, is that he made his application on 3rd August, the day before war was declared. His order of preference was the Wiltshire Regiment, King's Own Scottish Borderers, or the Scottish Rifles. In the event he was commissioned in the 2nd Battalion KOSB.

Gibson died at Hill 60 on 5 May 1915. According to his obituary he was a born teacher but "he always had hankerings after a life of action,

Gibson was a classics tutor and junior Fellow at Balliol when war broke out – five years older than Watson, Alec Hepburne-Scott, and Robert Whyte, he was the first of the group to die in action.

and the zest with which he threw himself into the war showed how fitted he was for such a life."

THE MOTORCYCLE ARTIFICERS

Cecil Stanley Burney (1884–1964) and Edward Alexander (Alick) Burney (1886–1971)

As vintage motorcycle enthusiasts we were in the middle of our research into the Blackburne – or Burney & Blackburne – motorcycle when we stumbled upon the Burney brothers' medals and photograph albums which we found in a country auction. That chance find led us into our long investigation into the extraordinary story of the 1914 despatch riders, and the lives and achievements of the motorcyclists of the 5th Division.

The Burneys had a dual rôle in the Signal company. They were both despatch riders and motorcycle artificers, responsible for maintaining and repairing all the unit's motorcycles. They were older than most of their colleagues, and had not enjoyed a university education like most of them.

Cecil and Alick were close to one another throughout their lives, though not inseparable. They were the only children of James Burney and his wife Gertrude. James described himself as a gentleman, though his profession (if any) is unknown. The youngest of 11 children of a Portsmouth educationalist, he was born in Bruges and died in Tenby at the youthful age of 35. The scant information we have suggests that the family was struggling financially. For example, James may have been born abroad because his parents had taken refuge from creditors by crossing the Channel.

There are other subtle indications that James Burney was born into a failing family. He moved around for no apparent reason – he married in London, and the family moved away from Hampshire. They were briefly in Berkshire where Cecil was born, then moved to Buckinghamshire where Alick was born, and they finally settled in a village near Ross-on-Wye.

By contrast with James Burney's uncertain financial background, his wife Gertrude Finlay was the daughter of a prosperous cotton merchant from Paisley who retired to live in Essex. Her father left most of his fortune to his eldest son, but Gertrude Burney probably enjoyed financial support from her family.

Little is known about the brothers' education save that Alick spent two years at Bradfield School in Berkshire. It was founded in the 1850s "for the careful education of boys as loving children of the Church of England", and the school offered an educational experience equivalent to a minor public school of that period, including fagging and cold showers. Perhaps

The Burneys photographed by Geoffrey de Havilland in December 1914 (Cecil on the left and Alick on the right) – to their fellow DRs they were 'Cecil' (or 'the older Cecil') and 'Grimers'.

more forward-looking than some public schools, Bradfield established an Engineering Class in 1900, which Alick joined.

After Alick left school, he and Cecil became apprentice engineers at Willans & Robinson in Rugby – a major firm which became better known under the name English Electric. There a life-changing event occurred, for they encountered an older apprentice who had built a home-made motorcycle. His name was Geoffrey de Havilland, later an aviator and founder of the de Havilland Aircraft Company.

De Havilland's motorcycle was an inspiration for the Burneys. In 1903 Geoffrey had built his first motorcycle from a set of instructions published in *The English Mechanic and World of Science*, using a proprietary kit of parts. However, this machine had been very disappointing in many respects, so de Havilland set about designing a new engine with mechanical valves, detachable head and a one piece crank. He constructed the prototype with help from the apprentice school at Willans & Robinson in Rugby, where the Burneys watched this machine being built with amazement. When de Havilland left Rugby, he sold the Burneys his spare castings and drawings, and the rights of manufacture – all for the sum of £5. The brothers made up two engines and installed them in copies of de Havilland's frame. With the robust design of these machines complemented by their own tuning skills, they achieved many competition successes and eventually conceived the idea of going into business to manufacture the 'de Havilland motorcycle'.

However, both the brothers moved on from Rugby before those plans bore fruit. Alick, for example, visited Buenos Aires in 1908, probably to oversee the installation of a stationary engine. By 1911 Cecil had a job as a motorcycle development rider and engineer with Rudge-Whitworth in Coventry, and Alick was working with Godfrey and Nash at Hendon, assembling the GN cyclecar in a shed on Archie Frazer-Nash's grandfather's farm.

In 1912 the Burneys fulfilled their ambition of setting up a firm to manufacture motorcycles. Cecil was already a well-known competition rider, and setting up their own firm allowed them to concentrate their energies on production. The aviator, Captain Harold Blackburn, provided them with £200 as working capital to establish Burney & Blackburne Ltd at Tongham, near Aldershot. They were soon joined there by a younger pair of engineering brothers. Cecil Quinlan Roberts, tall and burly, started an engineering degree at Cambridge in autumn 1910 but dropped out after only four terms, and Allan Quinlan Roberts, who was strikingly smaller than his brother, joined the firm too – he was just seventeen years of age.

No doubt the passion which the Roberts' brothers showed for engineering tested the patience of their father. George Quinlan Roberts, who was born in Australia, studied at Oxford as a Rhodes Scholar in the 1880s. He first came to public notice as an athlete and later held a prominent position in public life as Secretary of St Thomas's Hospital.

Burney & Blackburne quickly won a reputation for performance machines built to a high quality. After some experiments with valve gear, they adopted a simple sidevalve design closely based on the de Havilland engine. It also featured an outside flywheel, a one piece crankshaft made from a forged steel billet and a detachable head. Three machines were constructed and first shown to the press in February 1913. After adding some refinements, the Burneys and the Roberts showed the three prototypes at Brooklands in September 1913 (see picture on the next page).

When war broke out a year after this picture was taken, both pairs of brothers volunteered as despatch riders. The Burneys were the first motorcyclists to reach 5th Signal Company while the Roberts' brothers were assigned to GHQ Signal Company. Though many despatch riders went to France with motorcycles they had bought, the Burneys were probably the only riders to reach France on machines they had designed and built.

The quality of their work was immediately recognized by the other motorcyclists. Stanley Polhill, a Cambridge-trained engineer, wrote "the two Blackburns [were] an unknown but beautifully designed bicycle." Watson singled out the fine qualities of the Blackburne motorcycle, and his

The prototype Burney & Blackburne motorcycles were tested by *The Motor Cycle* at Brooklands in September 1913. From left to right, Alick poses on AR3348, a solo machine with a three speed Armstrong hub gear, Cecil holds AR3349, another solo with a fixed single speed belt drive, and Cecil Quinlan Roberts rides AA6327, fitted with a three speed hub, with his brother Allan in the sidecar.

testimonial was featured by the firm in its wartime publicity (see page 255). According to Sergeant Merchant, who was responsible for the Signal company's equipment, these two machines lasted longer during the war than any other in the company.

Generally the wastage rate among motorcycles with the Expeditionary Force was severe. Yet a report in September 1914 in *The Motor Cycle* weekly paper recorded that "the Blackburnes were among the few machines used by the despatch riders that had given absolutely no trouble…but E.A. Burney had lost his owing to its being driven over by heavy artillery". Alick's bike was written off only a month after landing in France – when Polhill was photographed late in September whimsically posing on the bike's frame, the registration number AR3348 is clearly visible!

The Burneys were recruited to the joint rôles of despatch riders and motorcycle artificers, on an enhanced rate of pay. Other men from the motorcycle industry were recruited as despatch rider/artificers – they included Howard Newman, who rode Ivy motorcycles in the TT, Frederick North, the Ariel competition rider, and Vernon Busby, who managed the Sunbeam team in the Isle of Man in 1914. In fact Busby arrived in France on one of the works machines which had been raced in the TT.

As summer gave way to autumn the Army Service Corps developed depots and workshops which supplied new machines, and where motorcycles were repaired and maintained. However, during the Retreat the whole burden fell on the artificers.

In addition to their responsibilities as artificers, the Burneys took a full share of despatch riding duties. At Le Cateau Alick fetched a knapsack full of fuses for the heavy artillery. On the lighter side he joined Watson and Danson blackberrying above Attichy. He was grazed by a sentry's bullet at Vinantes, and a few days after the Battle of the Marne, the brothers found themselves on duty one night, together with Watson in a forest. It was a difficult assignment particularly for Alick, because he couldn't see well at night, and he rode nervously with a loaded revolver in one hand. Perhaps he was as much a danger to his own side as to the enemy. The same night Cecil commented on the stench as he passed an obelisk in the forest, assuming that the source was the

The day after their arrival at Bailleul, Alick (back to camera) and Cecil Burney get down to repairs on one of the Signal company's Triumph motorcycles.

carcasses of dead horses. Watson informed him that what he hadn't seen was the bodies of eight German soldiers.

The Burneys were among the first to go on leave in early December. On their return, Alick hand-printed the menu for the despatch riders' Christmas dinner, and the CO instructed him to start planting vegetables for the spring. But long before the crop came up, the brothers left 5th Signal Company – Cecil was one of the first to be commissioned as a motorcyclist officer in the Royal Engineers in January 1915. As Watson put it, he went home "to train the despatch riders of the New Armies". A month later, Alick was commissioned in the Army Service Corps Motorised Transport Section (which Roy 'Moulders' Meldrum had joined in December).

Cecil served out the war with the Signals Service in France, reaching the rank of Captain, while Alick remained with the Army Service Corps. It seems that Alick emerged from the war in better shape than his brother, and by demobilization he was permanently based at the ASC depot in Bedford. In the final year of the war Cecil had a troubling pattern of unexplained absences. He overstayed leave in England more than once. Although he claimed this was due to debility and sleeplessness, he got an unsympathetic hearing at the resultant medical boards.

By 1919 Burney & Blackburne, the firm they had founded, was changed beyond recognition. George Quinlan Roberts appointed a new manager, Stanton Wilding Cole, when the Burneys left for France, and under Cole the firm won contracts to develop new technology for the War Office. When peace came motorcycle production resumed briefly, but the production of complete motorcycles was soon outsourced to the Osborn Engineering Company, known as OEC, in Portsmouth. Thereafter Blackburne concentrated on the manufacture of a range of engines for motorcycles and other applications. Blackburne engines were fitted to many vehicles, including boats, light cars, aeroplanes, and even lawnmowers.

Cecil (left) and Alick (right) pictured with their mother at Durrant's Farm, Northchurch. In the summer of 1915, they were both Second Lieutenants – the original picture in their album is ruefully captioned "Happy days when we were both equal!".

The Burneys prominently displayed this treasured photograph of Cecil, which was taken at the end of the war.

Alick posed with the prototype Burney 350cc motorcycle. This was made to Alick's design by Warrick of Reading, a long-established maker of trade bicycles. It featured an outside flywheel very similar to the original Blackburnes, but was not a commercial success.

Neither Cecil or Alick Burney, nor Allan Roberts (Cecil Roberts was killed in 1915) returned to the firm. It seems that the Burneys were left nursing a grievance, believing that the company's owners and managers had treated them unfairly. Alick joined Powell Brothers, an engineering firm in Wrexham, where he worked on a range of new motorcycles. However, the project was not a success and he returned south. In 1923 he went into business with Captain Oliver Baldwin, a Brooklands star, and he developed a motorcycle with a new engine along the lines of his original engine, still with an outside flywheel but with a one piece sidevalve barrel of more conventional design. They employed Warrick of Reading to manufacture these motorcycles, but they were not commercially successful.

The brothers' last known joint venture occurred in 1926 when they designed a new motorcycle, powered by 680cc JAP twin engines. It was sold as the Burney motorcycle but the venture was a failure. Cecil's own machine survives in a private collection, and it is rumoured that another machine, belonging to Alick, was destroyed in an air-raid during the World War.

Meanwhile, Cecil briefly went back to work for his old friends, Nash and Godfrey, as a GN works driver, competing with some success in trials and long distance events in 1920 and 1921. In 1921 he designed and built a cyclecar powered by an 8 hp Blackburne V-twin engine, but it was not a success. He then went to Scotland where he started a short-lived garage enterprise in Dunfermline with help from some of his service friends. This enterprise having failed, he started a long-running and successful business dealing in early cars and motorcycles of the sort he himself had manufactured and ridden. From its inception in 1930 he was involved in the Pioneer Run for veteran motorcycles, and in 1946, Cecil was invited by "Titch" Allen to be the first secretary of the Vintage Motor Cycle Club. In this rôle Cecil found lasting success in retirement, which he spent in Hampshire and Surrey.

Throughout their lives the Burney brothers remained close to one another but neither left any family. From surviving travel records we know that they holidayed together in Algiers in

1927, soon after winding up their mother's estate. Cecil never married. In middle age Alick wed Esme Davie, who had been widowed twice – her second husband Brigadier-General Davie died a year before she married Alick in 1943. Although Esme survived him, it's doubtful whether they were still together. She retired to Gloucestershire and was not mentioned in his will, while Alick moved to Haslemere where he died in 1971. Cecil pre-deceased him, dying at Godalming in 1964.

THE FIRST CASUALTY

Henry Goode Fielding Johnson (1894–1914)

Henry was one of the earliest British casualties of the First World War. He was last seen alive on 24th August 1914, the day after the Battle of Mons. The exact circumstances of his death will never be known. Although he was not declared dead until 1916, it is likely that he died shortly after he was last seen, on the second day of contact with the enemy.

Henry was one of the younger motorcyclists – far less travelled than Bagshaw who was only three months older than him, and with much less life experience than Trepess who grew up in a similar family in the neighbouring county. Henry was born at Goscote Hall in Glenfield, now a suburb of Leicester, third and youngest son of the owner of Fielding & Johnson, a worsted spinning business. An aunt who wrote their family history described him as full of energy and with a sense of adventure. The headmaster of his prep school in Brighton found him "cheerful and merry; not very industrious but with good abilities". He progressed to public school at Rugby, and with interests in Natural Science and Engineering, it was natural for him to apply to Pembroke College, Cambridge, a college noted for its engineering training, which had, and still has, strong links with Rugby School.

He began his university course in autumn 1913, studying mechanical sciences. War was declared on the August bank holiday, and that found him in Cambridge – probably in residence during the Long Vacation to catch up on his studies. We know that he had his own motorcycle because he rode to Leicester to ask his father's permission to enlist. Then he motorcycled to Chatham.

On August 7th he was sworn in as a despatch rider, and he was one of three 'Tabs' (Cambridge men) among the ten riders who left Chatham on 9th August. The following week the 5th Division sailed from Dublin, and both Watson and Sergeant Merchant mention his helpful presence at Le Havre.

His disappearance is referred to in several places, including, unusually, the Unit War Diary, where the names of 'other ranks' were rarely mentioned. He set off with a message at 6.30 am. When he failed to return, George Owen and Alick Burney were sent in his place. When they too failed, Watson set off. The ill-fated message was seemingly never delivered.

Henry Goode Fielding Johnson was the only one of the original 5th Division motorcyclists to die in service as a despatch rider.

Some hopeful information turned up in December 1914. Private Wade, from the Lincolnshire Regiment, who had been in action nearby that day, told Fielding Johnson's family that he had come across him on the roadside, lying among men who had been wounded in a skirmish.[1] He and his colleagues helped the wounded men to a nearby convent hospital, and they stayed with him while a doctor dressed his wounds and reassured him that he would be alright. Wade believed that the convent was soon over-run by the Germans, and he assumed the survivors had been taken prisoner. Owen, writing in 1926, recalled how it was thought that he had been "lanced by a roving patrol of Uhlans and then taken into a convent by some nuns."

Nothing more was ever heard, and after two years' absence he was declared dead. His loss is reflected in the poignant epigraph on the menu of the Christmas dinner, celebrating "the 10 surviving motor cyclists of the famous 5th Division". Owen remembered him as cheerful and companionable. During the short time he had known him, they got on very well. His disappearance brought home to them the fact that any of them at any moment might meet a similar fate.

As there were no eye-witnesses to confirm their son's death, the Fielding Johnson family suffered years of hope and uncertainty. Even after abandoning hope that he might be a prisoner, there remained the possibility that he had survived behind enemy lines. In the fast-moving actions around Mons and during the first days of the war, many men who were separated from their units survived behind the lines and then successfully rejoined their units days or weeks later. For example, one Bernard Montgomery, then a junior officer in the 1st Battalion Royal Warwickshires, brought a small group of men back after two days behind enemy lines.[2] Others, alone or in groups, headed for Antwerp or Holland. Some lived off the land for weeks, and others were sheltered by civilians. A handful survived for years as fugitives, only emerging from hiding after the Armistice, but many others who had found shelter with the local population were betrayed to the Germans. Most of these were executed as spies.

Happily, his brothers survived the war, and despite his early death, Henry Goode Fielding Johnson is still remembered. His great-nephew researched his disappearance and visited Mons in August 2014, trying unsuccessfully to locate the hospital where he was last seen. He is also commemorated in Leicester University. The Fielding Johnson Building, donated by the family to the newly founded University College in 1921, carries his name as a memorial to the son who did not return.

ONE OF THE DESPATCH RIDERS GOT AWAY

Eric Bagshaw (1894–?)

Eric Bagshaw was one of the three despatch riders in 5th Signal Company who was born overseas. His grandfather, William Bagshaw, emigrated to the Cape Colony in 1860, and spent 40 years in Port Elizabeth, returning to Manchester on retirement. Although William was trained as a mason, he set up a tannery in partnership with a man from Bradford. Industry in the Cape Colony was in its infancy, and the two Englishmen saw the possibilities in the leather business. Raw materials were plentiful, and there was a growing demand for locally produced leather goods, such as saddles, harnesses, and everyday footwear. Then, in the 1880s, gold was discovered in the Transvaal and their fortunes were made. Port Elizabeth became a major port of entry to the goldfields. It was known as the 'Liverpool of South Africa', and the long-term success of their business was assured.

Eric's father, Thomas Ponsonby Bagshaw (1864–1915) was William's only child, and he joined the business in his early twenties. A local historian who was commissioned to write a history of

---

1   See Timeline, Part 1, page 183.
2   Murland, Retreat and Rearguard 1914, p151.

This is the only known picture of Eric Bagshaw on his own rather than in a group. It was probably taken on a chilly day in December 1914 – Eric was brought up in a warm climate and would have found the French winter bracing.

the company trashed his reputation, describing him as "a thoroughly spoilt young man" with no interest in the business, whether tannery, retail shop or the leather trade in general. It was said that he only put in an occasional appearance at the office, and would look round briefly before disappearing; he was a heavy pipe smoker and avid sportsman, keen on team games such as cricket and shooting game. Yet his father's business partner tolerated this behaviour, and the business continued to thrive after he replaced his father.[1]

TP Bagshaw and his wife Edith had ten children – Eric was the eldest son. So, while his father had been brought up as an only child, Eric enjoyed a very different experience. There were two daughters before Eric, and he was followed by two more sons and five more daughters. In 1895, when he was aged one, the entire family sailed to England – the parents and their five children, along with the paternal grandparents and Edith's mother.

The occasion for that trip may have been TP Bagshaw's desire to reconnect his growing clan with their extended family in England – or perhaps they were just seeking a break from their home conditions. The owners of Bagshaw & Gibaud lived close to their employees in the leather works. The firm's original works, a primitive and noxious site, was sold to become the site for Port Elizabeth's new docks about the time that Eric was born, but the family probably still lived close to an unpleasant business.

That was the first of Eric's many trips to England. At the age of nine, he arrived in England to become one of the first pupils of the newly-established Bournemouth School. Although the school offered a boarding option, his father rented accommodation in the town, and Eric attended the school as a day boy from 1903 to 1909. He took part in the school production of 'HMS Pinafore' in 1905, and gained his first military experience in the Officer Training Corps.

---

1   Redgrave, In the shoes of William Bagshaw (2005).

George and Mrs Owen with King George VI. They were presented to the King in May 1947 at the British Industries Fair at Earl's Court which George was responsible for running.

despatch rider because they couldn't ride a motorcycle, George was able to get straight into the Royal Engineers and join the Expeditionary Force. His next brother, Francis, enlisted as a private in the Royal Fusiliers, and was killed in action in March 1916. His youngest brother, Ralph, was commissioned in the Royal Marines in 1917, and he too served in France.

George is one of the most memorable characters in 'Adventures'. Known simply as 'George', he is often the unofficial quartermaster or "the scrounger". He seems to have had more than his share of motorcycling mishaps and misadventures, and his War Office file contains a disciplinary record – he was reprimanded for disobeying an order in October 1914, and, after being promoted Sergeant, he was quickly reduced to Corporal again. Nonetheless his application for a commission was accepted in June 1916 and he served out the war as a Royal Engineers subaltern in Salonika, though he contracted malaria while there.

He was demobilized early in 1919, and married Doris Haines in 1920. Like Overton, he had an outstanding career in the Home Civil Service. As a senior civil servant at the Board of Trade, he went to Washington in 1943 as a member of the British trade delegation, and he ended his career as Under Secretary of State. He was appointed CB on his retirement.[1]

---

1   CB denotes Companion of the Order of the Bath, an order of chivalry reserved for senior civil servants and senior military officers.

Throughout his married life he lived in Hampstead. In the 1930s he shared a large house with his parents and his father-in-law Professor Haines who, with his father, was involved in the production of the Oxford Patristic Greek Dictionary. He and his wife spent their holidays in Devon where they had holidayed as children, but to their regret they had no children of their own.

His great-nephew wrote that he was remembered as very kind, witty and urbane and a real scholar. He said that George's sharp intellect caused him sometimes to give offence, and he wondered whether it was this characteristic which cost him the top job and a knighthood.

John Francis Danson (1895–1970)

Jack, nicknamed "N'soon," was the youngest of the 5th Signals motorcyclists, nearly two months short of his nineteenth birthday when he enlisted. He was one of a family of six – he had two elder sisters but he was the eldest son. Like all but his youngest siblings, he was born in Rangoon where his father was a merchant and businessman.

Although the Dansons returned to England when Jack was five, the family continued to have links and commercial ties with Burma. In the 1911 census his father recorded his profession as Director of the Rangoon Electric Tramway and Supply Company. His youngest brother and sister were born in England, and the family settled initially in London although their roots were in Cheshire and North Wales. By 1914 the family had moved to Gresford Hall near Chester. Only Jack and Edward were old enough to serve in the war, and Edward was also a survivor.

Jack Danson photographed in 1916 as a new Second Lieutenant – he was one of the last of the 1914 5th Signals despatch riders to be commissioned.

When war was declared, Jack was in the middle of his education. He spent seven years at Stonyhurst College in Lancashire. He left at Christmas 1912, and before going up to Oxford the following September, he worked for an engineering firm in London. The fact that he frequently rode home to Cheshire for the weekend was convincing evidence of his passion for motorcycling – a round trip of more than 400 miles would have been a challenge even 50 years later, let alone in 1913. At Oxford he shared his interest in motorcycling with an older undergraduate at Trinity, Cecil Hayes-Sadler, who took the younger man under his wing. However, whether or not his enthusiasm for motorcycling had any adverse affect on his academic career, Jack failed his first-year law exams. At least one other undergraduate at Trinity, Neville Baker, was an enthusiastic motorcyclist, and he too volunteered as a despatch rider in August 1914 – he was killed at Ypres in 1917. After the war Jack returned to Oxford to complete his degree, but he qualified as an accountant rather than a lawyer.

When he wasn't linked with Cecil Hayes-Sadler, Jack was often paired with Watson, who always wrote about "N'soon," the youngest member of the company, in warm and affectionate terms. He described him as 'dashing' and wrote about his 'tender skin' – and dealt tactfully with the medical problem which put him out of action for several weeks. In November 1914 Jack was diagnosed

Jack Danson (left) pictured at his family's country home in North Wales with Cecil Hayes-Sadler as a visitor soon after they were both commissioned – many years later, Cecil married Jack's younger sister, thus the old friends became brothers-in-law.

with blood poisoning, for which he was hospitalised. That kept him away from the company till January, thus missing the Christmas festivities.

Jack served out the war with the Royal Engineers. He returned home in December 1915 and it was not until June 1916 that he and the remaining three Oxonians were commissioned in the Signal Service. He was demobilised early in 1919. Afterwards he spoke little about the war, though he would remind those who asked that, for all his service on the front, he never went "over the top". The stand-out anecdote was his tragic account of an incident in a quiet area far from the front. He and a colleague were peacefully sharing a mug of tea when, without warning, a stray missile decapitated the other man.

After the war he returned to Burma where he was involved in a number of businesses. Passenger records show that he was a restless and frequent traveller in his 20s and 30s, sailing to the Far East and also to Australia and across the Atlantic.

Jack's life changed again in 1934 when he married Eileen Goold. They settled at Ingatestone in Essex. Their daughter was born in 1935, and their son, born more than ten years later, recalls his father as a contented self-employed businessman. Among other things he wrote a well-regarded tip-sheet for investors which had a large following on Wall Street. His principal hobby was gardening. He passed away peacefully at home in his mid-70s.

Cecil William Hayes-Sadler (1892–1964)

Cecil Hayes-Sadler was the only one of the twelve motorcyclists whose father was a soldier, but he happened to serve in the Army because of the call for motorcyclists on the outbreak of war, rather than any desire to follow in his father's footsteps.

"Sadders" was the third of four children of Major Reginald Hayes-Sadler and Anne Phillips. Major Hayes-Sadler was an officer, first in the Yorkshire Regiment, and then the King's Own Yorkshire Light Infantry. When Cecil's brother was born in 1896, their father returned to Africa, and he remained an absent father during Cecil's childhood and education. During his years in Africa, Major Hayes-Sadler filled a number of posts, such as Commandant of the Post Camp at Pretoria during the Boer War and staff officer with the Political Department in East Africa during the First World War. He didn't return to England until 1917 – by then, Cecil and his sisters, whom he had last seen as children, were grown up and Ralph, his youngest child, had been killed in action.

During his absence, the family lived near Windsor, and like Watson, who attended Harrow School which was conveniently close to his home, Cecil became a boarder at nearby Eton College. There he was in the Army class – it had a permissive regime under which students were allowed to drop more demanding academic subjects such as Greek. When he left Eton, he continued his education at Oxford, entering Trinity College in 1910 to read history. Having failed his first year exams, he took a year off. He came back to re-take his first year exams and succeeded at his third

A 'studio portrait' taken in France – probably during winter 1914 or spring 1915. The machine has been cleaned down, and Cecil is dressed for the portrait and not for riding. He was nearly blind without his glasses, and only passed his medical by memorising the optician's chart.

attempt, resuming his studies in 1913. When he enlisted and left for France, his degree was still unfinished.

In his last year, he met Jack Danson who had just come up to Trinity to study Law. They shared a common interest in motorcycling, and Cecil took the younger man under his wing. They were to remain firm friends for the rest of their lives. They served together as despatch riders, as Royal Engineers officers, and years later Cecil married Jack's younger sister Winifred.

Cecil brought back from France some items of memorabilia which he treasured all his life – including a blue and white brassard, a mud-stained despatch case, and a collection of the maps issued in 1914. His early letters home also survive (see Timeline), but the detailed narrative ceased after the 5th Division moved to Beuvry in October 1914. His willingness to put pen to paper may have faltered when two of his cousins were killed in late October 1914, not far from where Cecil was serving. Cecil's brother Ralph, who was nearly five years his junior, died on the Somme in September 1916.

Cecil was commissioned in the summer of 1916, one of the last four original motorcyclists to take that step. He served out the war in France, and after the Armistice served in the Occupation Zone. When he was demobilised, he applied to join the Colonial Service. His uncle Sir James Hayes-Sadler had been the first Governor of Kenya in 1909, and it was to that colony that he was assigned in 1921. His first posting was to Kisumu on Lake Victoria, but he had no interest in 'climbing the ladder', and soon accepted a transfer to Government House in Nairobi where

he spent the rest of his career. Colonial servants enjoyed home leave every two years – his photograph album records the war memorials under construction in France in 1923 when he visited his brother's and cousin's graves. On leave in 1931 he sought out Jack Danson who had returned from the Far East, and proposed to his sister Winifred. She accepted, and they were married at Government House in Nairobi in December 1931.

He expected to retire from the Colonial Service in 1941. By then he and Winifred had two daughters and were looking forward to returning home, but their plans were thwarted by the outbreak of the Second World War. No civilian travel was possible and no replacement officials were arriving, so Cecil was not released from his duties until 1945. Sadly he and Winifred lost their elder daughter in Kenya – she died of measles shortly before the family returned home.

When they finally reached England, Cecil and his family lodged with the Dansons in Essex before moving to Sussex. Cecil was in poor health – when they arrived in England he weighed only 6 stone – but he soon recovered. Though he didn't enjoy socialising, his

Cecil Hayes-Sadler in Sussex soon after he retired from the Colonial Service in Kenya in 1945.

daughter and niece described him as a happy but self-effacing man. He died peacefully at home aged 72, after suffering a heart attack.

Arnold Edersheim Overton (1893–1975)

Arnold Overton, slim, tall, and energetic, was known to his fellow despatch riders as "Fat Boy" or "Fatters" – no doubt inspired by word-play on 'Over-a-ton'. According to family lore, the Overtons were descended from an officer serving in the Parliamentary forces in the Civil War. Arnold's father was the Vicar of Ware, and his mother was the daughter of a distinguished Jewish scholar who emigrated from Vienna to the UK. His maternal grandfather Alfred Edersheim first joined the Scottish Presbyterian church but was later ordained in the Church of England.

Arnold was one of three brothers, and his generation enhanced the family's reputation with their achievements. His brother Thomas, just one year younger than Arnold, was killed at Gallipoli the day after he went into the front line for the first time. Marcus, the third brother, was born too late to serve in the First World War, but enjoyed a stellar career at the Bar between the wars. In his spare time he served as an officer in the Territorial Army, and he went straight into uniform at the start of the Second World War. He died in 1940 while serving with an anti-aircraft battery.

From the start of his education Arnold showed academic talent, winning a prize at

Arnold Overton (in light-coloured jacket) at Winchester College, aged 14 – on the left is Charles 'Peter' Portal, who also volunteered as a motorcycle despatch rider in August 1914. Portal was commissioned in 1914 and transferred to the Royal Flying Corps. As Viscount Portal of Hungerford, he served as Churchill's Chief of the Air Staff throughout the Second World War.

Winchester for Mathematics, as well as playing cricket, football, and golf. Then he won a scholarship to New College, Oxford, where he studied mathematics before changing to Modern History.

Overton was one of the last four of the original twelve 5th Signal company motorcyclists to be commissioned, at the same time as Danson, Owen, and Hayes-Sadler. Initially he returned to serve as an officer on the Western Front, but later went to Palestine where he was awarded the Military Cross. It's not certain how that came about, but it is rumoured that, as a very junior officer, he was attached to General Allenby's staff. When the General and his headquarters lost their way in the desert, Overton is supposed to have said: "Excuse me, Sir, I know the way" and led them to safety.

Interestingly his grandson recalled being told that Arnold was not too impressed by 'Adventures of a Despatch Rider'. Maybe the book's publication crossed the line between witness and self-promotion. If that was the case, he was admirably consistent, for his first surviving letter home, dated 10th November 1914, is prominently labelled: "Don't send any of this to the papers, please!"

He was demobilised in 1919, and after returning to Oxford to finish his degree he joined the Civil Service. He rose swiftly at the Board of Trade where he had a long record of notable achievements. In 1933 he was a member of Ramsay Macdonald's personal staff when the Prime Minister travelled to Washington to meet Franklin Roosevelt, who was then the newly-elected President of the United States. He led trade missions to the United States before the war, and during the war he was Permanent Secretary of the Board of Trade. In that capacity he played a major rôle in international trade policy. He assisted JM Keynes, and led the British team at the conferences

Arnold Overton (seated left) represented the British Government at the signing of the 1938 Reciprocal Trade Agreement between the United States and Canada. In the front row beside Overton is Sir Ronald Lindsay (British Ambassador to Washington), Franklin Delano Roosevelt, Mackenzie King (Prime Minister of Canada) and Cordell Hull (FDR's long-serving Secretary of State).

Sir Arnold Overton and Lady Overton returning from the Queen's Coronation in 1953.

where GATT (the General Agreement on Tariffs and Trade) was negotiated. This was conceived by Churchill as a way of securing better trading arrangements across the Atlantic, as the war had effectively destroyed Britain's trading with Europe. As a senior mandarin, he was a key player in Whitehall throughout the war, and would have had significant contact there with his old friend Charles Portal, then Chief of the Air Staff. He retired in 1963, having served as Permanent Secretary of the Ministry of Civil Aviation for ten years.

His honours included a knighthood in the Order of St Michael and St George. His obituary in *The Times* described him as a devoted servant of the public, "modest and retiring and apparently devoid of any personal ambition or of any desire to impress people with his own importance." He was survived by his three sons and a daughter. His eldest son, also knighted, was a diplomat who became Ambassador to Hungary.

TWO MORE CAMBRIDGE MEN

Stanley Frederick Philip Polhill (1891–1970)

Like many of the despatch riders, Stanley Polhill came from a family which claimed a rich and complex history of achievement. The Polhills were originally London merchants – for several generations they had been involved with politics, trade, and learning. In the 1780s an ancestor acquired Howbury Hall near Bedford, where Stanley's uncle brought up three sons. He and Stanley's father, Arthur, joined five other adventurers in a group known as the "Cambridge Seven". The Seven were young graduates, none with any strong religious background, who saw themselves as born-again Christians, and responded to an evangelist's call to become missionaries in China. They toured university campuses before leaving for China in 1885 on a wave of enthusiasm. Once there, they scattered to different missions but remained in close contact. Stanley's father married Alice Drake, the daughter of another missionary who attached himself to the Seven.

Stanley Polhill left Chatham for Carlow on a new Triumph, but is pictured here on a Douglas 2¾ hp machine, which was popular in difficult riding conditions – it was easier to manage on treacherous road surfaces, and lighter to pick up once a rider had come off, as frequently happened. This Douglas has been adapted by fitting Triumph front forks – the kind of neat fix which artificers like the Burney brothers pulled off in difficult circumstances to keep machines serviceable.

Arthur and Alice's five sons were all born in China. The youngest, Theo, was born on the eve of the Boxer Rebellion in 1900, when the family was forced to return to England for their own safety. Stanley's parents returned to China as soon as it was safe to do so. They left Stanley and his brothers with their uncle Cecil at Howbury Hall, while they travelled back to China overland across Siberia, taking only baby Theo with them.

At the age of 14 Stanley was enrolled at Trent College near Nottingham, a newly-founded public school. There he was an enthusiastic member of the OTC, and did well enough academically to go up to Jesus College, Cambridge in 1910. Stanley's older brother went into the Church, but Stanley chose otherwise. Maybe conscious of his father's precarious profession as a missionary, he chose to qualify in a profession that would provide a dependable income. He studied physics and engineering at university, and after he graduated in 1913 started a traineeship with a major engineering firm in Bedford. By that time he was an enthusiastic motorcyclist. He had run the motorcycle section of the Cambridge Officer Training Corps and owned a Scott motorcycle which he used for touring.

Stanley was one of the earliest volunteers to arrive at Chatham. Nicknamed 'Pollers', he made an immediate impression on the Royal Engineers. As may be seen from the OTC picture in Appendix ll, he was small in stature – indeed, his son describes him as diminutive. He had natural authority and was put in charge of the group of motorcyclists with whom he travelled to Ireland. On arrival at Carlow the commanding officer of 5th Signals company, Captain Doherty Holwell, immediately promoted him Sergeant.

Stanley had other pressing matters on his mind at that moment. He was courting Evelyn Davidson Wood, daughter of another missionary, and was on the brink of proposing marriage. When he set off for Chatham, he expected that, once recruited, he would be allowed a day or two at home to settle his affairs. However, he learned that he would have to stay at Chatham until he left for Ireland. So he put his proposal in a letter – apologizing for using the war as an excuse for not popping the question face-to-face!

Stanley photographed at Serches with an unknown Sergeant, probably a cyclist despatch rider (note the blue and white brassards).

Polhill is rarely mentioned in 'Adventures', but his own letters and photographs complement Watson's story. Stanley was probably the most proficient photographer in the group. He was also an experienced engineer, and in his letters (see Timeline) we find the authentic voice of the motorcyclist. As the Army would not accept his own motorcycle, he was issued with a brand-new machine. Riding it for the first time en route to Euston, he purred: "my Triumph is a perfectly *lovely* bike, extraordinarily powerful and smooth-running". Looking ahead to an early end to the war, he said he was "rather hoping to be able to take it off the Government at the end at an absurdly low price if the engine is still in good order". A month later, he is still enjoying the machine, but cautious of the wear and tear. "I've got a cracked front spindle which I have to nurse over pavé, but the engine has run beautifully every day and night." The Douglas he rode in 1915 was a much lighter machine, maybe better suited to a rider of his stature.

After the shock of the Retreat and then the bitter fighting and stalemate of late 1914, Stanley's mood seems to have changed. Two weeks into the campaign he was distressed by the sight of abandoned vehicles, but six months later, he talks about despatch riders' casualties almost casually. With the benefit of hindsight it seems that the gloomy casualty figures for motorcyclists were inflated, but there were daily risks to face, and Stanley writes about being "wonderfully fatalistic" about the fact that you can't hide from shells on a motorbike.

No doubt Stanley's leadership in 1914 contributed to the effectiveness of the Unit and the cohesion of the group in a warm and friendly atmosphere. After the turn of the year, members of the original group began to leave with commissions, and the motorcyclists, who had briefly enjoyed excellent facilities at Locre, were uncomfortable, to say the least, in their winter accommodation at St Jans Cappel. There, according to Overton, Stanley had a disagreement with the senior warrant officers and was transferred to the 2nd Army Signal company. Soon afterwards he was commissioned in the Royal Engineers, then shortly transferring to the Royal Flying Corps.

Stanley served on the Western Front as an observer for ten months, and then returned to the UK to train as a pilot. This was a potentially dangerous change of career, as pilot training was notoriously hazardous, more pilots dying in training than in action. After successfully gaining his wings, there was an opportunity for him to remain at Turnberry, training observers in the art of aerial photography. Stanley was joined there by Evelyn, whom he had married in September 1916, and their first daughter was born in Ayrshire.

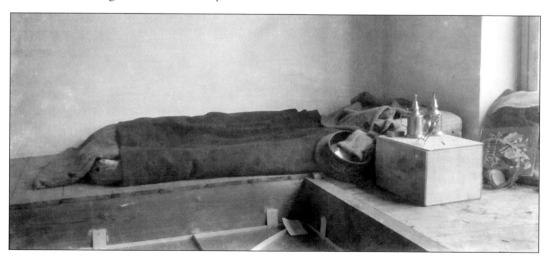

This carefully composed photograph was found among Stanley's negatives – probably now printed for the first time. This photograph depicts an improvised but tidy bed-space, its location unknown – we see his cap propped up behind the two spirit lamps.

Stanley Polhill caught at Beuvry Station. The image is from a damaged negative which spent years in the heat of Kenya, and has probably never been printed before.

Stanley Polhill in later life.

An atmospheric study of Evelyn when she and Stanley lived in married quarters at Turnberry in 1917, where Stanley learned to fly and subsequently worked as an RFC aerial photography instructor. The bed which appears in the picture was still in use thirty years later in the Polhills' home in Kenya.

After the war, Stanley continued to ride regularly, using a motorcycle to commute to work in London from a cottage near Epping Forest which he and Evelyn bought. Engineering work was hard to find, and in winter it was a long and cold hard journey twice a day. They now had two young daughters, and in 1921, when he was offered a position as engineer on a farm in the Kenya Highlands which was being mechanised, the offer was too good to turn down. Stanley set off for Africa with his youngest brother Theo, and the brothers worked for the farm as engineer and accountant. Soon Evelyn and the children followed them.

Unfortunately, their hopes of a secure long-term future were dashed. In 1925 Stanley sustained serious injuries in a bad farm accident – he got caught up in the unguarded moving chains of a harvester. He was fortunate to survive but, having lost a lung and several ribs, he was hospitalised for months. There was no prospect that Stanley would be fit for employment for a long time, so Evelyn took charge and found the family an abandoned farm where they could settle. Over the next twenty five years they turned it from a basic homestead into a productive business, and raised their four children there. In 1963 they retired to Lake Naivasha where Stanley died at the age of 79. After leaving for Kenya in 1922, he returned to England only once, to attend his son's graduation at Cambridge from the college where he himself graduated 45 years earlier.

Edward Farquharson Burkitt Orr (1895–1918)

Edward Orr, like Fielding Johnson, was an undergraduate at Pembroke College, Cambridge. Of the twelve despatch riders who joined 5th Signal Company at Carlow, only he and Fielding Johnson did not survive the war.

His father, James Orr, was the younger son of a Paisley cotton manufacturer. As a middle-aged bachelor, he left Scotland and moved to south-east England, where he married Mary Burkitt in 1882. James and his wife settled near her family in Tunbridge Wells, and they soon had a son and a daughter. Edward, their third child, was born nearly ten years later, when his father was in his early 60s. On the outbreak of war, his brother Esdaile Orr was serving as a Lieutenant in 1st Battalion Royal Berkshire Regiment, part of 6th Infantry Brigade. Thus Edward, who had just finished his first year as a law student, reached France only four days behind his brother, a professional soldier.

Like all the other original despatch riders, Orr applied for a commission, but he was the only one to join the artillery. He was sent for officer training late in 1915, and arrived on the front line as an artillery subaltern in January 1916. He served in 173 Brigade, Royal Field Artillery, a unit armed with the ubiquitous light and manoeuvrable 18-pounders. For six weeks before his death he had been acting as Reconnaissance Officer. There was copious intelligence warning of the coming German offensive – apparently, he returned from reconnaissance on the morning of the German attack and went on to a battalion headquarters. He was standing talking to the Colonel when he was hit by a bullet and killed at once. He is buried at Ham British Cemetery near St Quentin.

One of the few photographs of Orr, taken on Christmas Day 1914..

Orr is rarely mentioned in 'Adventures', and Watson uses Orr's name rather than a nickname. That suggests that the group simply knew him by his Scottish surname, which may have been perceived as a quaint and unfamiliar 'handle'.

After his death his family conducted a short but painful correspondence with the War Office. His sister Janet Orr complained that his possessions were not returned to them promptly. She mentioned that she was the only responsible adult in the family, for her father was too old – he was 85 – and her other brother was serving in East Africa. Orr's mother was a patient at the Holloway Sanatorium in Virginia Water, founded in 1880 for "the cure and care of mental and nervous invalids of the educated classes".

A LATE ARRIVAL

Roy Frederick Alexander Meldrum (1891–1949)

Roy Meldrum, nicknamed "Moulders", was another of the 5th Signals despatch riders who did not go to university. The only son of a naval officer, he was born and brought up in Portsmouth and educated at Rugby School. Roy's father died the year before he left school, and the 1911 Census records Roy living with his widowed mother and employed as a clerk at the Bank of England. He was still working in the City when he volunteered in August 1914, and with no obvious engineering credentials, he must have had some motorcycling experience to persuade the Signal Service that he would make a competent despatch rider.

He was the first of the 5th Signal company despatch riders to achieve a commission. He joined the Motor Transport section of the Army Service Corps, preceding the better-qualified Alick Burney by three months. As Watson put it, he "retired to the quietude" of the ASC, and Overton's comment about Meldrum's "somewhat mysterious commission in the A.S.C.M.T." may reflect his colleagues' uncertain feelings about his choice of career.

Over the remainder of the war he was to be found in a wide range of rôles. For example, he was Roads Officer for 4th Army Supply Column in 1915, officer

Pictured at Rugby School, Meldrum joined the 5th Signals motorcyclists when he was separated from the cavalry brigade he landed with – and he was the first to leave with a commission.

in command of the Caterpillar Tractor section of a Siege battery in 1916, and in charge of various stores and workshops units from then until the Armistice. He remained in the Army after the war, and as a serving officer in 1923, he applied to become an Associate Member of the Institute of Mechanical Engineers. To qualify as a member, he was seconded to Vauxhall Motors where he completed an engineering apprenticeship in his 30s, and he retired from the RASC with the rank of Colonel.

He married in 1918, and he and his wife Elise had a daughter who died as an infant. The newspaper reports of his death in 1949 suggest that his death was unexpected – he was standing for election to a Parish Council at the time. He was survived by his widow who died in 1968.

TWO REGULAR SOLDIERS

Raymond Vernon Doherty Holwell (1882–1917)

The 'Skipper' was a career soldier whose whole life was spent in and around the Army. He was the only child of Major Martin Doherty Holwell of the 2nd Battalion Worcestershire Regiment, and his wife Sarah. He was born near Cork where his father was then stationed. When his father retired, the family moved to Gloucestershire, and Raymond attended Cheltenham College from 1896 to 1899. He excelled in mathematics at school, and from there he headed to the Royal Military Academy at Woolwich. He was commissioned into the Royal Engineers in 1901, promoted Lieutenant in 1904 and Captain in 1911. His postings included the Balloon School – he was in charge of initial flight trials in 1906 – and a period of service with a field company in South Africa in 1911.

He was regarded with warmth and affection by the despatch riders, and it seems that the feeling was reciprocated. He was promoted to Lieutenant-Colonel but in January 1917 he became one of many senior officers who was killed in action, and he was buried in the cemetery at Poperinghe.

Doherty Holwell (back row, middle) was a popular commanding officer, and all the despatch riders who left accounts had only favourable words for him.

A candid photograph captures the moment when the Commanding Officer leaves the Signals HQ. Doherty Holwell (in tall boots, facing left) is about to enter his 'staff car' (the Barré which Alick Burney and Trepess liberated at Missy). The location could be Beuvry or Bailleul – the only identifiable despatch rider is Trepess (immediately to the right of the sentry with rifle).

Dear Mrs Burney,
    I am very sorry not to have written before and acknpwledged the cake and marmalade which turned up safely and which were toppingand very much appreciated. I hope your son gave you my message of thanks I do hope Alick will get his commision in the A.S.C. all right , I think he will. Both of them have done splendidly and I know our bikes have been the best looked afte in the army. They have never minded how much work they had to do and have always been so cheery.
    I was awfully sorry when Cecil left. I wish he could have st stopped on. I tried hardto get a motor cyclist officer allowed for my company but withput avail. I dont know what I shall do when your other don leaves. The original lot of motor cyclist in this company were perfectly splendid. I dont know how we should have got through the trying days at the beginning with out them. I am very glad that we got off with only one casual ty-Fielding Johndon. Please tell Cecil when you writethat I sh shall not be home on leave again as it is stopped from now on. I was hoping to see him again.
                              Yours sincerely,
24.2.15.   Raymond Holwell.

Doherty Holwell's courteous letter to Cecil and Alick's mother.

Francis Victor Merchant (1885–1968)

Like his Commanding officer, Sergeant Merchant was a Regular soldier who was brought up in an Army family. He was born in Nottingham, first child and only son of a senior NCO in the Lincolnshire Regiment.

His father, Jabez Merchant, signed up in his teens, and completed 25 years service in 1908. Regular soldiers in the Victorian army expected to spend many years in distant parts of the Empire, but Jabez saw relatively little overseas service – he spent only one year in Malta in the 1890s and two years in South Africa from 1901. Jabez was nearly 50 in 1914, but he returned to the colours, serving at home, first as a Captain in the Durham Light Infantry and then in the 5th Battalion of his old regiment, the Lincolnshires.

While he was an infant, Frank's time was divided between the regimental depot in Dublin and his grandparents in Cirencester and Nottingham. When he reached the age of five, his father's regiment moved to Aldershot, and the family settled there in married quar-

Pre-war studio portrait of Frank Merchant in uniform.

ters. He was a teenager when his father went to South Africa, and he himself joined the army not long afterwards. He married Madge Sharpe from Sleaford in 1912.

Sergeant Merchant first rode a motorcycle when the despatch riders arrived at Carlow. He preferred to use a combination for its stability and its capacity to carry equipment to the company's outposts. In this photo, the passenger is Sergeant-Major Tibble.

By August 1914 Frank was Pay Sergeant stationed in Carlow with 5th Signal Company. He became a father in July 1914, so, while deeply involved with his many responsibilities on mobilisation, he had to arrange his wife and daughter's journey to her parents' home in Sleaford, where they settled for the duration.

Frank was promoted CQMS in November 1914 and commissioned Second Lieutenant in April 1915. He remained with 5th Signals through the war and became its commanding officer in October 1918.

When he retired from the Army, he and his wife moved to the Isle of Wight. During the Second World War, he returned to military service like his father had done in the First World War – at the age of 58 he became a Lieutenant in the Royal Naval Volunteer Reserve. He died peacefully in 1950, survived by his wife, daughter and grandsons.

Francis Victor Merchant.

Major Merchant at his desk in Aldershot, shortly before his retirement.

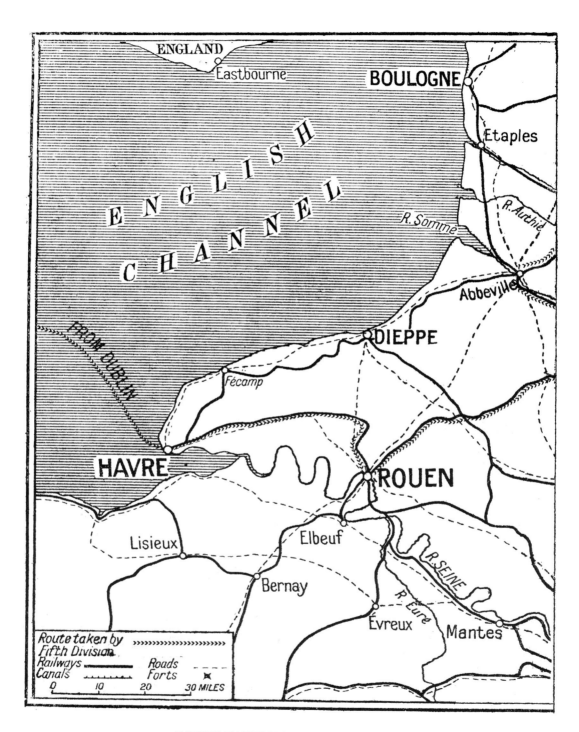

ROUTE TAKEN BY FIFTH DIVISION

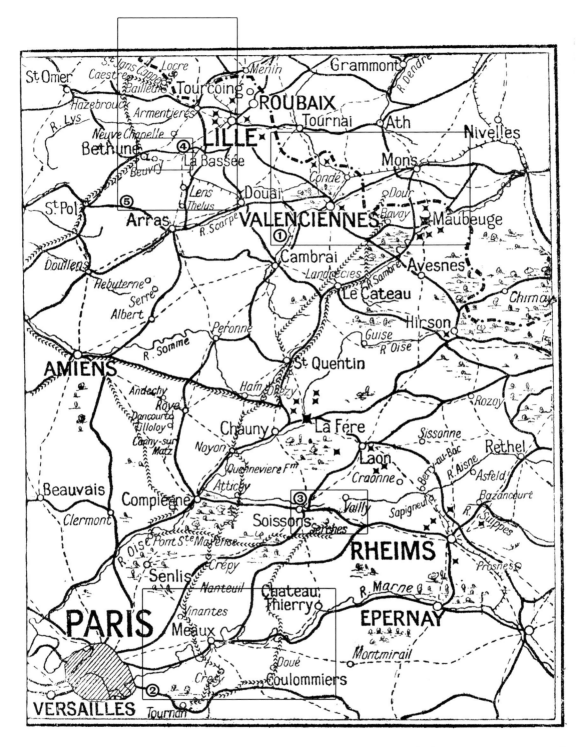

1 ROUND MONS | **2** THE MARNE | **3** THE AISNE | **4** ROUND LA BASSÉE | **5** YPRES TO LA BASSÉE

Timeline

Contents

Part 1

August 1914

GEORGE OWEN: 12 YEARS AGO – A DESPATCH RIDER AT MONS

Reproduced from the Owen family archive

George's reflections on 1914 were written in 1926, although the first paragraph seems to have been written in 1919. This substantial piece only covers the first month of the war – but it contains so much action and excitement that perhaps he had exhausted himself by the time he reached September.

While strolling across Trafalgar Square the other day to extort from my bankers yet another fraction of my dwindling fortune, I realised that I was standing on the exact spot as on the night of August 4th, 1914, and what I saw was a crowd clamouring for release from the army, a necessary but somewhat ironical corollary to the scene of four and a half years ago, of which it reminded me. Whereas now there was a low murmur, a forest of rifles and clanking of shrapnel helmets, then there was deafening cheering, a rare enthusiasm, and, what is still more rare with our crowds, an unself-conscious waving of hats; among those hats were those of three brothers, and one of these was mine.[1]

We were dazed, I remember, at the thought of war, but felt no doubt that war there would be. In the light of what I was told in Paris not many weeks later, of the sickening anxiety of France as to the attitude of England, the sincerity of this crowd is a touching memory. I doubt whether the violation of Belgium was uppermost in most minds, but there was certainly a great loyalty, loyalty to the Entente, loyalty to the abstract idea of justice, loyalty to self. And there, to help us in our doubt, were the first profiteers, the sellers of little union jacks; but we did not grudge them the reward of their foresight, for they had gauged the will of England before the politicians had voiced it, or their majesties on the darkened balcony of Buckingham Palace, to which we were swept irresistibly, had sanctioned it.

When England had spoken for war, we hurried to the Old Gambrinus,[2] not to hobnob with the many Huns who frequented it, but merely to satisfy an invincible regard for lager beer, which we badly needed at the time, and realized we should sorely miss in the years to come.

After a fruitless day of enlisting in infantry regiments who were entirely at a loss what to do with us, we came home next evening, and there I found a letter from Oxford saying that despatch-riders were urgently needed for the front. Now merely through chance I had once owned a motor-cycle (through a game of chance, as a matter of fact); for three short months I had maltreated an aged Triumph and bowed the knee to the grimy denizens of garages. So after a moment's hesitation dispelled once and for all by my brothers' rage at their inability to ride a motor-bike, I crawled into the first train to Chatham the next morning, a very sleepy traveller in bowler hat and tweed suit,

---

1   George's brothers were: Godfrey Elwin Owen (1890-1969); James Fountain Owen (1891-1952); Philip Henry Ashington Owen (1891-1917); Francis Whitwell Owen (1894-1916); and Ralph Everard Owen (1899-1968).

2   A German beer-hall in Regent Street, near Piccadilly, called "Ye Olde Gambrinus".

expecting to be allowed to come away for a day to say goodbye to my family, who were down in Cornwall, after enlisting. But this, of course, was impossible, and I handed in my suit-case and civvies, duly labelled, to the quarter-master, who confused my address with his own. But I learnt a lesson; this loss was my first introduction to the acquisitiveness of the soldier, a characteristic which I began at once to emulate: indeed the QMS[1] of the 5th Signal Company told me afterwards that I actually raised the standard

IRENE RANKIN: from DIARY 1914-1918

Extract from the diary of Irene Keightley Rankin (later Scott), Liddle Collection, University of Leeds

The author, who was staying overnight in Cambridge to attend Extension Lectures, was kept awake on the night of 5/6 August by the din of undergraduate motorcyclists leaving for Chatham. She later volunteered as a VAD nurse.

When the war broke out … we were staying on the corner of Mill Lane opposite Pembroke College. I remember it vividly because my bedroom window was on the street, and I could not sleep because motor-bikes kept starting up outside Pembroke making a terrific noise. I heard in the morning that many students were going to London in the hope of getting into the army as Despatch Riders.

GEORGE OWEN: 12 YEARS AGO – A DESPATCH RIDER AT MONS

Reproduced from the Owen family archive

Luckily my stay at Chatham was short. I did not like the idea of drilling, because it did me good. I did not like saluting by numbers in a tunic, bowler hat, tweed trousers, puttees and ammunition boots, because I did not consider the garb aesthetic: I did not like sleeping on the floor, because I had not learnt how to. I did not like listening to the lurid speculations of the subaltern who lectured to us on our future duties, because I thought suicide would be a saving of time, for they did not wonder whether we should be killed, but merely what form of death it was to be. They let their fancies roam in a most depressing way, till our teeth chattered, and the more sentimental clutched the photographs of their lady-loves in a last vicarious farewell.

Our instruction was most interesting in the light of actual experience. We were told how many Germans would pass a certain spot in a certain time, and on the side of the road to combine the duties of counting them and impersonating a mushroom. Later one of our number acquired the DCM,[2] not for counting a column, but for going back close to see whether they were German or not. Then we were told how we should be sent out to make maps. Later Count Gleichen[3] lent me his Mons map, and we were in the Paris environs before I had the opportunity – which I did not take, as it was autographed – of returning it. Again we were told how to get rid of our messages when surprised by the enemy. One of many amusing methods defies oblivion, that of eating them in a sandwich kept for the purpose. Imagine a motor-cyclist deliberately munching an operation order with a hun revolver pointing at a vital spot. It struck me that a desire for nourishment would be out of place in the circumstances, and most unlikely to deceive; moreover it postulated a credulity of which the enemy never gave a hint. It is not surprising that this policy of frankness

1   Quartermaster Sergeant.
2   Distinguished Conduct Medal.
3   Brigadier-General Count Gleichen commanded 15th Brigade.

about the dangers of our job, which was as necessary as it was disquieting, gave rise to a certain amount of melodrama. For instance, during a lecture, when I was trying to grasp the value of a compass in the dark and in unknown surroundings, I had the photograph of a girl thrust before my eyes by a disappointed suitor who explained to me in a whisper that unrequited affection was responsible for his presence at Chatham. I am sure that he has by now thanked the nymph for resisting his attentions with such unconscious patriotism, and hopes that he is now happy in the love of someone more appreciative. In an equally self-conscious manner I refused my brother's offer of money, loaded with which – though he could ill spare it – he came down to see me, on the plea that it would be of no value to a corpse. What saved me was a hurried visit from my father and sister, as representatives of my distant family, who caught me a few hours before starting to join my unit in Ireland. The desire to conceal from them my fears for my safety actually killed them outright, and thenceforward I tried hard to acquire the soldier's delightful philosophy of fatalism.

While seeing them off, we caught a glimpse of a small boy with his father – he told us he was only fourteen – who had come down to enlist in the West Kents. It is an incident we shall remember, as we have every reason to believe that that same boy saw the whole war, only to meet a tragic end only a few days before the armistice.

The three or four days vouchsafed to us at Chatham were spent in learning not to walk without a stick, saluting sergeant-majors, holding nightly farewell dinners, and memorising the respective positions to be allotted on our person to compasses, haversacks, water-bottles, mess-tins and revolvers. All except the last we had lost within ten days, jolted by the cobbled roads into the hands of the advancing Germans.

There is no need to describe in detail how ten of us a few days later, like so many khaki Christmas trees, journeyed to town, held up the Holyhead Express, landed in Ireland, were refused petrol, were stoned in a village, and billetted ourselves there for the night in a spirit of revenge, and how I was blessed by a nice old Irish peasant woman. Suffice it to say that we arrived at Carlow, and reported to the 5th Signal Company, which was mobilised there, and all but ready to start.

It is only one of my many reasons for respecting the memory of the late Colonel Holwell that we were treated with what must have been thought unheard-of consideration. For here we were twelve civilians – for two more we found had arrived before us – in the flimsiest of fancy dress, promoted with two unearned stripes apiece and five shillings a day, suddenly thrust upon an NCO's mess and the company at large with no knowledge of discipline or military law, but only a great desire to be of use. We might have been exceedingly uncomfortable, but we were not. There in a crowded tent, so hot that several collapsed fainting from the effects of a generous inoculation, we learnt some home-truths about the value of the individual in the army, which was new to me being an Oxford undergraduate, whose sole assets were a great self-regard and a marked disinclination to work. I do not accuse the rest of my companions of having the same undesirable characteristics, though they also were in the main from Oxford or Cambridge, with a few business men to leaven the lump. One could not have found a more sociable crowd in the whole British army; hereafter we ate, drank, slept, cursed, feared and hoped together in perfect harmony.

STANLEY POLHILL: LETTER TO MISS EVELYN WOOD

Reproduced from the Polhill family archive

Stanley left home for Chatham on 7 August to volunteer as a despatch rider. He expected to return home before being sent to his Division. Instead, he was deployed direct to 5th Division in Carlow. So, on 11 August 1914, he wrote to Evelyn to propose marriage, but apologised for doing so in writing rather than face to face. The letter continued:

This letter is partly the result of a hint from K[1] 'that our position was a trifle ambiguous & more of the news that we may be used for scouting; a distinctly dangerous game & I think unnecessary on a mobike & useless to boot, but that's not my business ...

We were to have gone off today in a party of 8, all nice men, whether school & Varsity. But we were delayed with kit so we move off tomorrow & catch the 7.30 or so from Euston via Fishguard to Carlow 51 miles below Dublin. My address will be Cpl. S. Polhill, RE motor cyclist, 5th Signal Company Carlow, Ireland. I've got my new Triumph all equipped. It's a beauty. I don't know how soon we shall move abroad but prob this week & straight from Ireland. Most of our men have left by now, some to Aldershot, some to Limerick & elsewhere.

I've practicing [sic] with my revolver whenever I have time. It's jolly heavy & kicks a good deal. We also have a rifle for scouting (not spying remember, we always work in uniforms). Over 200 men have been turned away these last few days & they still pour in to enlist.

STANLEY POLHILL: LETTER TO HIS FAMILY

Reproduced from Trident, the Trent College Magazine

Every ride, even those on home soil, was a challenge in 1914.

Wednesday, 12/8/14. 5th Signal Company, R.E. Carlow. – A most eventful day yesterday, 16 hours travel. We started at 6 a.m. from Chatham, and rode to Euston; it sounds simple – it wasn't! Our machines were brand new and untried, the traffic was very thick, and the tram-lines (which seemed everywhere) were wet and greasy. We all but one came off at least once. I kept up till we got to Euston and went down just turning into the station – no damage but a bent foot-rest. We caught the boat-train by three minutes, seven of us; the two others damaged their machines too much to continue, and came by night-boat.

FRANK MERCHANT: AUTOBIOGRAPHY written 1935

Reproduced from the copy deposited in the Royal Signals Museum, Blandford Forum

Frank Merchant wrote his life story for the benefit of friends and family in the 1930s. In August 1914 he was Pay Sergeant in 5th Signal company, based at Carlow.

On the first day of mobilization, the day following that on which the order was received, i.e. the 6th August, Nos 2, 3, and 4 Sections of the company had to march out and entrain for DUBLIN, CURRAGH CAMP and BELFAST respectively, where the headquarters of the 13th, 14th, and 15th INFANTRY BRIGADES, which they had to join, were then stationed. Headquarters and No 1 Section of the company remained the sole occupant of the barracks and stood by to await the arrival of reservists and new horses.

According to the war establishment, the company was to have 14 motorcyclists,[2] a type of soldier seldom met with in peacetime, so the despatch riders were something of a novelty – we were all looking forward to meeting this type of fighter.

On August 8th the first two arrived. They were both artificers from a well known firm of motorcycle manufacturers, and were thoroughly good and capable men. They brought their own

---

1   Field-Marshal Lord Kitchener, the newly-appointed Secretary of State for War.
2   5th Signal Company war diary for August 1914 records an establishment of 12 motorcyclists.

machines with them, and it is a significant fact that these two machines lasted longer during the war than any other in the company.

By the 12th a total of seventeen motorcyclists – too many by three – had arrived, but on enquiries being made it was found that the surplus three had to be sent to the 3rd Signal Troop R.E. at CURRAGH CAMP.

Personally I found the volume of work greatly increased owing to the influx of reservists and specially enlisted men and been kept very busy making out men's wills, pay allotments to relatives, separation allowances, and what not, and had at last got the clerical work well in hand and was able to finish work and take my first lesson in the use and abuse of a motorcycle before dark. The lesson took place in a quiet lane under the barrack wall and lasted about fifteen minutes.

The following afternoon I borrowed a motorcycle and, accompanied by OWEN, an experienced motorcyclist, went off to CURRAGH CAMP, a distance of 25 miles. This was my first serious run on a motorcycle, and strange to relate, the outward journey was accomplished without incident in 1½ hours. The return journey was completed in shorter time, and I was within 500 yards of home, crossing the CARLOW POTATO MARKET, when disaster overtook me – I ran into a cow. The animal did not appear to mind in the least but one of the footrests of the machine was bent slightly, otherwise the maiden run was a success. My wife was very pleased to see me return safely, for she distrusted motorcycles, especially when ridden by novices. Anyhow, the experience stood me in good stead, for later, during the war, I found the motorbike very handy and at times indispensable.

I spent the following day, Friday 14th August, in finally clearing up all peace work, and during the afternoon Madge busied herself packing up various articles of clothing for herself and Joan, our daughter but three weeks old, for her journey to SLEAFORD, her mother's home, was to commence that night.

That Friday night was memorable for rain fell very heavily, and the train was very late, so the travellers had to wait for some considerable time on the platform of CARLOW station, and as the waiting room accommodation there was rather meagre the wait was very comfortless. Four families from the barracks went off to their homes in England that night, and the parting was quite tearless although none were enthusiastic, for it was hard to realize that the men were off to war on the morrow.

GEORGE OWEN: 12 YEARS AGO – A DESPATCH RIDER AT MONS

Reproduced from the Owen family archive

Many of the motorcyclists had served in the Officer Training Corps at school or university. Other than that they had no military experience. George sets out how little training the motorcyclists received before they left for France.

After a day or two spent in painting out the bright spots on the machines, which we had been given at Chatham, and receiving base kit, which we left behind and never saw again; after one last real farewell dinner at which I was one of the few who could swallow the champagne after inoculation, we marched out to the strains of the village band, and early on the morning of the thirteenth of August the good ship Archimedes – the epithet is merely by courtesy – steamed slowly out of Dublin to the accompaniment of encores from the wise old soldiers, but that of 'Land of hope and glory' from twelve innocent young ones in the prow.

We took three days crossing to Havre, and it was our first touch of real discomfort. We had a lot of horses on board, and as I had never before shared a bedroom with a horse, though frequently with brothers, I found it beastly. There was no accommodation, of course, and we slept on deck – if fits of tortured unconsciousness can be called sleep – in coils of rope. It is significant to note that we had already assimilated the esprit de corps of the engineers, and resented sharing the boat with RAMC[1] details ("details" expresses a minority) who appeared to spend the day in ceaselessly lining up for meals.

I think it was on the second day that we sighted the coast of Cornwall. To all it was a sentimental sight, but for me it was more, because my mother and the rest of my family, to whom I had not said goodbye, were there. There I learnt afterwards on the top of a cliff stood my father with a pair of field glasses glued to his devoted eyes, searching the horizon for the ship which was carrying his son to the war. He was interrupted by a tap on the shoulder and was politely but firmly marched off, being informed by his captor that other enemy agents had availed themselves of clerical garb to work their horrid schemes; also, and this is a great touch, his borrowed glasses were confiscated. Although the incident was spoilt by the anti-climax of release and return of the glasses, it is a great tribute to the conscientiousness of our coastguards. One cannot help thinking that they must have been very busy in those first few months of war.

We landed on the 18th in a state of wild excitement and indescribable dirt, practically simultaneously with the rest of the convoy, which we had caught glimpses of on our way over, and were marched, mid scenes of touching enthusiasm, to an old factory above the harbour which was to be our billet for the night. It was absolutely bare, except for a stuffy attic, filled with cotton or wool, I cannot remember which. On this a few of us slept that night in preference to the bare floor and bumpy cobblestones which we observed the rest of the company to be patronising, thinking ourselves very cunning to have discovered it. As a reward for our initiative, next morning we were the unwilling hosts of a colony of fleas, whose vigour and health are unrivalled in my experience, except perhaps by the Bulgar variety, whose standard was certainly high.[2]

On the beach at Havre two of us were treated to a tent and bathing dress by a delightful French woman, to whose small and charming daughter I forfeited my heart and incidentally one of my tunic buttons. O,[3] who bathed with me, put his knee out during the swim, and had this, in addition to other hardships, to put up with in the trying times which followed. On the way up to Landrecies, where we finally detrained, I found that the incident of the button, which I fondly imagined to be an isolated instance of sacrifice and affection, was gloriously thrown into the shade by the behaviour of the company. Atkins[4] cannot resist the desire to give away, and at every level crossing station or town, the movement of the train being practically imperceptible, he had time to give away his hat badge, his buttons, his cigarettes. True, he received many cooling draughts of beer and cider, but it would be cynical to say that the gift was regarded in the light of an exchange.

To my great sorrow at the time, I was sent, immediately on detraining, to be attached to a brigade. I did not consider that it might be more thrilling with a brigade, though it unquestionably was, but I disliked leaving my new friends. So, with a heart sinking at the mutability of military affairs, I went off and reported to the brigade signal officer who employed me the greater part of that night carrying messages to divisional headquarters. As one of these jobs was the transport of a sack of nails I was hardly surprised to get a puncture; I was also annoyed, which was foolish, because there is nothing more conducive to the laughter of the gods than an enraged and weary person by himself at night.

I woke up next morning in the big double bed which I had hired for the night in the village – I think the name of it was Ors – and found the section gone and all the village deserted by troops.

---

1   Royal Army Medical Corps.
2   Roger West, a motorcyclist Intelligence Officer serving with the 19th Brigade, had severe problems with flea-bites, to the extent that his foot became too swollen to wear a boot. (Carragher, "The Man Who Saved Paris")
3   Probably Arnold Overton.
4   "Tommy Atkins", the colloquial name for the British soldier.

definitely how went the battle on our line. Later, when stationery ran out and verbal messages delivered in agitated tones by brigadiers were the rule, we really knew more than most, and the white and blue brassard shining out of a cloud of dust, stood for information.

All the morning and early afternoon I plied up and down that road, which was soon littered with dead chickens from a farm near the canal, tools and nuts from my motorcycle, and incidentally with the soles of my boots from cornering at speed in the village of Thulin.

Later in the afternoon, things began to look more lively. This would not have been apparent to the infantry, because they were in the thick of it the whole time, but to those who were keeping in direct touch with the infantry it was the first glimpse of actual warfare (to use a phrase happily coined by a friend of mine later at Salonika to point a contrast with operations in France). I had been sent to remain at a bridge spanning the canal, wait till the small detachment of RE's stationed there were ready to blow up the bridge, and then inform brigade headquarters of its destruction. On arriving I found a subaltern, and a few sappers in a fragile wooden hut by the side of the road fondling some suggestive looking square blocks of explosive. I had never had any experience of this sort of thing before, and being vastly interested, I questioned the men about it, but they were too busy to answer. They very rightly placed me in the same category as the small boy in the railway carriage who asks his patient mother why the wheels go round, and why they always travel third class. Then I heard the whine of bullets outside and understood. I went to the door and there in the middle of the road was the subaltern, his field glasses glued to his eyes shouting "There they are; there they are", I looked and he was certainly right, but I wondered why he used his field glasses. I was shortsighted and am still more so now, but the truth of his exclamation was evident. There they were, that swarm of grey blue devils advancing firing from the hip with the utmost inaccuracy, for the bullets were all passing over our heads.

People wonder what it feels like to be under fire for the first time. Well, this is my experience. First I felt very important. This was no Army manoeuvres; it was the real thing. I pitied all those OTC[1] fellows who had not been so fortunate as I. Then I felt afraid. There was one of the chickens I had run over during the day lying in the road. How funny it would be for the soul of the bird to see me lying by its own body in a few minutes. Previously, I had judged a building by its beauty and its ability to keep out rain and sun. Now it was bullets that must be kept out, and I realised that the wooden shanty in which we huddled from observation was simply challenging one to come through. Moreover, the bullets were coming clear down the road and this was my thoroughfare. The men had something to do, they had no time for morbid imaginings, as I had. For that I envied them and feared correspondingly for myself.

When all was ready, and they sat down to wait for the last moment, I was told to be off to brigade headquarters. This, I felt, was combining business with pleasure; but I remember the agony of dragging my machine out of the hut and pushing it along the road for what seemed miles before it deigned to start. I chose the left side of the road for my retreat and all but grazed each poplar on the way back to Thulin; in my back were a hundred eyes, each separately flinching at each separate bullet.

One word before I leave this incident. When the division moved from Ypres to the Somme in the summer of '15, I met one of those very sappers who were blowing up that bridge. When we had exchanged noises of surprise at our respective survivals, he told me that, the charge having proved insufficient, the subaltern had lost a hand in going back to complete the job: which goes to strengthen the conviction that the gallantry of the sapper is often unobtrusive, but never unnecessary. It is bravery, not bravado.

---

1   Officer Training Corps.

I found the brigade staff in the middle of the road, hatless and perturbed, I gave what little news I had, and was sent back immediately to the Cornwalls, being informed by my signal officer that they would be found by this time about two thirds of the way up to the canal. He patted me on the back as I left; I have never discovered whether it was a reward for my services or encouragement in view of my probable decease, but I value the memory of it inordinately. The donor was by the evening wounded and a prisoner.

I found the OC[1] Cornwalls at a farmhouse by the roadside, and behind it cowered the chargers of such of the infantry who were mounted. I noticed the calmness of the orderlies, and having witnessed the playful farewells exchanged by two infantry subalterns, who were prepared for, and expecting death, I tried to be unmoved myself; placing my bike in as safe a place as possible, I leaned against a tree and smoked.

It was by now evening twilight and the scene was picturesquely warlike. So unreal was it that it approximated very closely to a picture in a weekly illustrated paper. I was so excited, in spite of my efforts to calm myself, that the sights and sounds ceased to be terrifying. They were merely intensely absorbing. On the horizon glowed the flames of burning villages: straight as a die ran the road with the poplars motionless against the glare. Now and then arose the cry for stretcher bearers: suddenly an ammunition wagon would dash from a turning, the drivers crouching on the horses' necks, and hurtle in a cloud of dust up the road: a company of infantry would assemble behind the farm buildings. One by one they would crouch in the opposite ditch, glide across the road and advance in silent Indian file up the ditch on my side. There was a continued pop – popping noise which interested me very much. I turned to an NCO, one of those who, with fixed bayonets, were lining the road, and asked what that noise was. "Machine gun". Why did it seem so loud? "Cos it's pointing at you". I could not wish for a greater clarity of expression, nor a more convincing conciseness. I thanked him inwardly then, for confirming my suspicions, and I thank him outwardly now for his somewhat brutal frankness. It was the best policy. Similarly, though it is no more pleasant to the ear, it is better in the end to be told that we are wrong, or ugly, or going to die.

Nestling behind that tree, I smoked my last pipe of tobacco and pondered on the sudden change from the life of an undergraduate to that of a civilian soldier. I wondered whether my people were having supper in Cornwall; I wondered whether the old lady, to whose ward I was to have been tutor, had guessed where I was (because I had not told her). I also wondered where the Colonel of the Cornwalls was.

He must have forgotten me, because I was left getting more and more pensive, till company after company had passed shuffling wearily along the darkened road, and was advised by an officer to proceed on my own initiative. So with this object I started my engine, but was met with a torrent of most instructive oaths from Atkins and a forcible reminder from an officer that they were expecting an attack any minute and that the noise of my machine would give them away. Thus, with my great coat on that hot summer night and a stack of kit on the carrier, I pushed the machine for miles into Dour. Several times I fell down a three foot ditch with utter weariness, and once I prayed aloud to be shot dead. Prayers like this are not easily forgotten. Such another was that breathed silently on the voyage from Ireland that the war might never end if it were necessary to return by the same route and under the same conditions.

I found the other despatch riders in an outhouse at the station of Dour, and tried to tell them my adventures, but halfway through the first narrative I looked round and found them asleep. Piqued by their indifference, which of course, was actuated by physical fatigue, I threw myself down and slept the sleep of sheer exhaustion, which is as precious and rare as it is impossible to describe.

---

1   Officer Commanding.

It is impossible to give an adequate idea of the retreat which had now started without devoting a little space to the description of the conditions under which we worked. I have mentioned utter fatigue; this was our constant companion and in many ways our greatest friend. What rest we snatched was in the clothes we stood up in. More than one of us went to sleep on our machines and woke up in the ditch. None of us, with the exception of one bathe in the Oise, took off our boots for a moment. There was no time for washing. Besides, all the materials for a wash were lost with our kit after the first day or two. I remember once being washed by a Belgian woman, as I was lying half asleep on my machine with my head on the handlebars. Meals there were none. Fruit and chocolate thrown with a generous hand by the peasantry were our meals as a rule. I have cherished memories of simple meals given me by the divisional staff of the brigadier to whom I was attached, such as a cup of cocoa, a biscuit or an apple. My pre-war profession, smoking, was impossible to carry on owing to lack of supplies.

All day long we rode up and down the column with messages dealing with the rearguard actions or traffic control. But it was not till night that the real work began. Every unit of the division had to be found and given operation orders for the ensuing day. They were never, or practically never, at the exact spot which we were told, which meant delay and exasperation, for we had no lights. A common way of steering at night was with head in the air steering between the tops of the poplars which lined the roads. Again we had to carry our staff officers at night on our carriers with stable lanterns in their hands. For there were no staff cars in those days. It is difficult for the minor officials of non-combatant corps, who lately had cars for the transport of hospital nurses more attracted by the vehicles than the owners, to realise that there was but one car for a whole division. Moreover, we had no maps of our own and had to memorise in a moment a staff map thrust before our eyes, reddened and almost invisible for dust. It can be imagined how the infantry fared when we at divisional and brigade HQ were so placed.

So much for the permanent discomforts of the retreat, though there were many more incidental ones. I quote them mostly for my own benefit so that I shall not forget, so that they may remain fresh a little longer, these new wonders of beds and bowlers, tube stations and tablecloths, dances and "they come to goal at last, my wandering wits".[1]

Early on the next morning I was sent out with a duplicate message for the 15th Brigade. The original copy had been taken by Fielding-Johnson, who had not returned. He was a cheerful and companionable Cambridge undergraduate, with whom, during the short time I had known him, I got on very well. Nothing more was seen of him, though there was a story that he was lanced by a roving patrol of Uhlans and seen taken into a convent by some nuns. He was much missed by all of us, and his death brought home to us the fact that any of us at any moment might meet a similar fate.

I certainly had thoughts of this kind when I set out with a copy of his message. A brief account of my ride will give an impression of what motorcycling meant. To the infantry on the road, who saw us passing them, we appeared to be the only members of the force who did not work. We were cursed for raising dust, getting in the way, frightening horses, and for not marching. It was quite a natural point of view for them, dead-beat as they were with fighting and foot-slogging. To the staff, however we constituted practically the sole means of communication, and we were proportionately valued and employed.

My first difficulty was to surmount with my machine four five-barred gates securely locked and chained. For I had to cross the railway twice, and at each crossing a wild Belgian railway official was shouting "Allemands lá; Allemands lá" and doing all he could to obstruct me. As his

---

1   From G.K. Chesterton's poem "To Hilaire Belloc", the dedication of "The Napoleon of Notting Hill" (1904).

exclamations neither encouraged nor helped, I dragged the Rudge over them all,[1] in a state of excitement bordering on madness, and my tongue red hot with unintelligible obscenities. Then something went wrong with the lubrication of my engine with the result that the plug half sooted up, and I was enveloped in a cloud of oily smoke. Luckily, this happened on the top of the steep hill down into Paturages, where I passed a battery of field guns in action, and some kilted stragglers[2] plodding with set faces away from the scene of action. They must have been wounded, though I thought at the time that they were retreating. I turned sharp to the left at the bottom of the hill, and was about to dash under a bridge in front of me, when I saw a small knot of people huddled against the embankment. It was the staff of the 13th Brigade, and among them I recognised S.,[3] the despatch rider attached from Divisional HQ to the Brigade. I tried to borrow a spanner from him so that I could remove and clean my plug. It transpired however, that he had lost his machine in a hurried retreat from the Boche, because there was no time to mend a puncture, and he was at present sharing the use of a stolen civilian "push-bike". He told me that it was a happy thing for me that I had stopped, because there was hand-to-hand fighting going on only a few hundred yards the other side of the bridge.

So, with my engine misfiring badly, and still suffocated in smoke, I left that embankment. On it, I learnt afterwards, one of our operators stayed in an improvised signal office till the enemy was coming up one side. He then smashed the instrument, cut the wire, and descended coolly on the other.

I toiled on, searching every road, but repeated inquiries from stragglers and wounded only resulted in the discovery of a few men attached to the 15th. So I gave up after two or three hours and decided to report on what I had done to division. My bike gibbed, however, at the return journey up the hill, so I persuaded two weedy Belgian civilians to drag it up for me while I smoked a cigarette given me by a despairing tobacconist, who was throwing the entire contents of his shop as a gift to passing Englishmen.

On the way back I met W.[4] who had been sent out with a third copy of the same message. He was told by the general of the 13th that the 15th appeared to be cut off. As a matter of fact, they had retreated without being able to inform division.

I found the staff standing wild-eyed outside the station at Dour, collapsed in their midst, was helped into the building, gave a report on the roads I had searched in vain, was given a cup of chocolate and a biscuit, and sent off in hot haste to Corps HQ with the news. By the time W. was back all papers were being burned, the telephone exchanges were being smashed with a sledge hammer, and the wires being cut. It is sheer melodrama to look back upon, but it was merely commonsense at the time.

Not a few minutes after the delivery of my message to Corps HQ, the cars were purring, kit was bundled into lorries and they were ready to move. I asked the despatch-riders there what sort of time they had had. They said significantly they had had two wounded. I discovered afterwards from a friend, who was one of the wounded, that someone had been fooling with a loaded rifle; it accidentally went off and wounded both of them. I also consulted their artificer about my lubrication and found that, the oiling being operated by a foot pump, I had been, owing to the vast size of my boots, pumping oil into the engine every time I applied the brake. In self-defence I may say that the misfortune was not due to the length of my foot, but to the abnormally square toes of the ammunition boot, which made it impossible to press the levers separately.

---

1   The Rudge Multi was a heavy machine – it was an impressive feat to drag one over four obstacles.
2   Probably from 1st Battalion King's Own Scottish Borderers, part of 13th Brigade.
3   Cecil Hayes-Sadler.
4   WHL Watson, author of 'Adventures of a Despatch Rider'.

Divisional Headquarters, I had been told, were to be at Villers-Pol for the night, so thither I repaired with W., who had been sent to say that the retreat had started from Dour. It was a comfort to be with him, because he had an extraordinary *bump* of locality, as well as a swift eye for situations. So I followed him like a little dog.

On arriving at the village, we found no sign of life, so we tossed a coin to decide who was to catch a little sleep and who was to conduct investigations. I won. We both lapped a long drink from a pond and he disappeared, the bargain being that he should return and wake me when he had acquired information about headquarters for the night. I was waked in the evening by an ambulance crawling past the pond and outspanning, but there was no sign of W. I had a similar attack of panic as many days before, when at Ors I woke to find my brigade gone. By sheer luck I found the divisional signal company at the other end of the village, and, among the other motorcyclists, my friend W. who had volunteered for extra work and had been too busy to worry about me. I was told that another retreat had been necessary and divisional HQ was at St. Waast, whither we were ordered to move.

So far as we knew there was no one between us and the enemy. Imagine my excitement when you learn that I was taking down my gear when the order was received, having dropped a small but vital part of the mechanism; for this had to be substituted a nail filed down for me by the village blacksmith. The others very kindly waited for me to put my machine together, and we started off just before dark having more than a suspicion that we might be attacked by a stray patrol from the woods which fringed the narrow road. Johnson's disappearance had made us cautious. How near we were to capture can be judged by the fact that W., who was sent back for the CQMS[1] at Villers-Pol, found the ambulance unit I had seen, advised them to push on without a moment's delay, and actually saved them from an enemy patrol which entered the village at one end as they left by the other. Later, on the Aisne, the chaplain attached to it thanked W. personally for his sound advice.

We slept the usual chequered night of sleeping fitfully between the different jobs, and before full daylight were on the move again. During an exhausting day of column riding we were buoyed up with a hopeful story of a strongly-entrenched position to which we were even then supposed to be retiring. By the evening we were seen to be smiling a bland and knowing smile at the innocent Hun, unwarily advancing into our trap. It was astonishing then and thereafter during the retreat how the vaguest optimistic rumour was received with a joyous credulity, flashed along the column, and delightfully exaggerated. Throughout it was a strategic movement: the division was returning to a rest camp to re-equip; the fleet had secured a crushing victory; the Russians had dealt a smashing blow; the French had cut the enemy's lines of communication. Perhaps it was a policy, not an accident that such stories were circulated, just as propaganda at home started the tale of the Russians passing through England at night.

---

1   Company Quartermaster-Sergeant.

CECIL HAYES-SADLER: LETTER TO HIS MOTHER

Reproduced from his daughter's archive

After struggling to keep on the move with his machine, Cecil lost his motorcycle – and then the pushbike which replaced it.

Sunday 23rd August

The next day there was <u>plenty</u> of fighting and any amount of shells bursting close at hand. While I was mending my fourth puncture I saw an aeroplane being shelled, then, quite a novel experience. That night at 9.30 we received the order to move again, I was sent off with several despatches and then had to find my Signal Section consisting of an officer and about 20 push bike cyclists. No easy job! As no lights were allowed, consequently I had several falls and finished up by running into one of my own section! And so found them. My bike was quite done in.

Monday 24th August

I don't know what exactly went wrong and hadn't time to see, I was told to leave it and push on. I took my kit bag off and walked with the push cyclists. The other Trinity man [Danson] was with us, but he managed to keep his bike whole. No one except the officer knew our destination, and not even he knew the way. We got hold of a peasant as our guide, and I had to act as interpreter.

For hours and hours we crawled along in the dark over very rough country and along railway lines, and most of the time I had to push the other fellow's bike and lift it out of holes as well as carry my own kit bag. There was a good deal of talk about Uhlans being about on several occasions, but 15 miles on we arrived safely at a place called Wärmes [Wasmes]. There Brigade Headquarters took up a position behind a bridge. Several inhabitants made us some coffee and I was so hungry I ate a raw egg! There was much shelling and fighting, and as I had no bike I had to take my despatches on foot to the Railway station which was being shelled. They whistled and burst round me in all directions but none actually hit the bridge behind which we were stationed.

Suddenly, before anyone realised we were being pushed back, the firing line came back under our bridge. Headquarters received the order to move whilst a few infantry began firing through the bridge at the gentle Germans who were coming down the road in large numbers. I was ordered to leave; the other fellow offered me a lift on the back of his bike but like a fool I said "No". He was sent back to Divisional Headquarters with a message saying we were practically cut off. I was told to seize a stray push bike and to follow the General. I had to leave all my kit, and as I mounted my bike I saw the Germans about 100 yards off. Men close to me and all round were hit, but they too must have hit many Germans as they made a fine target. After pushing my bike a long way we at last halted on top of a steep hill. I sat down on a door step for a few moments rest. I heard a poor kitten mewing pitifully inside the house and was just trying to get it out when a shell burst yards from me.

No one was hurt, I received a scratch as long as a pin. Slowly but with great precision I took my bike again and mounted.

Tuesday 25th August

After riding for some time my poor bike had its back wheel pushed in by a loathsome artillery horse. More walking! Then a stray ammunition waggon that night carried me to St Waast, a village where my Div. Headquarters was. I was glad of a small amount of sleep. At 4 am we resumed the retreat, and I rode part of the way on a cart and walked the other part to a village called Reumont outside Le Cateau.

There we saw great preparations for a stand, but alas! The next day was to prove the German numbers were too large for us. That night we had a little sleep in a barn.

WALTER J WADE: LETTER TO FIELDING JOHNSON'S FAMILY

Reproduced from the Everard family archive

Private Wade served in 1st Battalion Lincolnshire Regiment – he responded to Fielding Johnson's family when they advertised for information about their son.

Thank you very much for the photograph of your son. I have no doubt about its being a photo of the Corporal we carried into a Convent at Mons on 24th August 1914. He was wounded in the shoulder and in the ankle.

The following no doubt will interest you. On Sunday, August 23rd, we were in action at Mons and retired about 6 p.m. We marched a roundabout way to take up a different position outside Mons. About 6 a.m. on Monday Aug. 24th, we took up a position by the sides of a road as follows:

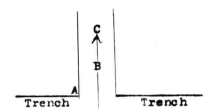

I was with ten men at "A". About 300 yards along this road at "C" I saw some "push" bicycles and two motor cycles and some of our own men lying by the side of the roadway. Seeing signs of life in some of the men, I went with 6 others and between us we returned with two wounded motor cyclists and 4 scouts. We had to make two journeys to get these men in and fortunately only two of our men were wounded. My chum and I had to carry the R.E. Corporal who said he was a despatch rider from the 5th Division. I particularly remember this because we did not know that the 5th Division was with us.

We carried him to the shelter of a low wall where I bandaged his wounds whilst my chum – since killed – went for a stretcher. I gave him a drink from my bottle and we had a few minutes chat. After about half an hour my chum returned with a stretcher and between us we carried him about 1½ miles to a Convent where there were beds, etc. for wounded. The doctor took off his bandages and re-dressed him. The doctor said he would be alright. The wound in the shoulder was a clean bullet wound, which would quickly heal. The wound in the ankle was small where the bullet entered and rather big where it emerged. At the convent there were three despatch riders of the R.E. and the Corporal we carried in entered into conversation with them. One of these men said: "Hullo Johnson have you stopped one."

My chum and I then returned to our trench to find our comrades killed and wounded. From the short conversation I had with Corporal Johnson I gathered that he and the other cyclists rode right into the German outposts and nearly all were shot down before they had time to defend themselves.

Apparently this young gentleman would be taken prisoner by the Germans when they passed through Mons. If this is not the case, it is quite probable that the Nuns at the Convent would shelter him, as they have been known to do with others. I sincerely trust this is the case.

GEORGE OWEN: 12 YEARS AGO – A DESPATCH RIDER AT MONS

Reproduced from the Owen family archive

Owen's fragmentary memoir comes to an end less than a week after he first saw action.

In the late afternoon, some of us, who had managed to pass the column and get on ahead, arrived at Le Cateau, a fair-sized and cheerful market-town, where we actually were shaved, and not only that but shaved by a woman. Though this luxury rendered the difference of colour between our necks and faces painfully evident, we were emboldened by a great hunger to dash into an inn, where we had an early dinner. The place appeared not at all disturbed. Perhaps, if their telegraph system is as leisurely as ours, they had not yet learned of the German advance. There was a sprinkling of French officers mounted and in cars, set on 'aperitifs' rather than retreat. The shops were open, in one of them I tried to get some seccotine and was shown an assortment of other glues. We expressed a feeling of confidence, though only a few hours later there was street-fighting in the town and a detachment of one of our cable sections was captured complete.

We slept at Reumont that night in a lofty barn chuckling to ourselves at the victory we should witness on the morrow. Moreover, we enjoyed a fair rest owing, I suppose, to the fact that the cables were laid and working to the brigade.

In the morning we were summoned to battle headquarters of the division, which was in one of a group of cottages outside the village on the right of the Le Cateau road. Leaning against the roof were some ladders, and a sort of rough platform had been fitted up for the General, the GSO1,[1] and the OC Signal Company, our captain. Dug into the road, with their head receivers on, were the telephone operators working like grim death.

The road sloped down for a mile or so, then rose again and disappeared over a crest. Along this crest was a row of poplars and parallel to it were shallow trenches hastily dug by civilians the day before under the supervision of a few British officers detailed for the job. This was the "strongly entrenched" position of the rumour. Naturally the enemy could range on the poplars and be sure of hitting their mark. Very near on the left – I say "very near" because a 60 pounder battery, when she speaks, is so audible that one minimises distances – was the 108th heavy battery in a hollow against a hedge with no protection. On the right of the road in front were a few guns waiting presumably for orders; a few, very few ambulance wagons completed the picture.

It was a morning of agonising indolence for us, as the wires worked well. I only rode once, while some did not ride at all. The story of the impregnable position having been exploded, another took its place. A corps of French cavalry was to relieve us at 11.30. I think this was the time mentioned; at any rate everyone looked feverishly at their watches from time to time, when the wounded began to limp past us along the road to the village church, where a dressing station had been improvised.

The reports buzzed along the wires and scribbled on to message forms by the operators became more and more discouraging, and our conversation became more trivial and spasmodic as the situation became more tense. A continuous line of shrapnel bursts was visible along the poplars on the crest, and the wounded said that the rest could not hold out much longer. Still no sign of the French. Later we were told that the commander refused to come to our assistance on the plea that his horses were too tired to move any further. The story goes – and it gives me great pleasure – that he was shot for it afterwards.

So we waited on cursing the French, speculating silently on the prospect of complete defeat, and staring fascinated at the wounded, who filed past with grey faces and reddened bandages, sometimes alone, sometimes supported by one or two comrades. Then began a procession which I shall

---

1   General Staff Officer Grade 1.

never forget, the remnant of a gun team without the gun, a team of horses with but one driver, frantic mounted orderlies, an officer with an arm shot off, a wounded bugler boy, whose horse had been killed under him, cheerfully riding a derelict bicycle, a loaded ambulance, an empty ammunition wagon. Fuses for the 108th battery had to be brought up by despatch-rider because the ammunition column could not or would not bring them themselves.

At about two came an order for some of us to retire to the farm where we had slept the night and simultaneously a sudden and sickening panic. I thought that the immediate cause was a round or two of shrapnel which burst near headquarters over some horses. The result was that lorries which were coming up with food and ammunition turned on their tracks, threw off their load, and infantry climbed on instead. Two men one after the other leapt on to the carrier of my machine, and I had difficulty in dislodging them. The road being very narrow, three or four of us, who had started to retire to the farm, were caught in the mob and were compelled to follow it through the village and beyond. It was only after some miles that we were able to dash into a farm-yard, eat a crust of bread while waiting for the road to clear, and make our way back. By this time the retreat had become official, our captain said good-bye and returned to try to establish communication with Corps HQ. We were told to shift for ourselves. He thought everything was up, and it certainly looked very like it. It was, however, hard to believe that we were entirely lost. I, for one, had been brought up to the quaint conceit that Englishmen are never beaten, but I cynically remarked to D.,[1] as we rode away together, that it looked precious like it this time. Our nearness to defeat in this war has been a great lesson to us. The history of the war might well be expressed in four sentences. We are defeated; we may not be defeated; we may defeat; we shall defeat. The peace conference will decide whether we have defeated.

We were told that the next headquarters would be at St. Quentin, but we never covered more than half the distance that night. It was one of black despair and, as if to match our forebodings, a drizzle started which continued the entire night.

It is impossible to adequately describe the scene on the road that night. We motorcyclists had stopped at a small cottage on the left of St. Quentin road, having made up our minds that further we could not go. The signal company bivouacked round the house, and one by one the divisional staff came in.

W. and I had collaborated in the slaughter of all the chickens in the outhouse and had plunged them straight into a pot to boil. Coffee was also found, which, with the chickens, made a reasonable meal, though I have since been told that an interval is generally allowed to fastidious people between killing and eating birds.[2]

The staff would only stay a little while. They were dazed and incoherent. One of them I could not get to answer me at all. They took a little to eat and went trudging along the road to St. Quentin. For most of the horses were either lost or killed. While I was holding one of the few remaining, I watched the column passing. It was not disorderly, but pathetically disordered. It was a string of remnants, not a procession of units. There would pass a hundred or so KOSB's[3] gnawing mangel wurzels or raw bacon, a little squad of Worcesters craving for water, a GS wagon[4] full of men too dead to march, a gun-limber, an ambulance. We could do nothing for them except give them water. Then think of the pitiless drizzle, the hunger, the fatigue, the thought of possible defeat, and you have the night after Le Cateau.

1   Jack Danson.
2   This incident described in more detail, page 40 of Adventures of a Despatch Rider.
3   King's Own Scottish Borderers.
4   General Service wagon.

CECIL HAYES-SADLER – LETTER TO HIS MOTHER

Reproduced from his daughter's archive

Cecil, still on foot, joined the throng retreating from Le Cateau to St Quentin.

Wednesday 26th August

The next night operations were resumed again in earnest. At 11.30 we were again ordered to retreat. The cart I was on got through the village just as the other end was shelled. It was raining hard and the traffic on the road was very mixed and in great disorder.

For about half an hour a German aeroplane buzzed about over our column, part of which had to take cover under a forest. However we were glad to see a French and an English machine bring the German down.

At 8.30 that evening we halted at a cottage but had no sooner settled down on some straw in the open with the rain pelting down than we had to move on again!

The motor cyclists were allowed to remain behind a little longer but I had to ride on a waggon or walk again. We got to St Quentin and I spent an hour or two that night in a barn there.

ERIC BAGSHAW RECALLS THE RETREAT

Reproduced from Michael Sadler's Memorandum of a conversation with Eric Bagshaw, in the Michael Sadler Archive, Leeds University Library Special Collections

Bagshaw's family was in South Africa, so he returned to Leeds for his first leave. The Vice-Chancellor's record of their conversation was marked PRIVATE & VERY CONFIDENTIAL. Sadler asked what had impressed Bagshaw most – Spuggy replied "Le Cateau."

They in the 5th Division had to stand the attack of the Germans alone. The numbers were overwhelming. They couldn't shoot them quick enough…. They fought to the last moment and then were ordered to make what was called a strategical movement. All the Tommies and apparently most of the officers believed that they could still beat the Germans where they were; but as a matter of fact they were surrounded. He and other motor cyclists were sent out to scout and were stopped by snipers on roads in every direction. Finally they made a bodyguard for the staff and forced their way through. That night was horrible. Limbers came in without guns; men running without arms; it was a rout … He saw some officers in hysterics, sobbing that the British Army was beaten.

ARNOLD OVERTON: LETTER TO HIS MOTHER

From the Overton family collection

Another despatch rider recorded the moment when the 5th Division started to withdraw from Le Cateau, and describes the level-headed reactions of the motorcyclists.

In the afternoon things seemed to be going badly for us, owing to the greatly superior weight of the German artillery, and we began to see our infantry retiring and being mowed down by shrapnel as they retreated. Up the road towards Le Cateau it was a ghastly sight to see men being mowed down and through my glasses I could see it all quite distinctly half a mile away. But we hung on expecting the French to come up and take the pressure off our flank, and it was not till about 3 o'clock that the order to retire was given. Divisional H.Q. stayed where they were till shrapnel started bursting round us, when the General "thought we had better change Headquarters". We motorcyclists were given vague orders and most of us got separated in the transport along the road. But 3 of us – Watson, Burney, and myself – waited in Reumont to get definite orders from the Captain. As we waited by the roadside there was a veritable panic among the transport and 10 yards from me a great van dashing down from a side road killed 3 men. Finally the Captain came up and gave us orders to get away as best we could – everybody thought there was no chance of the column getting away safely. After consultation among ourselves we decided to go to 2nd Army H.Q. and warn them of what was happening, as it was perfectly impossible to get past the column along the main road. On our way there we picked up most of our other motorcyclists, and when we got to 2nd Army, we were the first to inform them of what had happened in our division. We were placed under the orders of their lieutenant and started off for St Quentin. When we rejoined the main road about 3 miles along we found that the transport had been got into order – a wonderful feat – and we got on to Estrees where we waited till our Captain came up. Then we rejoined the Division and were told to sleep the night in a small hut by the roadside a couple of miles on. There members of the staff turned up one by one, each thinking he was the only one left, and we cooked some supper for them. Late at night the General turned up and the column got off again. But we were told to sleep the night where we were and come on early in the morning. We were lazy and did not get started until 5.30 when everybody had cleared off except a few stragglers. We made our way by by-roads to St. Quentin but everywhere were deserted lorries in the ditch and stores thrown out by the wayside. I filled up with petrol from one such lorry and smashed up its engine a bit so that the Germans should not use it.

WHL WATSON RECALLS HIS RETURN TO REUMONT

Reproduced from COMPANY OF TANKS (1920)

Watson's second book about the war described his service in the Tank Corps. In November 1918 he arrived back on the same ground he had covered as a despatch rider, and found little remaining evidence of the battle.

In the afternoon I ran over with Thomas to Reumont, where we hoped to find the 11th Division, but a relief had not yet been completed and its staff had not arrived. We spent our spare time in walking out to the cottage, which had been the headquarters of the 5th Division on August 26,

August 1914: 60 pounder of 108th Battery during the Retreat.

1914, but time had swept away every trace of that first battle. The pits which had been dug on either side of the road to shelter the signallers had been filled in. The tiles of the cottage, loosened by the scaling-ladders of our intelligence officer, had been replaced. The little trenches had disappeared. But there was the hedge from the cover of which our one heavy battery, the 108th, had fired – it ran short of fuses in the old-fashioned way, and Grimers was sent hastily down the road on his motor-cycle for more. In that barn to the left we had slept hoggishly among the straw on the night before the battle, the first night's sleep since we had detrained at Landrecies and the last until we reached the Aisne. To my amazement the church behind the barn was still standing, intact except for a couple of shell-holes. I could have sworn that four years ago, as I was riding out of the village, I saw flames bursting from the roof. The Germans certainly entered the village not long after I had left it. Perhaps they may have extinguished the flames and repaired the damage.

GEORGE OWEN: 12 YEARS AGO – A DESPATCH RIDER AT MONS

Reproduced from the Owen family archive

The motorcyclists discover the country has been stripped bare of food.

At the first glimpse of dawn we were up and rode by a side road to St. Quentin. On the way we caught up a small body of infantry under a subaltern, all that was left of a battalion. He begged us to commandeer all the bread in the town for his men who were starving. On arriving there we found after a long search a small patisserie shop with a tin of biscuits for sale. There were ten of us, and we shared them, and never have I needed bread and meat so much.

CECIL HAYES-SADLER: LETTER TO HIS MOTHER

Reproduced from his daughter's archive

After making do with substitutes Cecil at last borrows a motorcycle.

Thursday 27th August
Then the retreat was resumed. Every day was much the same, we started retreating about 3.30 am and billeted for the night about 7 pm. As the horses got more tired, so I had to do more marching.

During halts I took my turn as a despatch rider on a borrowed machine.

On the Thursday we billeted at a Chateau near Ham, and there were able to bathe our feet in a stream.

Friday 28th August to Saturday 29th August
The next night we were at Noyon and the next again at a Chateau at Carlpont [sic] where, I remember, I slept on a gravel patch with many horses in close proximity to my head.

Sunday 30th August
The next night we arrived at Attichy. I rode nearly all that night with despatches.

Monday 31st August
The next day we reached Crépy. Just before getting there in the evening we were supposed to be surrounded by Uhlans. All dismounted men were ordered to seize rifles. My Captain said me, "Oh, by the way do you know how to use a rifle?!" With much fear and trepidation four of us went down each of the roads from the cross-roads which we were told to hold at all costs!! Luckily

nothing happened, and we were soon recalled and the march resumed. That night as far as I can remember I slept on a pavement.

STANLEY POLHILL: LETTER TO HIS FAMILY

Reproduced from Trident, the Trent College Magazine

Polhill doesn't play down their problems but finds positive things to report from their current situation, with conscious pride in the Army's achievements.

Aug 28th. 9.30 a.m. Thursday. I feel I must write you a few lines to-day while I have time since, if you are at home, you will doubtless have read of our losses especially in the divisions. It was certainly no fault of our men, particularly the artillery, who were decimated but fought like true heroes. We were outnumbered five to one and more. We have retired each day since Sunday. What hurt me so was seeing the motor bikes and motor lorries abandoned on the road; there was no time to mend. Fortunately my motor bike has stuck to it nobly or I should not be here to write. My only trouble so far was a puncture the day before yesterday. I must stop now; troops are pouring in; the road for ten or eleven miles is crowded with our men. We re-organise here, we may rest a day or two. If I came out for experience, I am certainly getting it. Our captain says South Africa was a picnic to this! We were shelled at Headquarters by shrapnel yesterday, but I escaped unhurt. The shell has a peculiar whistle before it bursts. They got some good shots in yesterday, but we did better; their loss must have been heavy.

Part 2

September 1914

ARNOLD OVERTON: LETTER TO HIS MOTHER

From the Overton family collection

After describing the carnage at Le Cateau, the despatch rider notices indications of improved morale – the general in the front line, the resourceful artificer, and the despatch rider who fired his weapon in anger.

On the morning of Sept 1st we were attacked by German infantry before starting. The enemy must have thought we were absolutely demoralised, for they had no artillery to support their attack, and they were driven off with heavy losses. I was sent to the 13th Brigade with an important message and in order to find them went over country where our sergeant swore he was fired on by Uhlans! Personally I have my doubts. I found the General right up in the firing line and saw our infantry charging the Germans. After I had returned to Crepy our h.q. were ordered to move when I discovered my back tyre flat and a nail through it. Burney and I mended it in 7 minutes and we got off before the rearguard came through all right. We had great difficulty in finding h.q. again and came across some cavalry motorcyclists who had run into a patrol of Uhlans. They had got round and made off all right, but one had a cut in the top of his tank from a bullet, while the other had emptied his revolver into them. Having successfully beaten off this German attack, we made an easy march to Nanteuil and slept at a small village just beyond it. Next morning we rose at 3.30 and made a long march to Vinantes within range of Paris. We motorcyclists went on Vinantes by ourselves and failing to take the right turning arrived at Dammartin just inside the ring of Paris fortifications. After some difficulty we got breakfast there and after examining a deserted 3½ Douglas by the roadside, we rejoined the column to the East. I then took Bagshaw back on my carrier and fitted him up with the Douglas and we arrived quite early at Vinantes. Our quarters were very comfortable in a farm-house but there were heaps of messages going over narrow dusty roads. That night Burney II taking a message to 2nd Army H.Q. after dark, failed to notice a sentry and was fired at, the bullet whistling past his ear. After this we began a crusade against sentries firing on motorcyclists after dark, but this did [not] bear much fruit till later.

CECIL HAYES-SADLER: LETTER TO HIS MOTHER

Reproduced from his daughter's archive

After using – and losing – another borrowed motorcycle, Cecil at last is sent to collect a brand new motorcycle.

Tuesday 1st September

The next day I borrowed a bike and after a hard day's riding with messages, we halted at Nanteuil.

190

Wednesday 2nd September

The next day I had to take to a push bike again and arrived at a village called Vinantes, where got a little sleep on some straw in the open.

Thursday 3rd September

I hung on to my push bike the next day but about 11.30 arriving at a place called Trilbardou I was told to wait behind for my Captain. I turned my back for a moment and my bike was gone like a flash! After looking for it and the Captain for over an hour I thought it adviseable to walk on. Just as I started the bridge just behind me was blown up. After marching all by myself for a good many miles I came upon a few stragglers, and crossed another bridge was blown up soon after I had crossed it. I then walked about another 8 miles or so until I rejoined Div: Headquarters at Bouleurs.

Friday 4th September

On the Friday we proceeded to Tournan, one part of the way on a waggon.

After a long long ride that day I was sent to Le Mans with "Trepass", another motor cyclist, to get new bikes. After being conveyed in a motor to some station we got into a luggage van for Paris. Sitting in the van I found an Eton friend of mine. On our arrival in Paris that night we had dinner and then rushed across in a taxi to another station, and only just caught our train. I was sorry I could not have seen more of Paris whilst on my first visit there.

STANLEY POLHILL: LETTER TO HIS FAMILY

Reproduced from Trident, the Trent College Magazine

The writer reflects on how busy the motorcyclists have been in the Retreat.

Sept. 2nd. I must take this opportunity of our first slack day since war began of writing, or rather scrawling, you a few lines. I'm lying in some straw in a big farm-yard utterly at peace with the world. The sun is boiling hot, but there is a jolly breeze, and but for the sound of big guns in the distance nothing reminds one of war. Our little band has done no end of useful work, so several generals have told us, and we've certainly been kept busy enough, night and day. A lot of the roads are "pavé", which fairly knocks the bikes about. I've got a cracked front spindle which I have to nurse over pavé; but the engine has run beautifully every day and night. I hope to clean it out for the first time this evening, if I'm not too slack after tea. We eleven usually look after our own food; occasionally we draw bully beef and dog biscuits from the Company, more often we purchase bread, butter, and bacon in some village, or eggs from a farm. We are never very short of food.

4/9/14. I can't give you much news of the war though there is oceans to give. As you must have seen from the papers all is not well, and the turning point should be in a day or two now. We have been in three battles so far and fighting almost every day we've lost pretty heavily. However, the men are fit and well, especially the motor cyclists. We get through quite a lot of work, mostly night. The night before last we took one hundred-and-one despatches, some many miles. The weather has been just lovely for us, too hot for walking, and a full moon lately has helped us. It's incredible to think we've been out here just over a fortnight, it seems more like two months. We found two 3½ Douglas's on the road abandoned the other day, so collared them, and have made them go. We now have eleven bikes and twelve men. The fruit here is most abundant, often the road is lined for miles with apple and pear trees, and all the villagers supply us with fruit wherever we stop. So you see though the work is hard the fare is good. My bike is still running well. Yesterday they gave me paraffin for petrol and I didn't spot it till I was blue in the face trying to start it.

CECIL HAYES-SADLER: LETTER TO HIS MOTHER

Reproduced from his daughter's archive

Cecil repeatedly returns to recounting the varied places he has found to sleep.

Saturday 5th September

After a tedious journey, worse than our L.S.W.R[1] one to town, we arrived at Le Mans the next morning having taken 6 hours to do the last four miles!

Sunday 6th September

After much fuss we got two bikes and then were glad to learn that the English had started advancing.

Monday 7th September

At 8.0 the next morning we started off to rejoin. After riding hard with few halts we rejoined at Colomniers at 12.30 that night. The first hour of that night I slept in a wheelbarrow, the second on a gravel path, and the rest of the night I spent buried in the midst of a large flower bed!

Tuesday 8th September

All the next day we advanced, seeing everywhere many strange and dreadfully gruesome sights, we spent the night or part of it again at a Chateau where once more I slept in a flower bed.

Wednesday 9th September

The next night after a very hard day's riding we slept in the billiard room of another chateau, I was lucky enough to secure the sofa to sleep on.

STANLEY POLHILL: LETTER TO HIS FAMILY

Reproduced from Trident, the Trent College Magazine

The war of movement is coming to an end, and Stanley can see the munitions and supplies which are beginning to pour into the battle-zone from England.

15/9/14. We are now in the middle of a big pitched battle. I hear on good authority that one-and-a-quarter million men are taking part altogether on both sides. The enemy are most strongly entrenched on the hills opposite, but we hope to move them in a day or. We've had jolly cosy quarters here since Sunday morning, an open sided shed with plenty of straw. The weather was beautiful the first three weeks, but has changed, and we've had rain on an off for ten days now. The

---

1   London & South Western Railway

Sadders took this shot of his fellow despatch riders at Serches – they were housed in a yard at the back of the village school. Spuggy (centre) watches Cecil Burney with the frying pan.

The open-sided shed at Serches where the motorcyclists had their mess. Orr is behind the table second from left; on this side of the table are Alick and Cecil Burney. The despatch rider with his back to the camera (right) may be Trepess.

Alick Burney working on a Douglas at Serches – note that he is seated on a 2-gallon petrol can.

roads are in parts very bad and quite impassable, as one's mudguards get absolutely full of stiff mud every few yards. We've had gun fire all round us for two days, and can sleep through it now quite easily. The battle you refer to, the Battle of Mons, certainly was exciting, we were in the thick of it and retired at the last moment from Deuse [sic]. Thank goodness we're advancing again now, that fortnight of retreating was the limit.

18/9/14. As I write, we are tucked in straw in an open-sided shed, behind a hill. Big guns are going all round, and plenty of aeroplanes about. It's so windy to-day; I saw an aeroplane going backwards slightly instead of forwards. The enemy are very strongly entrenched over the hill on another range two miles away. There are nearly half a million here. Our job is to prevent them bolting up this valley while the French attack. No, I've not shot any Germans yet, nor been wounded, nor had trouble with the bike other than punctures. Our job is not killing Germans, but rather dodging being killed by them. So far, I've been eminently successful, though we've all been through plenty of shell and some rifle fire this week, we've not lost a man of the twelve yet.[1] Very dull, is'nt it? No, we don't get much time for bathes. Sometimes we don't wash for two or three days. I had a bath(e)? three weeks back and was lucky to get it, and I undressed yesterday, the first time since.

Sunday, 9 a.m. We should have some close fighting to-day. Somehow we always arrange our fights on Wednesday and Sunday. I went to H.C.[2] this morning, it was certainly unconventional with a ground sheet as altar cloth, most of us motor cyclists were present. Our big field guns roared out several times during the service.

Monday, 21/9/14. V. Div. H.Q. – You might enjoy the scene before me. The cyclists who are sharing this shed with us have got (I don't know how) a sheep, and are cutting it up with huge glee on a ground sheet: awful mess! My bike has stood things awfully well, only once in the six weeks has it failed to start up straight away and run non-stop; and that time a tappet stuck up with burnt

---

1   Has he overlooked the disappearance of Fielding-Johnson?
2   Holy Communion.

oil was responsible. That's pretty good, when you think they've stood out in all the rain day after day for a fortnight. The cylinder is bright yellow with rust; I've not even shortened a belt yet.[1]

25/9/14. V. Div. H.Q. - As I write the enemy are trying to bring down one of our aeroplanes with shrapnel, but we don't worry, they pot at it every day and never get it by any chance. They must have used hundreds of rounds on it by now. However it's amusing and we all turn out and watch how close the small pure white patches of smoke get to the plane. We're getting quite used to their shell fire by now, they certainly don't seem to be the shots they were made out to be. I suppose familiarity breeds contempt. We're having a fairly easy time of it here, after our energetic retirement and bustling advance. I think we deserve it. We're pretty well off for quarters, having straw in an open sided shed at the back of the village school, which is our headquarters (H.Q.). We feed on bully beef and biscuit, bread and jam, and a little bacon. The bread I'm told is made near Bristol, but we can buy fresh not far away. The biscuits are H. & P. Army No. 5, just at present, we change to ship biscuit often. The jam ration is instead of vegetables, and is quarter-pound per day. Altogether we don't do at all badly and have seldom been on half rations.

ANON: THE MOTOR CYCLE – October 8th 1914

The weekly papers for motorcyclists printed frequent reports from despatch riders.

The last news from the Burney brothers states that up to the 18th of last month they were well. The Blackburnes were among the few machines used by the despatch riders that had given absolutely no trouble to date, but E.A. Burney had lost his owing to its being driven over by heavy artillery during the night.

After the loss of Alick's Blackburne, Stanley Polhill posed whimsically on the frame which has been stripped of everything useful. Its registration number identifies it as the motorcycle Alick rode at Brooklands in 1913. Note the tank bottom left and the front wheel bottom right (Cast, page 134).

---

1   See Appendix ll, page 262.

Sadders no doubt aimed to picture a bullock cart bringing in the harvest amongst the military campaign – but the shadow cast by the motorcyclist reveals that nothing is normal in September 1914.

CECIL HAYES-SADLER: LETTER TO HIS MOTHER

Reproduced from his daughter's archive

After sharing more light-hearted information about his sleeping arrangements, Cecil gives a vivid description of the tasks the despatch riders undertook.

Sunday 13th September to Friday 2nd October

We arrived at a place called Serches, just south of the Aisne near Soissons on Sunday Sept. 13th. There we remained till Oct.2nd, sleeping when could in an open shed. While riding out [to] the Brigades from there I had several nasty experiences. One night I spent more than five hours trying to find the general, crossing and recrossing the river (Aisne) on a couple of planks, knee deep in water.

Another day I had to take despatches to two Brigades. After riding across a large open space which was being shelled I eventually got to a village, part of which was under cover and rest all knocked about, with heaps of dead men and horses, etc, all along the road. At the end of the village I turned a corner and went down a road about 200 yards to a farm where the first message had to be delivered.

The Germans very kindly stopped shelling the corner to let me pass, and then I went on again! After delivering the first message I was told the next Brigade Headquarters were in a village 1 mile away along the road. I set off and heard many cracks of rifles, but it was not 'till I heard the "zipping" of bullets all about me, that I realised the Germans were sniping me from on road on the left 200 yards from my road. I put on all speed and was glad to get under cover of the said village. There I was told that Headquarters was on the railway line and on the way to the village, and some 300 yards from the road running parallel to it.

An 'ambulance' (military hospital unit) in the valley above Serches during the Battle of the Aisne.

I licked back, and half way along the road left my bike at a farm and crept, under cover when possible, to the railway line. Then I started walking along the line to the village. After I had got some yards with bullets pattering all round me, I was told by some regiment under cover of the embankment that it was most unsafe! So as I had to get my despatch through somehow, I turned back and decided to try the road again. By the time I got to the village, being sniped all the way, I found Headquarters there. After running with two more despatches between the Brigades I went back to Divisional Headquarters, thinking to get a rest. A few minutes later I was sent off again to those two Brigades; when I got the first, I found that the second had been shelled out of its little village. I was told I should find the General in a ditch! which I could only reach by creeping under cover for some way and then bolting across a field for some 400 yards. I was able to do this with bullets whistling all round me and troops retiring in the opposite direction, but could not find the General, so had to do the bolt again and come back!

Part 3

October to December 1914

CECIL HAYES-SADLER: LETTER TO HIS MOTHER

Reproduced from his daughter's archive

Cecil's account of the first months of the war concludes with the move to the north. A few weeks later, towards the end of October, and not far from where he was serving, his cousins, Jack and Ernest Hayes-Sadler, were killed over a period of three days. No more of his letters from the Front have survived.

On leaving Serches I was again attached to a Brigade, and spent the night riding past long columns, but eventually reached a beautiful chateau at Longpont the next night where one dined fairly comfortably with the General.

The next night I did a lot more riding again and eventually got a little sleep at Bethezy St Martin [sic]. The next two nights we were at Béthancourt, the next at a chateau again.

The next day all the rest went by train to Abbeville. I remained with "Meldrum" and we had to follow two staff cars by road. We billeted at Verbine that night, and after riding hard all the next day we billeted at an old Chateau near Abbeville, where I actually slept in a bed! The next day we rejoined the Division at [Gueschart]. After two or three days we arrived at a railway station near Mlle Martin's home (Béthune). There we billeted in the tiny little waiting room for close on three weeks. It was quite near here that Jack was killed, also Ernest.

I had a good many nasty experiences there. Once I had to go to an observation station in a factory in a village, and my luck! just as I got there the English were being shelled out and driven back. Many bullets were flying and dead and wounded men lying all around, but I was luckily able to deliver my despatch and get away again. We have moved again since then but I've no more time now to write any more.

ARNOLD OVERTON: LETTER TO HIS MOTHER

From the Overton family collection

Like most of the despatch riders on leaving the Aisne, Overton enjoyed the long rides free of gunfire. After several days on the road through Longpont and Abbeville, the 5th Division engaged the Germans at La Bassée. There was four days' confused fighting before the Signal company was installed at Beuvry station.

On October 2nd our division was relieved by the 6th Divn. and we had 5 days or usually nights marching. The brigades were spread out over a length of about 20 miles & we had a succession of lovely long rides through delightful country with rather too much night work to be pleasant. The road was also used by French lorries & motor-buses packed with troops being pushed up to the left flank. Of where we were going we knew nothing, but the most persistent rumour had it that our destination was Antwerp. It was not till we detrained at Abbeville & found G.H.Q. there that we realised we should be pushed up towards Arras & that not only our division but the whole British Army was moved round at the same time.

Oct 9th. The following night at 9.30 pm Meldrum and I were sent on through St. Pol past numerous French motor buses which arrived late to transport our troops to be attached to the 14th at Diéval. For the last few miles there had been no signs of anybody & at Diéval found nothing. We got rather bad wind up, not knowing where the Germans might be & so retired to the Chateau at Brias & slept there in a horse-stall – very comfortable. Early next morning we went to Diéval where we found the 14th just arriving in buses which were 12 hours late. They did not want us, so we soon returned to the Division which had now arrived at Brias. That afternoon we spent on our bikes which badly needed overhauling, & in the evening we were very busy riding. That night I was attached to the 13th nearby, but most of the night I was out on messages & the rest I spent uncomfortably in a crowded & rat-infested barn.

Oct 11th. I was up very early & spent very nearly the whole day riding up and down the column between Brias & Béthune – an ugly industrial district crammed with 'civvies'. With darkness came no rest, as we had to hunt out brigades along the most complicated lanes, & I had to take all the messages to one brigade whose whereabouts I knew. That night we spent at Chocques Chateau – the motorcyclists & signals office being in the conservatory.

These 4 days of marching up from Abbeville were to me the most unpleasant of the whole war up to now. We were kept on the go practically the whole time, without actually fighting; we didn't know what was happening & whether or not to expect spare Uhlans; there was a lot of night work as the days were closing in so I was absolutely fed up with it by the time we arrived at Chocques.

Oct 12th turned out a glorious day, but in the morning it was very misty. H.Q. moved to the canal at Béthune & our brigades got into action, pivoting round on our right wing which rested on the French left, while on our left the 3rd Div. continued the movement. Beyond them were the 3rd and 1st Corps from which we kept hearing excellent news, for in the 1st week's fighting up here we had a great advantage over the Germans. Then they were reinforced & it was all we could do to hold our trenches, especially towards the end of the month when we were left with absolutely no reserve & under a heavy pressure

I think we were all heartily glad to be having another go at the Germans. Owing to the fog we motorcyclists were practically all unable to find the Signal Office & for about the first hour only two of us were there! The others I afterwards found out to my great indignation had not had equal difficulty in finding a patisserie!

Our brigades drove the Germans back several miles & by lunch time headquarters was able to move up to Beuvry station. Here in the waiting room – crawling with lice & strewed with filthy straw, we were to stay 3 eventful weeks. But we motorcyclists played a very tame part compared to that in the early fighting. The only risky job was done by Hayes Saddler [sic] who had to take a message to an observation post, past the ill-famed gap where the Dorsets were mown down in hundreds before his eyes by a German machine gun.

The nastiest job was being attached for the day to Chapman with the French brigade on our right, for round here bags of shells kept falling & not a few stray bullets, while a double battery of 'soixantes-quinzes' across the road always give one a headache.

The brigade jobs were very quiet, but when one was attached to brigades, there were a few spare shells round & I once had a Johnston[1] across the road 200 yards in front of me. I turned round & went to my destination by another road!

---

1   See footnote, page 105.

STANLEY POLHILL: LETTER TO HIS FAMILY

Reproduced from Trident, the Trent College Magazine

Stanley's letters range over many topics – he reports on the state of the roads and the condition of their motorcycles while reflecting on the prospects of eventual victory.

October 19th. As I write, our guns flash out every minute, and eight seconds after, you can hear the report, the whistle, and then the shell exploding in the distance. The roads round the three brigade headquarters are quite tricky at night, on account of the numerous large shell-holes in the road. One man dropped into one last night, on a "Triumph", and hopelessly kinked in the back wheel. We took him out our spare wheel, only to find it was a 1913 pattern and wouldn't fit. Luckily we've got a spare bike, which he's now got. I'm going over to 2nd Army Headquarters to get another wheel or another bike.

When you come to think of it, the Germans are putting up a jolly good show. With three powerful nations against them, they are holding their own extraordinarily well. Even the beggars in front of us are retiring only slowly, and the French have been held up by some machine guns quite a time. But they can't stand it indefinitely; we're grinding on and on, and our men are in topping health and spirits. When I was up passing the trenches this morning, the men kept shouting to me for news, and were all laughing or joking in their shelters, or curled up asleep.

At Beuvry Station Cecil's Blackburne is in the foreground of this picture. In the background, the motorcyclists watching an enemy aeroplane are gathering for the group photograph which appears in Chapter Nine (page 91).

Cecil's machine AR3349 (pictured here) is the only machine used in France in 1914 which is known to have survived the war – presumably Cecil took it back to England with him when he was commissioned in 1915, and it was photographed there in 1920.

Cooking breakfast at Beuvry station – Giblett (in a cap) and Alick Burney (wearing a light-coloured sweater) watch Polhill (crouching) and Watson (bent double) in front of him

BRIGADIER-GENERAL COUNT EDWARD GLEICHEN: BRIGADE HISTORY

Extract from "The Doings of the 15th Infantry Brigade" (1917)

This account by the commanding officer of the 15th Brigade probably explains why Stanley Polhill found French and British artillery near to one another.

October 19th

In the evening I went to examine a French 75 mm. battery, and had the whole thing explained to me. The gun is simply marvellous, slides horizontally on its own axle, never budges however much it fires, and has all sorts of patent dodges besides: but it is no use painting the lily!

Wilson, of the 61st Howitzers, was, by the way, a little aggrieved by this French battery coming and taking up its position close alongside him and invading his observing stations. The captain also got on his nerves, for he was somewhat excitable, and his shells were numerous that burst prematurely, whilst a house only 100 yards off, which should have been well under the trajectory of his shells, was several times hit by them. However, he doubtless caused much damage to the enemy.

4.5 inch howitzers in action – in all likelihood the three guns depicted are a battery of
61st Howitzer Brigade, mentioned by Count Gleichen, which formed part of 5th Division's
Royal Field Artillery detachment.

A French 75mm 'soixante-quinze' battery – in late October 1914 some French batteries were put under the command of one of the 5th Division Howitzer Brigades.

STANLEY POLHILL: LETTER TO HIS FAMILY

Reproduced from Trident, the Trent College Magazine

Stanley has forthright opinions about the conduct of the German army.

October 22nd. A slack day at last; a day of relief for mind and body, and I was jolly glad to get it. You know, I expect, that we usually keep one or two of our men at each of our Brigade Headquarters. Well, today, as everything seemed to be all right at Div. Headquarters, I've taken a day off and relieved one of the men at the fourteenth here. Brigade jobs are quite slack; it's only once in a blue moon that a message from a brigade is too important to send by wire, so our job is merely a nominal one and we take it in turn to come to the brigades and slack. This is my first opportunity of doing so. It's a tremendous relief to get away from the eternal call of "Next motor-cyclist." I think I shall trot back to-morrow after breakfast, but I guess things will go all right for a day. H.Q. (Headquarters) here are at an inn, which by some travesty of fate was named "Auberge de la Bombe". It's had plenty of bombs round it lately! Until this week it was the H.Q. of a German division, and three generals were quartered there. The old lady is still there and looks after the bar: but I hear they are to be shifted to-morrow as one of the daughters is suspected of being a spy. I've got a photo of the house among others taken here.

I'm told the generals behaved well and paid for all they drank; but it's a jolly different tale here at the house I am writing in. The other man Orr, and myself chummed up to the post sergeant and corporal here. They have a room and fire to themselves. We had lunch with these two, and tea. Tea was really almost like home. We had a *teapot* and cups and *saucers* and a sugar basin and all. And what *do* you think, we ended up with cake! The sergeant's wife had sent him out one. It's 7.30 now, and we're sitting by their fire – a fire in a proper grate, mind you! and writing letters at a big oval oak table. Many things truly look like home, but many *don't*. The mantelpiece mirror is smashed to atoms, all the cupboards are ransacked and the contents thrown on the floor. Upstairs looks positively awful; all the mattresses are torn open, the drawers turned out on to the floor, clothing of all kinds torn up and scattered about the room; wine glasses and half-empty bottles standing on the beds and tables, and all the looking-glasses smashed, and the basins and jugs ditto. It looks like the work of maniacs, and absolutely sickened me; I can't understand such absolutely wanton destruction. Nearly all the houses in the village, I'm told, are in a similar condition: how many of the inhabitants stayed on here beats me (this is a very different opinion from my other and earlier one of the German soldier). No words are too bad to describe the horrors that have taken place in this small village. Some of the girls and women have died from their treatment, and many are in our hospitals. The men have all left. But the Germans can fight, that's quite certain. They were through our trenches last night at one place and nearly through again to-day. Yes, they're brutes, some of them, but tough brutes! Thank God it's not in England. But if this sounds downhearted, don't think I am. These sights and tales sicken me, but we've none of us any doubt of the final result.

October 23rd. Early this morning I saw what looked like a solid cone of flame of enormous height showing above the trees in the distance. On enquiring I learnt that it was a church tower. The church had been burning all night and had left the tower, incandescent with heat standing straight up by itself like a gigantic candle flame.

Stanley also shares his views of the French.

Oct. 25. 11.50 a.m. You say you like letters from the centre of things; well, here's one. I'm writing this time from the H.Q. of a French brigade on our right. We keep an officer always at their H.Q. and one of us comes along for an attachment each day. I'm rather bored though, as I've struck a quiet day.

I've had my lunch, or whatever they call it. I jolly nearly missed it altogether, as I forgot that they have only two meals a day – 11 a.m. and 6.30 p.m., with coffee at 6.30 a.m. I must say they *do* know how to cook. I had the most lovely soup, roast beef, and potatoes, and coffee destined for the general. I've also cemented my friendship with the general by filling and mending his petrol mechanical lighter for him. They are an awful lot of chatterboxes here, and the house might be the parrot house at the Zoo. But they're a sporting lot and I get along famously as long as they don't talk too fast.

They are a funny crowd here, mostly captains; there seem to be swarms of captains. They get most furiously excited over nothing special. There's an old captain fairly bawling down the 'phone beside me as I write, because their motor-cyclist has been collared by some other officer for a job. They've only one motor-cyclist of their own here, on a prehistoric mount called the "Wanderer".[1] One thing I notice, the soldiers have the vaguest ideas about saluting. They do it when they think of it or when spoken to; but it's a slovenly affair at the best, and they just don't seem to take any *pride* in it. My friend the old general has just been along to ask if I've fed well; nice old boy.

The Indian Division arrived in late October and went into the line next to the 5th Division – and the English cyclists had a bad scare.

I'm afraid we shall soon be hearing of the English atrocities. The Indian beggars are awfully good fighters, but much too fond of souvenirs; ears are their speciality. When a shell bursts near their trenches they hop out and have a look at the hole; I expect they'll get into things later on. The day after I wrote you last (I was at the 14th. H.Q. you remember) the staff left the inn jolly hurriedly and it was smashed up by shell fire just twenty-five minutes after. The same day one of our men, Meldrum, was sent to the Manchesters, missed them, and before he realised it was well *in front* of our firing line. He turned amid a shower of bullets and got back with only a graze on one leg.

---

1   Appendix ll, page 261.

Pollers' picture shows a barricade – probably near Beuvry station – which would be impassable to any wheeled vehicle.

As he got a new puttee out of it he doesn't mind, and was at work again by the evening. Some of our divisional "push" cyclists (i.e. ordinary bicycles, not motor-bicycles) two nights ago were riding, lightless up to our trenches. By some extraordinary means they got a mile and a half into the enemy's lines before they discovered their mistake. The sentry had passed them *on purpose*. They turned and got back part of the way before being met by heavy rifle and machine-gun fire. Only one man was killed, all the bikes hit and dozens of spokes cut. One man went right back afterwards and returned with a wounded companion on his back, and wanted to go again for his bike but wasn't allowed. Shows how close our lines are here.

THE BURNEYS' VIEW FROM THE DESPATCH RIDERS' BILLET AT BAILLEUL

The despatch riders remembered this as one of their better lodgings – though their window faced east towards the Front.

THE BURNEYS RECORD CAPTURED GERMAN AIRMEN AT LOCRE – 27TH NOVEMBER 1914

For the despatch riders Locre was one of their best billets, but the Signal company moved from here because they were too near the Front – these captured German airmen would have been operating over the front lines.

ERIC BAGSHAW'S JOURNEY HOME ON LEAVE

Reproduced from Michael Sadler's Memorandum of a conversation with Eric Bagshaw, in the Michael Sadler Archive, Leeds University Library Special Collections

Michael Sadler enquired about Bagshaw's journey home on leave – even using the Channel Tunnel, it would be difficult to match this journey time today.

On the morning of the previous day (Sunday, the 29th) he went with dispatches [sic] from 5 till 7. At 7 he left his post near Ypres; was at Boulogne at 11; in England at 1.30; London at 4; Leeds at 9.30. He leaves Leeds next Saturday morning by the breakfast train and will be on duty on Sunday morning.

ARNOLD OVERTON: LETTER TO HIS MOTHER

From the Overton family collection

Overton returns from leave to the unpopular billet at St Jans Cappel.

Dec 13th. We woke up in the morning to find everything at St Jans Cappel just as we had left it. The British Army in France had not missed our presence as much as the shortness of the leave it gave us led us to expect. Meldrum who was due to come back, had not arrived & we afterwards heard he had got his leave extended by the W.O. pending his somewhat mysterious commission in the A.S.C.M.T.

   In December then we felt pretty sure that we should remain where we were for the next 3 or 4 months. It was obviously therefore our first business to make ourselves as comfortable as possible. But this under the conditions was no easy task. Between 10 & 12 of us, we were crowded into 2

Sadders contemplates "the big house" at St Jans Cappel – the despatch riders' quarters were on the first floor of the Lodge over the stables (pictured at page 210).

nasty little attics above the stable where the staff's horses were. Each of these little rooms measured about 14' × 9' & it was all we could do to crowd 6 into each. There were cracks in the floor through which came a strong stink of horses – especially when they had got wet. There was only a tiny little window in each room which we always had to keep wide open for it to be light enough to see or fresh enough to breathe. In spite of these disadvantages we managed to sleep 6 in our room & by rolling up our kits by day we had sufficient room for a folding iron table & iron collapsible chairs, which we had 'scrounged' from the summer-house. In our room were Trepess, Bagshaw, Owen, Hayes Sadler, myself & Danson when he came back from the base in February. We were all bridge-players except for Danson & Hayes Sadler which made things rather uncomfortable for them in the evenings, for it meant they always had to lie down on somebody else's kit.

We naturally collected a good deal of kit in this winter. Half of us had sleeping bags & Polhill always slept in pyjamas. The rest of us were content to sleep in our underclothes except George Owen who not until the spring could be persuaded to take his breeches off at night. Most of us had a spare pair of boots for when we got wet through & with slacks & our leather coats we all had a complete change.

Underclothing mounted up a good deal, for we were slack about getting it washed & it always made a soft warm mattress. Periodically however some had to be burnt owing to its getting infested with mice, or given away to the guard who were so far gone in this respect that they did not mind a few more.

THE GROUP PHOTOGRAPHS TAKEN ON CHRISTMAS DAY 1914

Hugh Trepess, Cecil Burney, Arnold Overton, and George Owen
begin to gather for the Christmas group photograph.

One of the photographs taken on Christmas Day 1914 – of the 12 men who joined the
Signal company at Carlow in August, Fielding Johnson was missing, presumed dead, and
Danson was absent on sick leave. From left to right, Orr, Polhill, Watson, Hayes-Sadler,
Trepess, Bagshaw, Alick Burney, Owen, and Cecil Burney. The picture above was
taken by Overton, the picture below by Polhill

THE MOTORCYCLE SHELTER AT ST JANS CAPPEL

Three of the despatch riders construct the motorcycle shelter, which was a lean-to against the company's stable. A fourth watches from their sleeping-quarters above the stable. The war diary for December, which Doherty Holwell asked Watson to write, recorded: "a garage for motorcycles was constructed on 29th December, blown down the next day, and reconstructed in a more sheltered position on 31st December."

Part 4

January to August 1915

ARNOLD OVERTON: LETTER TO HIS MOTHER

From the Overton family collection

In December 1914, things had begun to change – the despatch riders had become "mere postmen" and some of the motorcyclists who replaced those who had left didn't share their social background.

Of course during the winter we did a great deal of grousing, for we were in very uncomfortable quarters & had nothing much else to do. About the end of January we were told that there were a certain amount of motorcyclist commissions to be given to motorcyclists & of course we all rushed at it. In February the elder Burney obtained one of these commissions – he was much the best man for it – & went to England to train Kitchener's motorcyclists.

Finally about this time Polhill was transferred to 2nd Army after a row with the sergeant-major & Merchant, & Trepess was made Sergeant – the obvious man. Thus by the end of February Trepess, Owen, Hayes-Sadler, Orr, myself & Danson were the only originals left.

This break-up of our original set was quite the most annoying thing of the lot for us who were left. But before I begin on the phase which then began I must give you an idea of our life throughout the winter i.e. Dec to Feb. inclusive. After the bombardment in the middle of December there was literally no excitement throughout these months. The only thing that happened was occasional shellings of Neuve Eglise which became more intense in February so that brigade headquarters moved out of the village & troops were no longer billeted there. Our only danger was from a chance shell in Neuve Eglise if they happened to be shelling the place; and this was hardly enough to make one realise there was a war on. Church, one of the new motorcyclists who was attached to the Neuve Eglise brigade, was unlucky enough to get killed by one of these shells; but soon afterwards brigade headquarters moved back & one only had to skirt Neuve Eglise, instead of going into the square by a horrible corner where 17 men were killed one day by a shell. Personally I only passed Neuve Eglise once when it was being shelled, & so you can judge what small chances we had of being hit.

CECIL BURNEY AND HUGH TREPESS TAKE A TRIP TO ROUEN

JANUARY 1914

CECIL B. EN ROUTE FOR ROUEN

JANUARY. 1915.

C.S.B. RETURNING FROM ROUEN TO St. JANS CAPPELL

In the first week of January 1915 Cecil and Hugh (see Cast, page 143) went to Rouen for 'rest & recuperation' – a 250 mile round trip for which they used a Royal Enfield 8 hp combination. They enjoyed good weather on the outward journey, but seemingly returned in atrocious conditions. Cecil's caption, written when the album was being put together after the war, notes the date erroneously as 1914

WHL WATSON BECOMES A SUBALTERN IN A CYCLIST BATTALION

Reproduced from 'Tales of a Gaspipe Officer' in *Blackwood's Magazine*

After finishing the book version of 'Adventures', Watson began to produce the first instalments of his story as Cyclist subaltern, in which he appeared, in the third person, as "the Gaspipe Officer."

I Prologue

From the start his fellow officers challenge him to behave like an officer rather than the scruffy despatch rider he had become.

The village of St Jans, which is in French Flanders a mile or so from the Belgian Frontier, contains an *estaminet* that, to the best of my remembrance, has no name beyond the proprietor's, and the name of the proprietor cannot be pronounced and is never remembered. This *estaminet* almost faces the well-known *Maison Commune Estaminet* and the huge convent which in February 1915, both before and after, was filled with wounded and sick men and officers, who, for the most part, played good bridge.

In the main room of the nameless *estaminet* were living three officers, Bill, and M'Queen, and Jumbo. M'Queen, who was a captain, commanded the Divisional Cyclist Company.[1] Bill, who was also a captain, and Jumbo, ruled platoons. There was a third platoon with no officer. So the Gaspipe Officer walked down one evening from the top of the hill, reported himself to M'Queen, and, instead of eating, sleeping, and having his being in a tiny room together with five others, found himself an officer and a gentleman with a servant to wait upon him and thirty odd men of his own.

It was a famous Company. Before Mons it had pedalled in triumphantly from a successful little affair of outposts. It had waited for the Germans when some squadrons of a famous regiment had ridden through it in despair. Every day and every night of the Great Retreat it had kept unwinking guard on the rear of the Division. The men of the Company had never tired and had never been driven in. Then the Division advanced with the Cyclists merrily ahead of it. On the Marne they had rounded up a hundred and fifty German Guardsmen, and brought in eighty, although shelled by their own guns – they were then not sixty strong. On the Aisne they were out every night patrolling a sensitive sector of the line, and, near La Bassée, held as a mobile reserve, they were twice thrown against the German attack, and they stayed the attack. The Division went north. Every man was hurled into the firing line for the defence of Ypres. The Cyclists were put into the trenches at Hooge, and there they lost their commanding officer, a very gallant gentleman, who, being seriously wounded, passed through hospitals until he came home. And in February 1915 the Company was patrolling miles of wire and making innumerable fascines....

It was a famous Company. Also, it was a comfortable *estaminet*. The new officer nervously drew in his chair to the great blaze of the fire and ordered a drink. He thought without regret of the tiny stuffy room and Grimers laboriously frying a dab over a smoking, evil-smelling stove.

II Night-life in Paris

Watson's height – he was 6' 6½" tall – created the opportunity for his expedition. Paris was a destination for leave, as well as a place where he could have a uniform tailor-made.

It was M'Queen that raised the point.

---

1   Captain Donald McQueen Fraser (1879–1938) was a schoolmaster in Liverpool.

"You know, my dear Gaspipe, you were filthy and unshorn. Since you've become an officer, you've made attempts. … You have shaved, and, so far as I can see, you are clean. But I really can't have one of my officers going about in the tattered kit of a corporal. We'll try the Div."

M'Queen was right. And there was a further difficulty. The callow sub. had been a brother-in-arms to the men he was now supposed to command. He had sung choruses to the vile songs of Foster, that very Yorkshireman. He had been given tea at all times, and in all places. Jock, the Company tailor, was an honoured and frequent guest of the Despatch Riders' Mess. Had he not empurpled many an evening? A few days before the Cyclists had entertained their future despot to a fine meal – and odorous memories of Croucher and his pork chop still lingered. A little leave of absence and a lot of new kit might solve the difficulties of discipline.

The Div. was tried and found wanting. No leave and kit to be obtained through Ordnance. But the Gaspipe Officer possessed certain physical peculiarities for which Ordnance had never allowed.

The idea was Jumbo's. [Jumbo is a Territorial officer of fabulous girth, energy, and language. He had spent the early days of the war fiercely defending the coast of Yorkshire, and he filled us with such tales of day and night work without rest or food that we all firmly believed the real heroes of this war had never fired a shot – except at spying bushes in a doubtful light.]

"Paris is not so far from St Jans. It can be reached by rail or motor-cycle. He has a pass and can get a motorcycle. Send him to Paris for his kit!"

The Sergeant of the Despatch Riders, old Huggie, saw the point of the argument and turned a blind eye as the young officer prepared his old motor-cycle for a long journey. Then it began to rain, so the man who had been compelled to ride by night and day in every kind of weather sighed for softer methods of journeying.

Finally Tommy took him to Bailleul in the side-car. A supply train left for Paris at 6.30 P.M. There was interval for a good dinner and a final toast at the *Canon d'Or*.

It was strange to wait on Bailleul platform for the Paris train. The guns had ceased their grumbling, for the darkness had fallen and protective day had fled to let loose the night's grim little battles. There is night life beyond Wulverghem, and there is night-life in Paris. That was one of the obvious thoughts that flew into the Gaspipe Officer's head, for a platform beckons obvious thoughts. And the black trucks, like cows in Sussex, stood round patiently, filled with things for those men beyond Wulverghem. …

The Train Officer was kindly but irritable, and he wanted a Mess President; for, though he travelled between Bailleul and Rouen or Boulogne (there are good shops in these towns), he dined off a Maconochie. He also played Bridge, and entertained his fellow passengers with the complaint that, such were the hardships of his exigent service, he had been unable to obtain more than one rubber or so a week. He had a respect, though, for the combatant, and listened with open mouth to a Cyclist and an Infantry Officer swopping yarns.

The first-class carriage was luxurious. As they dozed the combatants heard the murmur of his voice: "Simpkins doubled, but we ran out with one to spare. But it's so rarely one gets the opportunity on this rotten job – is it very wet in the trenches just now …?"

The old supply train jogged on very, very slowly. There were occasional shoutings – the seats extraordinarily comfortable.

Amiens! Amiens!

The Gaspipe Officer stood sleepily on the platform, watched the old supply train flounder out of sight, then turned instinctively to the Restaurant. War or no war, it is the ἔργον[1] of Amiens Restaurant to produce good breakfasts and hurried drinks when the Paris Express has a moment to spare. The waiter was old and the cashier was ugly, but the omelette was good.

1　Literally translated, "core task" – freely translated, perhaps "business".

Once started it is easy to journey from Bailleul to Paris. A train marked PARIS came in, so without further ado he took his seat, and, though the pass he carried did not possess sufficient stamps and signatures to forward a cat from Clapham Junction to Earlsfield[1], the Cyclist Officer was not questioned.

There was no getting away from the war. At one place and another neat batteries of seventy-fives were drawn up in green fields, German prisoners, seemingly cheerful, were working in the yards, and dear old Frenchmen, with beards as long as their bayonets, stood impatiently on guard. The pass proved sufficient to enter Paris, and Paris smelt the same as ever, when the Cyclist drove to his favourite hotel in Montparnasse.

At first Paris seemed little different to the Paris he had known. Men in mufti still walked about the streets, and the *Taverne Royale* was as superlative as it had ever been. So while his uniform was being made, he went to the correspondent of a famous English daily and to an American artist.

The correspondent said nothing but asked much. The Cyclist remembered that he had been a Despatch Rider, and told many tales, of which a few fringed the truth.

The American artist lived in a delectable studio with his sister. They began about the war, talking of those worthy citizens who had fled to Bordeaux and shamefacedly returned; of the true and spurious widows that flocked the boulevards; of life in the trenches and the cause of it all; of Nursing and Art and the high price of food; of the models who were starving in the streets. Then wisely they abandoned war, and led the Cyclist through simple pleasures. It was a dream.

Mistily he remembers now the lobster and the artichoke at the *Clou* – an old thin man sang patriotic songs in a cracked voice and everybody laughed – with the fine walk back from Montmartre to Montparnasse. No one walks abroad in Paris now late of nights, and Paris is really dark; but the sleepy gendarmes smiled at "brav' Tommie," and let him go by.

Then there was the cosmopolitan tea-party with Marice, where French, American, and Roumanian met, and all proved more insular than the Briton. …

The dream becomes wilder and stranger, a very proper meal for the fancy of a young officer caged in an exiguous dug-out – afterwards he chewed the memory of Polaire, coldly untamed, chanting a too passionate song. At the Grand Guignol he sat between a corpulent general and a girl in black, each of whom would interpret the jokes confusedly. Add a tiresome walk to see the misty dawn from St Sulpice: the dawn was veiled with clouds, but the breakfast was good.

The maddest scene was the brown interior of a dilapidated cabaret in Montmartre, wherein Marice and her friends were giving a cheap and satisfying meal to artists and models for little or nothing. It was the opening night of the *Cantine des Humoristes*. The walls, covered with obscure drawings, rattled to their laughter. A fat poet sweated well with modest excitement, as in tones of screaming admiration he recited verses that praised vividly the charge of the British Lancers at the Marne. A squat-nosed Russian sang unintelligible ballads that had roaring choruses – and somebody's daughter danced. At the farther end of the room a monstrous wooden crucifix, wonderfully carved, stretched its kind shadow over a humorist and his model, who, replete with mirth and unexpected food, slept smilingly with gaunt faces touching. And through the half-open door, to complete the fantastic show, a crescent moon gazed in over the crenellated roof of a black and ruinous stable.

The dream continued. The Cyclist and his friends raced down the steps away from a worthy American girl who was solemnly collecting autographs, and two hospital orderlies of the same tribe, who stood husky with admiration for the British, to a lady that was said to smoke opium, and certainly preferred bull-pups to children. She was charming in her pink flannel dressing-gown, but received them with so transparent a hospitality and so cold a kindness that they left her

---

1   Why Earlsfield? Perhaps because Watson's father was Vicar of Earlsfield till his death in 1898.

in haste and, talking of the Hippogriff and other famous beasts, walked cheerily over the river to the studio. There they talked theories of art until the day dawned.

The uniform became rapidly ready, but it is easier to enter Paris than to leave her. It was only after interviewing countless railway officials that, coming at last to an ancient and sympathetic staff officer, the magic word "Mons" produced a pass. So, early one morning, Marice as the Cyclist's sweetheart, and the American artist and sister as his brother and cousin, were admitted to see the last of the Boulogne Express. …

An officer lucky enough after seven months in Flanders to find himself in Paris should make curious investigations into the state of the city and its gains and losses in time of war. It would have been interesting to compare London in December with Paris in February, for surely the observer should be unprejudiced, having seen neither city since the war began. Yet, I ask you, coming to Paris from Bailleul, how could Paris be other than a dream?

Paris seemed less calm and more sensitive than London. There was an eager and hourly anxiety – it was not fearful but rather a tightly strained interest – and THE WAR was not a great shadow to be avoided by pleasuring, or a subject as threadbare as the weather. In Paris a man never says, "What is happening in the war?" or "How are things going on in Flanders?" But rather, with a vivid acceptance of the phrase, "How did we do yesterday?" In London war is an entity outside man's life. It has an objective existence of its own. In Paris the fact and thought of war have become an actual part of life. It definitely flavours everything. London is at war – Paris is in the war.

Yet in some ways Paris has become curiously British. In February, the Parisians were ceasing to wonder at, and were beginning to understand, London's "More pleasure than ever." 'La Vie Parisienne' and more important journals were beginning to joke at London's assumption of the traditional French gaiety and the Parisians' assumption of the traditional London sobriety. So, though the artists were starving – *Bal Bullier* is a barracks and *Colorossi's* is shut – Paris awoke like a tired woman and wearily made herself gay.

And Paris vies with London in its suppression of enthusiasm. The Cyclist stood in front of the Madeleine and watched a battalion swing down the boulevards and into the Rue Royale. There was no cheering – only a rare self-ashamed shout, for this war is not a gasconading enterprise. In France, when sons or fathers go to the war they are not heard of for months and months. So the parade of soldiers is to many the parade of ghosts. …

The Express came to Boulogne late in the afternoon. The journey had not been dull, for the train was filled with American correspondents and French staff officers in their horizon-blue uniforms, who chattered with interest at the sight of prisoners and war material, or when the train barely crept over a newly repaired bridge. At lunch a friendly captain sat opposite the Cyclist, told him what was happening down Festubert way, and invited him to proceed from Boulogne in the car of a friendly interpreter.

Boulogne was unsatisfactory, as it always is in war-time, for Boulogne is neither Home nor Front. It overflows with ambulance drivers, and strayed officers, and men of mark in the I.M.S.,[1] who seem without work, and delicious nurses in delectable oilskins who flock the tea-shops and gladden the heart and eyes of a returning officer. Going on leave – Boulogne is only a place in which the bus or train stops a few hundred yards from the ship. To the wounded it may be a hellish or heavenly caravanserai, as the wound is light or serious – a purgatory for the convalescent on light duty, a space surrounding a Board of Officers who determine whether you may or may not be granted sick-leave at home.

---

1   The Indian Medical Service was deployed to France to provide medical support to the Indian Army units on the Western Front.

The Cyclist and his friend, the captain from Festubert, determinedly looked for the brighter side of Boulogne, and went near to finding it. Tea was at a tea-shop filled with I.M.S. and nurses. Then the interpreter and car arrived and they went to dinner, but outside the restaurant the Cyclist had seen a Staff Car of his own Division. This proved to be important, because there was little or no room for the Cyclist in the interpreter's car. An artist, fat, and with a certain enthusiasm, had come to Boulogne, and desired to paint battles at Armentieres – a simple wish. He was a friend of the interpreter, and the interpreter was stationed at Armentieres.

So the Cyclist went in search of the Staff Car and found Grimers, who with his usual tenacious pursuit after pleasure, had come into Boulogne on the car to buy fish for the Despatch Riders. Just after dawn – it was bitterly cold – the car called for the Gaspipe Officer. It was tricky driving, because the roads were frozen and the tyres were steel-studded. At St Omer they learned that Grimers had been given a commission, and beyond Cassel they knew certainly that the Canadian Division had arrived, because its immense green transport was woefully in the way. Before Caestre the clutch began to slip, and finally in front of that white farm where the Divisional Train used to make its headquarters – half way between Bailleul and St Jans – the engine that had been doing much work with no result found it could not heave the car out of a rut. So the Cyclist took up his baggage and walked.

In the main room of the *estaminet* Bill, Jumbo, and M'Queen sat over the fire in earnest consultation. When he entered M'Queen looked relieved, and, smiling uneasily, said –

"Glad you're back; thought the Division was beginning to smell a rat. Anyway, we've got some excellent news to welcome you home with."

"What's up?"

"The Cyclists," he read, "will take their turn with the Divisional Cavalry in garrisoning the trenches."

Jumbo, for no reason at all, roared with laughter.

CAPTAIN DOHERTY HOLWELL: LETTER TO MRS BURNEY

Reproduced from the authors' collection[1]

Cecil was commissioned in the Royal Engineers in January 1915, just a few weeks before Alick was commissioned in the Army Service Corps.

Dear Mrs Burney

I am very sorry not to have written before and acknowledged the cake and marmalade which turned up safely and which were topping and were much appreciated. I hope your son gave you my message of thanks. I do hope Alick will get his commission in the A.S.C. all right, I think he will. Both of them have done splendidly and I know our bikes have been the best looked after in the army. They have never minded how much work they had to do and have always been so cheery.

I was awfully sorry when Cecil left. I wish he could have stopped on. I tried hard to get a motor cyclist officer allowed for my company but without avail. I don't know what I shall do when your other son leaves us. The original lot of motor cyclists in this company were perfectly splendid. I don't know how we should have got through the trying days at the beginning without them. I am very glad that we got off with only one casualty – Fielding-Johnson. Please tell Cecil when you write that I shall not be home on leave again as it is stopped from now on. I was hoping to see him again.

Yours sincerely
Raymond Holwell
24.2.15

---

1   See Cast, page 159.

WHL WATSON LEADS THE CYCLISTS IN THE FRONT-LINE TRENCHES AND THEN PREPARES THEM FOR THE MOVE TO YPRES

Reproduced from 'Tales of a Gaspipe Officer' in *Blackwood's Magazine*

III Night-life Beyond Wilverghem

For the first time, Watson faced the prospect of defending a trench – acutely conscious of the risks caused by his height. He had seen the shallow trenches hastily dug by French civilians at Le Cateau, which were rapidly abandoned. Since the Battle of the Aisne in September 1914, Watson would have known many front-line soldiers learning hard lessons about the trenches.

It is no joke at all for Cyclists to be put in the trenches; trenchcraft cannot be learnt in a night. Cyclists have neither the knowledge, the experience, nor the appliances. Jumbo laughed, because, for many strenuous years a Territorial and for many packed months on home defence, he was at last to see real war. He talked boldly of listening-posts and crawling up to the German wire, but the Gaspipe Officer was filled with dread. The Despatch Riders whom he had left jeered at him, and pointed out – it was argument unanswerable – that the coming together of the trenches, his ignorance, and his physical eccentricities, would result in certain death. George said it was a shame. To put the Gaspipe in the trenches was simply to make a present of a might-be valuable officer to Fritz or Hans, or whomsoever the sniper of the day might be.

The cause of it all had occurred further up the Line. A Division composed of foreign service battalions had arrived and taken over from the French.[1] This Division was handicapped in many ways. First, a man who has been stationed at Hong-Kong, and then for a month or two at Winchester, cannot feel marvellously comfortable in Flemish trenches during a wet spring, even if his health does not actually suffer. Second, the trenches which this Division took over were, I am told, downright bad trenches. The Germans, knowing all this, attacked vigorously. So two of our warworn brigades were sent up north to restore the balance of power. This they did effectively and quickly; but in the meantime two very weak brigades came south to hold our sector of the line, which was comparatively quiet. They were so weak that the Cyclists had to go to their rescue.

Now the trenches of Flanders are known almost as well as the hotels. The *Faucon* and the *Canon d'Or* are familiar to many. So is trench *10b Support*. It is still, I believe, a comfortable and satisfactory trench. It was in February last – and the Cyclists rejoiced when they were bidden to garrison this trench and *10a*, another quite healthy ditch. The trenches themselves were safe. Casualties usually occurred going in or coming out.

The Divisional Cavalry, who were sportsmen, took the first shift, and lost enough men to make their Major tear his hair, for valuable N.C.O.'s trained in the work of Divisional Cavalry are not easy to replace. …

The evening came. M'Queen and the Gaspipe, cheered by a supper of champagne and oysters – for who can make a better Mess President than an ex-Despatch Rider? – embarked on waggons with half the Company, and slowly trundled along on bad and desolate roads towards the trenches. It was not raining, but the air was chill and dank. Dranoutre, never a cheerful village, looked like a melancholy dog that had come out of the water but forgotten to shake itself. The shattered

---

1 Foreign service battalions were Regular army battalions which had been serving overseas in 1914 – in order to supply trained units to the Expeditionary Force before the New Armies were trained, the War Office sent Territorial Army units as garrisons to overseas stations, thus relieving the Regular battalions which were sent to France.

trees cast dreary shadows. The men, who had been singing, became quiet and whispered among themselves.

Behind a slight, purple ridge ahead of them the pistol-lights were whizzing up and rifles crackled almost merrily. They disembarked near a little *estaminet,* and, while the men took their tea from a borrowed field kitchen, M'Queen and the Gaspipe swilled down many cups of *cafe-cognac,* admired the baby, and endeavoured to understand how many brothers, sons, and fathers of our hostess were serving. There was a filthy old man there, too, who cheered us by recounting the feats of German snipers.

At length they started off – M'Queen leading and the Gaspipe bringing up the rear. They crossed the top of the ridge and marched down a path which is marked on the map as being open to the enemy's fire. A few "overs" whirred harmlessly by and the Cyclists felt almost brave. Now, although the Cyclists were quite convinced that the Germans were filled only with the thought that the Cyclists were coming, the facts were that there were other troops also on the road and that it was very dark. The Gaspipe halted his platoon in the rear of some shadowy figures, and only after some minutes discovered that these figures had nothing to do with him. So he hurried on and caught up M'Queen in the main street of a ruinous village. There M'Queen told the men what to do. They were not to be frightened of stray bullets and duck. They were to bury their faces in the mud when the lights went up. It was easy to talk, but the village rustled uneasily with the zeep-zeep-ping of the bullets and multitudinous little crashes as they flew through the broken walls.

"I doan't loike this – place," murmured a man from Suffolk, and one officer at least agreed with him.

Again they forged on along a winding and slippery path. The zeeping grew more furious, and the Gaspipe, ducking his head to one that seemed viciously near, hoped that the darkness covered his sin and endeavoured to believe the obvious, – you cannot hear the bullet which hits you. So they stumbled forward, and having passed the stretch in which the Cavalry had suffered, grew more cheerful.

At last a weary "Halt. Wait here. It's dead ground."

It was dead ground – a flattish slope of black mud pockmarked with shell holes and lined with tiny streams. On either side were little groups of withered trees and bushes. Over the ridge were much light and noise for all the world like Port Meadow Fair before you cross the bridge. Instead of the shouting and the music of the merry go-rounds you heard the uproar of the rifles and the machine-guns. And the lights threw a sickly yellow glare upon every tree and bush and man.

M'Queen returned and led the way – planks over streams, round shell holes, and finally into a muddy ditch which was crowded with men. This was *10b Support.*

"Here's your dug-out," said the officer in charge hurriedly, eager to get away. "It's rather damp, but quite cushy. I've left some bread and pate-de-foie-gras. There's plenty of room for the men. The guard-room is here, and this is where you put your sentries. That's all – oh, one moment. There's a live shell just behind the parados.[1] Don't tickle it and Fritz enfilades this trench at a height of about 5 ft. 4 in. That's him! Keep down. Good-night."

Thus the Gaspipe Officer was left in charge of *10b Support.* He gave a few hurried orders, crawled into his dug-out, and determined to stop there until he was relieved. He disliked Fritz intensely.

The dug-out was constructed, like most dug outs, of sandbags filled in with Flanders mud which is a bad imitation of clay. The floor was of beaten earth. The length of it was five feet, the width three, and the height about two. Every inch of it was dripping, but inside a sleeping sack spread on the top of a groundsheet life was tolerable, though no arrangement could keep the dripping off the face.

---

1   A bank of earth built behind a trench to protect the trench from projectiles from the rear.

He had just snuggled into the sleeping-sack when a *chit* was brought from M'Queen – "Come and look me up."

He slid out of the dug-out with a curse, and, climbing wearily over a gap in the parados, was led by a friendly corporal to *10a*, where the Cyclists supported by a machine-gun section of Queen Vic's were engaged in what M'Queen called "obtaining a moral superiority over the Huns." Going back to his own trench, the Gaspipe slipped into a shell-hole, and he was very damp when he reached the comfort and shelter of his own dug-out. …

He slept soundly, and was wakened at dawn with the report that all was quiet along our front. It was a fine morning after the rain, and the birds sang cheerily. So here was he, a microscopic entity, in charge of one of those trenches, which stretch, as everybody knows, from the North Sea to Switzerland. Behind him was the dark hill covered sparsely with derelict trees. Eighty yards in front – you could see them safely through a certain loophole – were low-lying yellowish mounds faced with odd bits of wire and little heaps of grey. These were the German trenches – and the fact was not thrilling. Very occasionally rifles were fired: you would have thought they were fired at random if you had not listened to the ping of Fritz's bullet down the trench. And in the afternoon a few shells screamed like sea-gulls overhead.

So the troubled night came again. About eleven there were several sharp bursts of fire. The Gaspipe Officer grasped his revolver and wondered how on earth he was going to reinforce *10a*. He would be quite certain to fall into something on the way there. Before those Great Pushes that occur with such a lamentable frequency men do reach a high enthusiasm (it is given for the balancing of an enormous and immediate Death), but down "on the range," even when the surroundings are unfamiliar, the little emotions of nervousness, not fear, and miserableness, not misery, and a wee helping fellow called humour, creep into the dug-outs. The worst of war is that it is so rarely heroic. There are so few occasions which inspire a man to write a really fine letter.

M'Queen in *10a* had never needed the help of the troubled officer in *10b Support*. The "moral superiority" had been gained at the cost of much ammunition, and the Germans were aware – to look at the matter fairly and squarely – that new and green troops were in the trench opposite them. Besides, M'Queen had a telephone and knew everything that was going on up and down and behind the line. He also had a machine-gun.

The morning broke to a gorgeous day. Even the walls of the dug-out dripped less rapidly, and high in the heavens a lark sang with full glory. The German gunners began to try and hit Neuve Eglise, and the British artillery, longing for some excuse to unlock their stores of ammunition, determined to *strafe* the Germans' trenches and some villages behind the German line. The show began about half-past eleven with big guns, little guns, and all sorts of guns. Even "Granny," a howitzer quite as effective as any German, let out with one of her elephantine shells, which chortled through the air like an express passing through a tunnel beneath you, and brought down a church with everything near it. The field-guns banged and whizzed away at the trenches in front; it was a display more frightful than effective, for shrapnel burst on percussion does not do any great damage even to badly constructed trenches. The Germans replied mildly with some shrapnel that burst two hundred yards beyond *10b Support*. No one, except the Germans, knew exactly for what it was meant. Certainly no harm was done. When the morning's shelling was over, one of our aeroplanes flew along the trenches to inspect the result. The Germans were so intent on firing at it that M'Queen and his men, disregarding the aeroplane, fired at the Germans. One of the cyclists reported that a second after firing he had heard a German scream.

The Gaspipe Officer had been told that the work of him who is in charge of a support trench consists in keeping man and trench fit and dry. The man was the difficulty. The bottom of the trench was covered with nine inches of water, so planks raised on little piers had been laid along it and just above the surface of the water. The men, disregarding his advice and example, considered trench-life a huge joke, and gallivanting along the greasy boards, splashed splendidly into the water. Again, everybody knows that to get out of a Wulverghem trench in broad daylight and walk about behind it is to challenge a remarkably swift death. Yet two of his men did it and survived. Truly, the life of the cyclist is charmed!

To keep the trench dry and fit was not a difficulty, because it was impossible. A little digging might have been done: in fact it ought to have been done. But he had only once before been to the trenches – a fearful night, on which he had volunteered to help lay a wire, or rather watch a wire being laid from battalion headquarters to a fire-trench – and he knew so little about trenches that he dared not make a change. He might disturb something that had a name and was very useful. To exhume a gabion[1] would be indeed a crime. …

So the afternoon wore on, and the evening came when he was to be relieved by the eager Jumbo – and his courage failed him. Jumbo would not sit in a dug-out all the time. Jumbo would dig a new trench after he had improved the old. Jumbo would wander fearlessly up and down the slippery plank, careless of Fritz's cupronickel jibes, and hurl foul language at the Hun. For the rest of time Jumbo would be the warrior and the Gaspipe the craven in the hearts and mouths of the Company.

It was now quite dark, and still Jumbo did not come. Reliefs are always too late for the relieved and too early for the reliever: it is a curious temporal axiom. At last a message arrived from M'Queen:

"Leave your men in charge of Kay and wait for me at the solitary tree."

He scrambled with care through a gap in the parados, and slipping hastily over the black mud, walked with light heart to the solitary tree. The night was pitch-black. There was a low murmur of voices and the slop-slup of men marching over the mud. Then a pistol-light would flare up and the dead ground appear alive with black, stumbling files of men, some burdened with rations and water-bottles, some carrying loaded stretchers, some halted waiting to be guided in, and others tired but joyful coming out, very softly whistling. Soon a little party marched smartly up to the solitary tree the remaining half-company with Jumbo and Bill, Jumbo almost silent and tense. Soon they left, going trenchwards, and again the Gaspipe waited. The Devil's Fair it was with its light and music for sometime those low-lying yellowish mounds must be shattered to destruction by our guns, while the crowded men wait in *10b Support* and *10a*, and rush in a great charge. That will be but the beginning, for behind the German trenches a falsely gentle slope rises to the ridge of Messines.

M'Queen came along with his men, and together they tramped to the ruinous village. The path was quiet that night. Quite comfortably they reached the top of the hill and embarked on their borrowed waggons. It was bitterly cold, and they were delayed by an ambulance which could not be passed until they came to a soft place where the ambulance might draw aside easily; but the men, led by Jock the Tailor, sang all the songs they knew, beginning with the more innocent and finishing with the more crude. By the time they had reached the turning to Croix de Poperinghe all was silent except for a muffled curse at the cold. Four hours in a G.S. waggon on a freezing night is no pleasing journey.

The men were dismissed. M'Queen and the Gaspipe hurried to the nameless *estaminet*, where the inimitable Bland had a roaring fire going and a long and steaming dinner. …

When Jumbo returned three days later, the Gaspipe waited for an epic narrative, but Jumbo was short in his reply:

"Eh? I just lay close in that darned dug-out until somebody relieved me."

---

1   A wicker basket filled with earth used to fortify a trench.

IV Quiet Times
Watson and his company now relaxed, enjoying the calm before the storm.

So they came out of the trenches with no casualties save a few frost-bitten feet, and wrote home the most amazing letters of their prowess. Without doubt the Cyclists had made a noise.

The Company, content with itself, slid into a peaceful routine of play and work.

About a quarter to eight the Gaspipe Officer would be called, but getting up was difficult, because, after nights on the more repellent surfaces, a soft bed in a little cosy bedroom above the *Maison Commune* held out the most deliciously retaining hand. Breakfast and a pipe brought him to nine or a quarter past, at which hour Bill, with attendant subalterns – M'Queen had left them to buy eggs for a general – would walk briskly up to the Company's farm, dispense justice and sign multitudinous papers. After censoring the letters – a weary job – they would stroll round the country and watch the men making fascines, and so back to letters, papers, and lunch.

Later the order came from the Division for the Company to take a "refresher" course of training, and the morning would be spent in learning all the things a cyclist must know, to read a map, to fall off his cycle in the twinkling of an eye, to lay traps for cavalry, and to look like a company when riding and not like the Purley Pedallers. Some of these things the Gaspipe taught his men, but most of them he learnt from Bill and his platoon and the sergeant-major. On a pleasant morning, under the instruction of the sergeant-major, he would endeavour to shout orders across the greatest possible number of fields.

After lunch they might stroll into Bailleul or play football. Bailleul was never quite dull. In the spring Territorial Divisions began to arrive, and the Gaspipe with Jumbo or Bill used to saunter up and down the Square and criticise with a veteran air. A Division in column of route – the guns and limbered waggons rattling and groaning over the cobbles: the men grinning with happiness, for to many Bailleul was almost "the Front." Never will the Cyclists forget "Tango the Lion-Tamer," an officer who, to the pure joy of all the civilian and military inhabitants of Bailleul, appeared in a leopard-skin coat. Everybody asked everybody else: "Have you seen Tango?"

From the Square they would saunter into the dirty and smoky *Faucon* or the expensive Allies Tea Rooms for a drink. The more companionable *estaminets* were closed to officers, the Gaspipe found to his infinite sorrow. There was a little tavern that hung on to the side of the Hotel de Ville, where Chloe gently provided grenadines and made the most charming compliments to the brave corporals – and another down a narrow wynd not far from old Divisional Headquarters and much frequented by the London Scottish while they were in Bailleul. When these were full of men, it was difficult for a young officer, too sensible of his dignity, to enter.

Later a cinema was provided, while the North Irish Horse, finding life dull after their old free-booting days, started again the fine old sport of cock-fighting. …

About three afternoons a week the Cyclists turned out to smash their opponents on the football ground. The 3rd Divisional Cyclists were their great rivals; but the matches with the A.S.C. roused the bitterest feeling, for they played too professional a game. Bill excelled on the wing, and M'Queen's masculine coaching was beautiful to hear.

Even in those quiet days of March life was not all such pleasuring. There were wire patrols. The Gaspipe would borrow a motor-cycle and ride out to Neuve Eglise or Kemmel way. Then he would walk for miles, following a wire across fields that had been stirred with shells like porridge with a spoon or down near Wulverghem, or up from the ruins of Kemmel village to the top of Kemmel Hill – and see that his men were doing their work. It was laborious, unexciting, and infinitely melancholy. A dead and shattered man is a little horrible and almost unimportant, a thing defective, without soul, but dead and shattered country seems always to be suffering dumbly, as though it were a kindly beast in pain. And still it listens each night to the loud reports of the rifles and the whisper of the bullets as they fly complaining over the black and slippery mud. …

The rumour came that the Division was to move northwards to Ypres. Men freely cursed. The old Ypres salient was such a silly thing. Imagine for a moment one of those old Greek theatres, semi-circular. All the way round the Germans were on the top row of seats, and we were only half-way up. They could see everything that we were doing, while we, hemmed in, had to trust to aeroplanes. And down on the floor of the theatre stood Ypres, through which or by which nearly every road to the salient passed. It is not wonderful that the Germans shelled Ypres. It is amazing that they did not shell it more.

Jumbo went ahead to find billets, and we followed, trekking over Mont Noir – you can see from the smoke of Funes almost to Warneton, and from the towers of Ypres away to Sailly – and through Reninghelst to Poperinghe. There Bill was billeted on a "Wipers Widow" (a refugee lady whose husband still lives in Ypres), Jumbo on a priest, and the Gaspipe on a coal merchant whose brother was still "over there." In those days Poperinghe was a pleasant city, containing all that the heart of an officer could desire – good grocers, an excellent restaurant or two, and a delectable tea-room. The inhabitants, like all Belgians, are friendly to the point of embarrassment. The children sing "Tipperary" in the streets morning, noon, and night.

Coming in late one night the Gaspipe found the coal merchant urgent for a talk. First they discussed the price of coal, and the excellent system the British had of bringing their own fuel with them; then, as always happens, they started on the war, and the Gaspipe enlarged mightily on the merits of the voluntary system of enlistment. Finally, the coal merchant described how the Germans had left, and the French and British arrived.

"The last to leave were the German cyclists. We all kept sullenly within our houses, for the good God alone knew what the Germans might perpetrate in their defeat. The Germans left, except for one officer, and he rode round the town, firing at all of us, daring any one to touch him, for the Germans always returned. He was a brave man, and we, though we cursed and moved first forward a little and then back, did not dare. The women besought us to leave him alone for fear something should happen to them.

"Half an hour later the French cyclists rode through very quickly, then for many hours we were in suspense. There was much noise of cannon, but no one appeared. We opened our doors and flocked into our streets, talking anxiously.

"Towards evening the rumour flew round that the English were marching into Poperinghe. We ran to the street by which they were coming and waited. When they came, fine and brave men, we could not cheer for laughing, or laugh for cheering. Such funny little petticoats they wore."

Here the Gaspipe began hastily to talk of other things, for he knew the battalion and what had happened to them, and did not choose to laugh at their kilts. …

Bill, Jumbo, and the Gaspipe were comfortable enough in Poperinghe. A little training would be done in the mornings for the sake of appearances, and in the afternoons they would walk out of the town to have tea with some friends in an ammunition column, or watch the aeroplanes go up. They were, in fact, beginning to realise with shame that they might have belonged to the least combatant branch of the service, when the order came to shift into huts near Ouderdom.

They were well-constructed huts, because the Sappers had built them for themselves. You may curse the work the Sapper does for other people – nobody, however churlish he may be, can do anything but wonder when Sapper works for Sapper. There was even a large bath. …

ARNOLD OVERTON: LETTER TO HIS MOTHER

From the Overton family collection

The move from St Jans Cappel broke up the arrangements which separated the original despatch riders from the new drafts.

It was now that the problem of the 'A' mess and 'B' mess – otherwise friction between the original motorcyclists & those who had joined up since the beginning of things – first seriously arose, for at St Jans Cappel it had been staved off by our move into the billet. Of course we could not treat them quite like we treated each other, for we did not know them so well & also they were not of the 'public school' type though very nice chaps most of them. Of course they rather resented this & considered us 'snobs', but this was practically unavoidable. The solution we arrived at for the moment was to have 2 of 'B' mess, as before, attached to the 2 brigades – as the captain had always said we were to do – & to send the other 3 up to the advanced headquarters near Ypres, to be relieved when they wanted to be after a week or two. Thus 'A' mess & Tomlinson who was now incorporated in it & Curry the driver of the Singer which had just come up were alone at Poperinghe & very comfortable. Maddison, Bale & Sawtell were at the advanced headquarters in a dull & very uninteresting place, & Stubbs, Wagner & Cameron were with the brigades. 'A' mess were undoubtedly far the most comfortable at Poperinghe, but on the whole we had more work to do as we ran all the posts to the brigades, etc.

STANLEY POLHILL: PHOTOGRAPHS OF A WRECKED BE2A

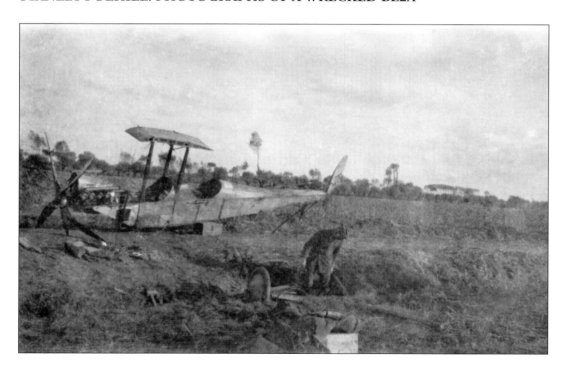

Stanley Polhill was serving with 2nd Army HQ Signal Company when he came across this wreck near Bailleul. The BE2a (its serial no 336 is just visible in the photograph on the previous page) was transferred to No 2 Squadron RFC on 4 March 1915 but it was wrecked the following day.

BE2a Serial no 336 was recommissioned after the crash and transferred to the RFC flying school at Netheravon where it was photographed in summer 1915.

WHL WATSON LEADS THE CYCLISTS INTO ACTION

Reproduced from 'Tales of a Gaspipe Officer' in *Blackwood's Magazine*

V A famous victory and dirty work at Ypres

The explosion at Hill 60 was one of the first mines to be exploded on the Western Front.

M'Queen came in with the news one morning.

"That Sapper fellow tells me we're mining a hill – enormously important place Germans can see all over the place from it. The show is going to take place at 7 sharp tomorrow evening. The hill's on our bit of the line."

The air was full of excitement. Even the gang of Belgian labourers that worked on the road outside the camp grinned, because they had heard the rumour of an attack. And in the tea-shops of Poperinghe everybody was talking about the mine and the attack after its explosion. A sergeant of the Cyclists heard exhaustive and accurate details from an old market-woman. The British officer is not expert in the keeping of secrets.

On the appointed evening the roofs of the huts in the Cyclist camp were crowded. The officers standing on a little rise swept the high country beyond Dickebusch with their field-glasses and looked often at their watches. At seven Jumbo swore he heard a dull thud. Two minutes later the guns spoke, hesitated, then broke out into an enormous fury of sound. Flash answered flash right along the horizon. The little black group of officers – it was deep dusk – watched the bursting shrapnel narrowly.

"That fellow's a bit high 'm – they're putting a few into old Wipers – a nice old salvo – put it into them, lads – give 'em hell!"

So they watched the bestial struggle for Hill 60 from Ouderdom, three and a half miles away, half joyful and half sick at heart. Not one of them would have confessed (it would have been mere sentiment), yet each had a great pride in the old Div., and a great anxiety that it should do well. Had the charge been successful? Had the gains been consolidated? They went back into their hut and sang any amount of music-hall trash until it was time to go to bed.

In the morning news came that the position had been rushed with slight loss; the Germans had been filled with such panic that they had fled from the trenches on either side of the crater: the Germans were heavily attacking: their guns and bombs were sweeping our new position: there was no wire down yet.

About nine the same night there was much cheering in the darkness of the camp. The remains of two battalions had returned from the hill. Then first were learnt the names of the fallen. Still there was no wire down.

At one place we had fought our way to the topmost seats in the theatre, but the cost of it was pitiful. It took five or six days before the wire was down and trenches properly made. During those days no battalion could remain for more than fifteen hours on the hill, and at the end of its shift it would return broken. The men could see the guns that were firing at them.

On the fifth day the Gaspipe was wakened very early.

"The Captain says dress at once and go and get instructions from him." It appeared that by luck or design the Germans had dropped a large shell, or more than one, on a certain street in Ypres and blocked it, with the result that many motor ambulances and some regimental transport had been shelled outside the city gate. The Cyclists were called upon to clear the street and keep it clear. They must ride to Ypres at full speed.

They started off, and the Gaspipe, to drown the thought that the unblocking of streets under shell fire was no job for a quiet fellow, rode as he had never ridden before. He flashed through

Vlamertinghe, and faster and faster along the magnificent macadam into Ypres. Just inside the city the Gaspipe threw himself off his bicycle, breathless, and looked round. There were only two men with him, and nobody else in sight! At that moment he learned definitely that to bring along a platoon or company of Cyclists at high speed is a fine art.

Leaving his corporal to form up the platoon as they came in, he rode to report. The Town Commandant, who was comfortably at breakfast, knew nothing about him, but believed that the idea of keeping the street clear was quite excellent. There did not seem to be any urgent need for the services of the Cyclists. The vivid picture which the Gaspipe had formed of monstrous labours in deadly danger and a cloud of dust disappeared. Ypres was quiet. He led his men to the Church of St Martin, and went forward to look round.

Beyond the church, an ugly red-brick building hitherto untouched, and a hundred yards or so inside the Lille Gate, there was a narrowing of the road. By craft or luck the German gunners had thrown a shell exactly on this spot, brought down the houses on either side and blocked the road. Some other Cyclists had worked right through the night to clear the street: it was the Gaspipe's job to keep it clear. The cycles were brought under shelter of the broad ramparts, and sentries were posted with orders instantly to report, if still alive, when shells fell near the objects of their solicitude.

Ypres was being shelled very lazily with big stuff, but nothing came near.

Bill and Jumbo arrived in an hour or so, and, like the Gaspipe, were bravely wishing for excitement. They first strolled up the street for a drink. Something dashed across the street just in front of the Gaspipe, and went with a crash through the door of a butcher's shop. For a wild moment the Gaspipe thought it must have been a great cat until the butcher noisily and triumphantly produced the fuse-cap of a German shell. They walked a little farther, then returned to the walls, where for the first time they experimented with chewing-gum, and disliked it.

It was pleasant on the walls, looking towards Zillebeke over the moat. They form a wide grass-covered mound sloping gently to the water. Trenches have been cut into them and dug-outs burrowed. On the other side of the moat, which by the Lille Gate is as broad as a lake, runs the infamous Sunken Road. Last October, when Ypres was being shelled very heavily, troops used to prefer the Sunken Road to a march through the city. This the Germans discovered, and the road became a slaughter house. The Cyclists knew it, for they had walked along it to the trenches of Hooge.

A couple of miles or more away the sky met a range of low and partly-wooded hills, on which the Germans live. They look down from them on to the dwellers in the plain, and because they can see and not be seen, dwell in a malign and abominable security. …

Before the war the old walls of Ypres swarmed on Sundays with burghers and their families in their best. I have always sympathised with fortresses that have become sights for the vulgar, and walls a public promenade. But the veteran ramparts, grown over and neglected, have revenged themselves on time, and, sighing for charge and affray, the creak of the cross-bow, and the hearty shouts of the bluff old warfare, have seen and heard such poor multitudes scientifically killed, that again they must be wearying for the gay Sunday quietude. …

They had tea in the *atelier* of a dressmaker, and then, having vainly searched their quarter of the town for a worthy drink, packed up their traps and cycled home to Ouderdom in the growing dusk. A guard was left to warn them if again the Germans should block that very important street to the Lille Gate.

All this time there had been bestial fighting on Hill 60. No battalion could remain on the cursed pile of dirt thrown out from a cutting for more than a day and a night. The Hill was death. But the Fifth Division has never let go, and never will. They stuck to the Hill while the sappers put up wire and made it defensible. Everybody had thought we had bitten off more than we could chew, but as nobody said it, we chewed.

So the spring came.

VI The afternoon of the twenty-second

On 22nd April the enemy's surprise attack on the French and British lines at Ypres was preceded by the release of chlorine gas – the first recorded breach of the Geneva Convention forbidding the use of gas.

Butcher, the new subaltern, arrived early in the afternoon with a draft for the company. The Gaspipe took him round and showed him the camp and the more important landmarks, Dickebusch Church, the towers of Ypres, the German ridge, and roughly where the Line was. Butcher was duly thrilled, and said a little sadly "Nothing doing just now, I suppose?"

"Nothing much. We lost a horrible lot of men taking a hill during the last week, but things should settle down now for some time. There's talk of a Push, but then there always is. Still, there's a Show this afternoon – French talking to what's left of the brigade that took the hill."

The Brigade, the old 13th, was drawn up in a square. Each battalion was about the size of a weakish company. The General came and told them simply that they were heroes – haggard, laughing men, who, glowing with pride, would afterwards joke about that "damned nuisance, the inspection." And the Gaspipe wondered bitterly how long he would remain to see the 13th again and again destroyed. In that maimed brigade there were, I think, about four officers and sixty men left of those who had come out in August; but the 13th was still a brigade that could be trusted, a brigade of steady and reliable battalions.

Just after the General had left, an aeroplane descended hurriedly on the parade-ground with a despatch. There was much consultation, and then a car started off at full speed. It was about four o'clock in the afternoon of the Twenty-second of April.

Bill and Jumbo went into Poperinghe. The Gaspipe and Butcher strolled lazily towards Vlamertinghe.

"Look there, Gaspipe," said Butcher "look at those flares going up away to the north. You told me if flares went up before dusk it was a sign of nervous troops. Well, they're durned nervous over there, because it's still quite light. Some cannonade you get, too, every evening."

The Gaspipe looked to the north. Flares were following each other in rapid succession, and the cannonade was become furious. Frankly, he was puzzled.

"I don't understand it," he replied reflectively. "It might be those Canadians who have just taken over from the French, but it's a bit too far north – and I didn't realise that the salient (the Ypres salient, you know) came round quite so far to the west. And, by G-d, listen to that!"

Butcher strained his ears and heard, above the noise of the traffic and shouts and laughter of the men, a swishing, thrilling, crackling sound. Suddenly it reached a sharper note. Beyond Vlamertinghe a vast tree of greasy black smoke appeared, and almost at once a great *bo-hoom* reverberated over the fields.

"That's a 'Jack Johnson, G.S., Tommy Atkins, for the use of,'" murmured the Gaspipe, "and what on earth's it doing over there? The Huns are getting uppish. Here are some of my men."

Half a dozen cyclists were riding in rapidly. They had just been relieved from duty on the important street at Ypres. The Gaspipe stopped them.

"Anything up?"

"Yes, sir." The man spoke with an anxious importance. "They've put some mighty big stuff into Ypres, and, as we was coming back we saw a lot of Frenchies with some transport and limbers, and Jim 'ere thought 'e saw a gun – they was tearing like mad across the fields to Vlamertingy."

"What's up?" said Butcher, when the men had been dismissed to their tea.

The Gaspipe thought a moment.

"Huns fed up with losing Hill 60, and bored with the Canadians, look for trouble start shelling Canadians and plumping a few behind the lines hit Belgian working-party rapid and amazed flight of same. Let's go and get some dinner. Rotten place, Ypres, though!"

They went back to their hut, and, after waiting some time for Bill and Jumbo, started dinner. The cannonade to the north grew louder and nearer. The Gaspipe was not satisfied with his own explanation. Butcher became excited and hoped that something would happen.

It was nine o'clock when Bill and Jumbo came in. Bill was a trifle pale, and Jumbo looked uneasy.

"Any news?"

"Any news! The Germans have broken through between the French and the Canadians! French transport, refugees, and infantry are pouring into Poperinghe from Elverdinghe! Huggie says the road is blocked for miles!"

The heart of the Gaspipe beat with enormous rapidity, and his knees seemed suddenly very weak. He tried to pull himself together. "If the Huns have broken right through," he said with a too admirable calm, "this old division is nicely cut off with one or two others, and there'll be some very pretty rearguard work on hand. You've struck oil fairly early, Butcher."

Bill gave orders for the company to stand to arms and everything to be packed up. Then they sat down to dinner, discussing the situation in detail.

It seemed queer to Butcher that a German breakthrough three or four divisions up the Line should affect the Fifth Division so vitally. The Gaspipe expounded with the aid of the rough diagram on next page (reproduced below).

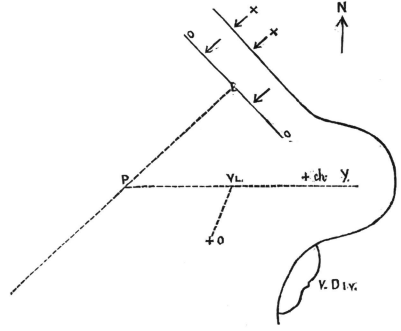

Y = Ypres.   E = Elverdinghe.   P = Poperinghe.   VL = Vlamertinghe.   O = Ouderdom.

Note.—The eccentricities of the line are exaggerated for the sake of clearness.

The Germans are reported to have broken through at XX, and to be pushing on towards Elverdinghe. Between XX and the Fifth Division the line is held by the 28th, the 27th and the Canadians. If the Germans push forward to the line OO the left of the Canadians will be badly in the air. Again, the line P–VL–Y is the road along which all supplies are sent up to the Divisions holding the salient. The German occupation of the line OO would literally threaten the British communications. Lastly, behind the line there are very few troops and very many valuable stores and staff officers.

The sergeant-major brought in a despatch. Two patrols each consisting of an officer and six men, were to report immediately at Advanced Divisional Headquarters, which were residing at a chateau (CH. on diagram) a couple of miles out of Ypres, on the Vlamertinghe road.

In five minutes Jumbo and the Gaspipe were ready to start. Back tyres were blown up; kit was tied on firmly; rifles were inspected. Jumbo shouted the order – "Prepare to mount! Mount!"

VII The night of the twenty-second

Watson was wounded by shrapnel on the day that poison gas was used for the first time.

The road to Vlamertinghe was almost clear. In front of an *estaminet* on the left of the road "Granny" and her train were drawn up for the night, monster masses of black tarpaulins. On from Vlamertinghe the road was a thick cursing crowd. For some obscure reason we never seem able properly to control the refugees from a bombarded town. It was hugely important to keep clear the road from Poperinghe to Ypres, the one good road running east and west. Yet in a critical moment an endless caravan of waggons and carts and panic-stricken men and women, loaded down with their burdens, shouted and jostled and moaned. Transport of every sort was drawn up on the pathway, and some batteries of guns, awaiting orders. The moon had not yet risen, and the night was blacker than hell. The only way to get through was to blast a way, and this Jumbo did. Walking and riding – almost feeling the road – the Cyclists cursed and damned a path through the craven burghers and the stolid gunners. And the refugees were whispering among themselves and shouting to the Cyclists as they passed –

"The Boches are shelling Ypres as they never shelled it before."

Over the shouts and the curses, the rumble and the creaking and the moans, came the shattering crashes of enormous shells bursting, and a funny slight sound of roaring the noise of flames.

They reached the gate of the chateau which was Advanced Divisional Headquarters, and rode up the drive. The Staff Room had a quiet and scholarly air. The Colonel, lean and black, took the Gaspipe and Jumbo over to an immense map which almost covered one wall of the room, and expounded the situation as if he were lecturing to a mixed audience on Ricardo's Theory of Rent.

All the information he had was that the Germans by employing gas had driven back the French from the Langemarck line. One of the Cyclist patrols was to ride through Ypres to St Julien and report on the position there. The Canadians might have been compelled to bring back slightly and adjust their left brigade. The second patrol was to ride along the western bank of the Yperlee Canal to Boesinghe, find out from the French there exactly what had happened, cross the canal, and proceed back along the road that runs a mile or so to the north-east of the canal.

"I do not think," he concluded judicially, "that the vague reports that have reached us and the surmises we have been compelled to make point to the fact of an enemy force on or in the neighbourhood of the north bank of the canal."

The Gaspipe was to take the canal patrol, for he spoke some pidgin-French. Outside the Staff Room, Smith, the A.D.C., met him.

"Have a drink, old man, before you go out?"

The Gaspipe refused. He was wondering what would happen if an enemy force was in the neighbourhood of the canal. …

He pushed off into the deserted outskirts of Ypres and turned to the left just after crossing the railway. There was a trifling lull in the shelling. He rode easily with eyes and ears well open. The moon was rising in a clear sky. Along the canal all was quiet. Some Canadian Engineers had heard only that the French had been driven back. A mile on he came to a temporary bridge held by Zouaves. Trenches were being hastily dug. There was a certain feverish activity.

"We do not know what is going on," an officer replied "but something terrible is happening on our left."

Ahead there seemed to be much noise of rifles and machine-guns and some shelling. The nervousness with which the Gaspipe had started left him. The affair was interesting.

Just south of Boesinghe the railway crosses the Yperlee Canal and the Dixmuide–Ypres road, which is the road that runs along the western bank of the canal. Fifty yards from the level-crossing is a ruined cottage. There the Gaspipe left four men and his sergeant, because the village was most undoubtedly being shelled. He walked into the village with the remaining man, and meeting a corporal, asked him the way to the French Headquarters. The corporal replied in a string of words, among which "marmite" and "chateau" predominated.

"Headquarters are in a chateau, and it is being shelled," murmured the Gaspipe wisely. "En avant, mon vieux."

The corporal cheerily led the way through the main street of the village, and he laughed out loud when the nose and eyes of the Gaspipe began freely to smart and water. Then the Gaspipe noticed that the village was filled with a greenish mist. Whatever it was, it was damnably unpleasant. He felt for a handkerchief and found he had none. It was awkward to interview a French general when one's nose was running and there was no handkerchief to hand. This artificially inspired rheum was a bore.

They came to the lodge gate of the chateau, so, taking leave of the cheery corporal, the Gaspipe and his man walked steadily up the drive. Now, if you hear a shell coming, you can do one of two things – get down or stop up. To get down is always the wiser course, but to get down and then to hear the shell pass harmlessly over your head and burst quarter of a mile farther on is to lose one's self-respect and the respect of others. To choose aright requires expert knowledge. On the other hand, if you know that with the very shell you hear the Hun is trying to slaughter you, don't think at all. Get down. The Gaspipe heard a shell coming and pressed himself flat to the ground. The Germans were endeavouring to hit the chateau, and the chateau was only fifty yards away.

The shell whistled and roared. The Gaspipe thought for a flash absurdly that khaki is invisible in the dark. There was a terrific explosion – just by his right ear, it seemed. All sorts of soft things fell on to his back. He jumped up before the smoke had cleared away.

"All right, Bloomfield?"

"I think so, sir" very feebly "but I can't see."

The Gaspipe seized him and dragged him at a run to the side of the chateau, determined in his panic that he would not be between the chateau and the Hun when the next shell arrived: but the next shell, disdainful of mere human reason, burst beyond the chateau. "Marmite" and "chateau" an unpleasant combination.

He was ushered ceremoniously along dark corridors, a door was flung open, and he stood in an immense room full of tarnished finery. At a table on the right sat the general and his staff. To the left were the orderlies behind some indefinite figures.

The general looked up and saw an immense, long, khaki figure, bespattered with mud and leaves, and wiping his nose continuously on the sleeve of his coat. Queer people, these British!

The Gaspipe advanced and made a ceremonious bow.

"Bon soir, mon general – les compliments du general du cinquieme division, le fameux cinquieme division qui etait a Mons (snuffle) – et il veut savoir que se fait – que passe – en bref, quelle est la situation ici."

The general, an upright white-haired old man, came forward, shook hands warmly, and began to explain. This is the drift of what he said, or rather what the Gaspipe understood him to say.

"Give my most respectful compliments to your general. I have heard much of your famous division. The situation is altogether horrible! The Boches are uncivilised brutes.

"At about five o'clock this afternoon there was a cannonade along the line of the brigade which I have the happiness to command. It was nothing much. Then my brave men, ready for anything in reason, saw approaching them rolling greenish clouds. It was the atrocious gas. They are brave, they are brave, I say, but they could do nothing. They were overwhelmed, crushed, massacred. The remnant retired, and the Boches pursued them. Ah, it was atrocious. We have fallen back about four kilometres, and now we are holding the line of the canal. The Germans are only two hundred metres on the other side of the canal here.

"Of the French division on my right between my brigade and the Canadians I have heard nothing, know nothing. Their headquarters are at Elverdinghe, but they have not communicated with me."

The old man sat down again very sorrowfully. His brigade-major murmured something in his ear.

"Ah, les contre-attaques! Yes, I have ordered counter-attacks at Het Sas and Steenstraate, and we hope that the Division on my right will attack the Germans at Pilkem, on their flank."

The Gaspipe made notes on his map, asked many questions concerning the tactical disposition of the French forces, and bowed himself out gracefully.

The shelling had ceased, but the village rattled and rang with rifle and mitrailleuse. Just before the railway-crossing there are no houses on the north side of the street. He hesitated then took to the ditch, but the water was deep, and stank so, pulling himself together, he took to the road again, and, running across the open spaces, came safely to the ruined cottage where he had left his men.

There he sat down, borrowed a handkerchief, blew his nose tremendously, and in a minute or so was able to see his notebook. In the meantime he was cheered by a shell which skimmed the cottage and burst harmlessly in a field on the other side of the road. He wrote a brief report, and gave it to Bloomfield, who was off in a flash.

Obviously it was impossible to cross the canal, because the Germans were on the farther side. He determined to ride back, and, crossing whatever bridges there might be, find out exactly where the line was.

They raced away to the first bridge. Leaving his men, he walked across. In five minutes he returned with the desired information, and made a mental note: Germans four hundred metres from canal.

The ride to the next (Canadian) bridge was not without excitement. The Germans had either pushed forward or woken up during the last two hours. Bullets zeep – pinged overhead, and shrapnel intended for the road burst just beyond it. There was an empty feeling in the Gaspipe's stomach. Charitably, he put it down to hunger.

They again dismounted at the Canadians' bridge. From an officer on the east side the Gaspipe heard roughly how the line ran. At this point the Germans were beginning to use high explosive, so, pushing through some Canadian waggons, he turned off westwards, picked his way through some lanes, and arrived triumphantly at the chateau.

Although his nose was running and his eyes smarted the first made him red and awkward: why hadn't he brought a handkerchief? – he determined to bathe in the academic atmosphere of the Staff Room.

"We have received your report," said the Colonel; "please tell the General the details of the situation."

Imagine, then, the Gaspipe holding forth bravely punctuating each sentence with a snuffle and a shamed wipe of sleeve across nose. On the way back he had put all the facts in fine order. A red-tabbed audience, a large map, and the academic atmosphere inspired him to produce what he himself felt was a nicely-rounded little lecture. ...

The French left brigade was back on the canal. He doubted whether the canal could be held, for the nerves of the men were badly shaken, and there remained only three weak battalions. The

French right Division had disappeared, save for a battalion or two who were holding a position in such-and-such a square. The left flank of the Canadians was badly afloat. Indeed there appeared to be a gap between the Canadians and the right of the French remnant. The Germans, however, did not seem to be pushing through. He suspected they had not looked for such success. Their position was in square so-and-so. …

He ended. Sundry questions were asked and answered, and then he was sent out again to keep a watch on the canal until the whole Company had time to ride up and take over.

So they started off back again, a little tired and stale. At the Canadian bridge there was more and more high explosive. They rode carefully northwards, cursing on the way some Cyclists of another Division who were careering madly along on the wrong side of the road. The German shrapnel was still bursting a hundred yards or so to the west of the road. Once more the Gaspipe felt that empty feeling in the stomach, and this time he put it down to fear. He was thinking too much of what would happen if the Germans registered accurately.

He had told the Staff that he would make a cottage just opposite the French bridge his head-quarters. Fifty yards from it Zouaves were holding a line between the road and the canal. The Germans seemed to be on the other bank, from the noise of the rifles and the fierce singing of their bullets across the road. He heard a little sad sob and then another. Two of the blue figures that had been standing fell to the ground and lay there.

He came to the cottage and, dismounting his men, began to lead them behind it. Suddenly the air was nothing but a sheet of white flame – an unbearable, monstrous crash, as if the world were falling to bits. Something pressed down upon him hard, and then his right leg gave way queerly. He hung on to his bicycle, trembling and stooping. He put his leg to the ground. It was all right, he could walk. Gently he murmured "By God, that was near. It does shake one up!"

His bicycle fell from his hand as he turned round and shouted, "All right, Ray?"

There was no answer only a low groaning and a wee scream. In the sallow light lay a heap of shattered bicycles and men, all muddled confusedly together. He limped into the middle of them.

"Ray, old man, aren't you all right? What's happened, Ray?"

There was no answer – only a groan and a wild loud cry – My leg! My leg!

Then a man slowly raised himself and stood up, shaking all over and holding his right hand with his left. The blood fell in great drops.

"Here I am, sir, they've got us this time. Oh, my hand!"

The correct thing under the circumstances, thought the Gaspipe grimly, is to get these men under cover before another beggar comes along. The road is distinctly unhealthy from (a) shells, (b) bullets.

They searched among the heaps and found a man who had been hit in the head. Very roughly they made him understand what he was to do. Then together, painfully and slowly, they carried the men, one by one, behind the farm and propped them up against the wall. The last time they went out a cow mooed. Both of them started violently – the Gaspipe laughed. He felt almost genial.

"Ray, old sport, our nerves are not what they were."

Leaving Ray and a Frenchman he had found in charge of the men, he picked up his bicycle and started for the Canadians to find a doctor. He had ridden a little way, when there was a crash behind him. Nearly falling from his bicycle, he pedalled furiously in panic fear to the Canadian bridge. There he waited until a doctor was discovered. After giving the doctor full directions, he turned off again past the Canadian waggons. A parting shell burst in a field beside him.

It was all so melodramatic. How could he report to the Division without being melodramatic? But the road was heavy and crowded, and his leg was weak. Near the chateau he looked towards Ypres. The Great Tower was silhouetted against vast tongues of crude flame. The city was burning fiercely as if some wrathful god had walked into it and lit monstrous bonfires. There was a rumbling and a clattering, and great distant thuds.

He walked into the Staff Room and leant against a chair, feeling sick. How absurd it would be to vomit in that academic atmosphere! The Colonel was dictating a long message. It seemed an age before he looked up.

"Yes?"

"I am sorry to report, sir, that my patrol has been knocked out – shrapnel. I thought I had better come back, sir, to report."

Then Baylor came in and took him into the pantry to have a glass of wine. He told his story, and finished with the great news.

"Baylor, I've got a cushy wound!"

They shook hands, and Baylor congratulated him jealously. The wound was displayed, a neat little red hole, and dressed. Everybody congratulated him.

"We'll send you along in the side-car to the nearest dressing-station," said Baylor, "and they'll hoike it out for you. Come along!"

VIII Cold chicken and champagne

Watson began the long journey from the front line to the Base Hospital.

The Gaspipe Officer squeezed himself into the side-car and waited fearfully for thrills: Tommy's eye judged in quarter inches, particularly when gunners with restive horses were about. They dashed fiercely down the drive, stopped abruptly for a divisional car, and swung off into the spate of traffic on the road from Ypres to Poperinghe. By this time it was flowing with some slight attempt at reasoned order. The monster waggons and high-loaded carts of the now resigned refugees were stranded hopelessly in the mud at the side. The military had usurped the firm centre. Guns and multitudinous ammunition limbers were moving up wearily, like people waiting their turn at the door of a theatre. Motor ambulances and empty waggons were hurrying west from the poor old stricken city. The flare of the great burning in Ypres cast queer little shadows.

Through it all Tommy steered a wizard course, charming to the trained eye of his cargo. There was a noise of great swearing – Bill and the rest of the Company.

"Hi, Bill! Patrol's knocked out. Got a scrap in my leg. Going to have it hooked out. Be with you in the morning. No, just a cushy wound. So long! Good luck!"

They wriggled in and out past the Cyclists, who were loudly worming their way through the crush, rattled into Vlamertinghe, and swung left on to the quietude of the Ouderdom road. "Granny" and her enormous train still lay inert close up to the friendly wall of an *estaminet*. Her slaves, the gunners, stared towards Ypres. …

Stopping outside the camp, Tommy ran in to fetch Brown and the Gaspipe's kit. A cable cart crawled hesitatingly along.

"Would you mind moving that side-car?"

"Sorry, I can't; [proudly] been hit in the leg."

Profuse apologies and interesting inquiries. A couple of men pushed the side-car very carefully out of the way. The hero was reminded of a time when he had pushed his grandmother down a steep place with a little violence.

Tommy returned, and they jolted over the painful pavé to the advanced section of a Field Ambulance. The doctor was hoarse, and talked mechanically, as men do when they are inhumanly weary.

The little room stank of iodine and blood and some cast or cut-off clothes that lay piled in a corner. Iodine was slopped into the wound and a careful injection made. Then the Gaspipe became heroic.

"I think I'll try and walk back to camp."

"All right," said the doctor carelessly.

The first ten paces were a triumph, the second a bore, and the third a torture. He hobbled back on the arm of the faithful Brown.

"Sorry to trouble you again, doctor; I'm afraid you must put me up."

"Thought so," replied the doctor dryly, and offered his own bed. The Gaspipe refused, and settled down finally on a stretcher. He slept a trifle, but for the most part spent the night in cursing his leg.

At the welcome dawn he was lifted into an ambulance, finding there Springett, one of his patrol, who had been hit on the head – not too seriously. This lad had walked a couple of miles on the unhealthiest of roads to obtain help and stretchers, when the doctor that the Gaspipe thought he had secured did not come, obtained them, and made a couple of journeys, carrying his comrades into safety. All this the Gaspipe heard afterwards from Bill.

They came to Reninghelst, where the Gaspipe was labelled and given breakfast, then on slowly to Poperinghe, the most wearisome of journeys. He was put on a little bed in an ante-room that formed part of a corridor. There was a door into it and a door out of it. Both were always banging, banging. A nurse smiled and asked if his wound were dressed. At last an orderly came and offered him food – cold chicken and champagne! He blessed the giver.

One door led down into a sunken hall crammed full of wounded officers. Most of them were waiting cheerfully for the hospital train, and a fair number left late in the morning, but cases kept coming in. An ambulance would arrive and be unloaded. This you knew by the intermittent shriek of pain, and the hectic complaints of the nerve-shattered wounded that reverberated horribly along the corridors. There would be a shriek and a long crooning wail – then little childish moans and chatter.

"Oh, do take care. It does hurt so. Move slowly. It burns like anything. Oh, it does hurt. G-d d-n you, man, be careful, be careful! Oh, it does hurt so."

The long crooning wail would begin again.

Some men were brought in, yellow and gasping. The noises they made shivered in your spine. These were the first victims of the gas. … The day passed with diabolical slowness. The staff, ever kind, listening reasonably to the most unreasonable of complaints, kept telling how overcrowded they were and how the hospital trains were being delayed by the supply trains with ammunition. The narrow ante-room begun to fill with "sitting-up cases." There was the subaltern who had blown up Hill 60, and a bunch of young Canadians who talked of affrays in western saloons, camping in far forests, and the price of land.

One lad stumbled in and sat down in a heap. His mouth kept twitching and his eyes were never still. They asked him where he had been hit.

"Not wounded. One shell just to right and one shell just to left. Picked myself up. Nerve gone."

At every sound he shuddered. When the door banged he started as if some one had struck him and cringed fearfully. He would forget himself for a moment and talk feverishly of gasconading days and purple nights in Canadian saloons. The door banged, and again he would cringe and moan and mutter about his nerves.

When it grew dark food was brought – cold chicken and champagne. They ate enormous meals; most of them had been without food for many hours.

There was talk of a hospital train at 8, and then at 10, but the summons never came. Restlessly they sat and could speak of nothing except the train. For the ante-room was so crowded that only a few could sit down. The rest leant against the wall or squatted on the floor. As it grew later they tried to settle themselves to sleep. The Gaspipe, hobbling out into the corridor, found a stretcher and Brown made him up some sort of bed. He dozed fitfully, wakened by the noise of motor ambulances loading and unloading, the groans and cries of the wounded, and a certain unpleas-antness in a nether limb.

About four in the morning he was wakened finally by a gruff voice – "Up with you! Get a move on! The ambulances are going."

Another long wait on the chilly steps and they were sitting comfortably in an ambulance. The convoy fled away along the Steenvoorde road, past dark columns of slow waggons, past interminable columns of French and English guns – away through Hazebrouck.

They reached St Omer in the grey of the morning and drew up at a forbidding-looking infirmary. They hobbled or were carried up innumerable steps and deposited in a cheerful ward, where they were given hot tea and put to bed. It was extraordinarily comfortable, and the Gaspipe, for one, never again wanted to move. There was no noise of guns and no endless rattling of transport over cobbles. Everybody was kind and quiet. Besides, being wounded, he had become a personage to be tended and cared for, a man whom all delighted to honour. …

In a couple of hours it was announced that the lighter cases were to go straight to Boulogne. So the Gaspipe dressed and, after telling the true story of the night of the 22nd to "Eyewitness," was bundled downstairs into a motor ambulance and thence into a hospital train.

They were cherished mightily in that train by a dear nurse who had the Bulgarian medal, and a young doctor who was pathetically eager to supply all wants. The lunch was foretold but the prophecy was false. The cold chicken came, just as good as it had ever been, and – beer. The Gaspipe travelled down with a young French Canadian and an oldish subaltern. Beyond Boulogne – the sun was setting – the subaltern exclaimed at the play of light on a pink-and-yellow cutting. It was A——, the artist.

So they came to Etaples. The Gaspipe was informed that he was going to the Hospital of the Duchess. He was lifted into a car with more tenderness than he required, and together with Mirfield, who had been shot through the arm, was whirled along straight, dimly lit avenues of dark trees to the glowing front of a Casino.

IX The Hospital of the Duchess

The Duchess of Westminster's Hospital, at Casino de la Foret, Le Touquet, was also known as British Red Cross No 1. The Duchess had a visible presence there – and after her divorce from the Duke of Westminster in 1920, she remarried Captain Lewis, an officer who was a patient about the time that Watson was there.

When the Gaspipe had been told that he was being sent to the Hospital of the Duchess, he did not know whether to laugh or cry. Behind the line rumours had trickled through of perfectly charming but perilously inefficient nurses, whose milk-white hands would nervously fumble with the wound, whose chatter was so delicious that it kept you awake, who sat on your bed just where it would hurt you, and then apologise so sweetly that you forgot the throb; who sometimes, when you were very good and kept yourself clean, kissed you goodnight. To an 'ero slightly wounded these were pleasant anticipations: yet behind them lurked the thought that a cushy and altogether gentlemanly wound can become a right royal disablement under ignorant care.

He had also heard of other hospitals, very different. In these, elderly and harsh featured spinsters with large red hands tyrannised with a horrible efficiency. You were regarded as a Case – and only those most painfully and interestingly disfigured were treated with any consideration. You would see a prophetic gleam in the nurse's eye. She would dose you and starve you until you were ready for the Operation, the high-water mark of hospital existence. Then, most indecently unarrayed, you would be stretched on a cold, white and shiny table, and, in the presence of a group of ghoulish spectators, be cut scientifically. Afterwards you were violently sick. …

During the first few moments the Hospital of the Duchess seemed surely of the former type. He was carried into an immense white entrance-hall where a few cheerful wounded sat critical

We're in tents and ours doesn't leak. There's a pond and a brook just outside. Woods and a lake a little further up the hill, the prettiest of tiny villages a little further down. At the top is the town of C— with good shops and a wonderful view right away to Dunkirk and the sea. We're still quite busy, as a lot of our men are busy filling casualty vacancies.

WHL WATSON RETURNS TO ENGLAND TO RECOVER FROM HIS WOUND

Reproduced from 'Tales of a Gaspipe Officer' in *Blackwood's Magazine*

X Wounded 'ero

This was the last instalment to cover Watson's service with the 5th Division. It was written at Pirbright in December 1915, when he was preparing to return to France in command of 16th (Irish) Division Cyclist company.

In the first December of the war those on leave experienced fully the quiet pleasure of being honoured. Just as when a murder is committed, everybody who can claims some acquaintance with the characters of the crime – the daughter of the murderer always makes a good marriage – so it was the delight of the Briton to cherish the man on leave. The muddied greatcoat had only to enter a car on the Tube and half the men would offer their seats. The women would nudge their husbands, and these, nervously daring, would sidle up and murmur in a deprecating voice: "You have been in France?" Of course nothing important resulted from this touching consideration. Only a few kindly and thoughtful men and women have tried to make leave worth its while. If you meet a gaunt, filthy, and joyous figure, you smile at him, naturally, and granted you are a gentleman of words, turn a neatly-rounded sentence on our brave defenders. You have never thought of organising a clearing house, of piloting your brave defenders safely home. And certainly you send your brave defenders back filled with the melancholy forebodings that are current among the best informed civilians. …

Still a wounded 'ero, particularly a wounded officer, has a tremendous time of it. When the boat reached Folkestone special constables swept on board, throwing everybody aside to make room for the poor fellow with crutches. On landing, the Gaspipe was fiercely attacked with offers of Bovril and cigarettes. He was despairing ever of reaching the train, when suddenly the mob evaporated. Afterwards he learnt the rumour had gone round that a certain Queen was travelling incognito by the same boat. He seated himself in a Pullman and graciously accepted lunch from a sympathetic manufacturer. London and a long ride in a taxi through black streets … that is a far cry from Boesinghe to Burford – from those pitted, ochreous fields and noisy roads and tumbled, broken houses, and nights alive with fighting. The Gaspipe was assured that the war had hit the fourth valley of the Windrush hard. Many had enlisted, and you never knew how late the local trains might be. There was no one in Northleigh or Witney or Burford or Widford who had not some friend or relative at the Front. Burford was full of tales. Timmins's Trouble, who before the war was ever playing truant and raiding orchards, had run away to Oxford and 'listed. Annie's young man had been blown out of his trench. The *Blue Goat* no longer rang on Sunday afternoon with the laughter and jests of the young gentlemen from Oxford. Mary no longer blushed at the compliments she had received for the cakes of her own making. And those lads and girls who had brought to life again those old dances and songs, which the village folk learnt so quickly that they seemed always to have known them, no longer came and danced and rioted and made merry with the *Blue Goat's* fine old ale.

The war had hit Burford hard!

Yet the Gaspipe, back again in the coffee-room of the *Blue Goat* with the proud gramophone, the soberly shining pewter, the hideous chairs, and Mary lightly telling stories of the village, could scarcely remember anything save that day, when, hearing laughter in the courtyard, he had jumped from his bed to the window, and jeered at Alec for a too early walk; of the stroll after tea across the meadows to the old mass-chapel of St Oswald's-in-the-Fields, and home in the dusk along the Happy Valley, and how the spire of Burford Church sticks up absurdly from behind the shoulder of a hill; of the talk by the light of the fire, and how they wrote a little note to her mother, who had gone to bed, asking if Mary might stop up a trifle longer and charm away the thought of "Schools" from their aching heads; of the sharp tramp over the hill to Shipton-under-Wychwood.

In the Happy Valley there was no noise of the transport interminably rattling over cobbles …

And Oxford, filled again with subalterns and gunners, Somerville become a hospital, and Oriel become Somerville – who will be left to carry on the traditions of wise folly and urgent, strenuous living? Will those who come after understand the thrilling pleasure in hiring the Masonic Hall for positively the first debate between Somerville and a college? They will never stroll down to the *Paviers* and play shove-ha'penny with the Ancient Order of Buffaloes, debate on the two main methods of wearing pyjamas, see how the walls of Holywell become yellow and pink in the arc-light, shout their curious war-cry under Trinity windows, explore Venice and the goodsyard, suspect their political opponents of illegal breakfasts, or choose with a careful ignorance their favourite Burgundy. No, they will be a military race and despatch essays to their tutors, with covering note:–

Herewith required essay on *Lancastrian Experiment* (University Form No. 101. Undergraduate Co-operative Series). For your information and early return, please acknowledge.

Oxford is full now of shrouded remembrances, very present vulgarities and fears. …

There is one strong link to old time. The appearance of the wounded 'ero, passing discreetly and affectionately through, brought forth courteous reminders from sundry interested merchants. One night in Flanders we talked together and pictured these solid burghers carefully putting on their spectacles, running fat fingers down the Casualty Lists, and reading the names in terms of indebtedness. Yet surely they must forgive us for our past omissions; their sons, too, are at the war.

We are doing our best to help, for Oxford is a broken city. The colleges are limping along, the weaker with the help of the stronger. But the landladies who used to batten on us have little custom. The dining places are silent and dismal. The shops charge "war" instead of "term" prices. Nobody now hires a horse. Nobody's motorcycle requires continuous repairs. The theatre is turned over to cheap varieties, and the streets that used to be gay are haggard – except for *Timmins's Trouble* and his fellows. …

So the Gaspipe, leaving Oxford and its kindly dons and sharp-eyed tradesmen, came to a certain suburb. All the manhood of it had gone to the war, but little had changed. The mothers did not arrive home so soon after church, for their sons' deeds had to be explained and compared. Tennis parties became feminine and croquet was re-learnt for the benefit of the wounded 'eroes. Yet all the small important policies and politics, alliances and enmities, came out again in the new warwork. The Supply Depot had to be carefully organised on a social basis, and discipline was enforced and regretted as discipline always is. The stringent class distinctions of the suburbs became loosened. Had not John, the butcher's son, got his commission? Suspected spies were treated with whispering coldness, and much alacrity was shown in the dimming of neighbours' lights. Everybody strongly represented to everybody else what everybody else's particular warwork should be. If some one came and spoke to you, the some one was interfering unwarrantably with your personal liberty. If you tactfully spoke to your neighbour, you were performing an unpleasant but patriotic duty. The conventions, too, were disregarded. Girls travelled up to London to their war-work by themselves – and the girl postwoman, who had never had a better time in her life, received much sympathy.

Then there was the burning question of military age and fitness. In such a friendly family suburb no one might decide for himself. Other people's chauffeurs were eyed darkly, and the age of one's own gardener was kept in misty doubt. Suspicion fell upon wounded officers who required too long a convalescence, and merely to drive a motor ambulance was more criminal than to remain at home and still flutter on the Stock Exchange. The Gaspipe had never before realised what the driving power of a community, bound together in mutual rivalry and composed mainly of women, can finally achieve. …

Again, there were optimists and pessimists and strategists. One dear old lady believed that the war could be ended if only the Kaiser could be captured. She could not understand why we did not concentrate on this all-important end. Another ran round her garden every morning before breakfast, so that if the Huns came she might run and hide herself in the jungle. A third practised vigorously with a revolver, so that she might shoot at least one German, even if in punishment the whole suburb were destroyed. The more dolorous papers were assiduously read, and in our suburb it is firmly believed that the Germans can detach a million from one front, throw it against another, wipe up the Serbians, land in Syria, and return before the absence has been noticed. Everything English is good, but silly: everything German is wicked, but wise. With a charitable toleration it has been decided that all Germans must be exterminated like rats, though at the same time we must, of course, retain our fair fame and fight only as gentlemen should.

The suburb is like a small, busy, contentious town of old Greece. The Gaspipe wondered idly what would happen if the suburb and Hulluch were suddenly to change places. …

So to London which swallowed up the war or thought of it. Tottenham Court Road was still that odd mixture of gross sensation and business. Cross & Blackwell's had the same ineffable odour. The bookshops off and on the Charing Cross Road had not changed. Leicester Square was still an oasis for a pipesmoker in a desert of convention. The top of Bloomsbury Square had not altered since that famous murder had been attempted for the delectation of a respectable old man. At dusk the river, the sky, and the chimneys of the Station were as blue as they had ever been from Cheyne Walk.

And a decadent review, full of the old audacities and clevernesses, came out to welcome us home. …

The reader must forgive this slight chapter. It is written for the pleasure of remembrance in a tiny workman's cottage – the country is the dirtiest in the world, and there is a distant rumbling of transport, and of guns, and humming of aeroplanes. He will soon return to France.

Watson's vivid account of his time at Oxford – almost a distant memory because of his time in France – returns us to the place he had so deftly described in his "Letter by way of Introduction". There were to be two further instalments of Tales of a Gaspipe Officer in Maga; his "Company of Tanks", published in 1920, recounted Watson's contribution to the war and the story of his return to England after the Armistice. What those later writings didn't recapture was the unique blend of wisdom, pride and humility which infused 'Adventures of a Despatch Rider'.

Watson's letter to George Blackwood containing the plan for 'Adventures of a Despatch Rider' is preserved in the Blackwood archive at the National Library of Scotland.

The book might consist:-

1. Of an <u>Introduction</u> or dedicatory letter containing amongst other things what the reviewer will probably call "a bitter diatribe against war." I want to make people realise that, despite the fact many of my letters were written for obvious reasons in a frivolous spirit, war is hell ghastly beyond man's imagining.

2. Of a <u>Prologue</u> describing some interesting experiences I had in London when I tried Wentlist and at Chatham after I had enlisted — thence carrying on the narrative to our entraining at Curlow.

3. Of the <u>Articles</u>. These I shall revise, correct and augment. I shall put in practically all the names.

4. Of The <u>Discourse</u> on despatch-riding.

5. An Index Nominum.

6. Two or three simple but good maps.
    a. Of the Great Marches.
    b. Of the Aisne District.
    c. Of the La Bassée District
    d. Of the line from Boesinghe to Vermelles.

The caricature Watson refers to in his plan, which appeared on the front cover of both wartime editions of the book in 1915 and 1917.

2

TEL.
HARROW 473.

LEAFLAND,
HARROW ON THE HILL.

These maps should, when spread out, lie flush with the page - so that the page need not be turned backwards and forwards. The print should be large, for the narrative is in many places condensed, and the page should have a fair margin. I have also an exceedingly clever caricature of myself and our fat signal sergeant, done by a Cyclist Officer on the Aisne. It would reproduce well & might act as frontispiece. The actual letter press should work out at about 65,000 words. The book would be published on the terms you stated. Unless I am worked harder than I have ever been in my life before, I might to get the fourth instalment, the Discourse and the making of the book done by the end of August at latest.

Sincerely yours.

WHLWatson.

Appendix I

The Despatch Rider in Print and the Story of 'Adventures'

Watson always described the production of 'Adventures of a Despatch Rider' as a compilation of his letters from France. He said in the first instalment of 'Adventures' in *Blackwood's Magazine* in April 1915: "The letters from which this account of events was taken were not written for publication. They were letters written home in the ordinary course, and they passed the Censor in the usual way. In consequence the narrative is not the whole truth. The account, as here printed, has also been submitted to the Censor." He repeated that explanation in the Introduction to the book, which was "made up principally of letters to my mother and [Robert Whyte]. …. I have filled in the gaps these letters leave with narrative, worked the whole into some sort of connected account, and added maps and an index." However, our examination of the different editions of the book, and the correspondence in Blackwood's Archive, reveals that the book's own story is a little more complex than that.

From the start of the war many members of the Expeditionary Force wrote long and detailed letters home. Friends and family wrote copiously in reply, and they also sent newspapers and topical magazines to the Army. Soldiers serving in France devoured printed material, and at home the press competed to publish material which came from the Front. Typically, local newspapers published material about soldiers from their region – either letters home passed to the newspapers by soldiers' families, or newspaper interviews with men on home leave.

The *Daily Mail*, which was then owned by the publishers of *The Times*, was the first national paper to publish a full-length account by a despatch rider – in December 1914 it featured Archibald Sproston's story of the campaign from Mons to Ypres in six daily instalments. Sproston's story, written in a breathless present tense, is full of tales of heroism, wartime carnage and the disgusting conditions suffered by the troops. They are a simplistic narrative of the trials suffered by motorcyclists, and they go into detail about their varied but mostly unpleasant living conditions. However, Sproston does not write about how the motorcyclists engaged with one another, or about the rest of the Army or the French.

If Watson was aware of Sproston's work, it's unlikely that it impressed him. A man with his background and education would have been sure that he could produce something better. However, he was set a sterner test by the first of his colleagues to appear in print. Stanley Polhill's family passed his letters home to his old school, Trent College. These letters were thoughtful and well-written, and the first extracts were published in *The Trident,* the school magazine, in November 1914 [see Timeline]. Polhill's copy of the issue which contained the first instalment of his letters probably reached him at Bailleul, and it's likely that the other motorcyclists would have seen his letters in print when they arrived.

Censorship at the start of the war was somewhat erratic. There were strict rules forbidding most types of publication by men in the forces, but breaches were often tolerated. The motorcyclists were novices in a professional Army, and they were three months into a war which was already bloodier, and looking likely to be more prolonged, than they had expected. While some wanted to spread the word about their experiences to their families and beyond, others understood the case for reticence. Interestingly, Overton's first surviving letter home, which was dated just after Polhill's letters were published, began with the stern warning to his mother: "Don't send this to papers please!"

It may have been seeing Polhill's letters in print that planted a seed in Watson's mind. However, Watson took no steps towards becoming a published author until February 1915, when he ceased to be a despatch rider on being commissioned. Presumably at his suggestion, Watson's mother, who lived in Harrow near his old school, called on his old tutor George Townsend Warner. She took Watson's letters to him, and conveyed his suggestion that they could be published in his old school magazine, *The Harrovian*.

Townsend Warner politely declined Watson's offer. He himself was a published author – a renowned historian who had also published a guide to English style. Furthermore, he was an agent for Blackwood's, the long-established Edinburgh publishers, which was then managed by the fourth generation of the founding family. It published quality literature, travel writing and history. As well as a traditional list of books, its output included a monthly journal called *Blackwood's Magazine*.

This periodical, nicknamed *'Maga'*, had been published for nearly 100 years, and was required reading for the educated public. Each monthly edition contained topical and scholarly articles on factual subjects as well as contemporary fiction. Early in its history the journal pioneered the serialisation of works which were later published in book form. Novels by many authors, including George Eliot and Joseph Conrad, first appeared in instalments in *'Maga'*, and John Buchan's topical novel 'The Thirty Nine Steps' was serialised there at the same time as 'Adventures'.

Townsend Warner wrote to George Blackwood in February 1915, sending him Watson's letters. He commended them as a publishing proposition, in his words "far & away the best thing I have yet seen from the front." Matters now moved very fast. On 6 April, Watson, who was still serving in France, replied to George Blackwood accepting his terms. And even before the first instalment was published, Blackwood asked Watson for more – he was sure that the articles would be a success. The lengthy first instalment, which was published anonymously, began with Watson's departure from Chatham on a "damp chilly morning", and covered Watson's journey up to early October and the Move to the North. However, it left out much of the detail about the Battle of the Aisne which appeared in later instalments.

At this moment, events beyond Watson's control intervened. He sustained a serious wound in the Second Battle of Ypres. After two weeks in hospital in France, he was repatriated to England in early May and convalesced at home until August. The first instalment was a popular success, and his long and uninterrupted spell at home gave him the ideal opportunity to pursue his literary plans.

When the first instalment appeared, Watson asked Blackwood whether it would be possible to turn his work into a book, suggesting that 'Adventures of a Despatch Rider' might be published in book form at the end of the war. Blackwood replied promptly – he wanted Watson to produce the book straightaway, and he offered to publish the book as soon as Watson had finished the instalments for *Maga*. So Watson set about finishing the instalments for the magazine, and at the same time turning what he had published into the book.

Watson's Plan

The book might consist:

1. *Of an* Introduction *or dedicatory letter containing amongst other things what the reviewer will probably call "a bitter diatribe against war." I want to make people realise that, despite the fact many of my letters were written for obvious reasons in a frivolous spirit, war is hell ghastly beyond man's imagining.*
2. *Of a* Prologue *describing some interesting experiences I had in London when I tried to enlist and at Chatham after I had enlisted – thence carrying on the narrative to our entraining at Carlow.*
3. *Of the* Articles. *These I shall revise, correct, and augment. I shall put in practically all the names.*
4. *Of the* Discourse *on despatch-riding.*
5. *An Index Nominum.*
6. *Two or three simple but good maps*
   a. *Of the Great Marches.*
   b. *Of the Aisne District.*
   c. *Of the La Bassée District.*
   d. *Of the line from Boesinghe to Vermelles.*

These maps should, when spread out, lie flush with the page – so that the page need not be turned backwards and forwards.

The print should be large, for the narrative is in many places condensed, and the page should have a fair margin.

I have also an exceedingly clever caricature[1] of myself and our fat signal sergeant, done by a Cyclist Officer on the Aisne. It would reproduce well & might act as a frontispiece. The actual letterpress should work out at about 65,000 words. The book would be published on the terms you stated.

Unless I am worked harder than I have ever been in my life before, I ought to get the fourth instalment, the Discourse, and the making of the book done by the end of August at the latest.

Blackwood accepted most of this proposal – generally the published version of 'Adventures' followed Watson's first ideas, particularly the layout of the book and the maps. However, no index was ever produced, and Blackwood rejected Watson's proposal to publish *The Discourse* as a section of the book or as a pamphlet. All Watson's material on despatch riding was thus woven into the text of the book.

In the book Watson filled in the full names of regiments and other units which had been left blank, and he identified most of the despatch riders by nickname rather than the initial letter of their surname followed by a blank. The only exceptions were George Owen – known as 'George' – and Orr, who was known by his surname. When Orr was killed in March 1918, the obituary in his local newspaper noted that Orr had been one of the despatch riders who appeared in 'Adventures', which is an indication that the book was well known in 1918.

The correspondence between author and publisher shows that Watson believed he had complied with all the censor's requirements. For example, he wrote to Blackwood's in August telling them that he had been given permission to put his name to the book. It seems there was a breakdown in communication between Watson and the censors, for most of the offending passages which were deleted from the expurgated edition were taken unaltered from the instalments in the magazine.

Watson completed his recovery by the end of August 1915. When he arrived in Ireland in September to train 16th Division Cyclist Company, the book was finished. He expected that it would appear in September or October, but publication was delayed until late in 1915 because the maps weren't ready.

Meanwhile, Watson continued to write instalments for *Maga*. *Tales of a Gaspipe Officer* was conceived as a continuation of 'Adventures' and was written for the same audience. However, 'Tales' has quite a different impact from the earlier work. The story is less dramatic than 'Adventures', and Watson chose to make a major shift in style – replacing the 'despatch rider' who narrated 'Adventures' in the first person with 'Gaspipe', a third person narrator. His identification with the 'gaspipe cavalry' – the nickname of the cyclists – is cheerful and irreverent, but Watson's account of what 'Gaspipe' did, or what happened to him, is less involving than the first person narrative of 'Adventures'. *Tales of a Gaspipe Officer* began to appear in December 1915 and instalments were published up to March 1916. However, as the correspondence with Blackwood shows, Watson was now serving in France with the Cyclist Company and was falling behind with the writing schedule.

Early in 1916, soon after the publishers ordered a second impression of *Adventures*, they received unwelcome news. Watson wrote to Blackwood telling him that he had been ordered to withdraw the book from sale. He would have to submit future material for pre-publication censorship and, if 'Adventures' was to be re-published, it would have to be expurgated. From the surviving fragments of correspondence between the censors, found on Watson's War Office file, it seems that 'Adventures of a Despatch Rider' had only reached the public in the first place because of mis-communications between the authorities.

The publisher complied at once with the War Council's order, and Watson published nothing more until the following January. Nonetheless, his breach of censorship rules doesn't seem to have affected his military career. He reached the rank of Captain in August 1915, and was promoted to Major in July 1916.

In late 1916 Watson moved to a new rôle in the Tank Corps, which seems to have consumed all his energies for a time. A final instalment of *Tales of a Gaspipe Officer* appeared in January 1917, but his next book, 'Company of Tanks', an account of the last two years of war, was not published until 1920.

The Shilling Edition of 'Adventures' appeared later in 1917.[1] There is nothing on the face of the book to show that the text had been altered from the first edition, but in reality it was heavily expurgated – on the censor's orders, Watson took out more than 2,000 words. Comparing the two versions offers a rare chance to see what caused offence in 1915.

The deletions, which are all indicated in the footnotes, fall into three main categories. First, the censor – unsurprisingly – removed accounts of incidents which one would expect the authorities to suppress, such as British soldiers shooting prisoners, and looting German dead.[2] The censor then removed almost everything which was critical of the French – including civilians as well as the French Army.[3] Finally, they ordered the removal of words which were critical of the British Army.[4]

Some of the deletions are clumsy – for example, they ordered the deletion of light-hearted comments on soldiers which were probably included in the first place to emphasise Watson's positive feelings for the Army.

---

1   The Shilling (1/–) edition actually sold for 1/3d due to rising production costs.
2   See Chapters Five and Six.
3   See Chapters Four, Five, Six and Seven.
4   See Chapters One, Three, Four and Six.

DR IDENTIFICATION

A white and blue brassard issued to Corporal Hayes-Sadler, and a laissez-passer issued to Sergeant Merchant by the authorities at Le Cateau – all despatch riders wore a two-tone brassard on each arm, and carried this document.

In addition despatch riders were issued with waterproof document cases, made from oilskin material with stitched reinforcement. This example belonged to Corporal Hayes-Sadler.

PROCUREMENT OF MOTORCYCLES

Army Form B 210A

The Army used this checklist for despatch riders bringing their machines for inspection when being signed on. It comprised a certificate to be completed by the inspecting officer, a list of spares required to be carried on the machine at all times, and a detailed schedule describing the actual machine being submitted for approval. (See below)

The form stipulated that:

a)   Motor cycles to be of a well-tried and approved make, of which adequate stocks of spare parts are available in the country, and to be fitted with variable speed gear and magneto ignition.

b)   Wheels to be 26 inches in diameter, with not less than 2¼ inch tyres for machines with engines of 500 cc and not less than 2 inch tyres for machines with engines of 350 cc.

c)   Engine to be of about 500 cc capacity and upwards, with one or more cylinders. A certain number of horizontal twin-cylinder machines of about 350 cc capacity will, however, be accepted.

d)   Magneto to be efficiently protected from the wet, and preferably of the waterproof type. Magnetos should, where possible, have interchangeable base and drive.

e)   Spring forks to be fitted.

f)   Screw threads used should be standardised as far as possible.

g)   Lamps and generator to be fitted with brackets for attachment to machine.

h)   If belt is used, it should have the standard angle and a section of 7/8 inch or 1 inch in the case of engines of 500 cc capacity, and ¾ inch for machines of 350 cc capacity.

i)   Spare parts, as specified below, to be carried on the motor cycle.

j)   Motor cycle to be fitted with suitable valise or bag for carrying personal kit.

k)   Machine to be effectively silenced.

Initially many types and makes of machine were accepted in August 1914. In late September 1914, the War Office announced that henceforth only Douglas, Triumph, P & M, Rudge, Rover, B.S.A., and James (single cylinder) machines would be accepted. In the event, it is unlikely any James machines were ever used on the Western Front, in all probability because of the lack of available spares to keep them running in the field.

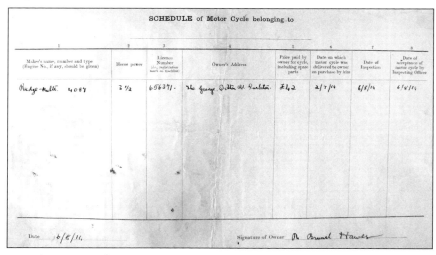

An extract of an Army Form B 210A with details of a privately owned
Rudge Multi being purchased for despatch rider use.

Burney & Blackburne, Ltd.,

TONGHAM, SURREY.

Extract from "Blackwood's Magazine," for July, 1915
(page 121).

"It was at La Bassée that we had our first experience of utterly unrideable roads.   North of the canal the roads were fair macadam in dry weather and to the south the main road Béthune-Beuvry-Annequin was of the finest pavé.   Then it rained hard.   First the roads became greasy beyond belief. Starting was perilous, and the slightest injudicious swerve meant a bad skid.   Between Gorre and Festubert the road was vile.   It went on raining, and the roads were thickly covered with glutinous mud.   The front mud-guard of George's Douglas choked up with a lamentable frequency.   **THE BLACKBURNE alone, the finest and most even-running of all motor-cycles,*** ran with unswerving regularity. Finally, to our heart-burning sorrow, there were nights on which motor-cycling became impossible, and we stayed restlessly at home while men on the despised horse carried our despatches.   This we could not allow for long.   Soon we became so skilled that, if I remember correctly, it was only half a dozen nights in all right through the winter that the horsemen were required."

*This is not an unthinking advertisement.   After despatch riding from August 16th to February 18th, my judgment should be worth something.   I am fully convinced that if the Government could have provided all despatch riders with **BLACKBURNES**, the per centage—at all times small—of messages undelivered owing to mechanical breakdowns or the badness of the roads would have been reduced to zero.   I have no interest in the **BLACKBURNE** Company beyond a sincere admiration of the machine it produces.

Watson's praise for the Blackburne machine he had encountered was used by Burney and Blackburne to market their machines during the war, but few were made until production restarted in earnest in 1919.

MOTORCYCLES

ARIEL 3½HP   500cc White and Poppe Sidevalve single. Three speed hub gear and clutch or countershaft three speed chain-cum-belt drive

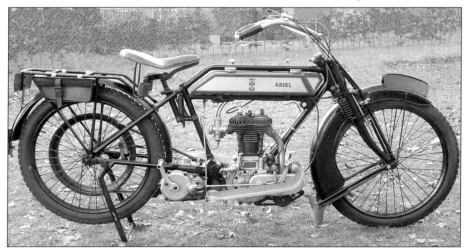

The Birmingham-built Ariel, featuring a proprietary engine made by White and Poppe with widely spaced side valves promoting cool running and reliability, was a powerful and well-made machine which was surprisingly popular in DR service with private owners recruited in 1914. The commonest model featured a three-speed hub gear of Ariel's own design. The chain-cum-belt countershaft model seen here, and an all chain drive model, were also available in 1914.

BLACKBURNE 4HP   500cc Sidevalve outside flywheel. Three-speed Armstrong hub gear

Based around an engine designed circa 1904 by pioneer aviator Geoffrey de Havilland, the Blackburne quickly established a reputation for smooth running and easy starting, and the distinctive outside flywheel played a key part in this. The two prototype machines were ridden by the Burney brothers and one survived the war intact. Several other examples were ridden successfully, and contemporary press as well as Watson and Polhill singled out the Blackburne as perhaps the best DR machine available, although in reality, very few saw active service with DRs.

BSA 3½HP   500cc Sidevalve single. Three-speed hub gear and clutch, chain-cum-belt

Built in Birmingham by Birmingham Small Arms, a cycle and weapons manufacturer, the BSA design closely followed the Triumph of the period, and was an early adopter of all chain drive, as seen here. They did also supply chain-cum-belt machines with countershaft gears, and three-speed hub gear belt drive models. Three-speed hub gear BSAs were in use with the 5th Signals Company, and no doubt Triumph spare parts could be used to keep them running due to the similarity of the machines.

DOUGLAS 2¾HP   350cc sidevalve flat twin. Two speed Chain-cum-belt

Douglas of Bristol introduced their flat twin 2¾HP model in 1910. Steadily improved, this relatively small and light machine became extremely successful, and was an obvious choice as a DR mount, having just sufficient specification to meet War Office requirements. Many of the 1914 DRs rode these machines, and several Douglas employees became DRs including Giblett, one of Watson's DR colleagues. Douglas machines were procured in large numbers by the War Office for DR use. Very light and smooth running, with the later Triumph Model H, these two were by far the most numerous DR machines in the First World War.

HUMBER 3½HP   500cc. Three-speed hub gear and clutch, belt drive.

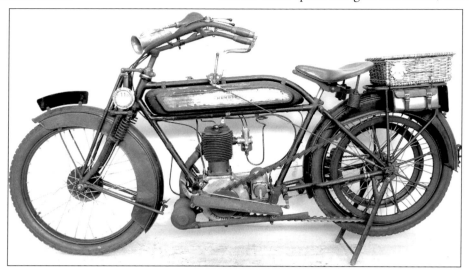

A well respected pioneering cycle, motorcycle and car manufacturer founded in the late Victorian era in Nottingham, Humber made very conventional machines in Coventry which featured their own design of engine with gear-driven magneto fitted behind the engine and hence protected from the worst of the weather. The Humber was amongst the first design to feature a kick starter driven by chain to the rear wheel, unlike the pedalling gear commonplace at the time. Although popular with motorcyclists of the period, they were not chosen by the War Office for DR use, so relatively few saw active service.

P&M 3½HP   500cc Sidevalve sloper single. P&M two-speed all chain drive.

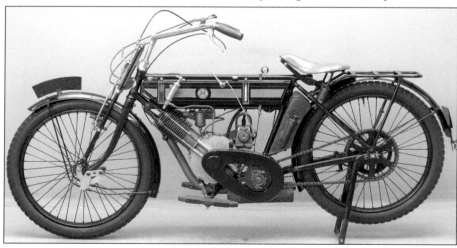

Phelon and Moore of Cleckheaton in Yorkshire were devoted to 'sloper' engines which formed a stressed member of the frame, coupled with a two-speed countershaft gear and all chain transmission. They were widely used in the First World War and were favoured by the RFC and RNAS, but less common on the Western Front. Being all chain drive, they did not suffer from the "dreaded belt slip" so common to belt drive machines in use in Flanders mud.

ROYAL ENFIELD 8HP   1000cc sidevalve V-twin JAP engine.
Three speed countershaft gearbox all chain or chain cum belt drive

The Redditch built V-twin Royal Enfield of both 700cc and 1000cc, combined with a wicker or coachbuilt sidecar, was a workhorse for DR duties, the sidecar being particularly valuable as an aid to stability during the very cold winter of 1914. An 8HP Enfield outfit was used by Cecil Burney and Hugh Trepess to visit Rouen during January 1915 (see Timeline, page 212).

RUDGE 3½HP Multi   500cc IoE single. 'Multi' variable speed belt drive and clutch.

Coventry-based Rudge Whitworth built their famous Multi, employing novel interconnected variable pulleys on engine and rear wheel combined with an all metal enclosed free engine clutch. It was a successful machine in 1914, winning that year's Senior TT. The IoE 'F' head engine was a powerful and reliable unit but the Multi transmission proved unreliable in DR use. The Rudge appears in Watson's story, but is usually referred to in unfavourable terms.

SUNBEAM 3½HP   500cc sidevalve single. Three-speed Countershaft gearbox all chain drive.

John Marston of Wolverhampton, makers of fine 'Sunbeam' bicycles and cars, introduced their all chain drive motorcycles in 1912 and they were immediately successful, being smooth, reliable, well finished and equipped with the famed 'Little Oil Bath' tinplate chaincases. The 3½ HP 500cc model was introduced in 1913 and many saw DR service in the hands of their owners in 1914, but they were too pricey to be purchased by the War Office.

TRIUMPH 3½HP   500cc sidevalve single. Three-speed hub gear and clutch, belt drive.

Triumph, based in Coventry, started manufacturing motorcycles in 1903 using Minerva engines, and introduced their own design of engine in 1905. This quickly became popular, and was widely used in competitions and by professional men as daily transport. Originally with fixed belt drive, a rear hub clutch was introduced in 1910, followed by a three-speed hub gear which was on the model widely seen in 1914 DR use, of both 500cc (3½HP) and 550cc (4HP) capacity. It also featured a simple girder front fork with rocking motion round the lower pivot and a horizontal spring rather than parallel linkage as was the norm. DRs used a heavy leather belt wrapped around the fork top to help reduce clash and prevent spring breakage. The successful 550cc 4HP Model H, with three-speed countershaft gear and chain-cum-belt drive, did not arrive till 1915, and with the lighter Douglas, was procured in large numbers by the War Office for the New Army, but in 1914, the belt drive hub gear reigned supreme.

WANDERER 3PS (HP) 439cc sidevalve V twin.
Two speed epicyclic gear, belt drive transmission.

Built in Chemnitz, Saxony, south of Berlin, the Wanderer was a popular machine on the Continent at the outbreak of the First World War, and sold in large numbers and was in use by both German and French DRs. A novel feature of the machine was its rear sprung frame, which made it very capable on rough ground and the poor roads of the day.

ZENITH 3½HP 500cc sidevalve engine. Gradua variable ratio belt drive.

The sporting Zenith, built in Finsbury Park, London, often with a V-twin JAP engine but seen here in DR-preferred single cylinder form, was highly successful due to its novel variable belt drive. Dubbed the 'Gradua Gear', this system had a variable engine pulley, and screw-jacks to move the rear wheel backwards and forwards to maintain belt tension. This was a very popular choice for competition use when first introduced in 1910, but was barred from competitions when deemed unfair. Zenith principal Freddie Barnes made much marketing capital from this ban.

DRIVE BELTS

Belt drive motorcycles employed rubber-impregnated canvas V-belting with a metal fastener to connect the cut ends of the belt. In use, the drive depended on the belt being taut enough to grip the pulleys – more so when the weather was wet or the conditions were muddy. When the belt slipped, restoring drive entailed removing the belt-fastener link and cutting out a section of belt, making a new fastener hole with a patent punch and then refastening the belt. Since it was now shorter and tighter, it would drive until it stretched or broke when a new belt would be needed. Motorcyclists carried a spare belt and a belt punch in special round cases or sometimes just strapped onto the rear carrier or around the steering head. A new belt could be expected to last many months of normal road use, but in DR conditions, perhaps considerably less. The use of V-belt drives effectively ceased in the 1920s.

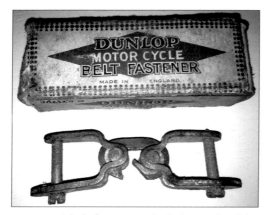

A belt fastener and a belt punch of the type that was carried by riders as part of their spares kit

HUB GEARS

Before the introduction of countershaft gearboxes familiar to modern motorcyclists, many marques of motorcycle were fitted with a three-speed hub gear, controlled by cables or a rod, a larger version of those still made for commuter bicycles. When the operating cables or rod became deranged or out of adjustment, the gears were 'down' and the motorcycle would be stuck in a high gear, necessitating urgent attention as lower gears were essential for riding on bad surfaces.

INLET AND EXHAUST VALVES

One of the most frequent problems encountered was valve failure which could break or simply burn the seat face if the tappet was maladjusted. DRs carried two spare valves in special holders made of wood in which replacement valves, springs and cotters were kept assembled ready for insertion through a removable cap. DRs became adept at changing a valve in order to ensure a safe return to base.

MAGNETOS

Ignition for motorcycles in 1914 was almost always provided by a magneto, a complex and costly electro-mechanical device invented by British engineer Frederick Simms but commercialised by German industrialist Robert Bosch. At the outbreak of war, supplies of German-made Bosch magnetos dried up, leaving a headache for British motorcycle manufacturers. Some Bosch magnetos were imported from their American factory, but UK magneto manufacturers, including CAV, EIC, M-L and Thomson-Bennett increased their output to compensate; nevertheless Bosch remained the 'best in class' well into the war. In order to assist with parts availability, certain aspects of magneto design were standardised on Bosch dimensions, so key components like slip rings and points assemblies were interchangeable. The waterproof 'ZE' model introduced by Bosch in 1912 made a big difference to the reliability of motorcycling in bad weather, and was copied slavishly by M-L of Coventry and others as can be seen when the M-L (L) and Bosch (R) units are compared. The two magneto designs were interchangeable.

PETROL

One logistic problem which continually exercised every DR was procuring an adequate supply of petrol for his machine, which had a relatively small capacity compared to modern motorcycles, typically around one gallon, enough for up to 100 miles on the machines of the day. Petrol supplies were usually in two gallon cans, roadside pumps being the exception rather than the norm.[1] When Watson disembarked from *Archimedes* in Le Havre, he ran out of petrol trying to locate the railway station from which the Company was due to travel to Landrecies. The French word for 'petrol' is 'essence' while 'petrole' means 'paraffin'. One can easily understand why, in the heat of the moment, DRs occasionally had their tank filled with paraffin in error. Although petrol engines can be made to run on paraffin, they are very hard to start.

SIDECARS

The DRs that landed in France with the BEF in August 1914 rode solo motorcycles, which were often difficult to ride safely on the treacherously slippery road conditions of northern France and Belgium with greasy or muddy *pavé*. Some months into the war, it was realised that the use of a sidecar would help reduce accidental spills and the 'dreaded side-slips'. Watson describes how the "Quarter-Bloke" (Merchant) managed to locate some French-built sidecars which were designed for right-hand fitting, unlike UK sidecars which were exclusively left-hand fitting. The artificers deftly fitted them and thus greatly extended the usefulness of the motorcycles in the worst of the 1914–1915 winter, which was notably severe. In January 1915, Cecil Burney and Hugh Trepess rode a Royal Enfield combination from St Jans Cappel to Rouen and back.[2]

---

1   See page 194 where Alick Burney is seated on a 2 gallon petrol can.
2   See page 212.

TYRES
Motorcycles of 1914 invariably used beaded-edge tyres, sometimes referred to as "clinchers". Instead of a wire-reinforced bead, these had a rubber and canvas moulded edge which engaged with the wheel rim to hold the tyre in situ. (The modern well-base wired-on tyre was still more than a decade away.) DRs kept a close eye out for slow punctures but tyre problems were a constant source of worry; only sufficient air pressure protected the rider from disaster when a deflated tyre came off the rim and could jam the wheel. The Company Quartermaster Sergeant was always on the look-out for replacement tyres and inner tubes, and his skill in procuring such items was part of the success of the whole despatch riding enterprise.

PHOTOGRAPHY

In 1910, the popular camera market was boosted by the introduction of the Vest Pocket Kodak camera, or VPK. Between 1910 and 1926, nearly two million were sold.

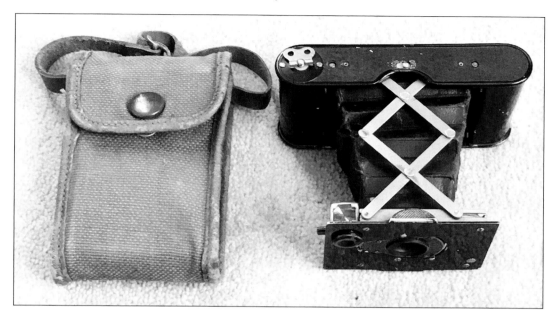

The VPK, measuring 4½in × 2½in × 1in (115mm × 63mm × 25mm) and weighing a hefty three-quarters of a pound (360 grams) was a sturdy, metal-bodied quality folding roll-film camera with a patent ball-bearing shutter. The 5th Signal company despatch riders had two or more VPKs between them. As some of the images in the Sadders, Pollers and Burney collections are identical, we conclude they shared prints from the same negative, but in each album there are images that relate to the owner alone.

While the images which they captured are not as good as contemporary studio photography could deliver, they range from action scenes to very informal group shots such as the Christmas day photoshoot, each DR in turn taking a shot of the others. Ironically Christmas 1914 proved to be the undoing of the VPK. In early January 1915, the *Daily Mail* published VPK images of the Christmas truce, and within weeks, the War Office had issued an order banning the use of cameras by serving troops in overseas conflicts.

DECEMBER 1914.

LT G de HAVILLAND R.F.C.

The VPK uses '127 format' roll film and most of the VPK images in this book are enlarged. The despatch riders, however, used contact prints in their albums, and for comparison, we reproduce at its original size the image that the Burney brothers took of their friend Geoffrey de Havilland, with Grimers' tiny hand-written caption on the album mount.

Appendix III

The 1914 Despatch Riders – Database

Introduction

While we were researching *Two Wheels to War*, we created a database covering all the men who were recruited into the Signals Service and served in the Expeditionary Force in France in 1914. The database contains vital data and mini-biographies of nearly two-thirds of the men whom we identified as motorcyclists – if we had extended this section to include all the information about the 1914 despatch riders, this would have been a very long book!

Recruitment of despatch riders

More than 400 motorcyclists went to France in 1914, of whom 200 landed before the end of August. One of the defining characteristics of the motorcyclists, particularly those who arrived early in France, was that they became despatch riders on an impulse. Very few were already serving soldiers or members of the Special Reserve. Nearly all were civilians who volunteered within a few days – or even hours – of the outbreak of war, leaving themselves no time at all to consider their options. Men recruited as motorcyclists by the Intelligence Corps, such as Roger West,[1] also shared that impulsiveness, which distinguished them from the thousands who followed them overseas as despatch riders from 1915 onwards. For example, Oswald Harcourt Davis[2] reflected for some time before committing himself to the Signals Service, while Albert Simpkin[3] left diaries which reveal how he shopped around in 1914. He was determined to join the Army, but he tried first to join the artillery regiment in which his brother was serving before he decided he would apply his passion for motorcycling to his military career.

Most of these early despatch riders were in their twenties or very late teens, but some were much older. Seven were born in the 1870s – and the oldest known motorcyclist, Ernest Longley, a GHQ despatch rider whom Roger West encountered at Le Cateau before the Battle of Mons, was born in December 1869. He joined the Royal Engineers in 1888, completed 20 years service in 1908, and in his retirement served as an instructor at Cambridge with the University OTC. He returned to the colours in August 1914 to serve as a despatch rider with GHQ Signal company.

We found that many of the 1914 despatch riders survived into the 1980s. John Perks, who died in 1995 aged 102, was the last known survivor, and he was, by some distance, the oldest former despatch rider. His account of the 1914 campaign is in the Liddle collection at Leeds University.

---

1   Roger Rolleston West (1891–1975), see Bibliography.
2   Oswald Harcourt Davis (1882–1962), see Carragher, "The Man who saved Paris".
3   Albert Simpkin (1885–1966), see Bibliography.

Our first stage in identifying a man as a 1914 despatch rider was finding a Royal Engineers corporal with a service number which fell within certain parts of the 28000 series. Corporal 28000 Malcolm Lincoln Taylor, with the first number in that sequence, was recruited at Chatham on 4th August, and many of the despatch riders had similarly low numbers. Cecil Burney was 28014, his brother Alick Burney 28035, and Watson himself was 28045. We have found nearly every Royal Engineers recruit with a number between 28000 and 28299 – only eight names are missing – and we have verified nearly all of them as motorcyclists. We have either positively identified them as motorcyclists from articles or letters or photographs, or there is corroboration in their military records. Their attestation form as a motorcyclist may survive in The National Archives (WO 339) or they were tagged with labels such as 'M.C.' or 'M Cy S' on their Medal Roll index cards (WO 372). Early motorcycle despatch riders are also found in two shorter sequences – from 28700 to 28799, and from 28965 to 29055.

From 28000 Malcolm L Taylor (1893–1970) to 29055 Lancelot B Dunford (1891–1956)

Malcolm Lincoln Taylor was an accountant when he enlisted as a motorcyclist. His attestation papers survive. He was wounded and repatriated to England in September 1914, but returned to France in November 1914. Later he was commissioned in the Royal Flying Corps and remained in the Royal Air Force after the war, ending his service career in 1945 as an Air Vice-Marshal.

Lancelot Babington Dunford can be securely identified as a motorcyclist from the annotation 'M Cy S' on his medal index card. He was commissioned into the Royal Engineers Inland Waterways and Docks section. In later life he was an agricultural produce broker in Norfolk, where he died in 1956.

28000 Corporal Malcolm L Taylor pictured in the Royal Flying Corps in 1916.

29055 Corporal Lancelot B Dunford was one of seven sons of a Tyneside shipbuilder.

THE TT CONTESTANTS

Many contemporary observers noted that a high proportion of the motorcyclists recruited to the Signals Service in 1914 had public school and university backgrounds – in particular, many had studied at Oxford or Cambridge. However, the Royal Engineers also recruited many non-graduates to this rôle – professional men or trained engineers with business skills such as Trepess or the Burneys.

It is less well known that at least 14 despatch riders who served in France in 1914 came from another elite group – those who had competed in the TT races, the ultimate motorcycle challenge. Riding in the TT in the Isle of Man was highly demanding. Just to finish the race was a great achievement, and riders needed the skills and stamina to handle a motorcycle over poorly surfaced roads and undulating terrain. Nor was it enough to be a great rider – contestants were unlikely to succeed if they didn't know their machine and its engine inside out, or didn't have the ability to carry out running repairs.

The recruits who had competed in the TT fall into two distinct groups. The early group landed on or before 16th August. Harold Kitchen, who had only started one race – he retired from the 1914 Senior riding an Abingdon – has the unique claim that he was the very first motorcycle despatch rider to reach France, landing there on 9th August. Others in the early group included Vernon Busby, who managed the 1914 TT Sunbeam team and who rode in the Senior TT, and Roy Lovegrove, who finished the 1914 Senior on a Scott. There were two men with formidable racing records – Archibald Sproston had ridden in three TTs between 1909 and 1911, and Howard Newman had ridden Ivy machines every year from 1912. Finally, two men who had been first time riders in 1913 – Frank Begley and Kenneth Clark – were assigned to the 3rd Division. Clark was killed in action in October 1914.

The 1913 Senior TT Rover team including despatch rider Duggie Brown (on the left).

MOTORCYCLE DESPATCH RIDERS WHO LANDED IN FRANCE IN 1914

• died while serving as a despatch rider
‡ died as an officer or in another service rôle
Names highlighted in grey are men who served with 5th Signal company in 1914

Name	No	Dates	Landed
Alexander, Samuel M	28298		30 Sept 14
Allen, William Shepherd	28181	1895– 1974	19 Aug 14
Amps, Leon Williamson	28215	1892–1989	15 Oct 14
Anderson, Robert	29036		7 Oct 14
Annoot, Basil Ernest	28167	1888–1962	27 Aug 14
Arlidge, George Edward	28117	1877–1971	13 Aug 14
Armytage, Kenelm Eustace	28156	1891–1968	25 Aug 14
Ashby, Kenneth Harold	28070	1893–1914 •	15 Aug 14
Atkey, Charles	27858	1891–1982	16 Aug 14
Ayling, William Frank	29054	1892–1944	26 Oct 14
Bagshaw, Eric	28018	1894–	17 Aug 14
Bailey, Walter	27862	1880–	15 Aug 14
Bailey, William Henry	28244		
Baker, Neville Ernest	28076	1895–1917 ‡	17 Aug 14
Bale, Herbert	29616		8 Nov 14
Banyard, Harold James	28178	1892–1988	19 Aug 14
Barlow, Alexander William Lancashire	28285	1892–1968	30 Sept 14
Barlow, Henry (Harry) Loftus	28236	1888–1918 ‡	12 Sept 14
Barnett, Victor	29005	1887–	26 Oct 14
Barnett, William Stuart	27868	1892–1914 •	10 Aug 14
Barratt, Charles Herbert	28027	1893–1915 •	1 Nov 14
Barrie, Vincent Norman	28083	1893–1917	16 Aug 14
Bass, John Gerald	28183	1895–1956	27 Aug 14
Begley, Frank	28009	1890–1963	16 Aug 14
Belfour, Algernon Okey	28065	1882–1975	16 Aug 14
Benedict, Frederick William	28047	1891–1952	15 Aug 14
Bennett, Edward William	28209	1893–1970	15 Aug 14
Bennett, Joseph N[eville]	28239	1887–1971	12 Sept 14
Berlandina, Herbert Hillel	28064	1887–1955	15 Aug 14
Best, Oswald Herbert	28042	1894–1980	17 Aug 14
Bethwaite, Isaac Greenhow	28199	1882–1930	12 Sept 14
Bevan, Arthur Wilson	29642	1895–1962	8 Nov 14
Bidlake, Alexander Guyer	29645	1895-1982	8 Nov 14
Bingham, Alfred Cyril	28038	1890–1974	19 Sept 14
Blackwell, Samuel Frederick Baker	29022	1888–1917 ‡	26 Oct 14

Name	No	Dates	Landed
Bleasdale, John	28989		15 Oct 14
Blower, Henry Blackburn	28134	1887–1974	15 Aug 14
Boulger, John C[orri]	28165	1882–1978	23 Aug 14
Bourke, Thomas McWilliam *aka* McWilliam-Bourke, Thomas	28214	1882–	12 Sept 14
Boyle, Patrick	28746		23 Sept 14
Boynton, Andrew	28194	1893–1973	16 Aug 14
Boys, Geoffrey Vernon	28033	1893–1945	16 Aug 14
Boyton, Godfrey George	28263	1891–1959	30 Sept 14
Breul, Oswald George Frank Justus	28087	1896–1917 ‡	16 Aug 14
Brew, Richard Vere	28062	1893–1963	27 Aug 14
Brocklebank, Charles Gerald	28031	1893–1940	15 Aug 14
Brooker, Sydney Francis	28980	1892–1929	26 Oct 14
Brown, Douglas McKenzie	28799	1886–1961	15 Oct 14
Brown, Edmund Louis	28204	1896–	23 Aug 14
Brown[e], Ernest Albert	28189	1885–1918 ‡	10 Aug 14
Browne, Hedley Goldsmith	28090	1888–1918 ‡	17 Aug 14
Bruce-Joy, Arthur William or Joy, AWB	29015	1891–1951	26 Oct 14
Buckell, William Dover Way	29046	1891–1970	26 Oct 14
Burdett, William B[rown]	28790	1890–	7 Oct 14
Burdin, Frank Amesbury	28228	1888–1915 ‡	19 Aug 14
Burney, 'Alick' (Edward Alexander)	28035	1886–1971	17 Aug 14
Burney, Cecil Stanley	28014	1884–1964	17 Aug 14
Burton, Eric	28282	1893–	30 Sept 14
Bury, Eric Lindsay	28075	1892–1918 ‡	16 Aug 14
Busby, Vernon Erle George	28224	1894–1918 ‡	10 Aug 14
Cadman, Charles Joseph	28061	1893–1917 ‡	15 Aug 14
Calvert, George Walter	28787	1890–	8 Oct 14
Cameron, Peter	28986		3 Sept 14
Cannon, Hugh Stanley	28754	1888–1914 •	22 Aug 14
Capper, Bass Durant	28262	1888–1917 ‡	30 Sept 14
Cargill, Richard Emil Dudley	28091	1894–1968	27 Aug 14
Chambers, E	29608		11 Nov 14
Channon, Ralph	28996	1884–1971	7 Oct 14
Chaplin, Joseph H[enry]	28276	[?? 1894–??	30 Sept 14
Chatterton-Dickson, Robert Charles D	28732	1893–1979+	30 Sept 14
Christon, Charles F[rederick]	29041	1880–	26 Oct 14
Clark, Kenneth Hunter	28132	1894–1914 •	16 Aug 14
Clarke, Sidney Hinman Cotterell	28990	1893–1962	15 Oct 14
Clarke, William Lionel Chipley or TWC	29023	1892–1968	26 Oct 14
Clement, Frederick	29017	1888–1957	7 Oct 14

Name	No	Dates	Landed
Cloke, Thomas	28792	1887–1972	15 Oct 14
Coates, Norman	28278	1892–	1 Oct 14
Cockburn, John Charles	28060	1890–1915 ‡	8 Sept 14
Cogger, William	28794	1883–1954	15 Oct 14
Coldbeck, Howard	29644	1893–1915 •	8 Nov 14
Collins, Robert Simpson	27855	1888–1918 ‡	13 Aug 14
Conaty, Desmond George	28133	1896–1919 ‡	15 Aug 14
Cooke, William Ingram	28019	1886–1947	16 Aug 14
Cooper, Charles Cecil	28115	1894–1973	15 Aug 14
Corbett, Percy Herbert	28108	1882–1961	11 Aug 14
Courtney, Geoffrey Stuart	28124	1892–1982	18 Aug 14
Coward, George M[ontagu]	28706	1886–1953	30 Sept 14
Craig, Hedley W	28290	1890–1917 ‡	30 Sept 14
Crawford, Hugh Cecil	28299	1896–1961	26 Oct 14
Cremetti, Maximilian Arthur Eugenie	28089	1892–1917 ‡	20 Aug 14
Crowther, Sydney Nelson	28164	1875–1914 •	12 Sept 14
Cuffe, George Eustace	28037	1892–1962	8 Sept 14
Curley, Charles	28979		26 Oct 14
Cutler, Harold Alfred	28102	1888–1961	15 Aug 14
Dainton, Percy B	27867	1884–1957	17 Aug 14
Daish, Thomas	28072	1892–1970	17 Aug 14
Danson, John Francis	28098	1895–1970	17 Aug 14
Dashwood, Lionel Albert	28168	1887–1915 ‡	12 Sept 14
Davies, Harold [sic] R	29027	1895–1973	26 Oct 14
Davies, Thomas Morecroft	28270	1882–1951	nd 1914
Day, Frank B	28162		16 Sept 14
Dean, Gordon William	27851	1894–1967	23 Aug 14
Deane, Arthur Denman	28280	1893–1916 ‡	30 Sept 14
Devine, Hugh F	29639		8 Nov 14
Disney, Thomas Brabazon Lambert	28080	1894–1959	17 Aug 14
Dixon, Charles Edward	28166	1894–	13 Aug 14
Dixon, George Russell	28222	1890–1918 ‡	20 Aug 14
Doyle, John			Aug 14
Drew, William Louis Guy	28122	1878–1958	12 Aug 14
Dry, William Frederick	28265	1890-1974	30 Sept 14
Duff-Stevens, Cecil James	28191	1893–1967	18 Aug 14
Duncalf, James [E]	28742		30 Sept 14
Dunford, Lancelot Babington	29055	1891–1956	26 Oct 14
Dyson, Albert Cyril	29032	1894–1981	26 Oct 14
Eade, Charles	28097	1891–1973	16 Aug 14
Edwards, Richard Barrie	30235	1894–1949	28 Sept 14

Name	No	Dates	Landed
Elliott, Stanley	27859	1892–1956	13 Aug 14
Ellis, Richard Garratt	29683	1888–1981	14 Nov 14
Elwell, Ernest Edward	28988	1891–1917 ‡	28 Oct 14
Elworthy, Thomas	28269	1892–1917 ‡	15 Oct 14
Enders, Frederick Albert	28129	1893–	19 Aug 14
Enstone, Thomas Clement	28203	1894–1982	26 Aug 14
Enticknapp, Percy J	28013	1894–1951	16 Aug 14
Erskine, John	28764		4 Oct 14
Erskine, William R	28284	1893–1916 ‡	30 Sept 14
Esgonniere, Ferdinand Robert	28200	1890–1947	15 Aug 14
Etherington, Hubert E	28752	1893–1980	22 Oct 14
Evans, Charles T	28142	1891–	16 Sept 14
Evans, Colin	27852		22 Aug 14
Evans, Thomas James	27871	1892–?1961	14 Aug 14
Evans, William Pearce	29008	1897-1920 ‡	26 Oct 14
Everitt, Bertram	28197	1887–1948	6 Sept 14
Ewart, Frank	28729	1887–1955	5 Nov 14
Farrow, William Hastings	28103	1893–1946	14 Aug 14
Fear, Percival Franklin F	28770	1893–1918 ‡	15 Oct 14
Featherstonhaugh, Geoffrey	28225	1889–	15 Aug 14
Fenwick, Harold Henderson	28105	1886–	24 Sept 14
Fetherstonhaugh, Francis Brian	28294	1892–	4 Oct 14
Fielding Johnson, Henry Goode	28050	1894–1914 •	17 Aug 14
Fisher, Wilfred	28069	1890–1915 ‡	11 Aug 14
Fitzsim[m]ons, Percy	28237	1889–1973	17 Aug 14
Foster, William Hayden	29040	1894–1969	26 Oct 14
Fox, Frank Arnold	28297	1888–1971	30 Sept 14
French, Stanley H[arold]	28714	1894–1982	15 Oct 14
Fulford, Horace Frederick	27860	1890–1967	16 Aug 14
Furniss, Cedric James	28745	1896–1980	14 Nov 14
Gamble, Robert William	28139	?? 1892–??	14 Nov 14
Gardner, John S	28158	1894–1964	2 Sept 14
Gardner, William Richard Halstone	29030	1884–1962	29 Oct 14
Gardner, Winston B	28757		15 Oct 14
Gates, Edward Percy	28722	1889–1952	7 Oct 14
Gaze, Ernest Yule	28288	1890–1951	30 Sept 14
Genllond, Frederick Donald	28068	1893–	22 Aug 14
Giband, Alfred Basstone	29048	1885–1962	26 Oct 14
Giblett, Henry Richard	28274	1892–1965	30 Sept 14
Gilbert, Ludwig	28708	1893–	4 Oct 14
Gilford, Alan	27864	1894–1949+	16 Aug 14

Name	No	Dates	Landed
Glendinning, William G	28762		4 Oct 14
Glover, Brian Edward	29640	1895–1916 ‡	8 Nov 14
Goddard, Frank Edward	28981	1889–1918 ‡	15 Oct 14
Goodhart, Eric John	28055	1894–1914 •	17 Aug 14
Goodman, Frank	28150		17 Aug 14
Goodman, Oscar Morris Berliner	29056	1890–1967	26 Oct 14
Gore, Robert William	28093	1891–1948	13 Aug 14
Gould, John Douglas	28767	1889–1914 •	29 Sept 14
Grayston, Hugh Stanley	28977	1890–1971	15 Oct 14
Green, George J	28718		30 Sept 14
Grubb, Lawrence Ernest Pelham	28026	1892–1914 ‡	16 Aug 14
Gundry, Arnold Guy Cuthbert	28023	1883–1949	23 Aug 14
Gurdon, William Nathaniel	7845	1891–1977	12 Oct 14
Gush, Charles Robert	28071	1895–1973	15 Aug 14
Haines, Alexander Crichton Cooper	28291	1895–1915 ‡	30 Sept 14
Hall, Henry	28002	1892–1944	22 Aug 14
Hall, Herbert Glynn	29051	1892–1975	8 Nov 14
Hallowes, James Brabazon	28128	1885–1961	16 Aug 14
Harris, Archibald John	28040	1892–1955	17 Aug 14
Harris, Arthur R	28249		16 Sept 14
Harrison, George	29045		26 Oct 14
Hart, John T	28793		5 Nov 14
Hawes, Richard Brunel	28121	1891–1964	27 Aug 14
Hawkins, Joseph	29050		26 Oct 14
Hayes-Sadler, Cecil William	28053	1892–1964	17 Aug 14
Hayes, William Edward	28020	1893–1960	20 Aug 14
Haywood, Clifford	28123	1891–1961	13 Aug 14
Hazel, Roland Henry	28114	1885–1960	16 Aug 14
Heath, George Alexander	28058	1893–1983	14 Aug 14
Heffer, Hubert Phillips	28771	1893–1924	15 Oct 14
Hemingway, George	28797	1886–1957	5 Nov 14
Hemming, Harold	28152	1893–1976	15 Aug 14
Henderson, George Lockhart Piercy	28976	1888–1930	16 Oct 14
Hepburn, Roger Paul	28034	1893–1917 ‡	17 Aug 14
Hewens, Cyril Jack	28725	1888–1956	7 Oct 14
Hill, Horace Leslie	28187	1891–1916 •	30 Sept 14
Hine, Sydney John	28101	1891–1989	21 Dec 14
Hirst, Sidney	28240	1895–1918 ‡	12 Sept 14
Hobbs, Walter Reynolds or Richard	28720	?1890–1958	8 Oct 14
Hobson, Frank	28782	1894–	26 Oct 14
Hobson, Frederick Greig	28025	1891–1961	17 Aug 14

Name	No	Dates	Landed
Hodder, Harold George	28066	1894–1952	17 Aug 14
Hodgson, Harold Kingston Graham	28092	1891–1960	16 Aug 14
Holder, Edward	28786		15 Oct 14
Hollis, William Pushee Bertram	28077	1894–1962	16 Aug 14
Holloway, Edward	27854	?1894–1980	12 Sept 14
Hollwey, James Bell	28289	1895–	nd 1914
Hollyoak, Arthur H	28985	1894–1968	15 Oct 14
Holmes, Percival T[homas]	28219	1894–1963	17 Aug 14
Holyoake, Ronald Hubert	28201	1894–1966	25 Aug 14
Hooper, Ernest	29026		26 Oct 14
Hope, Philip	28277		30 Sept 14
Horne, Frank Gordon	28965	1894–1960	7 Nov 14
Horner, Thomas L	28776		15 Oct 14
Houghton, John Rowland	28241	1895–1976	12 Sept 14
Howett, Alfred	29016	1893–	26 Oct 14
Hughes, T C	28715		7 Oct 14
Hugill, Valentine Francis Herbert	28161	1894–1916 ‡	16 Aug 14
Humby, Donald Charles Rumsey	28795	1895–1969	15 Oct 14
Humphreys, Daniel	28220	1893–1952	16 Aug 14
Humphreys, John G	28141	1892–1919 ‡	12 Sept 14
Hunt, Sydney George	28208	1889–1935	23 Aug 14
Hurlston, Francis Edward	28138	1885–1974	17 Aug 14
Hurry, Sydney Charles	28995	1893–1975	7 Oct 14
Huston, Gerald Marcus	28763	1896–1915 •	4 Oct 14
Hyde, John Stuart	30233	1890–	28 Sept 14
Innes, Donald Esme or Isaacs-Innes	28769	1888–1953+	15 Oct 14
Ison, Walter Leonard	29018	1892–1956	26 Oct 14
Jackson, Francis Joseph	27856	1891–	16 Aug 14
Jackson, William Guy	28245	1894–	20 Sept 14
Jacobs, Alfred	28202	1895–1972	15 Aug 14
Jameson, Charles	28232	1890–	15 Oct 14
Jennings, William F	28775		15 Oct 14
Jerman, Reginald Herbert	28100	1893–1969	16 Aug 14
Joanes, Walter	28172	1890–1955	18 Aug 14
Johnson, Edwin Henry Cross	28739	1890–1915 •	7 Nov 14
Johnstone, Edgar Stuart	28126	1894–1971	13 Aug 14
Jupe, Walter Ernest	28728	1892–1977	30 Sept 14
Keeble, Edward C	28781	1894–1968	15 Oct 14
Kent, George Herbert Stanton	28130	1892–1918 ‡	19 Aug 14
Kernick, John Wilson	28217	1891–1974	15 Oct 14
Kerry, Arthur Henry Goold	28067	1890–1967	15 Aug 14

Name	No	Dates	Landed
Keyes, Frank Ommanney	28702	1883–1961	29 Sept 14
Kington, Lionel	28768	1895–1945	30 Sept 14
Kitchen, Harold Leslie	28192	1893–1966	9 Aug 14
Knibbs, Albert E[dward]	28184	1890–1935	23 Aug 14
Krauss, Douglas Ernest	28211	1888–1965	15 Aug 14
Lalonde, Emile Claude Pollock	28246	1890–1960	16 Sept 14
Lalonde, Wilfred Pollock	28248	1894–1953	16 Sept 14
Lambert, Geoffrey	28169	1889–1957	17 Aug 14
Langton, Fred Kettlewell	28106	1890–1947	18 Aug 14
Larking, Ronald Guy	28078	1891–1918 ‡	15 Aug 14
Lawes, John Porter	28198	1887–1929	20 Aug 14
Lax, Charles Bernard	28063	1892–1966	2 Nov 14
Le Mesurier, Reginald Frederick	28717	1885–1946	4 Oct 14
Lea, Reginald Arthur Ernest	28144	1887–1939	17 Aug 14
Leather, Douglas John	28017	1894–1976	14 Aug 14
Lewis, Walter	28110		14 Aug 14
Littleboy, Frederick Graham	28008	1893–1915 ‡	10 Aug 14
Long, Arthur	28721	1890–1914 •	4 Oct 14
Longley, Ernest Albert	22876	1870–1963	13 Aug 14
Lovegrove, Roy William	28193	1892–1970	13 Aug 14
McClure, Ivor Herbert	29058	b 9/10/1890	Sept 14
McDougall, Percy	30278	1869–1942	28 Oct 14
McElroy, George Edward Henry	28292	1893–1918 ‡	30 Sept 14
McKibbin, Allen J	28761		5 Nov 14
MacKinnon, Angus Dow	28104	1888–1947	15 Aug 14
McKisack, Lawrence Hill Wilson	28967	1893–1916 ‡	15 Oct 14
MacLaughlin, Alexander Wilson	28987	1895–1917 ‡	15 Oct 14
Maidment, William J	27866	1892–1964?	17 Aug 14
Maillard, George Clement	28182	1883–1922	19 Aug 14
Major, Urban	28185	1885–1969	15 Aug 14
Malins, Harold	28774	1891–	15 Oct 14
Mallinson, George Scholes	28039	1893–1914 •	15 Aug 14
Mansfield, Ralph Sheldon	28024	1892–1964	15 Aug 14
Markwick, Edward Baguley	28798	1896–1918 •	15 Oct 14
Marshall, Alfred George	28044	1888–1973	18 Aug 14
Mason, Charles Leslie	27869	1893–1952	23 Aug 14
Mason, Thomas Godfrey	28791	1890–1959	5 Nov 14
Matthews, Hugh Percival	27853	1891–1967	16 Aug 14
Meldrum, Roy Frederick Alexander	28153	1891–1949	15 Aug 14
Mellor, [Robert] Rhubert William Henry	28054	1892–1964	16 Aug 14
Middleton, Leonard William	28707	1895–1917 ‡	30 Sept 14

Name	No	Dates	Landed
Milbanke, Edward C	28157	1893–	3 Oct 14
Miller, Alan W	29052		26 Oct 14
Milner, Geoffrey	28296	1893–1981	30 Sept 14
Mitchell, Robert S	28741		7 Oct 14
Mitchison, William Anthony	28032	1892–1917 ‡	14 Oct 14
Mocatta, Cyril Herbert	28022	1888–1966	14 Aug 14
Morrill, Henry J	29019	1887–1962	26 Oct 14
Morrison, John Stewart	28086	1892–1915 •	17 Aug 14
Myers, Ronald Maurice	28151	1890–1973	17 Aug 14
Needs, Francis Edwin	29009	1884–1946	26 Oct 14
Newman, Howard C	28190	1890–1956	15 Aug 14
Nichol, Robert William	28723	1893–1971	5 Nov 14
Nicholls, Walter Whitehead	27872	1884–1929	12 Aug 14
Norris, Thomas Pilkington [Watt]	28056	1892–1960	16 Aug 14
North, Frederick Charles	29028	1892–1964?	26 Oct 14
Oldershaw, John Harris	30232	1892–1965	28 Sept 14
Oliver, George F	29681		14 Nov 14
Oliver, Robert A	28748		5 Nov 14
Orr, Edward Farquharson Burkitt	28041	1895–1918 ‡	17 Aug 14
Overton, Arnold Edersheim	28095	1893–1975	17 Aug 14
Owen, George Sherard	28081	1892–1976	17 Aug 14
Palmer, Edward F	28118		17 Aug 14
Pask, Arthur W	28177	1893–1970	17 Aug 14
Patman, Frederick Arthur	27873	1883–1949	1 Oct 14
Patman, Roy	27874	1891–1979	1 Nov 14
Payn, Harold James	28221	1888–1961	17 Aug 14
Perks, John Noel Radcliffe	28073	1892–1995	17 Aug 14
Plumbley, John [Henry?]	27857	1890–1969	16 Aug 14
Polhill, Stanley Frederick Philip	28051	1891–1970	17 Aug 14
Pollitt, George Paton	28207	1878–1964	15 Aug 14
Portal, Charles Frederick Algernon	28028	1893–1971	14 Aug 14
Powell, Arthur G	28773		15 Oct 14
Price, Graham	29021	1887–1916 ‡	26 Oct 14
Price, James	28779		30 Sept 14
Prideaux-Brune, Lancelot Grant O	28998	1894–1987	20 Nov 14
Pryor, George Hawson Deen	28079	1894–1963	22 Aug 14
Pyemont, Winthrop	28206	1890–1981	15 Aug 14
Quill, John Jerome Patrick	28783	1883–1972	15 Oct 14
Raggett, Bertram Robert	28030	1890–1918 ‡	14 Aug 14
Rason, John William	29053	1884–	8 Nov 14
Reid, Kenneth Barnard	28016	1892–1972	17 Aug 14

Royal Signals Museum

Frank Victor Merchant, MS personal history of his war

Trent College Archives, Long Eaton

Stanley Polhill letters in *The Trident* 1914–1917
Officer Training Corps, photographs

Private Papers & Photographs

The Burney brothers – photographs, photograph albums and Raymond Holwell's letter
Jack Danson – photograph, letters
Cecil Hayes-Sadler – photographs, letters, and memorabilia
Arnold Overton – letters and photographs
George Owen – letters and family photographs
Stanley Polhill – photographs and letters

PUBLISHED SOURCES

Books and Journal Articles by Soldiers, Their Families and Their Contemporaries

Anon, *The English Mechanic and World of Science*, a series of 16 weekly articles entitled 'How to Build a 1 1/2 H.P. Motor Bicycle' published in issue Nos 1867–1882, 4 January–19 April 1901.
Anon, 'The Best Motor Cycle War Story, "Adventures of a Despatch Rider"' in *The Motor Cycle*, No 691 Vol 16 (February 3rd 1916), pp. 106–7.
Anon (Staff of "Motor Cycling") *Motor Cycling Manual,* first edition (London, Temple Press, 1911) (particularly Chapter XXVII, Military Machines).
Busby, V article in *The Motor Cycle*, September 3, 1914.
Carey, G. V. (ed), *The War List of the University of Cambridge: 1914–1918* (Cambridge: University Press, 1921).
Coleman, Frederic, *From Mons to Ypres with French: a personal narrative* (Toronto: William Briggs, n.d.).
Corcoran, A.P. *The Daredevil of the Army: experiences as a "Buzzer" and Despatch Rider* (New York: E P Dutton & Co, 1918).
Craig, E. S. (ed), *Oxford University Roll of Service* (Oxford: Clarendon Press, 1920).
Davis, Oswald Harcourt, *Triumph on the Western Front: Diary of a Despatch Rider 1915-1919*, edited by Philip Holdway Davis (Brighton: Firestep, 2015).
Drinkwater, Harry, (Added authors, Cooksey, Jon, and Griffiths, David) *Harry's war: the Great War diary of Harry Drinkwater* (London: Ebury Press, 2013).
Dunn J. C., *The war the Infantry knew 1914–1919* (London: Jane's, 1987).
Gleichen, Edward (Count), *The Doings of the Fifteenth Infantry Brigade* (London: Blackwood, 1917).
Gordon, Huntly, *The Unreturning Army, A Field Gunner in Flanders 1917-18*, first published 1967, new edition edited by Gordon, David (London: Transworld, 2013).
Malins, Geoffrey H., edited by Low Warren; introduction by Nicholas Hiley, *How I filmed the war: a record of the extraordinary experiences of the man who filmed the great Somme battles etc,* (London: Imperial War Museum, Department of Printed Books in association with Battery Press, 1993).
'Phoenix' (Chas S Lake, AMIMech E), *The Motor Cyclist's Handbook,* second edition, (London, Percival Marshall & Co, 1912).
Polhill, Arthur T, and Cecil, *Across Siberia with a baby, & A visit to a Chinese prison* (London and Cambridge: Deighton, Bell, 1904).

Priestley, R.E., *The Signal Service in the European War of 1914 to 1918 (France)* (Chatham: W & J Mackay & Co, 1921).

Rogerson, Sidney, *Twelve days on the Somme: a memoir of the trenches, 1916.* (London, Greenhill, 2006).

Simpkin, Albert, in Venner, David (ed), *Despatch Rider on the Western Front 1915–18: the diary of Sergeant Albert Simpkin* (Barnsley: Pen & Sword Military, 2015).

Sproston, Archibald, 'Four Months under Fire', *Daily Mail* 14–19 December 1914.

Stewart, Herbert A., *From Mons to Loos: being the diary of a supply officer* (Edinburgh and London: William Blackwood & Sons, 1916).

Warner, George Townsend, *On the Writing of English*, (London, Blackie &Son Ltd, 1915).

Watson, WHL, 'Adventures of a Despatch Rider', *Blackwood's Magazine* 1915.

Watson WHL, 'Tales of a Gaspipe Officer', *Blackwood's Magazine*, 1915–17.

Watson, WHL, *Company of Tanks* (Edinburgh & London: Blackwood's, 1920).

Watson, WHL, (compiler), *Tales from English History: Part 1, Early Times – 1600* (London: Philip Allan & Co, 1925).

Secondary Sources

Atkinson, Diane, *Elsie and Mairi Go to War: Two Extraordinary Women on the Western Front* (London, Cornerstone, 2010).

Beckett, Ian F W, *The First World War – the essential guide to sources in the UK National Archives* (London: Public Record Office, 2002).

Bird, Antony, *Gentlemen, we will stand and fight: Le Cateau, 1914* (Marlborough: Crowood, 2008).

Bond, Brian, *Survivors of a kind: memoirs of the Western Front* (London: Continuum, 2008).

Brown, Malcolm, *The Imperial War Museum book of 1914: the men who went to war* (London: Pan Books, 2014).

Carragher, Michael, *San Fairy Ann? Motorcycles and British Victory 1914–1918 (*Brighton: Firestep Press, 2013).

Carragher, Michael, *"The man who saved Paris": Roger West's ride 1914* (London: Uniform, forthcoming).

Clayton, Anthony, *Forearmed: a history of the Intelligence Corps* (London: Brassey's (UK), 1993).

Crockford's Clerical Directory 1898.

Downing, Taylor, *Secret warriors: key scientists, code breakers and propagandists of the Great War* (London, Little, Brown, 2014).

Gegg, Martin, *War Bike: British Military Motorcycling 1899–1919* (Lulu.com, 2015).

Gilbert, Adrian, *Challenge of battle: the real story of the British Army in 1914* (Oxford: Osprey Publishing, 2014).

Gudmundsson, Bruce, *The British Expeditionary Force 1914–15* (Oxford: Osprey Publishing, 2005).

Halford, Julia Elizabeth, *The Grand Old Man – before and after*, (Braunton, Merlin, 1984).

Ham, Paul, *1914: the year the world ended (*London: Doubleday, 2014).

de Havilland, Geoffrey, *Sky Fever: the autobiography of Sir Geoffrey de Havilland* (London: Hamish Hamilton, 1961).

Hart, Peter, *The Great War* (London: Profile Books, 2014).

Hastings, Max, *Catastrophe : Europe goes to war 1914* (London: William Collins, 2013).

Holmes, Richard, *Riding the retreat Mons to the Marne – 1914 revisited* (London: Pimlico, 2007).

Holmes, Richard, *Shots from the front: the British soldier 1914–18* (London, HarperPress 2010).

Hutton, John, *August 1914: surrender at St Quentin* (Barnsley: Pen & Sword, 2010).

Jones (ed.), Spencer, *Stemming the Tide: Officers and Leadership in the British Expeditionary Force 1914* (Solihull: Helion & Company, 2013).

Kendall, Paul, *Aisne 1914: the dawn of trench warfare* (Stroud: Spellmount, 2012).

Laws, Felicity Jane, *War on Two Wheels* (self published: revised edition, 2011).

Lewis-Stempel, John, *Six weeks: the short and gallant life of the British officer in the First World War* (London: Orion, 2011).

Macdonald, Lyn, *1914* (London: Penguin Books, 1989).

Mallinson, Allan, *1914: Fight the good fight: Britain, the army and the coming of the First World War* (London: Bantam Press, 2014).

Mallinson, Allan, *Too Important for the Generals: losing and winning the First World War* (London: Bantam Press, 2016).

Messenger, Charles, *Call to arms: the British Army 1914–18* (London: Weidenfeld & Nicolson, 2005).

Murland, Jerry, *Retreat and rearguard 1914: the BEF's actions from Mons to Marne* (Barnsley: Pen & Sword Military 2011).

Neillands, Robin, *The Old Contemptibles : the British Expeditionary Force, 1914* (London: John Murray, 2004).

Newton, Douglas J., *The darkest days: the truth behind Britain's rush to war, 1914* (London: Verso, 2014).

Nicol, Randall, *Till the trumpet sounds again: the Scots Guards 1914–19 in their own words* (Solihull: Helion & Company 2016, 2 volumes).

Pierson, Melissa Holbrook, *The perfect vehicle – What is it about motorcycles* (London: Granta Books 1997).

Redgrave, J J, *In the shoes of William Baghaw – a centenary history of Bagshaw Gibaud & Co of Port Elizabeth (1872–1972)* (South Africa: W R Harding 2005).

Richardson, Matthew, curator *1914: Voices from the battlefields*; foreword by Peter Liddle (Barnsley, South Yorkshire: Pen & Sword Military, 2013).

Senior, Ian, *Home before the leaves fall: a new history of the German invasion of 1914* (Oxford: Osprey, 2012).

Spencer, William, *First World War Army Service Records* (London: The National Archives, 2008).

Strachan, Hew, *The First World War: a new illustrated history* (London: Simon & Schuster, 2003).

Strong, Paul, and Marble, Sanders, *Artillery in the Great War* (Barnsley: Pen & Sword Military, 2011).

Tarplee, P.A. 'The Atlas Works, Bookham and Blackburne Engines', *Leatherhead & District Local History Society Proceedings*, Vol 6, No 6 2002, pp 129–138.

Terraine, John, *Mons The Retreat to Victory* (London: 1960) (Barnsley: Pen & Sword Military, 2010).

Tombs, Robert & Chabal, Emile (ed), *Britain and France in two world wars: truth, myth and memory* (London: Bloomsbury, 2013).

Tuchman, Barbara, *August 1914* (London: Pan Macmillan, 1994).

Venables, Ralph, 'CS Burney Recalls – The History of the Blackburn Company', in *Motor Sport* (March 1948), pp. 69–71.

Vincent, M W, 'The Role of Blackburne Engines in Road and Air Propulsion', in Newcomen Society, *The Piston Engine Revolution, Proceedings of a conference at the Museum of Science & Industry Manchester, 2011* (N.p.: Newcomen Society, n.d.)

Watson, Nigel, *L.W. Cole (Distributors) Limited – a history of the company and its founder* (London, The Book Guild 1995).

Zuber, Terence, *The Mons myth: a reassessment of the battle* (Stroud: History Press, 2010).

Websites

Army Service Numbers 1881-1918 http://armyservicenumbers.blogspot.co.uk/2011/08/royal-engineers-1881-1914.html

Baker, Chris. The Long, Long Trail, http://www.1914-1918.net/4div.htm.

Grant, David, The Auxiliary Division of the Royal Irish Constabulary (website at http://www.theauxiliaries.com/index.html accessed 6/1/2017)

Acknowledgments

The Despatch Riders of Fifth Signal Company in 1914 and their Colleagues

First and foremost we want to give credit to the men whose story is told in this book – and to remember their courage, hard work, and spirit. We honour the sacrifice of those who died and acknowledge the losses sustained, even by those who survived.

Our Families

We're deeply grateful to Eleanor and Joan for their unfailing encouragement and support, and to Jill, Philip, Robin and Anna who've all generously given us help and assistance whenever we've asked

Families of Despatch Riders and Other Soldiers

Many thanks to all the men and women we've met – in person or by phone or internet – in the course of this research, all of whom have offered interest, kindness, and support, including:

Roger Polhill
Sue Elphick
Roselle Bonney
David Danson
Valerie Upton
Harry Upton
Erica Dunster
Mark Wastell
William Watson
Stephen Lowe Watson
Andrew Watson
Tim Owen
Pickard Trepess
Richard Everard
Sandra Moon
Alan Aburrow
Felicity Jane Laws
Felicity Russell
Elsie (Patman) Burton

Institutions

We would like to thank these organisations and their staff for their research and assistance provided to the authors.

Museums, Archives and Libraries

The National Archives, Kew
The Royal Engineers Museum, Gillingham (Danielle Sellers)
The Royal Signals Museum, Blandford Forum (Martin Skipworth, Head of Research and Archive)
The Imperial War Museum
Special collections of The Brotherton Library, University of Leeds (Nick Brewster)
The National Library of Scotland (Alison Metcalfe)
University Archives, Cambridge University Library
Vintage Motor Cycle Club Library, Burton-upon-Trent (Annice Collett and Peter Hill)

Schools and Colleges

Bournemouth College (William Pyke)
Stonyhurst College (David Knight)
Trinity College, Oxford (Clare Hopkins)
Rugby School
Pembroke College, Cambridge
Eton College
Haileybury School (Toby Parker, Archivist)
Winchester College (Suzanne Foster, College Archivist)
New College, Oxford (Jennifer Thorp, Archivist)
Rossall School (Claire Moore, Archivist)
University College, Oxford
Merton College, Oxford
Trent College, Long Eaton (David Pinney, volunteer School Archivist)
Jesus College, Cambridge
Bradfield College
Warwick School (Gervald Frykman, Archivist)
Harrow School (John Dale Vargas)
Balliol College (Anna Sander, Archivist)
Repton School (Paul Stevens, Librarian and Archivist)
Magdalen College, Oxford (Robin Darwall-Smith, Archivist)
Cheltenham College (Christine Leighton, College Archivist)

Researchers and Friends

Sarah Allen
Professor Stephen Badsey
David Barry
Geoff Brazendale
Michael Carragher
Neil Chadd
John Clemence

Steve Corbett
Richard Duffin
Edward Gilbert
David Grant
Bill Harding
Philip Holdway-Davis
Kathy Hoy
Maurice Johnson
Tam Large
Philip Lecane
Gordon Mabb
Paul Meade
Paul Morley
Geoff Morris
David Oxlade
Rick Parkington
Chris Roberts
Michael Ryan
Brian Thorby
Graham Turner
Ian Westerman
Nick Yeomans

Internet Resources

Great War Forum
The Long, Long Trail
Rootschat
Europeana
Roads to the Great War

Picture Credits

From the Authors' Collection

The Burneys' album – pages viii, 57, 71, 89, 103, 125, 132, 135, 136, 137, 142 (lower), 143 (upper), 156, 159, 160 lower, 187, 201 (upper), 205, 206, 208, 209 (lower), 210, & 212

Other pictures – pages vi, 225 (lower) 253, 255, 260 (upper), 262 (upper), 263, 264, 265, 268

Individuals and Families

Alan Aburrow: page 160 and 161
David Danson: page 146
Sue Elphick: pages 26, 29, 76, 78, 83, 91, 93, 99, 127, 140, 147, 148, 149, 153, 194, 195, 200, 201 (lower), 207, 209 (upper)
Geoff Morris: 262 (lower)
Richard Everard: page 138
Tim Owen: pages 144 & 145
Patman family: page 269

Roger Polhill: pages 27, 31, 100, 115, 152, 154, 155, 196, 197, 202, 203, 205 (upper), 224, & 225 (upper)
Felicity Russell: page 272
Pickard Trepess: page 143 (lower)
Valerie Upton: page 142 (upper)
Mark, Paul and David Wastell: page 151
William and Stephen Watson: pages 16 and 128

Organisations

Balliol College: page 126 (the photograph has been reproduced by kind permission of Gillman & Soame Photographers)
National Library of Scotland: page 244
Repton School Archives: page 131 (upper)
Royal Aero Club Trust: page 267 (left)
Royal Signals Museum: page 158 and 253
Rugby School: page 157
Stilltime Collection (www.stilltimecollection.co.uk): page 134
The National Archives: page 254
Trent College, Long Eaton: page 252
University of Glasgow Archives & Special Collections, University Collection gb248 ch4/4/2/2/82: page 131 (lower)
The Warden and Scholars of Winchester College: page 150
Yesterdays NL: pages 256-261

All the research required to produce this book was undertaken by us in our spare time. If there are errors of fact or opinion, we are beyond a shadow of a doubt responsible for them.

We welcome feedback from readers about any aspect of the content of this book. Please email us at **twowheelstowar@gmail.com**